The psychology of religious behaviour, belief and experience

The Psychology of Religious Behaviour, Belief and Experience is the most comprehensive survey available of theories and research on religion from the perspective of psychology. Religious belief is never evenly distributed, and is correlated with such variables as social background, gender and personality characteristics. Beit-Hallahmi and Argyle use findings in these areas to test numerous explanations of the origins and functions of religion in human culture. They also consider social consequences of religiosity, religious experience, religious attitudes, the effect of religion on health, the acquisition of beliefs, conversion, and the benefits or otherwise of religion. Their main conclusion is that religiosity is first and foremost social, and is learned like other kinds of social acts.

Benjamin Beit-Hallahmi and Michael Argyle are renowned for their clear, analytical approach, and this new state-of-the-art study of psychology and religion is no exception. It will be welcomed as an update to their previous work in the area by social psychologists, sociologists and theologians worldwide.

Benjamin Beit-Hallahmi is Professor of Psychology, University of Haifa, Israel, and the author of several books, including *The Social Psychology of Religion* (1975) with Michael Argyle. **Michael Argyle** is Emeritus Professor of Psychology, Oxford Brookes University, and has written over twenty books, including *The Social Psychology of Everyday Life* (1992) and *The Psychology of Social Class* (1994).

The psychology of religious behaviour, belief and experience

Benjamin Beit-Hallahmi and
Michael Argyle

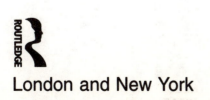

London and New York

First published 1997
by Routledge
11 New Fetter Lane, London EC4P 4EE

Simultaneously published in the USA and Canada
by Routledge
29 West 35th Street, New York, NY 10001

© 1997 Benjamin Beit-Hallahmi and Michael Argyle

Typeset in Times by Keystroke, Jacaranda Lodge, Wolverhampton
Printed and bound in Great Britain by Mackays of Chatham PLC, Chatham, Kent

British Library Cataloguing in Publication Data
A catalogue record for this book is available from the British Library

Library of Congress Cataloguing in Publication Data
A catalogue record for this book has been requested

ISBN 0–415–12330–5 (hbk)
ISBN 0–415–12331–3 (pbk)

Contents

List of figures ... viii
List of tables ... ix
Preface ... xi
Acknowledgements ... xii

1 Religious phenomena and their interpretations ... 1
The phenomena: ecstasy and routine ... 1
Defining psychology and religion ... 5
Relevance of psychological data and findings ... 7

2 Explanations and research hypotheses ... 10
Origin hypotheses ... 11
Maintenance hypotheses ... 24
Consequence hypotheses ... 31
Testing the explanations ... 33

3 Research methods: methods of studying religious phenomena, their correlates, causes and effects ... 34
Variability in religiosity ... 34
Direct and indirect ways: learning about religion by looking at either the believers, or the beliefs ... 36
Rules of the game: admissible evidence ... 37
Descriptions, surveys, and measures of religious behaviour ... 39
Experimentation ... 47

4 Ritual and clergy ... 49
Rites of passage ... 49
Worship in groups ... 54
The clergy ... 63
Conclusion ... 71

5 Religious experience ... 73
Surveys of religious experience ... 73
The varieties of religious experience ... 76
Demographic variations in religious experiences ... 80

Traditional methods of arousing religious experiences   81
Experimental induction of religious experiences   85
The effect of religious experiences   89
Background and personality factors   90
Explanations of religious experience   93
The social aspect of religious experiences   95
Conclusions and final comments   96

6 Acquiring religious beliefs: socialization and continuity   97
Religious socialization: social and interpersonal influences   97
Family influences   98
Parental images and the deities   106
Formal religious education   109
Differences in denominations and traditions   111
Conclusions   112

7 Changing beliefs and identities: conversion, religious movements, and defection   114
Conversion   114
Recruitment   123
Recruitment campaigns   128
Religious movements   130
Apostasy, atheism, and disbelief   135
Conclusions   138

8 Religion as a dependent variable: gender, age, class, and community   139
Gender differences   139
Age and religiosity   147
Social class and community size   155
Conclusions   162

9 The effect of individual differences in personality and ability   163
The effects of heredity   163
General personality traits   164
Self-esteem   165
Authoritarianism   165
Dogmatism and cognitive complexity   167
Suggestibility   171
Locus of control   173
Intrinsic and extrinsic religiosity   173
Personality and intense forms of religiosity   175
Dynamics of handling guilt and anger   176
Intelligence and other abilities   177
The religiosity of academics and professionals   178
Conclusions   183

10 The effects of religiosity: individual level   184

Happiness and the quality of life   184
Health   187
Mental health   189
Religious ideas in psychiatric disorders   191
Fear of death   193
Suicide   197
Helping, compassion, honesty, and altruism   200
Sexual behaviour   204
Summary: individual functioning   206

11 The effects of religiosity: group level   208

Fertility   208
Divorce   210
Crime and deviance   211
Work and achievement   213
Prejudice and ethnocentrism   218
Political involvement   221
Social integration or social exclusion   226
Conclusions   229

12 Evidence, inferences, and interpretations   230

The problem of cross-cultural generalizations   230
Other problems in testing theoretical explanations   231
Evidence for specific propositions   232

References   257
Author index   303
Subject index   316

Figures

4.1 A predictive model of evangelism   58
4.2 Personality of male and female Anglican ordinands as measured using the Eysenck Personality Questionnaire   66
6.1 Models of male and female adolescent religious belief and commitment   104–5
6.2 Path analysis of the predictors of attitudes to Christianity of 15–16 year olds   110
8.1 Experience of God's nearness   149
8.2 Frequency of church attendance 1972–91, for ages 18–88, of male/female white Protestants/Catholics   153
9.1 Theoretical model of religion and support for corporal punishment   166
9.2 The effect of 'dogmatism' on the tendency to reject members of other religions   168–9
9.3 Degree of certainty of judgments on (a) non-religious, (b) religious propositions   170
10.1 Religious buffering of uncontrollable negative events   190
10.2 Percentage of household income contributed by contributing US households for total, religious, and non-religious contributions   202
11.1 Total marital fertility rates for US Catholics and non-Catholics from survey data, 1951–75   209
11.2 Prejudice and church attendance   219

Tables

2.1 Proposed theoretical explanation 11
2.2 Types of projection 19
2.3 Proposed relationships between deprivation and the development of religious groups 30
3.1 Items on the intrinsic and extrinsic scales of the Religious Orientation Scale used by Allport and Ross (1967) 44
3.2 Quest scale 46
4.1 Non-verbal symbols used in rites of passage 50
4.2 Glossolalia in Australia 56
4.3 Ministerial activity scale 70
5.1 Greeley's descriptors of religious experience (RE) 76
5.2 'Psychic' experiences reported 78
5.3 Religious experience in Britain 79
5.4 Denominations and REs: response to the question, 'Have you ever been aware of or influenced by a presence or a power?' 80
5.5 Triggers of REs 81
5.6 The Marsh Chapel miracle: the effects of psilocybin on mystical experience 86
5.7 Religious imagery during psychedelic (LSD) experience 87
5.8 Religious experiences under LSD 87
6.1 Effect on behaviour or attitude of US students of that of their parents or friends 100
7.1 Percentages of audiences responding at Billy Graham's meetings in Britain, 1954–5 129
8.1 Proportion of women and men in different Christian denominations in Australia and the USA 141
8.2 The effect of employment on ritual attendance in the USA and Canada 144
8.3 Percentage of adolescents holding traditional beliefs 151
8.4 Correlations between estimated per caput disposable income and estimated conversion ratios in four authoritarian and four non-authoritarian denominations 159

9.1 Personality traits correlated with intrinsic and extrinsic
     religiosity   174
9.2 Religious affiliation and selected measures of intellectual
     orientation   179
9.3 Religious affiliation of American scientists (1954), their parents,
     and US population (1957)   180
10.1 Scores on an index of adjustment, and church membership   185
10.2 Mortality rates of regular church-goers and others   188
10.3 Relation between mental health and three kinds of religiosity   189
10.4 Correlations between death perspectives, modes of death
     transcendence, and intrinsic/extrinsic religiosity   194
10.5 Death perspectives scales   198
10.6 Religion and sex in the USA   204
10.7 Attitudes to sexual acts   205
11.1 Divorce rates by church and attendance   211
11.2 Intrinsic work ethic scores by country   215
11.3 Denomination and achievement in the USA   216
11.4 Median per caput income for groups of nations classified by
     dominant religious tradition, 1957   216
12.1 Factors sustaining interest in Christian Science, by sex and
     problem   247
12.2 Individual religiosity: a general model   255

Preface

The aim of this book is to offer a comprehensive review of the psychology of religion and religiosity, through the presentation of research findings and the support in these findings for current theories in the social sciences. The book surveys both the research literature and current theories and hypotheses. It is first descriptive, in the sense of presenting data about the social and psychological reality of religion, and then analytic, theory-driven, in the sense of formulating and testing explanatory hypotheses. Our approach is eclectic in both argument and evidence. We shall first present theoretical explanations and then present the main research findings from social surveys, field studies, and experiments about religious behaviour, beliefs and experiences. We will look at the literature produced by psychologists, sociologists, historians, anthropologists, and political scientists. The qualitative methods of ethnography and historical analysis will share our attention, together with a variety of quantitative data.

We shall use these findings to test psychological and sociological theories about the origins, functions and effects of religious behaviour. The final products of this effort are generalizations about the causes and consequences of religiosity.

Acknowledgements

The authors would like to acknowledge their debts to numerous organizations and individuals who have made the writing of this book possible.

Work on this book was started when the first author was serving as *directeur de recherche* at the Centre d'Etudes Trans-Disciplinaires (CETSAH), at the CNRS, Paris, and a significant part was accomplished while he was Visiting Professor at King's College London. The Research Authority at the University of Haifa offered much needed technical support, and the library at the University of Haifa, as always, was not only most friendly but also extremely useful.

Important materials, suggestions, ideas, and support were generously offered by Gordon Claridge, Peter B. Clarke, Michael J. Donahue, Zmira H. Heizner, Bruce Hunsberger, Lee A. Kirkpatrick, Etan Levine, Dan Littauer, Kate M. Lowenthal, Brian Mountford, Raymond F. Paloutzian, Kenneth I. Pargament, Paul Ritterband, and Stanley Stark. We are particularly grateful to Professor Laurence B. Brown, with whom we have had many discussions, and who played an important role in helping us with the early stages of work on this book. His special contribution is reflected in most of the chapters.

While we are thankful for the generous help we have received, all remaining faults are our sole responsibility.

The authors and publishers are grateful to the Parapsychology Foundation, Inc., as publisher and copyright holder, for granting permission to reproduce the table on page 86.

The authors and publishers have made every effort to contact copyright holders of material reproduced in this book. If a proper acknowledgement has not been made, the copyright holder should contact the publishers.

Chapter 1

Religious phenomena and their interpretations

THE PHENOMENA: ECSTASY AND ROUTINE

The term 'religion' brings to mind countless baffling scenes and images, from saintliness to cruelty, and from art to madness. The wealth of religious behaviours and experiences seems to cover most areas of human culture and society, from great art to bloody conflict. Complexity and multivocality characterize religion at every level (Turner, 1974). For the individual, there are heights of joy and depths of depression and guilt. There are many claimed miracles, and some events and human accomplishments which may be judged as truly miraculous. Religion has served for most of human history as the inspiration for the finest art, from pre-historical cave art in Lascaux to not only the greatest compositions by J. S. Bach and G. F. Handel but also the greatest paintings in the history of Western art, by Michelangelo, Leonardo and countless others. Such works are capable of moving all audiences, regardless of religious affiliation or faith.

There is no intrinsically religious meaning in anything. Any object, person, time, or place may become imbued with holiness and thus gain religious meaning. Religious actions are defined solely by their relation to the religiously defined realm of holiness. Holiness is a realm of content, not psychological function or structure (Beit-Hallahmi, 1989). The idea of purity and pollution, a dimension of distance from the holy, serves as the starting point for numerous rituals, bringing about psychological gratification to individuals as well as benefits to group cohesion. Hindus, Orthodox Jews, and Moslems come to mind, but elements of ritual purity traditions are everywhere. All religions have created sacred space and time, structuring day-to-day life, and connecting secular activities with gradations of sacrality.

Religion in reality is joy in fellowship, warmth and belonging. We are touched when we experience the community of believers, conjoined in faith, security and camaraderie. At the same time we remember that such heightened community ties may also lead to depths of suffering and rivers of blood. At the social and communal level, religion has served as the inspiration to the heights of altruism and devotion, while being also the declared source of cruelty and moral depravity. For society there are schisms and conflicts, as well as unity and brotherhood, and actions that range from the sublime to the horrifying, from the absolute reverence for life of the Jains, to fanatic massacres committed by groups of believers in all societies and in all times.

History and current events show us that religion, or at least religious claims and identities, are involved in large-scale violence. A closer look at history shows us that violence rarely occurs in the context of small religious groups. It is tied to mass movements and large mobs, as in the Crusades or in more recent religious riots in India. In this respect religion is no different than other mass identities, such as nationalism, as a cause of violence and cruelty. In the cases of the conflict in West Asia between Israelis and Palestinians, or the conflict in Southeast Europe between Serbs, Croats, and Bosnians, or in Northern Ireland, religion does not seem to be the real cause, despite all appearances, but it clearly is not conducive to tolerance.

While we are prone to bring up cases where religion is implicated in violence and conflict, numerous instances of the opposite are quite important historically. Indian religious traditions show a potential for conflict, together with its total opposite. The Jain tradition of absolute respect for all forms of life has been an inspiration not only for Gandhi but also for (often secular) individuals and movements all over the world. In many religions we may find non-violence, but even more often we find the turning of aggression inward towards the self. This is, of course, already a psychological way of putting it, but this seems quite compelling, even obvious. Asceticism in its strong forms seems masochistic, and while its social consequences are more positive than that of religious violence, similar psychological questions must be raised. The most extreme form of religious self-sacrifice is martyrdom, encountered throughout human history. Group suicide as a form of martyrdom is the rarest form of turning aggression inwards. Often it is the result of total devotion to a 'charismatic' (or psychopathic) leader.

While dramatic acts of martyrdom are naturally short-lived, and only their memory lingers, less extreme ideals of charity and humility lead to continuous miracles of devotion and altruism. It seems that only religion has been able to produce these examples of unselfish service to others. The continuous, everyday martyrdom of religious altruism remains a shining example even when it is only rarely encountered.

One intuitive meaning of 'religious' is the spiritual, in the sense of being otherworldly, indifferent to material necessities or power relations in society. But we do find a tremendous range of differences in worldliness, first on the individual level, and then in terms of groups and movements. Some religious individuals do follow an ideal of withdrawal from the world which most of us find stunning. Others, while truly committed to religious ideals, manage to be very much in this world, not needing the structures of separation to bind them. While we see religious movements which aim at changing the world through prayer and charity, there are others who are ready to enter political struggles and dream of creating totally religious states, such as the Islamist integrists who are today active in North Africa and West Asia.

The dream of creating a truly religious government, unifying the political and the religious institutions, has always been part of human history. Revitalization through religious revival has been a common hope in many cultures. It is only that at the end of the twentieth century such an idea strikes us as out of place, but many are still ready to die for it.

What we call religious behaviour, that is, observable, measurable activity, which today can be easily filmed (if allowed), preserved, and then leisurely analysed, consists mainly of rituals. Ritual behaviour includes an enormous range of actions, all focused on worship, expressed through feasts or fasts, prayer or silence. The ideal of sacrifice is central to many forms of ritual. The worshipper is expected to give of himself or herself as evidence of true devotion.

Pilgrimages may be regarded as an elaborate form of ritual and sacrifice. On the road to the shrine of Santiago de Campostella in northern Spain, immortalized in countless works of art, pilgrims march for hundreds of miles in the hope of spiritual salvation and regeneration. Other pilgrimages all over the world are initiated in the hope of finding miracle cures, visiting relics (a hair from the beard of the prophet Muhammad in northern India) or tombs, places in which apparitions have been reported, or just a mountain considered sacred since time immemorial.

All over the world humans worship their ancestors within the family circle, and those worshipping today know, or hope, that they themselves will be the objects of such veneration in some future time. Humans also worship other humans who, they believe, have become divine, as they have moved up the ladder of sacredness and have become saints. Such saints, who are believed to provide protection from various dangers, are represented in shrines, pictures, and statues. Some entities are believed to have always combined human and divine qualities, and Christians worship the mythic figures of the Virgin Mary and Jesus Christ as both human flesh and blood, and supernatural. Not only humans but also animals are worshipped everywhere. In India devout Hindus maintain the goshala, which is a rest home for sacred cows past their prime. All rites and sacraments are held and performed to ensure eventual salvation at some final time of reckoning.

We are most struck by religious virtuosi and religious 'professionals', those who have decided to devote their lives to living out a religious ideal. It seems to us that to some clergy, and certainly to many members of religious orders, all of life is a ritual. When we observe the monks on Mount Athos, or nuns who have chosen to become the brides of Christ, we are stunned by their total commitment, and by the ritualized structure of their lives. We may get the same feeling from observing closed communities of believers, such as the Amish or Orthodox Jews. While the power of the Sufi brotherhood or any such religious community is striking, even more surprising is the solitary Jain monk reaching the heights of self-negation.

Solitary experience marks also the testimonials of great revelations and the ecstasy of the great mystics. These private miracles make up what we call the religious experience, when an individual is struck as if by lightning. These mysteries sometimes turn into torments, but most often are the source of individual redemption and great beauty. Conversions seem like another kind of miracle, unplanned initiations into certainty in old or new beliefs. But both religious experiences and conversions are ultimately social in their sources and consequences. Sharing infrequent private revelations and conversions with the majority of believers becomes a major ritual and a source of confidence. The ideal of metamorphosis for individuals and collectivities is nourished by the example of individual conversions.

Religion is about dreams and promises deeply believed and awaited, voyages to the realm of imagination where all things are possible. There are millennial dreams of heaven on earth, as well as promises of resurrection, and expected immortality. All promises are tied to the private and public calculus of sin and expiation, without which eternal punishment is expected. The idea of reincarnation as punishment or reward is extremely popular among humans, as well as the idea of nirvana, the final release from the endless chain of metamorphoses and metempsychoses.

For individuals, religion is experienced most vividly in such dramatic events as possessions, exorcisms, visions, apparitions, dream visions, and similar experiences. But we should resist this temptation to dwell on what is extravagant. Let us mention the non-dramatic, mass phenomena which make up the majority of religious behaviour. Most individuals experience religion through routine rituals, which are very much tied to security and structure. Dramatic quality is relative. Cow worship seems amazing to Europeans, while being totally routine to hundreds of millions in India.

Despite widespread secularization, especially in the developed world, religion is not just history. A global view reminds us that most humans regard themselves as followers of a religious tradition, even if their commitment to specific commandments may be partial only. They make up a clear majority of humanity, and two main traditions claim about a billion followers each (Islam and Hinduism), while Christianity in several varieties can claim even more, including almost one billion Roman Catholics.

As we observe this panorama of humanity engaged in religious actions, we may want to ask what do all of these have in common. Is there a red thread connecting Jains, Hindus, Moslems, Sikhs, Shintoists, Jews, and Christians? Religious ideas travel well. They move from one continent to another, finding new audiences and hospitable cultural environments. Mormons, coming from the New World of North America, find converts in old Europe, Africa, as well as Oceania. African ideas have found a home in the New World.

We are struck by the prevalence of similar customs, ideas, myths, and rituals. Syncretism seems to be the rule, rather than the exception, in all traditions. An ancient Judaic taboo about the mixing of milk and meat is found in East Africa, and stories told in India about Krishna are being told in Europe about Jesus. So what is the common core and the basic unity? In the next section we will try to specify this uniqueness.

DEFINING PSYCHOLOGY AND RELIGION

An academic field is defined by (a) a set of problems, topics, or questions, and (b) a range of research methods. The two sets, (a) and (b), create a unique field, whether it is chemistry, sociology, or psychology. The field of academic psychology is defined through its two components. In academic psychology set (a) includes questions about regularities in the behaviour of humans, that is, in their observable actions, as well as in human consciousness. Beyond looking for regularities, we seek to explain them by using various measurement techniques included in set (b). These consist of using experiments, questionnaires, and systematic observations. The verbal behaviour of individuals is a major source of data, but is treated as material to be weighed and analysed, not as evidence in itself. As will be very much in evidence throughout this book, concern and doubt about the adequacy of measurement techniques are always on psychologists' minds, as they share many interests with the other human sciences, such as anthropology, sociology, cultural studies, folklore, and history.

Delineating the boundaries of the phenomenon to be studied is our next task. What do all religious phenomena have in common? The common denominator of all religious actions is made up of beliefs and claims. Some definitions of religion are very broad and include most systems of beliefs, philosophy or ethics. Religion is clearly an ideology, meaning 'that part of culture which is actively concerned with the establishment and defense of patterns of beliefs and values' (Geertz, 1964, p. 64). But it is clearly different from all other ideologies we know, such as left-wing or right-wing worldviews in politics, in the nature of its claims. Religion is a very particular kind of ideology, involving the individual in a unique commitment, in the absence of evidence or rational argument, and in a unique network of relationships, real and imagined. The working definition of religion we use here is the straightforward, everyday description of religion as a system of beliefs in divine or superhuman power, and practices of worship or other rituals directed towards such a power (Argyle and Beit-Hallahmi, 1975).

The irreducible belief core common to all religions contains the belief in spirits inhabiting an invisible world, and our relationship with them (Beit-Hallahmi, 1989). We will use the presence of the supernatural premise, or supernatural assumptions (Stark and Bainbridge, 1987), as the touchstone for defining certain human behaviours as religious. What is this premise?

It is the premise of every religion – and this premise is religion's defining characteristic – that souls, supernatural beings, and supernatural forces exist. Furthermore, there are certain minimal categories of behavior, which, in the context of the *supernatural premise*, are always found in association with one another and which are the substance of religion itself.

(Wallace, 1966, p. 52)

All religions promote the idea of an invisible world, inhabited by various creatures, gods, angels, and devils, which control much of what happens to us. Ideas about the external control of the self are, of course, much more prevalent, and much older than ideas of human self-determination. Religion and occultism emphasize access to external forces controlling human destiny. 'Magic suggests aid from sources lying in the unseen and in the unknown' (Loomis, 1948, p. 3).

If our emphasis is clearly on a particular kind of belief we follow a respected tradition. William James described a separation of the visible and the invisible worlds:

Religion has meant many things in human history: but when from now onward I use the word I mean to use it in the supernaturalist sense, as declaring that the so-called order of nature, which constitutes this world's experience, is only one portion of the total universe, and that there stretches beyond this visible world an unseen world of which we now know nothing positive, but in its relation to which the true significance of our present mundane life consists. A man's religious faith . . . means for me essentially his faith in the existence of an unseen order of some kind in which the riddles of the natural order may be found explained.

(James, 1897, p. 51)

Thouless (1971) stated that what distinguished religious individuals from others is that they 'believe that there is also some kind of spiritual world which makes demands on our behaviour, our thinking and our feeling' (p. 12). And if we believe in the existence of the unseen world, then religion as a social institution is for us the mediator between the invisible supernatural world and the visible, human and natural world; but that institution, with the behaviours tied to it, does not exist without the belief in the supernatural.

While this definition may be too narrow to include some belief systems, it is broad enough to cover what to most human beings is connoted by religion, through their concrete historical experience. Our definition has the advantages of being concrete, historical, and close to the direct experience of the proverbial person on the street, the common believer. The psychological definition of religion has to be close to that which real people experience and recognize immediately, and such substantive definitions are in line with the traditions of scholarship in the study of religion.

The emphasis on the supernatural assumption in defining religion gives us first a clear distinction between religious and non-religious behaviours, and then a valid cross-cultural definition. The universality of our definition is based on the universality of beliefs in the world of the spirits. Despite the cultural variations and the claims for uniqueness, the description of supernaturalism is valid not just for Westerners, but also for Shintoists, Hindus, Moslems, Sikhs, and members of the thousands of other religious groups.

We should also discuss here the sphere of parareligious beliefs and practices, often referred to as superstitions (Jahoda, 1969). As stated above, there is a psychological and cultural continuity between normative religious beliefs and parareligious beliefs which are constituents of the occult folklore in every society. Religious and occult beliefs share the quality of offering certainty and completeness, in placing the self within a cosmic order (Zusne and Jones, 1982). In cultural praxis, parareligious beliefs are transmitted unofficially and orally, as folklore, whereas religious beliefs are part of an official sacred lore transmitted purposefully and officially and found in scriptures. The content of the two classes of beliefs and of the consequent practices is similar, contiguous, and consistent. Beliefs, as well as attitudes, tend to become organized structures and one may speak of an 'occult ideology' (Zusne and Jones, 1982) which parallels normative religion. The empirical correlates of the occult ideology are similar to those of normative religiosity.

RELEVANCE OF PSYCHOLOGICAL DATA AND FINDINGS

Why do people engage in religious acts? Is there a 'pure' religious behaviour, with no ulterior motives? These are the questions put before the psychologist of religion. What can we say about individuals who are of high religiosity, in any religious tradition, in terms of personal qualities? And then what can we say about the real world consequences for individuals of high religiosity? When individuals tell us that they espouse a certain belief system, what can we say about the relevant psychological antecedents, and about the relevant behavioural consequences?

Our goal is to determine whether religion is either a definite cause or a definite effect in regard to any significant human behaviour or psychological variable. The theoretical debate focuses on the issue of whether religion plays a truly causal role in history and in human behaviour. We are going to treat religion, and religiosity, first as an independent variable causing or determining other behaviours, and then as a dependent variable, being the final result of non-religious processes.

The psychology of religion is, by definition, empirical. It offers observations and explications of the phenomena of religion, using the terminology of psychological theories. Where shall we start, and where do we get our ideas? The main sources of ideas are in social psychology, personality theories, developmental psychology, psychopathology, and evolutionary psychology. Some social psychologists have used religious beliefs as the subject matter for their research and theorizing, not because they were interested in the uniqueness of religion, but because they saw it as just one system of beliefs and attitudes among others (Bem, 1970; Brown, 1973a; Deconchy, 1980; Fishbein and Ajzen, 1974; Rokeach, 1968). However, most empirical studies in the psychology of religion are done by psychologists who are interested in the uniqueness of the topic, and not because they are asking questions of general interest to psychological theory.

Going outside academic psychology, we also find important questions and ideas in anthropology, psychoanalysis, history, and sociology. Historians, sociologists and anthropologists may study 'our' psychological variables or use them in explanations. Our relations with the fields of sociology and anthropology are especially close. While anthropology supplies us mostly with data on traditional, pre-modern societies, sociology looks at modern society, but also offers general theories of religion and secularization. What are the differences between psychological factors and socio-historical ones? Can religion be understood outside cultural and social structures? Anthropologists quite correctly view religion as part of a comprehensive meaning system called culture, and suggest culture as the correct unit of analysis. Sociologists, with much justification, see religion as embedded in a social system of power and status. Religious ideas cannot be separated from their historical, social and cultural contexts.

Our basic assumption is that religion is always both individual and social behaviour, as meaning is created culturally and individually, and individual dispositions meet social processes. It is both a collective, cultural configuration, and a personal assimilation of that configuration. As an illustration we can look at what is supposedly the most personal in religious behaviour: mystical experiences (see Chapter 5). The content of private religious experience is totally predictable from culture. Only Catholics have visions of the Virgin Mary. This is the cultural part. But then comes the individual causative part. Not every individual will have such an experience, even within the same cultural tradition, and we assume that personality factors play a role in creating this behaviour. Our perspective must be essentially and unavoidably multidisciplinary, informed by research in all the human sciences. We can enjoy the overlap in interests and the crossing of boundaries into other disciplines.

Chapter 2

Explanations and research hypotheses

Believers claim that religion, as a human activity, is a natural human response to the reality of the supernatural world, and to the reality of divine revelation. Researchers, approaching religion from an academic vantage point, see it as a part of human cultural evolution. As psychologists we view religion as a human response, but the stimuli we consider are all in the natural and the social worlds, both external and internal.

The researcher's gaze is always at odds with the direct experience of the actors; there is a wide gap between the language of the observer and that of the actor. Where the actors see devotion the researcher finds underlying motives and causes which are economic, political, or personal. Researchers assume that actors are not necessarily aware of the true forces leading to their behaviour. As we observe developments and changes in religious traditions, whether Rastafarian, Shinto, or Hindu, we are compelled to go beyond the actors' personal accounts. Otherwise all we are left with are mere personal experiences and conflicting claims. The actors' conscious conceptions of their behaviour and its causes are certainly important, but they are only partial, and sometimes quite misleading explanations if we are looking for the overdetermined motivations involved.

This is assumed in historical research, as well as in sociology and anthropology, and in this respect all social and historical research deals with unconscious motives. How do historians explain the Protestant Reformation or the European Crusades? They do so through human needs, some of which are undeclared by the actors themselves, or even denied and ignored at the time, if not totally unconscious in the psychological sense. Scholars have offered non-religious explanations for public positions and doctrinal changes in various traditions. Thus, Darian (1977) explains the rise of Buddhism in India 2,500 years ago through the ability of Buddhism (compared to Hinduism) to satisfy better the political and economic needs of rulers and merchants (cf. Houtart, 1977). Similarly, Hynes (1989) suggested that a coincidence of interests between clergy and tenant farmers helped to spread Catholicism in Ireland, tying it to national identity. White and White (1980) offer mundane needs and pressures as an explanation for a contemporary 'divine revelation' affecting Mormon doctrines. Many more such examples could be easily provided (Wilcox and Jelen, 1993).

Our intuitive model (Table 2.1) is one in which multiple motives and multiple gratifications are at work, for both individuals and cultures. Over the past few centuries, traditions of description and analysis in the study of religion have created numerous interpretations and researchable propositions. Explanations of religious behaviour can be divided on the basis of three categories: there are *hypotheses of origin*, which attempt to explain the psychological sources of religion; there are *hypotheses of maintenance*, which attempt to explain why certain individuals, or certain societies, hold certain belief systems; and there are *hypotheses of consequence*, which deal with the effects of religious behaviour for either individuals or social groups. Hypotheses of consequence, which deal with the effects of religious behaviour, also serve as hypotheses of maintenance, which explain the continuity and survival of belief systems.

Table 2.1 Proposed theoretical explanation

Origin hypotheses	Maintenance hypotheses	Consequence hypotheses
Neural factors	Social learning	Personal integration
Cognitive need	Identity and self-esteem	Social integration
Cognitive styles: evolutionary optimism	Deprivation explanations	
Cognitive styles: religion as art	Personality factors	
Adjustment to anxiety		
Fear of death		
The effects of early childhood		
Projection and religious beliefs		
Super-ego projection and guilt		
Sexual motivation		

Origin hypotheses emphasize the significance of particular ideas, but it is possible that the original ideas, developed many centuries ago, are less important today, and the forces of social maintenance still operate to keep the system going.

ORIGIN HYPOTHESES

Neural factors

This approach starts with the correct notion of humans as having a biological, pre-cultural systemic endowment. Neural substratum explanations posit universal species-wide capacities as well as individual differences in brain structure and function, leading to exceptional behaviours. All humans, like other animals, do have automatic neural responses to certain stimuli, which explain the effects of music, for example.

Explanations based on the structure and functioning of the nervous system as the biological substratum of religion suggest that humans are 'hard-wired' for non-rational experiences that are perceived as the building blocks of religion.

Beyond 'normal' irrationality, neural factors seem responsible for exceptional religious behaviours, such as trances and visions. The temporal lobe of the brain has been identified as the location for neurological mechanisms which cause religious experiences (Persinger, 1987).

Cognitive need explanations

Humanity has been described as 'the questing beast', always seeking answers to difficult, maybe unanswerable, questions. And humans may be marked not only by a quest, but by a tendency to believe, preferring credulity to doubt (Gilbert, 1991). All belief systems serve 'to understand the world insofar as possible, and to defend against it insofar as necessary' (Rokeach, 1960, p. 400). Human ideations impose order on the chaos of direct human sensory experiences.

Humans have apparently found it adaptive to impose order on our complex environment. There is a ubiquitous tendency to organize our world according to simple cognitive structures (Fiske and Taylor, 1991; Markus and Zajonc, 1985). A need for cognitive closure has been hypothesized to operate in humans. This need for closure has been described as 'the desire for a definite answer on some topic, *any* answer as opposed to confusion and ambiguity' (Kruglanski, 1989, p. 14).

The apparent human need for coherence or for coherence imagery, which seems vital for thinking and experience, takes the form of an imposition of causality and purpose as part of human perception (Heider, 1958). Direct observations of young children show a universal tendency towards egocentrism, causality, and animism in the attempt to make sense of the world (Inhelder and Piaget, 1958; Piaget, 1962, 1967).

Faced with meaninglessness, there is a danger of despair and disintegration. The refusal to accept meaninglessness leads to a search for a framework of meanings and values, which provide overall sense of the world. Religion meets the need for a meaningful cosmos and a meaningful human existence, as all religions claim to offer a comprehensive explanation of the universe and the place of human life in it. Weber (1922) maintained that religion is concerned with the meaning of those irrational aspects of life – evil, suffering and death – that are insoluble by science. Religion provides a socially shared set of cognitions which supply an interpretation of reality, a definition of self, and a source of directions for behaviour (Berger and Luckmann, 1967).

Here is the basis for some of the main psychological theories of religious beliefs (Spiro, 1966). Religion seeks to offer us 'the meaning of suffering, or, more exactly, the difference between suffering which made sense and senseless suffering' (Koestler, 1940, p. 224). Thus, the native American cultures of the Sioux, Navajo, and Hopi possess a belief in immanent justice. The universe is inherently just, and sickness or misfortune occur in retribution to failure to adhere to sacred prescriptions (Thompson, 1948). Such beliefs are found in most cultures, as common suffering is endowed with meaning, within a human-centred universe (Fisher and Fisher, 1993).

One limitation of the cognitive need explanation is that it accounts for a general need for answers, but not for the unique style and the unique content of religious answers, which seem to be fairly similar in all religions and places in the form of the supernatural premise. We are still left with the problem of explaining the content of religious beliefs.

Another problem is that cognitive need explanations are 'intellectualist' (cf. Skorupski, 1976), and seem to imply that religions have been created through an intellectual, or philosophical, process. No religion has ever claimed that, as religious authority relies on revelation alone. Supposedly rational, or logical, reasons are introduced much later. Might it not be more reasonable to imagine the process through which religion has been first formed as rather emotional, laden with anxiety, and leading to complete certainty, which in itself seems to indicate emotionality rather than intellectual work?

Cognitive styles: evolutionary optimism

Religion, found in all cultures, may be a successful evolutionary adaptation, otherwise it would have been lost a long time ago. Evolutionary psychology predicts that this adaptation is universal because all humans have always had to face the same adaptive problems. Human evolutionary inheritance may include rituals which reduce aggression and produce awe and sub-ordination, observed among animals (Lorenz, 1966). Such rituals might have also contributed to the development of religion.

Malinowski (1935, p. 238) defined magic as 'the institutionalized expression of human optimism, of constructive hopes overcoming doubt and pessimism'. In the face of death and of life's many difficulties, humanity must come up with a basic optimism, a persistent hope, which has essential survival value (Tiger, 1979). This evolutionary optimism is reinforced by the experiences of infancy (see p. 17). The experience of the past few centuries has shown that an extremely optimistic world view is possible within an atheistic framework, but, historically, religion has been the cultural institution embodying and expressing the propensity to be hopeful, which is selected by evolutionary pressures (Greeley, 1981).

Hebb (1955) hypothesized that higher mammals are vulnerable to emotional breakdown. The greater the development of intelligence, the greater the susceptibility to imagined dangers and unreasoning suspicion. Humans are protected by the protective cocoon of culture. Illusory beliefs, rituals, and art seem to have no survival value, but on reflection we realize that they may play an important role in relieving anxiety and allowing culture to survive.

At what point does evolutionary optimism turn into irrationality and wish-fulfilment? The content of religious beliefs may be related to a basic irrationality, displayed by humans on many (often secular) occasions. The human tendency towards magical thinking, errors in judgment, and distortion of reality has been often documented. Observations of children's thinking (Piaget, 1962, 1967) have noted its domination by magical notions, false causality, egocentricity, and animism. Both psychoanalysis and cognitive psychology agree on the basic human inability to pay reality its dues (Tversky and Kahneman, 1973).

In this case inherited coping strategies may be detrimental and mis-applied. If human nature, as sociobiologists claim, is a 'hodgepodge of special adaptations for an environment largely vanished, the world of the Ice-Age hunter-gatherer' (Wilson, 1978, p. 196), part of this excess baggage may be our magical over-reaction to the environment. History provides us with some examples in which religious faith has led to extremely non-adaptive behaviour. At the same time, observations of religious individuals and communities show that their adjustment to reality is, in most cases, not guided solely by blind faith. One explanation is that religious beliefs are used selectively and kept marginal in everyday life, and believers know well the limits of acting on faith. It is possible to conceive of them as a 'regression in the service of the ego' (Beit-Hallahmi, 1989).

Testing the hypothesized connection between religiosity and irrationality may be done, nevertheless, by looking at the findings regarding possible relationships between measured dogmatism, suggestibility, and religiosity.

Cognitive styles: religion as art

The analogy between art and religion is based on observing basic psychological processes common to both. Art offers both direct emotional relief and a kind of cognitive meaning. Religion is viewed as a form of art, a symbolic product of human anxiety, desire, and imagination expressed in a social milieu. This is tied to the psychoanalytic view of religion as wish-fulfilment.

Like any art, religion is a product of tension – between the individual and the mass, between the urge to satisfaction and life, and recognition of the inevitability of suffering and death. Its most effective expressions are generated, as in all arts, by individual creative effort, but they depend more than other arts upon tradition and membership in a community.

(Firth, 1981, p. 584)

Religious thinking can be compared to artistic thinking, reflecting a 'regression in the service of the ego' (Kris, 1952). All humans share this readiness to regress from reality in favour of imaginary solutions. The process of artistic creation is a model for understanding the process of religious creation. In the dreamlike thinking of the prophet and the artist, all things are possible, and artistic solutions become preferable to changing reality the hard way (Beit-Hallahmi, 1989). Any religious belief is a fantasy, created to serve the needs of both the creative artist and the audience. To be acceptable to the audience, it has to be reliable from a psychological point of view, not from any other viewpoint. This is the artistic, psychological, truth of religion. Through identification, so essential to art, every member of the audience participates in the unfolding drama on stage: in the case of religion, he or she can participate in a drama set on a cosmic stage.

Predictions derived from this explanation suggest that the audience for art is going to be similar to the audience for religion, and that emotional involvement in religion will be produced by 'aesthetic' processes.

Adjustment to anxiety and insecurity

The hypothetical process which created religious belief systems does not seem to be a purely cognitive search for meaning, but more like an anxiety-laden adjustment reaction to external and internal pressures. The picture of religion as a defence against anxiety is reinforced by the often ambivalent and defensive nature of religious acts (Freud, 1907). Vollmerhausen (1965) describes religion as a neurotic claim, which grows out of the child's helplessness and basic anxiety (Horney, 1964). Geertz (1966) argues that religion attempts to cope with the ungovernable forces in human experience: ignorance, pain, and injustice. The transience of life itself (see p. 16) leads often to feelings of emptiness and despair. Humans are subject to 'existential anxieties', about death, suffering in life, and meaninglessness (Freud, 1927). La Barre (1970) states that religious behaviour is a neurotic reaction to stressful times. Responses to anxiety may include specific fantasies or the denial of existential concerns.

It does not take much contemplation to see that the only permanent thing in life is uncertainty about every aspect of existence, and there is nothing philosophical about it. We tend to forget that fear is still, for most humans, an emotion experienced more often than any other. Existential insecurity is not some intellectual abstraction, but the reality of everyday life. Human life is filled with the primary emotion and the primary experience of fear, real, realistic, and justified. Most humans have had and still have lives that are short, precarious, nasty, and brutish. Going to bed hungry and cold every night is the lot of innumerable humans all over the world as we write these words. And for most humans physical suffering and misery is accompanied by much ignorance about the world about them, which only increases a justified sense of helplessness. This reality is a major component in the creation and maintenance of religion.

But sources of pressure may not only come from the outside, and internal impulses may cause conscious and unconscious anxiety. Ostow (1958) described religion as a major complex of instinctual control. To achieve control, the mechanism of regression in the service of the ego is utilized most effectively. Instinctual controls imposed by religion are only of relative value, and far from effective, because of the power of instincts. This explanation may be tested by looking at the findings on religion and religiosity in stressful times and situations.

Fear of death

If religion is a response to life's sufferings and anxieties, the fear of death must figure chiefly among them. The finality of life is the main challenge to religion as a meaning system.

> Religion, whether it be shamanism or Protestantism, rises from our apprehension of death. To give meaning to meaninglessness is the endless quest of religion . . . Clearly we possess religion, if we want to, precisely to obscure the truth of our perishing . . . When death becomes the center, then religion begins.
>
> (Bloom, 1992, p. 29)

> What came into existence beside the dead body of the loved one was not only the doctrine of the soul, the belief in immortality and a powerful source of man's sense of guilt, but also the earliest ethical commandments.
>
> (Freud, 1915, p. 295)

The encounter with death is viewed by Freud as the source not only of religious beliefs, but of all human morality. Wallace (1966) also suggested that the origins of religion are to be found in pre-historical burial rites, where the earliest rituals were the response to death anxiety.

Greenberg et al. (1986) suggest that death induces terror in our minds and religion, among other cultural systems, offers death-transcendence. The denial of death as a finality is one of religion's strongest 'compensators' (Malinowski, 1925; Stark and Bainbridge, 1987). The religious response to the reality of death is its most improbable message, which also seems to be the most attractive to believers (Becker, 1973). All religions state that death itself is only a passage, a transition point in the existence of the soul, as it comes out of a particular human body. Then various religions offer differing accounts of the soul's further movements, whether up to heaven (or down to hell), or to another human body, or to a non-human body, or to an inanimate object, and so on. Most religions promise a return of the particular soul (or even a particular body) to earthly, and much improved, existence.

The idea of immortality and the promises of after-life rewards have the added consequence of denying or reducing the importance, and the impact, of life here on earth. If this life is just the less important trek through the cosmos, if it is only a preparation for the next one, then we can look with equanimity at suffering and success, defending against common anxieties.

Could any other ideology enable humans to face death? Some secular ideologies, such as nationalism, clearly do that, but they do not ever promise resurrection to fallen heroes. Religion offers both an individual and a collective victory over death. The individual one comes with the soul's survival of bodily death. The collective one will come with cosmic salvation, the *eschaton*, the coming of a messiah and the end of human existence in this vale of tears.

How can this explanation be tested? It is not clear whether religious individuals should be more fearful of death, and therefore religious, or less fearful because religious faith has reduced their fear. It is probable that the denial of death will be more important to older than to younger people, but it should also be important to society as a whole. Terror-management theory (Greenberg *et al.* 1986) predicts that any reminder of our mortality is a threat to religion and will lead to a vigorous, often hostile, response (Greenberg *et al.* 1990).

The effects of early childhood

Intensive parenting and dependency, characteristic of the human family, have deep implications for several of the theoretical explanations proposed for religion. Specifically, they may encourage optimism (or illusion?), provide materials for projections, and lay the groundwork for social learning, identity, and authoritarianism as factors. Children learn from their parents (see p. 99, Chapter 6), but this learning is done in a special way, which binds ideas to emotions.

La Barre (1991) suggested that the prolonged human childhood, while adaptive in many ways, leads to the formation of illusory beliefs, because of the child's dependence on powerful, seemingly omnipotent creatures. Erikson (1963) offered a theory in which religion is linked to basic trust and to the mother's role in creating (or not creating) that feeling. The banishment from the Garden of Eden, in the Genesis myth, is a reflection of the first ontogenetic catastrophe, which occurs with teething, and the eventual separation from the mother, creating a basic conflict between feelings of trust and evil. Religious institutions reaffirm that sense of basic trust: 'All religions have in common the periodical childlike surrender to a Provider or providers who dispense earthly fortune as well as spiritual health' (Erikson, 1963, p. 225). Religions create faith, which is necessary for adults who need to create basic trust in their children. Similarly, Klauber (1974) stated that religious faith has its origins in the fantasies which the infant creates to justify its confidence that the mother will continue to protect and rule its world, and which are then affirmed by symbolic means. The symbols have to be taken as literal truths because this provides the only means of conveying the truth of the experiences. Ferenczi (1926) suggested that it is the natural experience of every child to ascribe omnipotence to others surrounding it. Projection of this experience later on is the foundation for faith.

Hutch (1990) explained the experience of the sacred as stemming from the *residuum*, which is the sum total of prototypical affect-laden traces or images which, arising from infancy, remains the person's more or less fixed projection on the world and others. This *residuum* 'is the psychological origin of all religious myths, rituals, doctrines, communities and ethics'. Lutzky (1991) suggests that the 'numinous' experience stems from early object relations. The internal object world of the infant is proposed as the prototype of the sacred.

Out of this theorizing tradition, a major hypothesis would be that the relationship with one's parents, and more specifically one's father, for better or for worse, would play a major role in religious beliefs and activities. Good parental relations, or bad relations, or losing a parent would lead to varying levels and kinds of religiosity. Parental relationships are connected to authoritarianism, not only extreme authoritarianism but also the normal kind, which expresses itself through the acceptance of tradition, authority, and conventions, without critical thinking of any kind (Fromm, 1941; Adorno *et al.* 1950).

Projection and religious beliefs

Projection hypotheses are those approaches which attempt to explain the specific content of any religious belief system, as opposed to a presumed general need for meaning. If the gods, devils, and spirits, or other tenets of faith, are a product of the human mind, how are they conceived of and formed? How do specific religious ideas, images, and beliefs develop? A limited number of repeated themes and beliefs are found across time and space, across history and cultures. These beliefs are not invented by each individual on his or her own, but are received from a source, believed, accepted, and passed on to other believers.

In general, projective hypotheses explain the content of religious beliefs as reflecting specific human experiences and fantasies, perceived, or claimed to be perceived, as external to ourselves and our world. But what is really the presumed, if symbolic, content of these ideas, the essential building blocks of religion?

The idea of concordance, homology, or correspondence between symbolic systems on one side and social systems or psychological structures on the other side is often found in the social science literature on religion. The reflective projection notion views religious beliefs and rituals as symbolic re-enactments of psychological states, or a mimetic–isomorphic representation of a social situation. Notions of correlation, reflection, or projection vary in terms of their emphasis on the personal, the cultural (social), the isomorphic (reflective) or the compensatory. The argument is over the source of the unique potency of myths and beliefs. Psychologists naturally point to the internal psychic landscape as the source of religious ideas, while sociologists and anthropologists point to the social landscape as their likely origin. The possible origins and functions of religious ideas, according to projection hypotheses, could be isomorphic or compensatory, and personal or social, as presented in Table 2.2.

Table 2.2   Types of projection

Isomorphic	Compensatory

Personal:
    Internal processes and structures, private internal experiences
	Personal:
	    Universal internal experience – ideal father, Oedipal solutions

Social:
    Projection of social realities and social arrangements
	Social:
	    New world coming, heaven and hell

The isomorphic explanation suggests that religious ideation parallels or reflects cultural practices (Fortes, 1959), social structure, family dynamics (Jones, 1951), or personality dynamics (object relations theory). Sociologists sometimes interpret religious beliefs as projections of social systems (Winter, 1973). Isomorphic, parallelistic reflection, expressed as ritual or belief, may also be a source of legitimation. The idea of religion as an isomorphic representation of social reality is related to Durkheim's notion about God as a projection of the group. According to the isomorphic–parallelist view, 'religion is not a compensation, but a fair representation of the social reality', and 'religious forms as well as social forms are generated by experience in the same dimension' (Douglas, 1973, pp. 34, 110). Different social conditions are said to correspond to religious styles, thus, 'when the social group grips its members in tight communal bonds, the religion is ritualist; when this grip is relaxed, ritualism declines' (ibid., p. 32). 'The man who has been raised up seeks symbols of his high estate; the one who has been degraded seeks symbols of debasement . . . Thus we should expect that those who have the sense of living without meaningful categories, and who suffer from being treated as an undifferentiated, insignificant mass, will seek to express themselves by inarticulate, undifferentiated symbols' (ibid., pp. 182–3). And indeed in research on contemporary religious movements, the claim has been made that the individual has become sacred, paralleling the extreme individualism of modern society (Westley, 1983).

Even if we accept isomorphic representation as an explanation, there is the question of motivation. Is there a basic motive for isomorphic expression of social and psychological status? Isomorphic theorists do not explain the need for projection, unless we assume that projection is just a celebration of the self and the community. Compensation theorists assume that any compensatory fantasy is self-explanatory, a reaction to harsh reality. Religious ideas are regressive mechanisms designed in response to the problems of the secular world. Salvation dreams, so common in every religion, do not just reflect, but promise a radical change. So any notion of compensatory projection is connected to deprivation as the initial condition.

Psychoanalysis specifies the psychological mechanism involved in the development of religious ideas. In psychoanalytic writings, projection is either a defence mechanism, externalizing an internal threat, or a general perceptual mode, externalizing internal processes or needs, pressing to be expressed. In both cases the result is perceptual distortion (Guthrie, 1993). Projection as a general perceptual mode, which externalizes internal needs and leads to distortion, has been demonstrated in various laboratory studies in psychology.

There is a universal readiness for projection, which is first expressed in the animism found in every child, and projected on the universe. The root metaphor of animism, as Pepper (1942) stated, is the human being. Anthropomorphic thinking is its sole explanation. Every event in nature comes about just as we feel our own behaviour does, as the result of a wish or conscious intention. This is a direct projection of human conscious experience. This animistic world hypothesis is what all religions have in common.

Psychoanalysis suggests an 'iconic correlation' between the internal world and religious ideas, so that these ideas are a reflection of the internal psychic landscape. Psychoanalytic theorists have provided us with various content hypotheses, specifying what is projected. Psychoanalysis also implies a recapitulation mechanism, through which early experiences in the family are recreated as cultural products. The presumably projected humans are the 'significant others': father, mother, family relations and dynamics. The hypothetical psychological structures presumably projected include so-called internal objects, the super-ego (see p. 22), and the self.

The father-projection hypothesis

Among the various Freudian hypotheses regarding the sources and the functions of religion, the one suggesting the connection between one's earthly father and the idea of a divine father has been most testable and the most tested. In *Totem and Taboo* (1913), where it was first stated, Freud suggested rather emphatically that 'God is in every case modelled after the father, and that our personal relation to God is dependent upon our relation to our physical father, fluctuating and changing with him, and that God at bottom is nothing but an exalted father' (p. 244). The same idea was expressed in Freud's other major writings on religion (1927, 1939).

The mother-projection hypothesis

Psychoanalytic object relations theory led to ideas about the projection of early experiences in the mother–child complex, which determine the adult pattern of human relations, real and imagined. In contrast to Freud's hypothesis about father projection, other psychoanalytic theorists have been emphasizing the major role of the mother in infancy, and her possible role in projection (Weigert-Vowinkel, 1938). Schoenfeld (1962) suggested that the concept of God may be not only a father-projection but also a mother-projection, based on early childhood experiences, and especially on the importance of the mother in relieving anxiety. The young child may hallucinate the mother's presence in moments of great anxiety, which is the precursor of religious experience. Hutch (1990) suggested that the hub of sacred authority in life is a powerful mother-imago. Obeyesekere (1984) interprets the pervasive myth of the mother-goddess (who is still a virgin) and the death and resurrection of her son (and often lover) as expressing a wish to identify with the mother. If indeed the image of the mother is so central, we should expect it to emerge in both religious traditions and psychological research as superior to the father image. Attachment theory (Kirkpatrick, 1992) would lead us to view all religious objects as projections of one generalized internal object, which becomes the target of a permanent search, as a compensation for the early failure to develop secure attachments, or as a continuation of the early pattern. Thus, particular cultural images would be less important than the constant yearning for a relationship.

Projecting family relations and dynamics

Because of the centrality of family dynamics in early childhood, psychoanalysis suggests that all religious traditions would contain projective fantasies which construe the 'cosmic environment' in the shape of the family drama. A general version of this suggestion was presented by Jones (1951): 'The religious life represents a dramatization on a cosmic plane of the emotions, fears and longings which arose in the child's relation to his parents' (p. 195). La Barre (1970) suggests that the monotheistic god (one and eternal) is a denial of Oedipal wishes, because one cannot kill him and he does not have a wife whom one may covet. Spiro (1968) suggested that the belief among the Trobrianders in a spirit-child which enters the womb, thus causing pregnancy, and the Christian belief in the Virgin Birth are both attempts at Oedipal (re)solution, in which individual fantasy turns into cultural structures.

Viewing religion as a cultural projective system (Kardiner and Linton, 1939) has to take into account cultural relativism. Since parental care varies in different cultures, the child's concept of the parents will similarly vary, and so will the resultant image of the deity. Not only are the images of the gods likely to vary in accordance with early concepts of the parents, but also the means of communicating with them and soliciting their help (Kardiner, 1945). The relativist version of the parental-projection hypothesis states that there is in every society a correspondence between early socialization experiences and beliefs regarding supernatural beings (Spiro and D'Andrade, 1958).

Secondary projection

A more complex view of the projection process notes that religious images come before us ready-made as part of social learning, but then we as individuals project our personal, unique experiences on them. What a religious tradition teaches is an ambiguous stimulus, and we develop it in the image of our own private history (Rizzuto, 1984; Spiro 1978).

Projection of self

'The first being of which we are aware is our own being ... in loving God it is ourselves we love, and by loving ourselves ... we render to God the appropriate homage' (Lacan, 1982, p. 142). Similarly, La Barre (1970) suggested that the idea of god is a projection of the omnipotent baby.

Evidence for testing the various projection hypotheses will come from looking at religious ideas in relation to social structures as well as in relation to individuals' images of parents, family, and themselves. Individual differences in the images of religious objects should be related to other personality differences.

The super-ego projection theory and relief of guilt

The basic theory of the development of the super-ego, according to psychoanalytic theory, may be summarized briefly. The child is punished by his or her parents, either physically or by the withdrawal of love, for indulging in certain behaviour, and later experiences anxiety, when he or she behaves so again, because of anticipated punishment. The child identifies with the parents and wishes to be like them and to conform to their demands. Parental requirements become 'internalized' and the child now feels guilty even if the parents are absent. The psychological structure which represents the parental demands is called the super-ego. The super-ego is harsh and irrational, because aggression towards the parents is redirected to the self; this is particularly likely to happen when the parents are kind, but frustrating in subtle ways. When physical punishment is used, children feel more able to express their frustration in outward aggression.

Flugel (1945), among others, postulated that the super-ego is 'projected' on to God. A later formulation of the super-ego projection hypothesis states that 'There is a being, God, and an institution, religion, that serve the adult as magnified parents who enter the conscience and punish and reward, helping to maintain the adult's typical balance between desire, morality, and action' (Ostow and Sharfstein, 1954, p. 76). Beit-Hallahmi (1973) suggested that the internalization and formation of conscience occur with the image of God serving as a 'portable punisher', while Skinner (1971) observed that an 'all-seeing God' is uniquely effective, because escape from the punisher is impossible. In the search for self-control, external supports are often utilized. This psychological reality is reflected in the familiar philosophical debates about whether morality is at all possible without belief in God, and in many cultures, religion is identified with law and morality.

The super-ego is likely to come into conflict with instinctive desires, particularly sexual and aggressive desires. Flugel's (1945) theory is that this conflict can be relieved by projection of the super-ego which now appears as God. For example, the super-ego can be projected on to a doctor, teacher, leader or priest; the repressive demands of the super-ego are then thought to be prohibitions imposed by the person in question, who is felt to be coercing and looking down on the subject. In Flugel's formulation a more radical type of projection is postulated, in which the super-ego is projected on to the universe as a god, and the instinctive desires similarly as the devil (Flugel, 1945; Fenichel, 1945). Alternatively, instinctive desires can be projected on out-groups such as Jews or Africans who are then thought to be highly sexed and aggressive. The gains for the individual are that the conflict is reduced through being no longer an inner one, while the person feels that he or she can deal with the situation by overt action, instead of by changing him/herself (cf. Adorno *et al.* 1950; Horney, 1946).

The presumed role of religion in impulse control is highly relevant to testing this hypothesis. Findings on the effects of religion in controlling aggression, sex, and drug use and in promoting pro-social behaviour are relevant to the testing of this hypothesis.

Several psychoanalytic writers mention the function of religion in relieving guilt feelings. Guilt feelings have often been interpreted as the direction of aggression towards the self, and there is evidence that it is connected with internal conflicts between the self and the ego-ideal (Flugel, 1945; Rosenzweig, 1945). We may want to see whether religious individuals are more likely to engage in habitual self-blame. Most often, guilt feelings are aroused, rather than relieved, in prayers and sermons. Ostow and Sharfstein (1954) suggest that guilt is used by religious groups as a means of controlling people, in the interests of both religion and social control. Data on the prevalence of guilt feelings among the more and the less religious would be relevant to testing this explanation.

Sexual motivation

The sex-repression (or sex-frustration) theory of the origin of religion proposes that religious activities are sublimations of sexual impulses. Leuba (1925), supporting this view, pointed to the prominence of sexual symbolism in religion, which seems to be almost universal, and the erotic nature of religious frenzy. Mol (1970) and Taylor (1959) suggested that sex and religion were two alternative, mutually exclusive, ways of self-expression and satisfaction. Conservative politicians (e.g. Rees-Mogg, 1992) often extol the virtues of religion as the one tradition which has proved powerful enough to control sexual appetites.

Thus, religion may be related to sexual motivation as a response to frustration or by way of sublimation. We can then test this explanation by looking at the correlation between religiosity and sexual activity.

MAINTENANCE HYPOTHESES

Social learning

In discussion of religious acts, we often tend to forget that all religion is socially acquired. The vast majority of believers have been born into whatever tradition they now follow. Their current behaviour and displayed commitments are tied to the accidents of birth, geography, and history. Belief systems are not acceptable to most people unless they are shared with members of a social group. Religious behaviour, beliefs, and experiences are simply part of culture and cultural experience, and so are regularly transmitted from generation to generation. We postulate here that religion is learned by the same processes of socialization as any other attitudes and beliefs. It is learned as a part of a given culture, which can be described as the human-made part of the environment (Herskovits, 1948) or learned and shared systems of meaning (Rohner, 1984). Triandis (1972) described subjective culture as including norms, roles, and beliefs about several areas of life, among them religiosity.

It is socialization which makes particular religious ideas plausible. The psychological mechanisms involved are conformity and the replicative transmission of behavioural repertoires. Even mystical experience can be accurately predicted from cultural background; all religious behaviour follows closely role expectations and definitions. We learn from authorities and accept what they say without hesitation or reflection. So religiosity may be simply a form of social conformity. To some extent we assume this explanation when we talk of the different religious traditions of different countries, since it is taken for granted that these are relatively unchanging and will persist in time.

Theoretically and logically, socialization is preceded by basic psychological styles, described above among the theories of origin, but then learning is crucial. If social learning is indeed the more important variable in creating religiosity, then social variables, rather than personality variables, should be more successful in predicting it.

But in addition to this major factor much is left to be explained, as we have already seen in earlier sections. One crucial question addressed earlier is that of the particular content of (socially learned) religious beliefs and rituals, or intense religious experience. Beyond that we must look at the question of individual differences. Within the same tradition we can observe individuals who have been exposed to the same teaching but who display differing levels of religiosity. In trying to account for such differences in behaviour, our framework must be personality theory. We must ask whether levels of religiosity, within the same tradition, or changes in religious identity are related to personality variables.

Identity and self-esteem explanations: religion as a social membership category

Believing is participating in a social system, belonging to a community, and achieving intimacy with real and imaginary others. If above we described the mechanism of social learning as being the most important for the maintenance of religion, we might want to ask about the content of that social learning. How does one learn to become religious? Most individuals learn their religion in childhood, as a specific identity, within a specific community (Beit-Hallahmi, 1989). They are 'cradle' Roman Catholics or 'cradle' Moslems. For most individuals, learning their religious identity (and belief system) is like learning their native language. And children do not have more of a choice in learning religion than they have in acquiring a mother tongue. Religion, in most cultures, is ascribed, not chosen, and this identity label is impossible to remove in many of those cultures.

When we observe the maintenance mechanisms of religion, it is clear that religion is expressed through identity and social roles. A social role is expressed through scripts for actual behaviours, guided by cognitive schemas. Religious individuals identify with and participate in a cohesive community, sharing norms, beliefs, and actions. It is quite natural then to speak of loyalty, or defection, in a religious context. It has been observed that young children first learn a religious identity and role (Beit-Hallahmi, 1989), and only then beliefs and rituals. Children learn about their ascribed identity very early, and only later do they adopt beliefs. 'If you are a Catholic, then you believe in the Virgin Birth.' That is the logic and the order in which things develop.

The theoretical sources for the understanding of religion as a form of identity and as a way of attachment come from modern psychoanalytic theories and also from social psychology. Our social persona, or identity, is composed of numerous social identities, or sub-identities, which make up our social position. Religious identity together with age, sex, and class status are in many cases an obvious, public part of the persona.

Is there a need for identity? Is the unconscious need for group identification and support a significant motive for religious faith? Burton (1990) suggested a list of universal needs, which include identity, bonding, security, and meaning. They supersede cultural requirements, and always demand satisfaction. It is obvious that the need for identity and belonging is often quite conscious as well. The need for identity and meaning within a culture becomes most pressing at life's turning points. Indeed, it is religion which provides rites of passage in most cultures.

Lewin's (1948) conception of group identity focuses on in-group solidarity, group boundaries, and intergroup relations. An individual's identity, denoting group membership, is a background determinant of individual behaviour in many settings. The structure and the content of identity are determined by forces external to the individual and are not tied or related to personality dynamics. Zavalloni (1975) listed the following elements in a 'social identity cluster': sex, nation, religious origin, political ideology, social class, family situation, age group, and profession. Tajfel (1981, p. 255) defined social identity as 'that part of the individual's self-concept which derives from his knowledge of his membership of a social group together with the value and emotional significance attached to that membership'.

The work by Tajfel (1978, 1981) showed that social categorization based on minimal similarity is a sufficient condition for in-group solidarity and discriminatory social behaviour. The simplest dichotomization into 'we' and 'they' creates a division of our social world into one in-group and at least one out-group. The reality of social categorization, whether in the case of religion or in other identities, leads to various cognitive distortions in deductions about the self and others such as out-group homogeneity bias, in-group favouritism and stereotyping (Fiske and Taylor, 1991). Social categorization is accompanied by evaluation, and intimately tied to the management of self-esteem. Individuals express an overvaluation of the in-group, thereby enhancing their self-esteem, and a parallel systematic under evaluation of the out-group. The result may even be described as in-group narcissism. The imperatives of insecurity and self-enhancement, individual and social, may lead to conflicts which are identity inspired and automatic.

Religion has 'identity functions' in being a source of legitimation for group identity and for individual self-esteem (Rosenberg, 1979). Bellah (1967) stated that religion provides a sense of identity for individuals and groups, i.e. a definition of self as well as environment. Belonging to a religious community is often tied to the experience of belonging to one's family. Group identity is connected to personal identity and to self-esteem. Any slight to the collective identity is an insult to the self, and thus a most powerful attachment is formed. 'Faith and family, blood and belief, are what people identify with and what they will fight and die for' (Huntington, 1993, p. 190).

Each of us enjoys the experience of belonging and acceptance, and many would enjoy the feeling of superiority often provided by religious groups. The idea of being elected and belonging to a superior group is a powerful compensation for any psychological deprivation. Religious identity may be more forceful than other kinds, because of the notion of election and superiority. The idea of being chosen is found in every case of religious ideology. Members of all religious groups believe that their group has been chosen to share in revealed absolute truth, and that their group is the vanguard in a cosmic project to save (or damn) all of humanity. The belief that one is playing a role in this cosmic script must have a powerful effect on self-esteem.

Deprivation explanations

Explanations linking religious activity to deprivation, frustration, and personal deficiencies have been the most common in the research literature, even before Karl Marx formulated the best known among them:

> Religious suffering is at the same time an expression of real suffering and a protest against real suffering. Religion is the sigh of the oppressed creature, the heart of a heartless world, and the soul of soulless conditions. It is the opium of the people.
>
> (Marx, 1964, pp. 43–4)

While deprivation and frustration are situational, personal deficiencies are assumed to be internal and constant.

It is important to keep in mind that deprivation may be both 'objective', measurable by income and education, and 'subjective', measured by self-esteem and attitudes and not always expressed publicly. Very often 'deprivation' is misinterpreted as being just economic, but status deprivation may be just as important (Hill, 1971a, b). The term 'frustration' may be more useful in this context. Feelings of frustration are often hidden from sight, and must be inferred. Social science literature abounds with such terms as estrangement, depersonalization, isolation, loneliness, marginality, alienation, or anomie to describe the context of religious yearnings.

The idea of relative, rather than absolute, deprivation has been used increasingly to explain the growth of sects, and seems relevant to this case. Schwartz (1970) postulates relative deprivation to explain why people join religious sects: 'People join sects because they seek to redress the lack of deference and esteem they feel is rightfully theirs' (pp. 40–1).

Psychoanalysis, in many of its notions about religion, does use the concepts of deprivation and compensation. Freud (1927) developed a similar view of religious beliefs as reactions to both individual and collective deprivations. All psychoanalytic theorists take a tragic view of life and agree that it is a continuing frustration of both instincts and humanity's dreams of immortality. It has been suggested many times that religious ideas about heaven, the coming kingdom of god, or reincarnation are but compensatory mechanisms, offering peace of mind to those suffering in the real world. And indeed deprivation explanations predict the appearance of compensatory fantasies, and predict the need for projection of any kind, isomorphic or compensatory. This is the direct tie between projection explanations of the content of religious beliefs and the deprivation hypothesis accounting for the basic need for any such projections.

Basic research on responses to frustration has shown that these include aggression, fantasy, and withdrawal. According to psychoanalytic theory, as well as general psychological theory since the 1940s, stress and frustration lead to regression, which may be expressed through magical thinking and fantasy. An inverse relationship is predicted between readiness and opportunity for instrumental coping on the one hand, and involvement in religion and magic on the other (Beit-Hallahmi, 1989). Religion offers first psychological compensation through fantasy, and then sociability, community, the feeling of power, and an experience of belonging and acceptance, which all serve to reduce frustration. Social isolation and loneliness are a powerful form of psychological deprivation, which would lead to religiosity, among other possibilities. The feeling of social superiority and 'chosenness', often provided by religious groups, must be viewed as a compensation for social frustrations. Fromm (1941) described the general tendency to follow powerful entities outside the self (individuals, groups, or institutions) in order to enhance one's sense of power. Religious believers are expected to obey cosmic forces and be rewarded by feelings of vicarious participation in the power and wisdom of those forces.

The sociological deprivation–compensation theory of religious involvement was most clearly expressed by Davis (1948), as follows:

The greater his [man's] disappointment in this life, the greater his faith in the next. Thus the existence of goals beyond this world serves to compensate people for frustrations they inevitably experience in striving to reach socially acquired and socially valuable ends.

(Davis, 1948, p. 532)

This echoes, of course, Marx's (Marx and Engels, 1957; Marx, 1964) view of religion in relation to the real world. This view leads to several predictions derived from Marxian ideas, both social and personal. The basic prediction is that people who experience actual deprivations are more likely to be religious. Stark and Bainbridge (1987) describe religion as providing 'supernatural general compensators', imaginary rewards wished for when real rewards are unavailable. They describe the human condition as inherently frustrating, leading to the need for compensators, but they also predict a direct relationship between specific unmet needs and religious involvement.

In a way, all secular explanations of religion are based on the notion of deprivation, as they all assume the presence of unmet needs. All psychological explanations of religion are based on some form of deprivation or felt need, from cognitive need (see p. 12) on. Explanations based on general anxiety, death anxiety, or sexual motivation are all based on something that is missing, a lack, or frustration of human needs and human functioning. It seems that all 'need' theories of religion are really deprivation explanations. Such explanations are not just theories of maintenance, but theories of origin. Deprivation seems to be a general explanation for the origin of religion.

It should also be recalled that most social science explanations for most human behaviours, individual and social, especially secular ideologies and movements, political action and private behaviour, are based on deprivation or deficiency. The terminology of strain, crisis, deficiency, and dislocation is used in the literature of history and social science not just to explain religion, but to explain ideological commitment, secular ideology, and secular political movements (Smelser, 1962). If we examine historical and social science research on nationalism, revolts, revolutions, political attitudes, or psychotherapy, deprivation explanations are most common (Beit-Hallahmi, 1992). Trauma serves as a major explanation for many human actions, and more often of the dramatic kind.

In psychology, the concepts of frustration, deficiency, and compensation are often used to explain individual behaviours (Adler, 1956; Rattner, 1983). Criticism of the deficiency, or deficit, model of human behaviour has been expressed in psychology, especially since the appearance of the so-called humanistic school, originated by Maslow (1970), Rogers (1961), and others in mid-century. Self-actualization theorists have stated that humans are motivated by growth and actualization, positive urges, as opposed to deficiency needs. These ideas have had some impact, but they are hard to measure and test, and so deprivation explanations have remained dominant.

One criticism of deprivation theories is that they are circular, and too general, despite their apparent attraction for scholars in all disciplines. Deprivation is indeed universal. Life is filled with anxiety and insecurity (see p. 15). Under the human condition frustration is endemic. We are all deprived but we do not all choose religious solutions. This criticism can be met by suggesting that personality factors (see p. 31) determine responses to universal frustration, together with social circumstances. We will see such combined explanations used in Chapters 8–11.

Is there a relationship between specific deprivations and particular forms of religious compensation? Glock (1964) distinguished between five kinds of deprivation which may give rise to religious reactions: economic, social, organismic, ethical, and psychic. Economic deprivation has to do with the relative distribution of material goods; social deprivation relates to the perceived uneven distribution of socially valued attributes (age, race, intelligence, status); organismic deprivation stems from illness or disability; ethical deprivation stems from the perceived conflict between ideal and actual behaviour; and psychic deprivation occurs when cognitive needs for meaning go unmet. Their relationships to religious groups are shown in Table 2.3.

Religious reactions to deprivations are either inaccurately perceived or are beyond the control of those subject to them. Therefore, states Glock,

Table 2.3 Proposed relationships between deprivation and the development of religious groups

Type of deprivation	Form of religious group	Success expectations
Economic	Sect	Extinction or transformation
Social	Church	Retain original form
Organismic	Healing movement	Becomes cult-like or is destroyed by medical discoveries
Ethical	Reform movements	Early extinction due to success, opposition or becoming irrelevant
Psychic	Cult	Total success resulting in extinction through transformation, or failure due to extreme opposition

Source: Glock (1964)

religious activities 'are likely to compensate for feelings of deprivation rather than to eliminate its causes' (p. 29). One prediction derived from Glock's theory is that multiple deprivations (e.g. being of an ethnic minority, with low income, and less education) would make religious involvement more likely. Social isolation and loneliness are a powerful form of psychological deprivation, which would lead to religiosity, among other possibilities. Deprivation predictions will be tested against the findings presented below.

Personality factors

Most of the explanations presented so far are based on the notion of universal needs or conditions, which would lead to uniform levels of religiosity in a given social and historical situation. Psychological approaches to religion tend to look for individual differences in religious behaviour, which are assumed to be related to individual differences in personality. Is there a 'religious personality', which pushes individuals towards religious involvement? Is there a personality style, a cognitive style, or a way of viewing the world, which is connected to religiosity? Brown (1962) proposed the independence hypothesis, positing complete isolation of religious beliefs from personality factors. The individual differences hypothesis is especially relevant to higher levels of involvement. Some interesting ideas have not yet been explored. Thus, it is possible that differences in the need for closure may become expressed in religiosity (Kruglanski, 1989). Findings related to sex differences in religiosity are relevant here as well.

CONSEQUENCE HYPOTHESES

The expected consequences of religion for both individual and collective functioning derive from the hypothesized effects of religion in controlling individual impulses, providing meaning, providing identity, and relieving anxieties and frustrations about life and death. Every one of these should have both individual and social consequences. Some functions of religion, such as that of providing identity and meaning, seem crucial to social integration. We do not imply here any 'functionalism', in the sense of a theory that describes effective integration and stability at individual and social levels. There are attempts at integration, but their success is far from certain.

Individual integration

The notion that the function of religion for the individual is to induce better personal integration and personal adjustment is a reflection of older religious traditions, but has also been stated in modern psychological terms (e.g. Allport, 1950).

Hartmann (1958) saw the main function of religion in the individual as the integrative function, through which the inner mental processes are synthesized with social adaptation. Another view of the integrative function was offered by Draper (1969), who emphasized the sublimation of aggressive and libidinal drives through religion, while Spiro (1978) suggested that neurosis and psychosis are not the only means for resolving intra-psychic conflicts. There are culturally constituted defences, which serve to maintain the sociocultural system. In traditional societies, religion is the cultural system *par excellence* for achieving conflict resolution.

Religious beliefs should help with coping, because they provide security and meaning in an insecure world (see pp. 15–17). On p. 27 we listed numerous causes of deprivation and tension in the human condition. Meaning systems, be they religious explanations, political ideologies, or a 'sense of coherence' (Antonovsky, 1979), serve as 'stress buffers', if not real immunizations, against life's stresses. The contributions of religion to personal integration will be assessed by looking at the data on the effects of religion, presented in Chapters 10 and 11.

Social integration

Sociologists of religion, ever since Durkheim (1915), have explained the function of religion in terms of its ability to provide legitimation for social arrangements or the 'social constructions of reality' (Berger and Luckmann, 1967). Religious beliefs are maintained as a kind of 'social reality', based on the beliefs shared in the group, and religious experiences have as their contents a feeling of unity with others and a desire for harmony with them (see Chapter 5). Durkheim (1915) suggested that the origin of religion lay in 'collective effervescence' in groups, that is, intense emotional arousal which strengthened social bonds and beliefs and also produced new ideas. By providing a unified and unifying value system, religion is expected to contribute to the integration of the whole society and the functioning of other social institutions. Religion has been described as 'the most general mechanism for integrating meaning and motivation in action systems' (Bellah, 1970, p. 12). As such, it will contribute to social stability and to a better adaptation of the whole social system.

Parsons (1960) described the 'core' function of religion in the social system as 'the regulation of the balance of the motivational commitment of the individual to the values of his society – and through these values to his role in it' (p. 302). Yinger (1957) offered a more limited theory of integration, emphasizing the role of religion in creating political stability. Similarly, Ostow and Sharfstein (1954) offered a psychological version of the integration-through-control theory. They suggest that since most members of a stable society must be obedient and accepting, religion is used to make them this way. Freud (1927, 1930) was among those who thought that the masses (but not intellectuals like himself) needed religious controls to help them to behave and he worried about the social disintegration expected with secularization. We know that this social and moral disintegration has not taken place (Campbell, 1971).

All predictions of religion's contribution to both individual and social integration are related, of course, to the explanations presented above in terms of search for meaning (p. 12), response to anxiety (p. 15), the reality of dying (p. 16), as well as the notion of religion's role in controlling individual impulses (p. 24). This explanation will be tested by looking at the findings presented in Chapters 10 and 11.

TESTING THE EXPLANATIONS

How much can the findings presented below contribute to a definite validation of the theories? Not all hypotheses are easily testable. As we have already seen, some concepts are rather abstract and hard to test by using clear measures. Sometimes any validation is difficult, as in the case of hypotheses about the origins of religion as a belief system. Explaining the behaviour of humans at the hypothetical moment at which religion first appeared is by necessity speculative. That is one reason why discussions of the ultimate origins of religion have not been very popular. Any verification of such theories must be done with the help of historical, archaeological, and anthropological methods. What we are dealing with when we speak of origins are the psychological antecedents of religion, rather than its historical origins (cf. Spiro, 1966). Looking at the correlates of religiosity today lets us reflect on its presumed psychological origins, as we may ask why particular ideas have always seemed so plausible.

Chapter 3

Research methods

Methods of studying religious phenomena, their correlates, causes and effects

VARIABILITY IN RELIGIOSITY

Religiosity is a continuous, rather than a discrete, variable. This means that for most humans, it is not an all or none question, but a matter of degree. So on a questionnaire we will ask the respondent to indicate levels of agreement with various statements, and not just 'yes' or 'no'. Even when the respondent is allowed only a 'yes' or 'no' answer, the findings may be significant. If, in a public opinion poll, 98 per cent of Americans and 62 per cent of Britons said 'yes' to the question 'Do you believe in God?', both the percentages and the clear difference emerging here are significant social facts.

There are some general psychological hypotheses (some would say axioms) about regularities in religious behaviour. The first one is the normal distribution hypothesis, which suggests that religious behaviour in any society shows a 'bell curve'. In classical social psychology, we find the important notion of ego-involvement (Sherif and Cantril, 1947; Beit-Hallahmi, 1989). Individual differences in ego-involvement create the bell curve of religious commitment and activity. At the high end we find testimonials of conversion and ecstasy, while in the middle and low end we find the common believers and just nominal members. This means that even if we are looking at a religious minority, or a new religious movement, the distribution will be skewed. A few members will be at the extreme ends of the distribution, while most will be around the middle. Most believers are average in their religious activity, rather than virtuosi. Experiences of ecstasy are rare, and will be followed by less dramatic behaviour. William James (1902) spoke of those for whom religion is 'a dull habit' and those for whom it is 'an acute fever'.

Behind this tension between the few and the many lies a major issue in the psychology of religion as it looks at the individual: the question of religion as motivation. When is religion really the sole motive for a given act? We all realize that religious acts may be prompted by non-religious motives and reasons. We all seek to study behaviour that is 'purely' religious, where it can be agreed that no other motivation is involved. We search for pure religious motivation, where religiosity is the independent variable, and no other motives involved.

Distinguishing between religious and non-religious motives is far from clear or easy. This central issue has been studied by using the theoretical distinction between intrinsic and extrinsic motivations, which is discussed on p. 44. Another approach to the same issue assumes two psychologies of religion (Beit-Hallahmi, 1989). Based on the notion of ego-involvement, it describes two distinctive styles of religiosity. The difference between the two styles is denoted by the terms of high involvement vs. identity. This 'dual', or 'parallel', theory does not necessarily seek to tie our findings about the intense minority of virtuosi to the low-involvement majority. Most of the time, for most individuals, religion is just an aspect of social identity, that is, implying low involvement (see p. 25). Holding religious beliefs while keeping them marginal in one's life-space, as opposed to keeping faith closer to the centre of one's existence, should have some measurable consequences. This brings to mind the classical sociological distinction between sect and church, and between sect-religiosity and church-religiosity. The former is marked by commitment and emotionality, the latter by routine and structure. Quite often, we have found that nominal believers just do not know much about the religious tradition they seemingly espouse, nor do they report much in the way of emotional experiences.

Most religious behaviour is rather undramatic, but our natural tendency as observers and researchers is to look at exceptional, exemplary cases. Religion's hold on the masses is created through minimal involvements in myth and ritual. Why pay attention to extreme and unusual behaviours? Some may claim that they are unrepresentative, but others may state that their behaviour only magnifies more normative phenomena. Maybe we should look only at leaders, founders, clergy, virtuosi, because they represent high ego-involvement.

Are we too obsessed with the minority quests for otherworldly personal salvation, at the expense of normative, routine, majority experience? The psychology of religion has been fascinated by such minorities, because we assume that in them we find a purity of motives. In the cases of saints and converts there are fewer doubts about motivation, at the psychological level. Conversion has been such a major subject because it seems 'pure' (see Chapter 7). We are naturally affected by the religious ideals of saintliness and martyrdom. Those proving their faith by their readiness to commit their lives to it or to die for it are an object of admiration and wonder.

Those demonstrating a readiness to sacrifice by joining belief minorities are a challenge that psychological theories should meet, and those committing their lives to the service of religion constitute another intriguing minority. That is why we will look closely at converts and members of the clergy. We will make special effort to look at the virtuosi, while at the same time dealing with majority behaviours. While in searching for 'pure' religiosity and its effects we regard it as an independent variable, we will look as well at religion as a dependent variable, determined by age, social status, and personality traits.

DIRECT AND INDIRECT WAYS: LEARNING ABOUT RELIGION BY LOOKING AT EITHER THE BELIEVERS OR THE BELIEFS

The questions which empirical studies of religion ask and what we find today in the writings of psychologists about religion constitute really two separate traditions representing two kinds of questions:

1 Questions about the content and origins of religious beliefs, leading to the psychology of religion, which focuses on the psychological explanations of religious phenomena (e.g. Spanos and Hewitt, 1979; Freud, 1927).
2 A social psychology of religiosity, studying the social and psychological correlates and context of religiosity (Argyle and Beit-Hallahmi, 1975; Beit-Hallahmi, 1989).

The majority of studies in the literature of academic psychology deal with questions of the second variety. We might use the term 'circumstantial evidence' if we want to ask about the implications of the latter for the former. And eventually we do want to use religiosity in order to understand religion.

In developing a social psychology of religiosity we are interested in religiosity levels, rather than religious affiliation. Group membership should be our focus only when it is tied to psychological variables and has theoretical implications. The effects of religious affiliation on economic or educational success seem relevant, as long as they are tied to psychological variables. Survey findings, such as the percentage of Australians who believe in the devil, are not of much use, unless they are correlated with or explained with the help of psychological variables and theories, or compared to data at another point in time.

The expression of religious beliefs is our main measure, which is then related to other beliefs, and to psychological and behavioural measures. Beliefs are not distributed randomly or equally in the population. Beliefs and attitudes can be correlates of primordial roles, such as age and sex, social status measures, and personality measures. Much of the research presented in this book is about the antecedents of religious behaviour and beliefs.

A second kind of research is concerned with those correlates of religious behaviour in other spheres of behaviour, which can be regarded as the effects of religiosity. The basic question here is, 'Does religiosity make a difference?' The answer is given in terms of both individual and social behaviour. We will attempt to see where religiosity operates as an independent variable, affecting other behaviours. Naturally, the eventual usefulness of data on religiosity lies in their meaning for the content of religion itself.

Looking at the content of beliefs directly is tied to several theoretical traditions, mainly the psychoanalytic one, of proposing and analysing projections, needs and gratifications. Testing the origin or direct meaning of beliefs is harder to do than finding their correlates, because we cannot go back to the point in time where these beliefs were first created. The psychological meaning of particular beliefs can be assessed through looking at some correlates and at behavioural evidence.

Evidence for psychological conflict around some aspect of religious behaviour, such as ritual purity or sexual activity, would be a sophisticated measure of psychological involvement, but obtaining such evidence is difficult. However, researching the presumed symbolic and unconscious content of religious beliefs and images can be done with behavioural measures. Classical psychoanalytic interpretations of the Catholic cult of the Virgin Mary have been tested on 71 non-Catholic males in the USA. They had to evaluate independently crucifixes and representations of the Virgin Mary. As forecast, a measure of early maternal care and protection, assumed indicative of repression, best predicted the selection of both a suffering Christ and an erotic/nurturing Virgin Mary (Hood *et al.* 1991).

RULES OF THE GAME: ADMISSIBLE EVIDENCE

Academic traditions have been historically connected to particular research methods. Anthropology and sociology use exploratory or illuminative observational research. Sociology of religion often uses systematic surveys, in which large amounts of data are collected and related to social variables, as well as surveys of particular groups, tied to identity labels. Political science also uses survey research, in which large amounts of data are collected and related to social variables. Psychology boasts of a tradition of laboratory experiments, and of quasi-experimental intensive studies, looking at relatively small groups by means of highly reliable instruments, such as standardized questionnaires. Studies coming from various disciplines and using all of these methods are to be surveyed in this book.

Desirable methodologies are those that allow replicability, openness, and evaluation by peers. To be considered rigorous, research has to meet the criteria of adequate sampling, careful measurement, and appropriate data analysis. The ideal research methodology in psychology would involve the use of control groups, and the careful specification, in advance, of all variables involved or implied. It is clear that some of our evidence does not come from sources which meet these standards, or even aspire to them. Some of our data are 'naturalistic', i.e. taken from real-world settings. We will refer to descriptive and exploratory evidence from historical, sociological, and anthropological studies of particular events and time periods.

At the case study level, we find individuals and groups closely observed in their own right. The personal history and personality approach to religion has enriched us by presenting a gallery of fascinating individuals. Case studies do not come only with a psychological orientation. Historical, sociological, and anthropological researchers use this method. We will use case studies, not as definitive proof, but as systematic illustrations of more general claims, based on a broader body of data. A case study is a 'critical incident' analysis, chosen for a closer analysis because the people concerned are considered representative, or because more information about them is available. In a way, this kind of event analysis is an improvement over the finding of a general association in a number of cases, because the processes involved are more closely observed. However, measurement errors in single cases may invalidate their conclusions, while statistical analysis helps us to avoid such pitfalls. When we look at a body of historical studies, which each constitutes just a case study, the weight of their collective evidence cannot be ignored, and represents a form of statistical validation.

Most studies rely on convenience sampling, i.e. they use an easily available group (university students) that is assumed to be representative. Students are so often used because they are a captive audience on university campuses, and are ready to cooperate with professors doing research. Another kind of convenience sample may be a religious congregation, whose leader has agreed to cooperate with the researchers. Questionnaires are then collected from members, but their representability is undetermined. The best rule of thumb is to regard with caution the results of any single study, and to rely on consistent findings when they are obtained from samples of convenience. We are keenly aware of the many methodological limitations, which hamper the ability to generalize, and so we proceed with much caution. But being too cautious about generalizing beyond the data will eliminate much of relevance.

One conclusion that will easily emerge from surveying the research literature is that the best controlled studies (often done by psychologists) used US college students, while less elegant data collection (often by sociologists, historians, and anthropologists) involves other segments of the population. It is easy to conclude that although data from the 'real world' (i.e. off the US campus) are more often less reliable, they bring us closer to appreciating social complexities.

While the difficulties in obtaining reliable data have been pointed out, the reader should keep in mind that in many areas of research on religiosity and its correlates we do have a reliable body of findings. Our body of accumulated knowledge comes from varied sources: historical case studies, anthropological observations, sociological surveys and psychological experiments.

DESCRIPTIONS, SURVEYS, AND MEASURES OF RELIGIOUS BEHAVIOUR

In this section, measures of religiosity and religious activity will be described, and in each case two questions will be discussed: how satisfactory the index is as a criterion of religiosity; and how accurate the measurement is likely to be in terms of actual, as opposed to merely reported, behaviour.

Broadly speaking, social science studies of religion use:

1 Behavioural observations of activities, or direct measures (donations, participation rates).
2 Self-reports of beliefs, feeling, and experiences on researcher-designed questionnaires.
3 Self-reported rare and unusual experiences (visions, conversions).

It is clear that these three methods may reflect different levels of involvement, but they must not produce unrelated findings.

Asking individuals about their religious beliefs and acts means touching something which is often personal and intimate. But as researchers we are faced with an additional problem. Because much of this behaviour is private and the research relies on self-report, we may wonder about its value. Will not a response bias in the direction of social desirability, the wish to achieve a 'proper' self-presentation, affect what people tell us? Our concern about this issue is met by two strategies: first, by using a variety of sources and checking for consistency and, second, by noting differences across time and place in responses to similar questions, which assure us that responses are far from mechanical and express personal involvement. The fact that certain reactions may be considered socially desirable in a particular historical moment is in itself an important social fact. Thus, the reported differences in levels of religious belief and practice between the USA and Britain (Argyle and Beit-Hallahmi, 1975) indicate that research studies have touched on significant social and historical issues. 'Yes, but do they really believe?' This is a comment openly heard in response to findings obtained in many surveys studying religiosity. The question of construct validity can be answered only through using other religiosity measures, as well as other, non-religious behaviours. Construct validity is indicated by the variance in responses, and by differences in religiosity which follow theoretical predictions. Such predictions, found in Chapter 2, lead us to expect differences in religiosity indices based on a variety of factors, and such differences are indeed reported in the chapters below.

The most commonly used method in the research literature, not only in the empirical psychology of religion but also in sociology and political science, is that of questionnaire surveys. The use of this instrument was pioneered by Edwin D. Starbuck (1866–1947), who in 1893 distributed two questionnaires (or 'circulars' as they were called then), one on 'conversion' and the other on 'gradual growth', among students at Harvard University. Since then hundreds of thousands of questionnaires have served to build up our data base. Structured interviews, done by trained interviewers, are a variant of the same method.

As to the content of research questionnaires, multi-dimensional measures of religiosity have become widely used. Since it has become clear that being religious involves several discrete kinds of behaviour, which are possibly measurable as dimensions, the idea that a good measure of religiosity has to include several criteria has gained popularity. Glock (1962) suggested the following four dimensions: ideological, intellectual, ritualistic and experiential.

Measuring the four dimensions

Ideological, covering religious beliefs

Belief is the main measure used in the literature, because that is how religion itself measures its successes or failures. Every religion wants more believers, even if they do not follow all its commandments. A public statement of faith is considered sufficient for membership in many religious groups, and this makes sense from a social-psychological point of view. A public stand means public commitment, and that is what any group would wish to have. Data about both rituals and beliefs should not be based on official dogma, but on what believers say. Large scale surveys of beliefs sometimes produce inconsistent and contradictory results. Thus, in a 1968 Gallup poll, 15 per cent of a random sample of Americans expressed belief in heaven, but not in an after-life (Hertel, 1980).

Anthropologists and historians argue that the term belief is unhelpful and should be used carefully when talking about people of non-Western faiths. Ethnographic accounts of 'beliefs' do not reflect 'inner states' of individuals but are instead reports about collective representations. This does not mean that every individual who is part of a collectivity actually 'believes' what the collective claims to believe, as 'people do not necessarily believe what their culture trains them to say' (Needham, 1972, p. 5). This has serious implications for the validity of ethnographic reports which refer to the collective representations that prevail in particular cultures. Some Thai Buddhist monks were found to be unaware of some Buddhist doctrines, and acted sometimes contrary to explicit norms (Piker, 1972). As Needham rightly argues,

There is no point ... in speaking of collective representations, or dogma, which are true of a culture as a whole as 'beliefs' if it is not implied that the individual human beings who compose the social aggregate in question actually and severally believe them. Something that is believed by nobody is not a belief; and if we are to accept that collective representations are believed, we have to be provided with evidence that individuals believe.

(Needham, 1972, p. 6)

The ideal solution to this problem would be to ask, as much as possible, individual believers, as individuals and not as representatives of any particular culture, what they believe in.

Intellectual, covering religious knowledge

Religious knowledge, that is, the knowledge of a religion's scriptures and traditions, is not considered a good measure of religiosity, simply because the majority of believers surveyed, in Western countries at least, seem to be quite ignorant of what are considered basic elements of religious tradition, and, one might even say, of Western civilization (Brown, 1988). Discussing the USA, two leading researchers have stated: 'The public on the whole is amazingly ignorant ... For example, 79 per cent of the Protestants and 86 per cent of the Catholics could not name a single Old Testament prophet' (Stark and Glock, 1968, p. 161). Such ignorance is not found for all denominations, but assuming that nominal members are familiar with their group's doctrine is risky. As mentioned above, ignorance about beliefs on the part of nominal believers is found in non-Western cultures as well (Piker, 1972).

Ritualistic, covering participation in religious rituals

Frequency of attendance in religious services is another common index of public religious practices. There may be some attenders who have no real religious beliefs or feelings. However, these people would not be expected to be active in more private kinds of worship, such as saying prayers or reading the Bible. In the case of church attendance it is also possible to count the number of people who go to church, and this has been done in a number of local studies by sociologists.

Most studies using data on attendance at religious services rely on self-reports, which raises the obvious question of reliability. Should we trust what people tell us about their public worship attendance? Doubts have always been expressed, and found justified in research. It was found in one English survey (Odham, 1947) that people who claimed to go to church 'weekly' actually missed an average of seven Sundays a year.

In the USA more than 40 per cent of the population were reporting having attended services ('in the last seven days') since the 1960s. Many have thought such findings physically impossible (i.e. not enough space in places of worship to accommodate 100 million attenders). Using actual counts of attendance, rather than self-reports, Hadaway *et al.* (1993) demonstrated that a more realistic figure would be about 23 per cent. Does this mean that self-reported attendance should not be used in research? Not at all. The first thing we learn from this over-reporting of religiosity is that it reflects a strong cultural norm, which reflects the reality of US culture (and not the reality of behaviour in the USA). We may still want to use attendance as a variable, because it correlates with other measures and with other attitudes. We should think of responses to questions about worship not necessarily as reflecting reality, but as part of a complex of attitudes and other behaviours, which should be looked at and correlated. As we will see below, those who claim regular worship attendance are quite distinct in many ways, as compared to (self-reported) non-attenders, and this is of great interest to us. The mere fact of claiming to have attended religious services in the past seven days, or other specific period, is tied to other significant variables, such as political attitudes, sexual behaviour, or prejudice.

The saying of private prayers, and other forms of private religious act, cannot easily be validated against direct observations of behaviour. As things are, it is difficult to interpret the reported frequencies. Like self-reports of attendance, they should be correlated with other data.

Experiential, covering intense religious experiences

The experiential dimension covers intense religious experiences such as conversion, 'speaking in tongues', or mystical experiences. Back and Bourque (1970) used the question, 'Would you say that you have ever had a religious or mystical experience, that is, a moment of sudden religious insight or awakening?' Findings on this dimension are reported in Chapter 5.

If a number of religious items of various kinds are factor analysed they form a general 'religiosity' factor. For example, Wearing and Brown (1972) gave 32 such items to 420 Australian students and found a first factor which had very high loadings on religious fundamentalism, belief in a personal god, frequency of prayer and attendance, the religious value from the Allport–Vernon–Lindzey Study of Values, and belief in an evil power. The second, smaller, factor was about moral issues. The first factor included reported behaviour and beliefs as well as purely 'attitudinal' items. Other studies have also found that a general pro-religion factor correlates with or includes church attendance, holding traditional, orthodox beliefs, and a generally conservative attitude (Brown, 1988; Wulff, 1991). Kirkpatrick (1949) and others devised series of items to measure 'religionism', consisting of questions covering a wide range of conventional beliefs and having a high degree of internal validity.

Liberal vs. fundamentalist attitudes

Fundamentalism and 'literalism' consisted traditionally of believing literally all that is written in the Bible or other sacred book. There are also a number of scales for measuring 'orthodoxy' of beliefs. In Christian churches, fundamentalism is usually associated with an Evangelical attitude, emphasizing human sinfulness, the need for atonement, and a personal relation with Jesus. Liberalism consists, under this name or others, of a more open and critical attitude to religion; some liberals are probably less active or committed or devoted compared with fundamentalists, but others have equally strong commitment, and serious devotion to a religious life; the difference is that their beliefs are held in a more complex and questioning way, sometimes as metaphor or myth (Hunt, 1972). These positions can be measured by attitude scales based on the factors which have been found. However, these attitudes are held by entire movements, and in many studies comparisons have been made between members of different denominations. In the USA the Southern Baptists are fundamentalists, and Episcopalians and other major Protestant churches are known for their liberalism. As well as Southern Baptists, there are many smaller fundamentalist Protestant bodies, such as Seventh Day Adventists, Pentecostalist groups, Hutterites, and Mennonites. And there are some Hindus, Moslems, or Jews who may be classified as 'fundamentalists' in their religions.

Fundamentalist groups and their members are different from others in being on average of lower occupational status, education and income, and these factors need to be held constant when other comparisons are made (see Chapter 8). When this has been done, there are a number of striking differences between fundamentalists and liberals, confirming that this is an important distinction (see Chapter 9). As we shall see in Chapters 10 and 11 fundamentalist churches have more influence on the behaviour of their members in a number of spheres. For example, the strict rules about drinking and other health-related behaviour result in better health. They are also different from liberals in sexual activity outside marriage, in family size, even in average happiness. On the other hand members of fundamentalist churches are more prejudiced both towards other ethnic groups and towards followers of other religions, and the more active they are in the congregation the more prejudiced they are. They also differ in terms of personality, such as being more authoritarian than members of more liberal churches.

Intrinsic vs. Extrinsic attitudes

Allport (1950), following James (1902), suggested that there might be two ways of being religious, and these styles were translated into attitude scales by Allport and Ross (1967) in their Religious Orientation Scale (ROS). Those whose religion is intrinsic see religion as an end in itself; they really believe it, and take it very seriously. Those whose religion is extrinsic see it as a means to other ends; for example, they think that church is a good place to make friends. The ROS is given in Table 3.1. Such scales have been widely used, and revised versions published. The two dimensions have been found to have quite different sets of origins and consequences.

Table 3.1   Items on the intrinsic and extrinsic scales of the Religious Orientation Scale used by Allport and Ross (1967)

Intrinsic scale

1 It is important for me to spend periods of time in private religious thought and meditation.
2 If not prevented by unavoidable circumstances, I attend church.
3 I try hard to carry my religion over into all my other dealings in life.
4 The prayers I say when I am alone carry as much meaning and personal emotion as those said by me during services.
5 Quite often I have been keenly aware of the presence of God or the Divine Being.
6 I read literature about my faith (or church).
7 If I were to join a church group I would prefer to join a Bible study group rather than a social fellowship.
8 My religious beliefs are what really lie behind my whole approach to life.
9 Religion is especially important to me because it answers many questions about the meaning of life.

Extrinsic scale

1 Although I believe in my religion, I feel there are many more important things in my life.
2 It does not matter so much what I believe so long as I lead a moral life.
3 The primary purpose of prayer is to gain relief and protection.
4 The church is most important as a place to formulate good social relationships.
5 What religion offers me most is comfort when sorrows and misfortune strike.
6 I pray chiefly because I have been taught to pray.
7 Although I am a religious person I refuse to let religious considerations influence my everyday affairs.
8 A primary reason for my interest in religion is that my church is a congenial social activity.
9 Occasionally I find it necessary to compromise my religious beliefs in order to protect my social and economic well-being.
10 One reason for my being a church member is that such membership helps to establish a person in the community.
11 The purpose of prayer is to secure a happy and peaceful life.

How far are they independent? Donahue (1985) reports a meta-analysis of research with the intrinsic–extrinsic scales; the mean correlation for 34 studies was –0.06, but for those using the original ROS it was –0.20. And for members of evangelical or conservative churches, or for groups high in intrinsic religiosity, the average was –0.44. So for fundamentalists, being extrinsic is a negative index of religion. However, for the general population of Western believers the scales are essentially independent; this means that intrinsic and extrinsic are not alternatives, and individuals could hold any combination of them, including being high on both. This generalization has been more recently challenged by Burris (1994).

The intrinsic scale correlates consistently with other measures of religious activity, such as frequency of attendance, and measures of orthodoxy and commitment; the extrinsic scale does not. When we review findings about the relation between religion and personality (Chapter 9), we shall see that the extrinsic scale correlates with authoritarianism and dogmatism, while the intrinsic scale correlates with other aspects of personality such as internal control. When we review findings about the effects of religion (Chapters 10, 11), we shall see that the two scales have quite different effects on altruism, mental health, prejudice towards racial minority groups, and fear of death.

The Intrinsic–Extrinsic (I–E) line of research has been sharply criticized for both conceptual and empirical reasons (Kirkpatrick and Hood, 1990). It looked for a while as if intrinsic religiosity was a more 'positive' or 'sincere' way of being religious, as Allport believed originally. However, Batson *et al.* (1993) are critical of intrinsic religiosity, and argue that it goes with a closed mind and commitment to orthodox doctrines, with no questioning. Studies of the relationship with dogmatism mostly show no relation with the intrinsic scale, either positive or negative. Leak and Fish (1989) and Burris (1994) found that high intrinsic scores reflected both a tendency towards self-deception and an effort at impression management. It was this line of criticism which led Batson and co-workers to develop a third attitudinal dimension.

The Quest dimension

The scale for this new, third, dimension, 'Quest', is given in Table 3.2. The intention was to discover a dimension of religiosity which was more open-minded than the intrinsic dimension, and which placed more emphasis on complexity, doubt and tentativeness. It has been found that the Quest dimension is independent of both intrinsic and extrinsic, and has a small negative correlation with measures of orthodoxy. It has a negative correlation with a scale measuring 'cognitive bondage', that is, being totally committed to and unable to change religious beliefs (–0.28), while intrinsic has a positive correlation (0.47).

Table 3.2 Quest scale

---

1 As I grow and change, I expect my religion also to grow and change.
2 I am constantly questioning my religious beliefs.
3 It might be said that I value my religious doubts and uncertainties.
4 I was not very interested in religion until I began to ask questions about the meaning and purpose of my life.
5 For me, doubting is an important part of what it means to be religious.
6 (–) I do not expect my religious convictions to change in the next few years.
7 (–) I find religious doubts upsetting.
8 I have been driven to ask religious questions out of a growing awareness of the tensions in my world and in my relation to my world.
9 My life experiences have led me to rethink my religious convictions.
10 There are many religious issues on which my views are still changing.
11 God was not very important for me until I began to ask questions about the meaning of my own life.
12 Questions are far more central to my religious experience than are answers.

Source: Batson *et al.* (1993)

A number of doubts have been raised about this dimension by Donahue (1985) and others, of which the most important is to question whether it is a measure of religiosity at all, or whether it is simply tapping the sceptical and questioning views of US undergraduate students. In reply Batson *et al.* (1993) report two small validity studies: one showed that Princeton theological students (rather liberal) had higher scores than other students, the other that both a small group of charismatics and a small Bible study group also had high scores. It has been suggested that many or most high scorers, being low on orthodoxy, probably are not committed members of any religious tradition. Spilka, Kojetin and McIntosh (1985) suggested that what Quest really measures is religious conflict; high scorers are indeed found to be in a state of religious conflict, but this is not what the scale is supposed to measure, and it is argued that it measures an active search to solve these conflicts (Batson *et al.* 1993). If we have in mind the masses of religious believers in society, this measure may be of little relevance.

Batson and colleagues have carried out a series of studies to investigate whether, as they predicted, Quest would be a better predictor of altruism, mental health, and absence of racial prejudice than intrinsic, for example. In Chapters 9–11 we will examine these and other studies carefully to see whether Quest or Intrinsic are correlated with a number of 'positive', pro-social traits and behaviours. Despite the extensive work done using the concepts and measures of intrinsic religiosity, extrinsic religiosity, and the Quest orientation, debates continue over their significance. The issue for us remains the relevance of the findings to the great masses of believers all over the world.

EXPERIMENTATION

Much research on religiosity and its correlates has been 'naturalistic', in the sense of being carried out in various social settings. In such cases the analysis is correlational, and a correlation does not necessarily indicate a causal connection. The preferred methodology in academic psychology is that of the laboratory experiment, of course, but religion has been the topic in only a few laboratory studies.

Ideally, all hypotheses in the psychology of religion should be amenable to testing by direct experiment. The true virtue of the experiment lies in the extensive control over all aspects of the experimental situation, ability to manipulate causal variables, and the random assignment of subjects to groups. The controlled experiment is also replicable, and replication is essential to verification of results.

In practice, experimentation requires much effort, imagination, and resources. The subject of religion seems too complex and too 'soft' for the laboratory. It is filled with much fantasy and feelings, two topics which academic psychology finds hard to approach. One solution is to report on a naturally occurring quasi-experiment. In the first celebrated quasi-experiment in the literature, Francis Galton (1883) looked at the effects of prayer on health and longevity. He found that members of royal families, who were regularly wished long lives in their subjects' prayers, did not live longer than those same subjects. They even died, on average, younger than their subjects! Similarly, relatives of the 'prayerful' did not recover any faster from illnesses than other people. Experimental studies of religion in humans are also fraught with ethical and practical problems, and not much 'experimental' or 'quasi-experimental' work has been done in the psychology of religion, using the dominant laboratory model in psychology (Deconchy, 1977, 1985; Osarchuk and Tate, 1973). There are, however, a few examples in the literature of successful experiments in the psychology of religion.

Darley and Batson (1973) wanted to test whether the parable of the Good Samaritan, taken from the New Testament and presented as a model of true altruism, would affect helping behaviour. In this story a traveller, robbed and severely beaten, is saved by a kind stranger. Christian seminary students, who had just read the parable, and some of whom were supposed to give a talk about it, were put in a situation where they could help someone in apparent distress. The experiment was well designed. There were two experimental variables, being exposed to the parable (or not) and being told to hurry, or not to hurry, in going to another office in order to help the experimenter. On their way to the other office, after having met the experimenter and been asked to help, the students ran across a man who was clearly incapacitated. The results showed that the parable of the Good Samaritan had no effect on the students' readiness to help, while the instruction to hurry did.

There have been several quasi-experimental studies which take advantage of real-world events. Festinger *et al.* (1956) did an observational study of a religious group, seen as an ideal laboratory for testing social-psychological theories. The researchers were participant observers in a group founded by 'Mrs Keech' in the early 1950s in a major USA metropolis. The founder claimed to have had information from a source that was both extraterrestrial (from outer space) and divine (Jesus in Christian tradition) about the coming end of the world. On a specified date, which she announced to the world, all of humanity would perish, save the group members, who would be taken away in a spaceship. The researchers watched what was happening to the group, following the inevitable failure of the prophecy. The group did not survive this crisis, but its disintegration was not immediate. Actually, the disconfirmation caused some committed members to proclaim their faith even more vigorously by proselytizing. This unexpected (by most commonsensical observers) development was viewed by the researchers as a confirmation of cognitive dissonance theory. Here the cognitive loss in terms of physical reality led to a need for change in social reality. In this celebrated study, religion was not the focus, but it was simply a field in which a general psychological theory was tested. As we will see (p. 134) other cases of the disconfirmation of prophecies have been studied, with important implications for the understanding of religious movements.

As the examples above demonstrate, experiments and quasi-experiments, designed by psychologists, seem to reflect, in most cases, something of the lived reality of religion. Experiments can be used as a contrasting setting, which can illuminate distinctive properties of 'real-world' observations. However, one should not overlook the limitations of experiments, and their obvious dissimilarity to religious activities outside the laboratory. Critics point to the limited usefulness of results obtained in such a controlled situation, which ignores the complexity of natural behaviour. This is known as the ecological validity critique, which insists that methods and findings should be lifelike, rather than contrived. Experiments can rarely match the complexity of the social world. What is most lacking in the laboratory situation, as we try to make it ecologically valid, is the living religious community, with its benefits and its pressures.

Chapter 4

Ritual and clergy

We start this chapter with the forms of religious behaviour which involve large numbers of participants, and often low levels of commitment. These are the rites of passage such as initiation, marriage and burial. Then we look at several aspects of worship, the regular religious behaviour of the body of believers. Finally we turn to the clergy, those who have adopted religion as a career.

RITES OF PASSAGE

Being initiated into human society, married and buried are the most widespread forms of religious behaviour, since they are very often done in a religious context, sanctioned by religious authority. These are all examples of 'rites of passage', that is, rituals which mark a change of state, from single to married, from this world to the next. Thus, religion provides what we might call life-cycle ceremonies, celebrated at points of crisis, or potential crisis, in life. The research evidence which we can use here consists of anthropological case studies of rituals and their symbols, though we shall be able to cite some quantified cross-cultural studies. On the other hand the ideas and theory here are highly relevant to the psychology of religion.

Rites of passage are just one kind of ritual. By rituals are meant standardized patterns of social behaviour, which are symbolic rather than instrumental; they are not pieces of rational behaviour, and they always contain strong non-verbal elements, such as putting on a ring, in addition to verbal ones, such as marriage vows. A common ritual is shaking hands, in greeting, to mark the beginning or end of an encounter; this is not normally religious, but it could be, if it were the custom for a priest to bless it and give his approval. Rituals have the power to bring about social changes, in the relationships between people as in marriage, or changes of state as in burial. The non-verbal symbols used in rites of passage, which often include bodily contact, are summarized in Table 4.1.

Table 4.1 Non-verbal symbols used in rites of passage

Ceremony	Bodily contact	Symbolic meaning

Graduation
Confirmation
Ordination
	Places hands on
	  initiate's head
		Passes on continuous
		  chain of authority

Healing ceremonies	Anoints with oil or other substance	Application of medicine

Wedding	Places ring on bride's
	  finger
		Ring stands for marriage
		  bonds

Monk taking vows	Puts his new clothes
	  on him
		Clothes represent his new
		  status

Prize-giving	Presents cup or other
	  prize, shakes hands
		Prize is mark of groups'
		  recognition for success

Adolescent initiation	Inflicts physical damage	Test of manhood

Source: Argyle (1988)

Religious ritual is 'a stereotyped sequence of activities involving gestures, words, and objects, performed in a sequestered place, and designed to influence preternatural entities or forces on behalf of the actors' goals and interests' (Turner, 1977, p. 2). Religious non-verbal symbols include red wine for blood, washing for purification or removal of guilt, prostration on the floor for humility and reverence. These symbols have meaning as simple metaphors. Others have arbitrary meanings through magical and mythical associations, as in the case of sacred relics, revered in many traditions, and animals or flags standing for social groups. Turner (1967) argued that symbols can have two meanings at the same time, one formed through bodily analogy, and the other through standing for a group. In this way group values become charged with emotion, and emotions become ennobled through being linked to group values. The reason that these non-verbal symbols are used is that they have more emotive power than mere words. Their influence may lie in the ritual performance, which affects feelings and beliefs more directly than by the use of words (Argyle, 1988).

Food or drink substances which have been consecrated ('Holy water'), and other holy objects, are regarded as 'sacraments', that is, symbols of the sacred, which have spiritual power and can convey grace to the participants in rituals. Such sacraments are found in all religions. For example in Zoroastrianism, Haoma, the son of God, was believed to be incarnate in the sacred plant haoma, which was pounded to death to extract its life-giving juice, so that those who consumed it would become immortal; the son was believed to be both victim and priest, an intermediary between God and humanity, in this sacramental banquet. The connection to the Christian sacrament of the Eucharist seems clear.

Rites of passage are where most individuals encounter religion most directly. The basic transitions through the life cycle, from birth to death, through initiation and family rites, provide meaning to existence, or consolation and encouragement.

The main religious rites of passage correspond to the stages of life: birth/naming, becoming adult/initiation, marriage, and burial. These are more than biological processes – the period of childhood varies among cultures, and it takes more than getting older to become accepted as an adult – usually a public ceremony is needed too. In some societies there are many more such rites; among the Todas in India a woman has to go through twelve of them after childbirth before she can return to normal life. Secular ones include graduation and retirement; religious ones include being ordained, and becoming a monk or nun.

Rites of passage are used to do 'ritual work', that is, effect the desired social change (Goffman, 1971). The religious element makes the ritual more powerful, because a religious official has the 'charisma' to induce feelings of awe. Weber (1922) thought that charisma is acquired by a religious leader demonstrating supernatural powers; it seems to us more likely that charisma can be generated by further non-verbal symbols, in this case impressive costume, together with an elaborately decorated building, dim lighting, powerful music and the rest.

Do rites of passage work? They are universal to humankind, suggesting that they do have some important function. They probably do succeed in making people feel that they are indeed joined in marriage, or that they have graduated, and this is partly through the changes in perception of the others present at the ceremony. Sociologists believe that these rites have the social function of creating a new social equilibrium, after the disruption of transition. In addition they may strengthen the social order, with its roles and statuses, since these are often dramatized in the ceremony. Family rituals are seen as strengthening families, by bringing them together, providing enjoyable occasions and shared memories (Meske *et al.* 1994). From a psychological point of view rites of passage may reduce anxiety by helping people through a difficult transition. There is some evidence that this works too, in that family rituals lead to higher adolescent self-esteem and reduced anxiety (Fiese and Kline, 1993). Rites of passage are more prominent in primitive societies; this may be because the same people are involved in several overlapping role systems, so that ritual is needed to clarify their roles (Gluckman, 1965). It has been argued that in modern society the lack of rituals has resulted in anomie, so that more ritual is needed now (Durkheim, 1912/1976). This received some confirmation in a comparison of 148 societies in which it was found that increasing population density led to a greater number of calendar rituals (Reeves and Bylund, 1992).

Van Gennep (1908) noticed that rites of passage usually had a three stage pattern. In the first the candidate or candidates for change appear in their existing state, shown by their usual clothes for example, and with their friends. In the second stage some clothes are removed; there may be initiations; individuals may be told secrets, and may have temporary licence to misbehave. In the third, final stage, they appear again, in new clothes to mark their new status, in new company, and are publicly seen as changed. The Oxford University degree ceremony is rather like this. Turner (1969) developed an analysis which focused on the second, or liminal, stage of rituals. He described the play, joking, deviance and creativity of this period; there may be status inversion, in which future leaders are humiliated, and novices humbled. In this liminal stage there is ritual creation of an ideal state of society, called 'communitas', where there are no status divisions and no property, and there is love, equality and harmony among all. This is a religious and ecstatic condition in which people are liberated from the strains of office, and the sinful state of selfish and hierarchical society. Of course the world cannot be managed without an administrative structure, and even the Franciscan monks had to have a leadership hierarchy. Both aspects of society are necessary, though they are totally incompatible. Religion is able to keep communitas alive, especially at religious services; it gives 'recognition to an essential . . . human bond, without which there could be *no* human society' (p. 99). This is a religious state which is able to purify candidates for transformation. Turner suggests that whole groups are permanently in this state – Franciscan monks in the original form, holy beggars, poets, clowns, and others who do not recognize status or property; they are taboo because they cross social boundaries and threaten the social order, but are also a source of innovation. It is significant that two of Turner's taboo categories are religious.

Male puberty rites, when boys become men, are the most typical rite of passage, which the theories are really based on. In all preliterate societies this is a religious affair, and in the modern world religious denominations have placed their own rite at the same time, as with confirmation, adult baptism and bar mitzva. In primitive society, boys (and less commonly girls) at the age of puberty are separated from the world of women and children and are initiated into the world of men. They spend a period of time living outside the boundaries of the tribe, having been stripped of clothes, sometimes disguised or wearing masks. A senior male figure officiates, with other men; there is instruction into the ways of adults, including religious knowledge hitherto secret, and they may be expected to go into trances or have religious experiences. But above all they are initiated into sexuality; the boys are also subjected to painful and frightening ordeals and mutilation, often including circumcision. They are 'born again' into the male adult world. Part of the purpose is to separate them from the world of women and childhood; cross-cultural comparisons have found that these initiations are more common and more severe in societies where infant boys sleep with their mothers during the first year of life

(Whiting *et al.* 1958); but it has also been found that initiations take place only where there are male organizations for war or hunting; in both cases there may be concern about boys being able to play the male role (Young, 1965). Circumcision may be to mark the boys' sexuality, one of the ordeals to test and prepare them for the life of men.

Adolescent rites like this are rare in modern society, and those which we have are not religious, though religions still have their rites; there may be initiation ceremonies for college, sometimes at places of work, and both of these can involve ordeals and sexual experiences, and some have had to be banned because of fatal consequences. An experiment in which college girls had to undergo an embarrassing experience to join a very dull club found that their desire to join was enhanced if this was more severe, a case of cognitive dissonance in action (Aronson and Mills, 1959).

Marriage is universal to human societies; 92 per cent of people in Britain, for example, get married, many of them in churches. The main ritual is the marriage service, but there is a series of others before and after. There is the engagement, in many places the payment of the bride price, instruction to the bride on how to be a wife by the mother-in-law, where there is an extended family, before the wedding. The service itself is designed to achieve a change of relationships: the couple are separated from their kin and joined to each other, and bonds are also created between the two groups of kin. The attachment between man and wife is strengthened by the emotional power of the service, the social support of the other participants, and the religious authority of the priest.

Funerals are held in all human societies, and this is often a religious occasion. Most cultures believe in an after-life, and the main purpose of the funeral is to effect the passage of the deceased from this world to the next. How the body is processed depends on beliefs about what is going to happen; it may be elaborately equipped for the journey, as the ancient Egyptians did, or there may be rites to prevent its return such as by pointing its feet away from the house. It may be thought necessary to purify the corpse if it is believed to be polluted, for example, by blood, by violence, or simply by belonging to a lower caste. Thanks and praise are offered for the life of the deceased, and his or her achievements noted, so that they can thus live on in memory at least. A second function of funerals is to help those who are left behind, the bereaved, who must adjust to life without the deceased. Social solidarity and human relatedness are shattered by the death of someone close. Cultural mechanisms must serve to reintegrate the bereaved into society. There is a period of withdrawal, after which they return to normal life. The period of mourning allows some readjustment, by publicly licensed grief. The ceremony itself may help, since there is often a party with food and drink, and in some cultures dancing; these are cheerful occasions when social support is offered to the bereaved (Brandon, 1989).

The tendency of individuals in modern society who lead totally secular lives to resort to religious rites of passage has been noted. We find that non-believers apparently feel the need for a traditional rite when they are faced with a life-cycle transition. Pickering (1974) suggested a distinction between 'ritual' and 'ceremonial' to explain the persistence of rites of passage in modern society. 'Ceremonials' are the elaborate or stylized form of social behaviour on such occasions, which can be utilized by the non-believers, while the believers on such occasions experience 'ritual', which includes the religious element. The non-believers need the ceremonial structure, and use traditional rites to obtain it, which religious organizations are happy to provide.

WORSHIP IN GROUPS

Most religious behaviour consists of the meetings of groups of believers to engage in worship and related activities. Worship may consist of hymns of praise or other music, prayers, sacrifices or other rituals, readings from sacred books, creeds, as well as charismatic activities such as speaking with tongues, 'healing', dancing and clapping. The balance between these activities varies among religions and denominations. Group worship often takes place in a temple, but household worship is also common around the world. The intention of worship is probably to maintain relations with the gods, by gifts and sacrifices, in order to preserve life, to maintain the social cohesion of the group and pass on its traditions and doctrines (Harrelson, 1989).

Durkheim (1915) held the view that the origin of religion lay in 'collective effervescence', that is, intense emotional arousal which strengthened social bonds. These ideas receive some support from those preliterate societies where it is common to hold ecstatic religious meetings. Csikszentmihalyi (1975) argued that communitas and collective effervescence are both cases of what he called 'flow', a state in which participants are absorbed in the activity and lose awareness of themselves, as in challenging activities such as rock-climbing. Others have argued that religion is a social event such as making music together, where the participants share the same experiences in the course of a complex sequence; 'religion like music is a social event' (Schutz, 1951).

Charismatic worship

Ecstatic religious meetings are found in many cultures. In a cross-cultural study Hayden (1987) found that this is more common in societies where it is important to hold groups of men together as they do dangerous hunting or fishing; he argued that the ecstatic rituals suppress individual identities and enable strong bonds to form. He said: 'Masked monsters or spirits, flames and darkness, bullroarers, drumming, and the whole panoply of sensory effects insured total involvement and the forging of some of the strongest emotional bonds the human race has known' (p. 86). This could be a case of 'social evolution', that is, a social pattern persists if it is found to work. In a study of 44 urban communes, Carlton-Ford (1992) found that where there was evidence of shared emotional rituals – i.e. collective effervescence – the self esteem of the members was higher. Having a charismatic leader helped too, but only if there were few rituals.

Worship in Pentecostal and charismatic bodies in the West has attracted much attention. In the early days of American Pentecostalism, shortly after 1900, 'at nearly every meeting there was speaking in tongues, prophesying, healings, exorcism, hand-clapping, uncoordinated praying aloud, running, jumping, falling, "dancing in the Spirit", crying and shouting with great exuberance' (Anderson, 1987, p. 230). Since then Pentecostalists have become more restrained, healing has declined, and there is concentration on speaking with tongues, which is taken as a mark of 'baptism in the spirit'. More recently, since 1960, there has been a world-wide charismatic revival, affecting some mainstream Protestant churches and the Roman Catholic church. An Australian survey found that Pentecostalists now make up 18.5 per cent of Christian church attenders, and that 14 per cent of attenders speak in tongues (Kaldor, 1994). Originally Pentecostal churches were mainly drawn from lower class or African Americans. British Pentecostalists are still mainly working class, and in Australia they are less likely to have university degrees, and more likely to be immigrants and not to be able to speak English than mainstream church members, but there are also many middle-class Pentecostalists. In the USA and Britain charismatic members of mainstream churches are similar in background to others.

The ecstatic states characteristic of charismatics can be induced in a number of ways – inspirational preaching, arousing music, and above all Bible reading, according to Poloma and Pendleton's (1989) study of 1,275 members. In revivalist meetings the contents of the sermon can be very arousing, describing the prospects of imminent death, and of going to hell. 'In ten years' time a quarter of you will be dead' (Billy Graham); 'Hell has been running for six thousand years. It is filling up every day. Where is it? About eighteen miles from here. Which way is it? Straight down – not over eighteen miles.' (John Wesley). In snake-handling cults in North America, this activity produces arousal to the point of collapse (Sargant, 1957).

Glossolalia

Speaking in tongues and the other charismatic behaviours appear to be signs of joy in groups of shared religious enthusiasm, just as described by Durkheim and by Turner (Buckley and Galanter, 1979). It is the distinguishing feature of contemporary Pentecostalism and charismatic worship. It has become more prevalent and more acceptable in some Western countries since the 1970s. Table 4.2 shows the extent of tongue speaking, and of approval for it, in Australia. It can be seen that 57 per cent of members of Pentecostal churches spoke, and another 37 per cent were in favour, but there was a certain amount of it in mainstream churches too. Originally, it was claimed that glossolalics were speaking some foreign language, which others present were able to interpret, but linguistic analysis has made it clear that there is no actual language here at all, in that there is no vocabulary or grammar, though some biblical names and words from other languages may be included. Samarin (1972) provides an example:

kelalaiyanamo, kelalaiyenayeno

Saying 'alleluia' three times is not very different. However the utterances do follow a regular pattern, and seem to have informal rules; there are regular lengths of speech between pauses, each starts on a stressed syllable, and there is regular rising and falling intonation (Samarin, 1972).

Table 4.2　Glossolalia in Australia

	Necessary for all %	Approve and do speak %	Approve but do not speak %
Overall	6	14	17
Pentecostal	25	57	12
Mainstream	3	7	17
Anglican	3	8	18

Source: Kaldor (1994)

Two opposing points of view have been put forward. Samarin argued that glossolalia is a learned form of religious behaviour, following the rules of the group, used in order to be accepted by the group. In favour of Samarin's position is the finding that speaking with tongues is learned quite easily. Goodman (1972) argued that it is a speech automatism produced by extreme emotion and near trance states in which the language centres in the brain are disconnected from speech production. In support of Goodman's position are her observations in an ecstatic Mexican church group. However, Stanley et al. (1978) analysed 120 letters describing glossolalic experiences and found that there were several different types. For some it was a necessary activity for membership in their group, while for others it was the result of a crisis, was an optional extra in their group, or was a joyful experience in private, a form of private prayer.

Another point of view has been that tongue speakers are psychologically disturbed, but this has been strongly disconfirmed; no difference can be found on standard personality measures. On the other hand, as we have just seen, they are often undergoing a crisis, and some studies have found evidence of some anxiety or conflict, and a desire for close relations in groups (Richardson, 1973; Kildahl, 1972).

Several studies have traced the conditions which produce glossolalia; Poloma and Pendleton (1989) carried out a path analysis, using a sample of 1,275 members of the Assemblies of God, with the results shown in Figure 4.1. The main predictor of glossolalia and other charismatic behaviour was devotional activity, and in turn charismatic behaviour led to evangelism. Other studies have found that a desire for a deeper spiritual life, disillusionment with existing traditions, a life crisis, and the encouragement of friends were the best predictors (Malony and Lovekin, 1985). Holm (1991) recorded several hundred Pentecostal meetings in Finland and found two different kinds of glossolalia. 'Prayer glossolalia' was by individuals either alone or in groups, sometimes for the first time. 'Prophetic glossolalia' was given loudly by leaders at meetings, and was followed by an interpretation of what was said. The typical conditions for someone to speak for the first time were an emotional meeting, prayers, laying on of hands and a strong expectation that this would happen. Despite these powerful social influences the event is experienced as a gift from God, and the recipient is said to be 'baptized in the spirit'.

Speaking in tongues is regarded in Pentecostal circles as a way of establishing religious credentials, through showing that those concerned have been 'baptized in the spirit', but it is less important in charismatic sections of mainstream churches. Ball (1981) found that glossolalia did not become part of the self-image of tongue speakers, perhaps because they wanted to emphasize their membership of the church and wanted to minimize the differences. We can sum up by stating that glossolalia is not really verbal behaviour, it is more a kind of non-verbal behaviour. It expresses intensity of religious devotion, and tone of voice, facial expression, and posture can convey further aspects of the worship being expressed.

Religious healing

'Healing' is often associated with religion, from pre-historic times onwards. There are still many faith healers, healing cults and practitioners of 'alternative medicine' in industrialized countries. Health is of great importance to all, and it is one of the roots of religion.

In traditional cultures there is little medicine, and religious healing takes its place. There are a number of features common to different cases of traditional healing: there are group settings with an intense degree of emotional arousal, strong social pressure from leaders of the group, strong expectations that the healing will work, and a theory about what is going

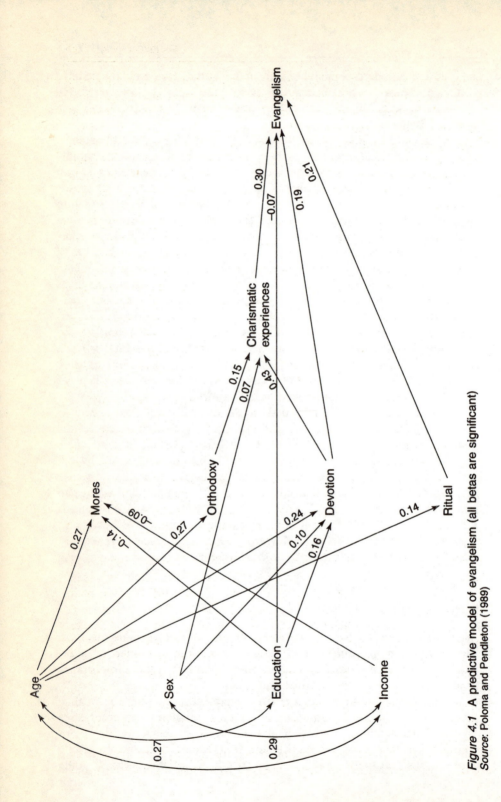

Figure 4.1 A predictive model of evangelism (all betas are significant)
Source: Poloma and Pendleton (1989)

on. As Frank and Frank (1991) observe, 'healing' operates like a placebo effect, well-known in medicine, in its use of suggestion and expectation. Often there is some strong symbolism; Turner (1967) describes a Zambian ritual for healing barrenness, which used red clay to symbolize menstrual blood, figurines for infants, carved calabashes for wombs, castor oil which is used to massage new-born infants, and the death of a cock to represent the ending of being troubled by a spirit. A further factor is that only certain individuals become healers, and some of them seem to be very successful.

Purification is often part of 'healing' practices, and is associated with certain shrines, rivers such as the Ganges, or springs as at Lourdes. There are pilgrimages to these places, and to the saintly individuals who are believed to have the power of healing. The Lourdes situation has much in common with traditional healing but on a vaster scale: 40–50,000 gather each day for the main service, in an atmosphere charged with religious emotion and positive expectations, and with the sight of piles of abandoned crutches as apparent evidence of past success (Cranston, 1957). However, as Paloutzian (1996) pointed out, actual cure rates at Lourdes are lower than expected from what we know about spontaneous remissions of serious illness.

Some fundamentalist sects practise 'faith healing' at the end of regular services, in a similar emotional atmosphere and with the prayerful support of the congregation. There have been some careful follow-up studies of some of those treated. Glik (1986) interviewed 176 individuals who had attended charismatic and other healing groups, and compared them with 137 who had received regular primary care. Those who had been to healing groups reported better health and subjective well-being, though their actual physical state was unchanged. Pattison *et al.* (1973) analysed 71 cases of healings at healing services; 62 'recoveries' took place during the service, half of them suddenly; 50 had been suffering from serious illnesses. Again there was no actual change in physical condition or life style; what had changed was their faith and their subjective condition. They believed that they had been healed by the casting out of sin. MMPI (Minnesota Multiphasic Personality Inventory) scores showed that these 'recovered' individuals engaged in denial and disregard of reality. In both of these studies the changes were towards improved subjective health, and not in actual physical condition. Miettinen (1990, cited by Holm, 1991) studied extensively 611 cases of 'healings' in Finland. The findings were that there was no evidence of any physical improvement, but that the clients (450 women and 161 men), who were of limited education and social status, experienced a subjective change, attributed to suggestibility and personal instability.

There is also psychological healing. Traditional priests and priestesses are often successful through their knowledge of what is going on in the community, usually a village, though they also use sacrifices and other rituals, sometimes symbolism such as purification or rebirth, and may put clients in states of high emotional arousal (Huxley, 1966). It has been suggested that shamans are like primitive psychiatrists, 'wounded healers' who have been ill themselves, who have some understanding of what is troubling their clients, and who organize 'dance psychodramas' in which the latter are led to act out their troubles symbolically (Lewis, 1989). Traditional healing may also involve strengthening bonds with the group, by the patient providing a feast, or by confession and forgiveness. Focusing attention on the patient is also likely to restore self-esteem. McGuire (1983), in a survey of Christian healing groups, suggested that mobilizing a sense of self-empowerment was a key factor in healing.

While there is no evidence for religious faith as curative, in Chapter 10 we have evidence for its effects as preventive and stress reducing. Findings about the psychology of mental health can throw some light on claimed cures. Mental ill-health, more than physical, is greatly affected by stress, and social support can do a lot to prevent or cure. Discussion of problems may lead to solving them; sympathetic support can lead to enhancing self-esteem; the availability of a supportive network can lead to a feeling of mastery, an ability to cope with things; but above all acceptance and companionship of others, a feeling of being loved, may be the most therapeutic of all (Argyle, 1992). Where does religion come in? We shall see later that the religious community is a powerful source of social support, and that the presumed relation with God is another effective means of coping with emotional problems. There are often feelings of guilt, failure and low self-esteem in mental ill-health, and religion is a means of relieving people of such feelings, by confession, counselling, and acceptance into the community.

Sacrifice

This is a ritual which is found in palaeolithic times, in preliterate societies, and is central to Christianity, ancient Judaism, the religion of ancient Greece, Indian Vedic religion and that of Japan, as well as many other traditions. Sacrifices are carried out by priests or other qualified elders, after they have been ritually cleansed. Animals (but sometimes humans, as in ancient Mexico) or vegetables are sacrificed, usually by first killing and then burning them or sometimes eating them. The common element is the giving or offering of living possessions to the gods (Henninger, 1987). It is done at an altar, at regular times or at special events such as rites of passage. Sacrifices are offered to the gods, to spirits or to the departed, for a number of different purposes. When there is propitiation of evil, the animal represents this and is completely destroyed. When there are offerings to gods of the underworld, blood is poured into the ground or streams.

Anthropologists have put forward a number of theories of the motivations for sacrifice. There are several main types of sacrifice:

1 Gifts in the hope of a return of favours.
2 Propitiation, forgivenesss, avoidance of god's punishment.
3 Seeking communion, a closer relation with god, by sharing a meal, for example.
4 Killing the god, to prevent his becoming senile, so that he can be reborn and maintain the fertility of crops.
5 Eating the god, in the hope of ingesting his powers.
6 Funeral sacrifices to help the departed on their way to the next world.

These ideas are all more or less conscious, but psychoanalytic writing proposed that sacrifice serves to placate the super-ego, derived from the parents and projected on to the gods, and thus to relieve guilt feelings, and to make further licence possible (Fenichel, 1945).

We have seen that one purpose of sacrifice is for propitiation of the gods, and forgiveness of sins. Ancient religions made extensive use of sacrifice, and it was intended 'to impress on the person bringing the sacrifice the enormity of his sin, to the extent that whatever happened to the animal that was sacrificed should by rights have happened to the sinner' (Wigoder, 1989). 'Sacrifice as a religious act was part of the mental furniture of everyone in the ancient world, Jew, Christian and Pagan' (Hanson and Hanson, 1981, p. 107). However, it ceased to be so for Europeans when 'at the very end of the eleventh century, Christian thought permeating European culture could no longer take for granted the ancient concept of sacrifice' (ibid., 1980, p. 108).

It is believed that sacrifices release a positive force of social cohesion in the group. Can we understand this process in terms of psychology? The specific effects of sacrifice have not been isolated but we can use some well-established psychological findings to throw a little more light on this phenomenon. Research on reciprocity shows that there are strong expectations and pressures that gifts will be reciprocated, and that giving gifts is a means of obtaining benefits from another. In close relationships, however, we also give gifts to those we love, partly because it will strengthen or sustain the relationship, but also because there is concern about the needs of the other. And doing things for others induces positive feelings and self-esteem in the giver; so there are several bases for the 'positive force' to which anthropologists refer. Gifts for the gods are expected to be reciprocated, and also to strengthen social bonds and individual psyches.

Music

Music and religion are closely linked; music is used in worship in all religions. Music is found in all preliterate societies, often with dancing, accompanying not only religious acts but also feasts, war, and other co-operative activities. Song and dance draw groups together, generating intense, sometimes trance, states and feelings of group unity (Blacking, 1987). Both are believed to come from the realm of spirit. Music is used in several ways. In shamanism, frenetic drumming is used to work people up into states of frenzy and trance; in Voodoo there is prolonged rhythmic dancing and drumming; in charismatic religion music is part of the means of arousal of similar states. In ancient Greek religion music was believed to affect the state of the soul, and in particular to generate states of celestial harmony; later religious music is used similarly to produce elevated states of mystical experience – 'a flame of emotion that is kindled by the thought of holiness' (Scholes, 1955). Music is often used to recount beliefs or mythology, as in the Mass or requiems. Hymns play a central part in group worship, as those present share in proclaiming their beliefs and generating shared emotions. Hymns are enjoyable and can therefore be used to attract new members to the church (Ellingson, 1987). They are used at revival meetings; Billy Graham, in his mass meetings, used highly emotional gospel hymns, sung by a choir of 1,500.

The human voice is the preferred source of religious music, probably because words add to the meaning, and human emotions are directly expressed. The earliest Christian music took the form of hymns; in the sixth century unaccompanied plain-chant was established, and in the sixteenth and seventeenth centuries Palestrina and Bach wrote music for the mass which became the 'religious sound' of the West for several centuries (Perris, 1985). This was later added to by numerous hymn writers, so that hymn tunes became another religious sound. Churches adopted organs, partly to distance themselves from the secular music of the roisterous jongleurs; later on instruments became acceptable, and now evangelical churches have abandoned organs in favour of guitars, drums, keyboards and wind instruments, and use choruses instead of hymns, probably to distance themselves from traditional worship. It is partly a matter of convention which sounds are regarded as religious, but there may also be a definite sound quality which generates religious feelings. Research on the sounds of the human voice when experiencing different emotions has found the physical properties of sad, happy, or angry. Religious emotions are probably aroused by special kinds of music, which will be familiar to composers. If people are asked to describe how they interpret pieces of music, it is not only 'religious' music which receives a religious interpretation. Beethoven's 'Pastoral' Sonata was described as the 'joyful uplifting of the oppressed soul that feels itself released from the depths of anguish' (Valentine, 1962). The 'Dream of Gerontius' gives the experience of the soul ascending to heaven. And Beethoven's last quartets, not usually regarded as religious music, are also experienced as a glimpse of heaven or eternity.

THE CLERGY

As stated above, one of our goals is to study those who could be defined as religious leaders, or at least as professionals, those for whom religion is not just a label but is the centre of their lives, a major investment and commitment. Looking at the clergy is one extension of the classical approach in the psychology of religion that has focused on converts. Both converts and clergy are members of a minority that has made a unique commitment to religion. In the case of the clergy, we have individuals who are *professionally* religious, which implies a special kind of religiosity. What can we learn by looking at them? Adopting the role of a virtuoso (clergy, converts) dictates strong behavioural constraints, which should lead to strong identification with the role, and to related beliefs. Social-psychological theories of dissonance are relevant. This may be why religious traditions force members (in minority religions) or clergy to adopt special dress, life style, chastity rules, and so on.

Religious leaders emerge in preliterate societies; those chosen are individuals who are judged to have the greatest magical or religious powers. In preliterate societies this is often a shaman, who uses his own powers to heal the sick and see the future, usually by going into ecstasies or trances while dressed as an animal, and by frenetic dancing, drumming or singing, sometimes induced by drugs, and thought to be due to spirit possession (Lewis, 1989). Priests, on the other hand, make contact with and try to influence transcendent powers, by means of sacrifices, worship, and ritual; they are experts in these matters and have acquired religious knowledge, sometimes secret, through being trained by the priesthood. The criteria for selection for these religious roles vary; sometimes shamans are chosen because they are epileptic or have an unusual number of fingers (Eliade, 1964). Priests direct worship and other rituals, which are conducted in a formal place of worship, which is the centre of ritual activity.

The pay and status of the clergy, once high in Europe, have declined during this century, but their image, in popular fiction at least, is of 'sincerity, unselfish concern for the poor and outcast, fearless denunciation of evil from the pulpit, and wise, sympathetic counsel to the erring and perplexed' (Voigt, cited by Moberg, 1962).

Recruitment

The clergy are recruited rather differently from other professions. In the case of the Roman Catholic clergy, it is of course unlikely that their fathers will be priests, but often there are other relatives in the church. The main source of influence for Roman Catholics is the local priest, who recruits suitable young people, often at an early age, and most while they are still at school. The second major influence is the mother (Fichter, 1961). In a survey of Anglican clergy the main influence in deciding to be ordained was clergy, followed by mother and then friends (Towler and Coxon, 1979). Some had fathers who were clergy, and often there is an experience of being 'called'. In a large sample of American Protestant clergy 38 per cent reported this, but for sect-type clergy the figure was 85 per cent (Moberg, 1962). Some Christian denominations insist on it, as the main qualification, though there is some confusion about how it is defined. In later life all clergy have a strong sense of 'vocation' compared with other professions (Ranson *et al*. 1977). In all religious groups, those who become clergy had attended services often as children, had been active in religious youth groups, and had been judged by others to have the right qualities for ordination.

For some it is seen as a good job, for some it was a source of social mobility, at a time when the clergy were better paid and seen as community leaders. There are class differences in the origins of clergy of different traditions, reflecting the class composition of the laity; Anglican clergy in Britain are more middle class than other clergy, and Catholic clergy are drawn from all classes. It has been found that many more women join religious orders in those continents such as South America and Africa where there is little education for women, and poor alternative career prospects (Ebaugh, 1993). Ordinands wear special uniforms, and through changes in self-image become increasingly committed. As with trainee doctors they practise their new skills, in this case taking services and giving sermons; taking on the new role in this way will further enhance alterations in self-image, since they will be perceived by others as clergy.

For millennia most leaders and clergy in all religious traditions were male. During the twentieth century Christian Protestant denominations have increasingly recruited women, though there has been massive resistance to this change. Near the end of the century, half of the ordinands in some theological colleges are women, and we face the feminization of the clergy in the twenty-first century. In the USA women clergy are older than the men, with an average starting age of 35, having either been mothers or had other jobs first. They did not have 'role models', though many had been encouraged by a clergyman or a professor, or by their fathers. Their motivation has been found to be a little different too; women ordinands want to 'develop spiritually' whereas men primarily want to be parish ministers (Charlton, 1987). In a comparative study of male and female clergy in mainstream US Protestant denominations, Lehman (1993) found only a few differences between them. Men preferred exerting power and using structured decision making, as well as legalistic ethics. Lehman (1980), in a study of American Baptists, found that resistance to the ordination of women was a function of theology, sexism, and the views of reference groups; those holding oppositional views stereotyped women, in a way which made them unsuitable, and sheer contact with clergywomen made no difference. In a US study in which subjects rated the acceptability of imaginary clergy with various combinations of attributes, being female produced a rating 3.8 points lower on a 100 point scale; being black was 7.7 points lower, and being divorced 9.7 (Schreckengost, 1987).

Personality

It has been claimed that the clergy are neurotic or inadequate in some other way (Spilka, Hood and Gorsuch, 1985). However, these assertions are often based on inadequate samples, for example, of clergy receiving therapy. Several studies have used the Eysenck Personality Questionnaire (EPQ). Francis (1991b) tested 252 Anglican ordinands with this measure, and the mean scores are shown in Figure 4.2. It can be seen that the male ordinands were significantly more introverted than the population mean, and scored lower on the lie scale – which is usually taken to measure acquiescence and conformity. The female ordinands on the other hand were *more* extraverted and less neurotic than the population mean. Since men are usually more extraverted than women, and less neurotic, Francis concludes that male clergy are more feminine and female clergy more masculine than the averages for their sexes.

There are other possible interpretations of the personalities of female clergy. Another explanation, which we use in Chapter 8 to account for the greater religiosity of women, suggests that religion stresses the 'feminine' values of kindness, empathy, and compassion, and does not value the masculine characteristics of aggression and dominance. It may be that clergy of both sexes form a new norm, i.e. more masculine than the average woman, but more feminine than the average man.

Are clergy more neurotic or mentally disturbed than other people, as has often been claimed? The findings above suggest that they are not. Some studies have used the Personal Orientation Inventory (POI), which is a test to measure self-actualization, self-acceptance, maturity and personality integration. Webster and Stewart (1973) found that New Zealand clergy scored above the published norms for this test, especially for the scales measuring ability to live in the present, self-acceptance, integration and being good at interpersonal relations. The clergy who were theologically liberal, less dogmatic, as opposed to conservative, had higher self-actualization scores, and had higher job satisfaction. On the other hand, Kennedy *et al.* (1977) gave this test to 271 American Catholic priests and found that they were *lower* than the norms; 57 per cent were classified as 'underdeveloped', especially in their relations with others, and in their faith. Ferder (1978, cited by Wulff, 1991) tested 211 Catholic women who wanted to be ordained, and found that they were *more* developed than the female norms, again probably because they were a determined and self-selected group.

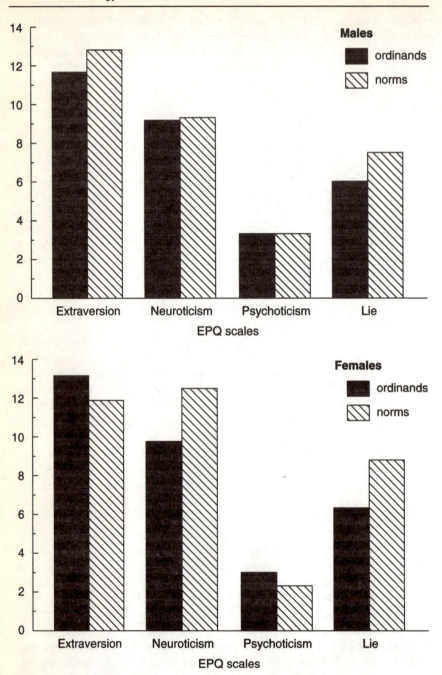

Figure 4.2 Personality of 155 male and 97 female Anglican ordinands as measured using the Eysenck Personality Questionnaire (EPQ)
Source: Francis (1991b)

We have seen that female clergy scored markedly higher on measures of adjustment and extraversion, and lower on emotional disturbance. They have also been found to be more assertive and intellectual than women teachers for example, i.e. more like men in personality. This is all probably because those who succeeded in becoming ordained during the period of conflict must have been particularly determined and able to cope with the stress of this situation.

Sexuality

Clergy seem to be different from the general population in terms of sexuality. It has only been possible fairly recently for data on homosexuality to be obtained, and there are still no proper surveys. Wolf (1989) concluded that about 40 per cent of American Roman Catholic priests are gay; this was the average estimate of the gay priests interviewed. Sipe (1990) interviewed 1,000 Catholic priests, half of them in therapy, and 500 of their sexual partners, and concluded that 20 per cent were in a homosexual relationship, and 20 per cent in a stable relationship with a woman. In Britain there are reportedly many homosexual priests in the Church of England too, especially in the High, or Anglo-Catholic, branch. Fletcher (1990) studied a sample of these and found that they were under great stress, mainly from the fear of being found out. Despite the absence of proper sampling in these surveys, it is clear that homosexuality is common among the clergy of some Christian churches, well above the usual rate of 2 per cent. If so, this is an interesting fact to be explained. The most obvious explanation is that joining the celibate clergy is a respected role in which being unmarried is normal. If this explanation is correct, now that homosexuality is more widely accepted perhaps fewer homosexuals will seek this role.

There are further sex problems; Loftus and Camargo (1993) reported on the treatment of 1,322 male clergy sex offenders in Canada. About 10 per cent had been in trouble with children, presumably boys; they were not otherwise abnormal (cf. Berry, 1992). Some of these sex problems can be explained by the tradition of celibacy, and the close contact with young choirboys.

Stress and satisfaction

The sources of stress are fairly clear, for example from Dewe's survey (1987) of 486 New Zealand clergy. They are:

1 Work overload, for instance from looking after several parishes; shortage of time; not enough time off or with family.
2 Low incomes.
3 Loneliness, for unmarried priests, and the desire to marry.
4 Conflict with the congregation, and the latter's lack of commitment.

In his sample of Anglican clergy Fletcher (1990) found that 42 per cent were stressed by 'always having to please others', and 52 per cent by being on call 24 hours a day. They share with other leaders of leisure groups the problem of having to manage an organization with no sanctions to punish or exclude and very little powers of reward (Argyle, 1996). The resources for dealing with stress can be inadequate. There is too little time for leisure, unmarried clergy live alone and lack social support, and there may also be lack of support from the hierarchy. Catholic priests report being under most control from the hierarchy, and subject to enforcement of rules, Anglican clergy least and Methodist ministers in between (Ranson *et al.* 1977).

Despite many reports of the stresses experienced by the clergy, overall their level of stress appears to be well below the average. Rayburn *et al.* (1986) in a study of 250 American Roman Catholic clergy found an average stress level of 123 on the Osipow and Spokane scale, compared with 138 for the general population. And Fletcher (1990) with 230 English clergy found a level of mental health above the working population average; they did better than the norms for the Crown and Crisp inventory, only 5 per cent being at a 'case' level of disturbance. There was also a high level of satisfaction in that only 3 per cent were thinking of leaving, whereas 53 per cent 'would not dream of doing anything else'. In some cases, it is possible that the role of the clergy may fit particular individuals because of their psychological problems. Spiro (1965), in discussing the role of the Buddhist monk in Myanmar (Burma), describes the way in which individuals having tendencies for withdrawal, regression, and self-absorption find the prescribed clergy behaviour an ideal solution, and a way of precluding serious pathology.

If we look at the bodily health of the clergy, it seems again that the stress cannot be too high. Clergy, monks and nuns have a lower death rate, that is, they live longer, and are less likely to die from heart attacks, most cancers, suicide and accidents. The health of Protestant clergy is better than that of Catholic priests; Japanese Zen priests do well too. The difference is now less than formerly and the longevity of the clergy is similar to that of school and university teachers. It is partly due to better health behaviour, such as smoking less (Jarvis and Northcott, 1987). In a large survey of the mental health of American Catholic nuns it was found that they had a lower rate of hospitalization and of schizophrenia than the rest of the population. However, the rate for cloistered nuns was considerably higher, it has been suggested because the life attracts those with a tendency to withdraw, i.e. with incipient schizophrenia (Kelley, 1958).

Reported happiness and job satisfaction are high for the clergy. Among the elderly, church members are happier than non-members (see Chapter 10), and church leaders are happier still; this includes clergy (Moberg and

Taves, 1965, shown in our Table 10.1). Other studies show that the clergy have a high level of job satisfaction, similar to that of university teachers and social workers, and higher than that of managers, clerical or manual workers. Their job satisfaction is high for the same reasons. Nelsen and Everett (1976) found that ministers were less likely to consider moving (an index of low job satisfaction), or leaving the church, if they felt that they were appreciated or that the pay was sufficient; those in large city parishes were the most contented. Hoge *et al.* (1981) studied 659 Protestant clergy in Chicago and found that personal fulfilment was greater when they felt that they were challenged and could use their skills. Two further factors which probably enhance clergy satisfaction are the high degree of autonomy and social recognition they have (Argyle, 1989).

However, some clergy do resign, and in the US Roman Catholic church many have left since 1960. Between 1966 and 1984 as many as 37 per cent resigned in the first 25 years of their ministry (Schoenherr and Young, 1990). Those most likely to go were the younger ones in large city parishes. Another predictive factor was loneliness and the desire to get married (Verdieck *et al.* 1988). In the study of British clergy, only 3 per cent wanted to leave, and the most discontented were the homosexuals (Ranson *et al.* 1977).

The religious life of the clergy and members of religious orders

One of the main points to be made about the clergy is that they live a very active religious life (see Table 4.3). Religion is a full-time job for them, and they have a religious identity, supported by their title and costume. They are recruited from young people who have already been seen to be very active in their congregations, many feel that they had been called, so have a strong sense of vocation; they underwent intensive religious education, often under semi-monastic conditions for several years, in a regime of physical and spiritual discipline, often celibacy, so that they became dedicated to a religious life (Oxtoby, 1987). They acquired a great deal of religious knowledge, and this is added to by having to expound their faith week after week. They conduct regular services, often daily, in which they play a central part in the ritual, and are publicly committed to what is done. And they spend time alone in study, to prepare sermons and classes, and in prayer, and in private services and devotions.

Religious orders are found in Christianity, Buddhism and elsewhere. The life of monks and nuns is very different from that of the clergy. While the main work of the clergy is with their flock, the main work of members of religious orders is ritual and prayer. They usually attend several services a day, and also spend some hours in prayer and meditation. As a result they

Table 4.3   Ministerial activity scale

EVANGELIST (Reliability: alpha = 0.87; split-half = 0.90)
 1 Maps out objectives and plans the overall church strategy and programme.
 6 Helps people to develop the desire to have their congregation grow in size.
14 Visits new residents and helps to add new members.
21 Helps to set membership goals for the congregation.
29 Urges people to see the need for sharing their faith with others.
35 Leads people in the process of reaching out to the unchurched in the community.
10 Urges people to become involved in the mission challenge of the church-at-large.

MINISTER TO YOUTH/CHILDREN (Reliability: alpha = 0.88; split-half = 0.90)
 2 Teaches and works directly with children.
 4 Helps the congregation to keep in touch with disinterested youth.
10 Conducts worship services in a way that is meaningful for children.
11 Teaches and works directly with young people.
12 Talks with individuals about their spiritual development.
13 Teaches youth in confirmation instruction.
22 Helps youth to identify their goals and evaluate their adequacies.
28 Treats children and youth as individuals entrusted to his spiritual care.

PERSONAL/SPIRITUAL MODEL (Reliability: alpha = 0.80; split-half = 0.82)
24 Follows a definite schedule of reading and study.
25 Shows interest in teaching subject matter with religious content.
27 Maintains a disciplined life of prayer and personal devotion.
38 Cultivates his home and personal life.

COMMUNITY-MINDED MINISTER (Reliability: alpha = 0.83; split-half = 0.85)
30 Cooperates with social, legal, medical and educational workers.
34 Participates in denominational activities.
39 Participates in community projects and organizations.
41 Mixes socially to develop contacts.
43 Assists victims of social neglect or injustice.
44 Speaks to community and civic groups.

PREACHER/PRIEST (Reliability: alpha = 0.77; split-half = 0.86)
 3 Leads public worship.
 7 When teaching, keeps class members interested.
16 In teaching, relates God's activity to everyday life and happenings.
23 Preaches sermons.
33 Administers baptism and communion: conducts weddings and sacred rites.
34 Participates in denominational activities.

PERSONAL ENABLER (Reliability: alpha = 0.91; split-half = 0.93)
 5 Ministers to the sick, dying and bereaved.
 9 Fosters fellowship at church gatherings.
12 Talks with individuals about their spiritual development.
14 Visits new residents and helps to add new members.
15 Supplies ideas for new activities and projects.
17 Works with congregational boards and committees.
18 Recruits, trains and assists lay leaders.
19 Helps lay teachers.
26 Promotes and creates enthusiasm for church activities.

Table 4.3 continued

31 In group discussion, stimulates people to participate.
37 Counsels with people about their moral and personal problems.
42 Maintains harmony, handles trouble-makers, averts or resolves problems.

ADMINISTRATOR (Reliability: alpha = 0.82; split-half = 0.83)
 1 Maps out objectives and plans the overall church strategy and programme.
17 Works with congregational boards and committees.
20 Manages the church office – records, correspondence, information centre.
32 Helps to manage church finances.

TEACHER (Reliability: alpha = 0.86; split half = 0.85)
 7 When teaching, keeps class members interested.
12 Talks with individuals about their spiritual development.
13 Teaches youth in confirmation instruction.
16 In teaching, relates God's activity to everyday life and happenings.
31 In group discussion, stimulates people to participate.
36 Teaches and works directly with adults.
45 Teaches adults in confirmation instruction.

EQUIPPER (Reliability: alpha = 0.85; split-half = 0.86)
 1 Maps out objectives and plans the overall church strategy and programme.
 5 Ministers to the sick, dying and bereaved.
17 Works with congregational boards and committees.
18 Recruits, trains and assists lay leaders.
19 Helps lay teachers.

VISITOR/COUNSELLOR (Reliability: alpha = 0.80; split-half = 0.78)
 8 Counsels with people facing the major decisions of life – marriage, vocation.
27 Maintains a disciplined life of prayer and personal devotion.
37 Counsels with people about their moral and personal problems.
38 Cultivates his home and personal life.
41 Mixes socially to develop contacts.
46 Visits regularly in the homes of the congregation.

OVERALL EFFECTIVE – Complete Scale (Reliability: alpha = 0.96)

Source: Nauss (1994)

report a high level of religious experiences (Stifler *et al.* 1993). They have to follow a life of asceticism, including poverty and celibacy, humility and obedience (McGinn, 1987). Some spend all of their time on such religious activities, while others will spend some of their time on teaching, nursing, or other good works, together with gardening, candle-making or other monastic manual work.

CONCLUSION

Religion creates a real community, not just an imagined one. This is done through rituals expressing identity and common fate, and through ties to other believers and group leaders. In this chapter we have looked at the building blocks of the religious community in its living reality. In the next chapter we will look at the most intense and rare cases of religious action: religious experiences.

Chapter 5

Religious experience

SURVEYS OF RELIGIOUS EXPERIENCE

William James (1902), in one of the best-known early studies in the field, investigated the intense experiences of a number of exceptional individuals 'in their solitude'. Later work sampled the whole population, and was not confined to solitary experiences. There are several ways of assessing religious experiences (REs). The method used in most surveys is to ask a single, carefully drafted question. The version used in British surveys by the Alister Hardy Research Centre in Oxford, known as the 'Alister Hardy question' (Hay, 1982), is:

Have you ever been aware of or influenced by a presence or power, whether you call it God or not, which is different from your everyday self?

The version used by Greeley (1975) and colleagues in the USA was:

Have you ever felt as though you were very close to a powerful spiritual force that seemed to lift you out of yourself?

A second way of studying REs is to obtain descriptions of them and analyse their contents. Alister Hardy (1979) advertised in newspapers and obtained several thousand replies; he reports an analysis of the first 3,000 in his book. Another way is to provide sample descriptions of REs and to ask people to say how similar their experience was to these. This was the method used by Hood (1970) to develop his Religious Experience Episodes Measure (REEM), which has been used in a number of studies.

A number of national sample surveys using the Alister Hardy question or the Greeley question, or others like it, have produced 'yes' answers from 34 per cent or more of the British and American populations (Hay, 1990). Back and Bourque (1970) reported the results of three American national Gallup polls, which had asked the question:

Would you say that you had ever had a 'religious or mystical experience', that is, a moment of sudden religious insight or awakening?

The percentages saying 'yes' were 20.5 (1962), 32 (1966) and 41 (1967), suggesting a sudden and so far unexplained increase in the frequency of REs. Hay (1982), using the Alister Hardy question in Britain with a sample of 1,865, found that 36.4 per cent had been influenced by a presence or power. This was repeated in 1987 and 48 per cent gave positive responses, though not all interpreted these experiences as religious. The figure of 34 per cent or so may be an overestimate since not all of those who gave a positive answer were describing REs in the usual sense; some were describing experiences of the beauty of nature, some were reporting 'psychic' experiences (see Table 5.2). On the other hand most of those who said 'yes' to these surveys were describing experiences when they were alone, not experiences in church, and the intense experiences which some people have in some churches should certainly be described as REs. From the contents of the experiences, to be described in more detail later, it looks as if there is only a difference of degree between these widespread REs and those described by famous mystics in the past.

Is there a core RE?

There are quite a number of 'varieties of religious experience' as William James (1902) recognized. On the other hand they may have a common core. A number of authorities have listed the features of REs from different religions, cultures and historical periods; the most widely recognized list is that of Stace (1960):

1 Unifying vision, all things are one, part of a whole.
2 Timeless and spaceless.
3 Sense of reality, not subjective but a valid source of knowledge.
4 Blessedness, joy, peace and happiness.
5 Feeling of the holy, sacred, divine.
6 Paradoxical, defies logic.
7 Ineffable, cannot be described in words.
8 Loss of sense of self.

Several investigators have used these criteria. Thomas and Cooper (1978) used them to rate the experiences described by 302 adults; only 2 per cent were classed as mystical experiences. This suggests that there are other experiences outside the central core, which are commonly experienced and reported as religious. Stace says that he deliberately omitted from his list visions and voices, and trances and ecstasies, which he did not believe belonged to the universal core experience.

There is another important division between two aspects of REs; perhaps there are two types of them. One variety is of contact with a transcendent being, outside oneself, of awe and dependence, the 'numinous' experience, described by Otto (1917). The other, sometimes described as 'mystical', is of the immanent unity of all things. Stace's list appears to be biased towards the immanent as opposed to the transcendent type of RE (see Hood, 1995). Hood (1975) had used these categories to construct a 32-item scale for measuring mystical experience, with factor analysis showing two factors, though these were correlated with each other at 0.47. The first factor was of General Mysticism and contained most of the items, the second he called Religious Interpretation, and contained his religious, noetic and positive affect items. The religious and noetic items are the closest to transcendence in this list. But major religious writings have often described REs as: a feeling of unity with God, fear, awe and reverence, dependence, a journey inwards or upwards, love and marriage, the goal of union with the Divine (Smith and Ghose, 1989). Here is an example:

> At this time, if I'm lucky (during yoga exercises), I seem to latch on to something akin to a pure emotional state, a sense of happiness. There is definitely some sort of power there which seems to greet me, to embrace.
>
> (Hay, 1982, p. 134)

Concepts like these do not appear on Stace's list.

There is a second area of possible omission from Stace's list, suggested by the anthropological research into the 'liminal' state described in Chapter 4. In traditional rites of passage those involved experience a fusion with the others, a feeling of love, equality and 'communitas'. This is also found in modern REs, when people feel a heightened unity with others, enhanced feelings of love and concern. One of Hardy's subjects said:

> I was overtaken by an intense feeling of affection for and unity with everyone around as they ran to catch buses, took children shopping or joyfully met their friends . . . This sense of oneness is basic to what I understand of religion . . . The effect of the Experience has been, I think, a permanent increase on my awareness that we are members of one another, a consequent greater openness towards all and a widening of my concern for others.
>
> (Hardy, 1979, p. 58)

The Stace list and the Hood scale do not mention imagery or visual aspects of REs. In the Alister Hardy collection, 8.8 per cent mentioned light, 4.5 per cent being bathed in a glowing light, and 18.3 per cent visions, while others mentioned sensations such as music, voices, and warmth. A great variety of images have been reported in REs, at least partly the result of different religious education or other social influences. Here is an example from Hardy's collection:

> On the first night that I knelt to say my prayers, which I had now made a constant practice, I was aware of a glowing light which seemed to envelop me and which was accompanied by a sense of warmth all round me.
>
> (Hardy, 1979, p. 34)

We conclude that the core RE probably exists but needs to be amplified to include more transcendent components, more of the heightened concern for others, and sensory images. These are reflected better in the list obtained by Greeley (1975) in his national US sample of 1,467 people (Table 5.1).

Table 5.1   Greeley's descriptors of religious experience (RE)

Description of RE	Percentage out of those reporting one or more RE
A feeling of deep and profound peace	55
A certainty that all things would work out for the good	48
Sense of my own need to contribute to others	43
A conviction that love is the centre of everything	43
Sense of joy and laughter	43
An experience of great emotional intensity	38
A great increase in my understanding and knowledge	32
A sense of the unity of everything and my own part in it	29
A sense of a new life and living in a new world	27
A confidence in my own personal survival	27
A feeling that I could not possibly describe what was happening to me	26
The sense that all the universe is alive	25
The sense that my personality has been taken over by something much more powerful than I am	24
A sensation of warmth or fire	22
A sense of being alone	19
A loss of concern about worldly problems	19
A sense that I am being bathed in light	14
A sense of desolation	8

Source: Greeley (1975)

THE VARIETIES OF RELIGIOUS EXPERIENCE

Evidently there are a number of varieties of RE, but as yet there is no agreed way of categorizing them. While there may be a common core as described above, there are variations within it and other experiences which fall outside it. We have seen that there may be a distinction between immanent and transcendent REs; but Hood (1975) found a correlation between his two types which to some extent correspond to these. There may be another important distinction between REs in solitude and those which are experienced in a group, for example in a charismatic service. For a time it was assumed, perhaps following William James, that REs occurred when those concerned were alone. In Hay's (1982) survey 61 per cent were indeed alone and only 7 per cent in a communal setting. Perhaps those carefully drafted questions for some reason suggested solitary rather than communal events. Moehle (1983) asked subjects to classify a broad sample of REs and found that *social–individual* was one of the main dimensions needed to classify them. Sociologists such as Poloma (1995) have drawn attention to the importance of social factors and social setting in generating these experiences.

It may be that all of these varieties are elaborations of the common core. It is widely accepted that all experiences, including religious ones, are mediated by social learning, and that there has been a historical development within all faiths of the content and character of experiences. Religious experience is in part at least the product of historical development and of the religious training and education of individuals in each tradition. However, it has been argued that the social constructions involved are based on a central core experience (Proudfoot, 1985), as described above.

One reason that the single question surveys found 34 per cent or more of respondents reporting REs while Thomas and Cooper (1978) found only 2 per cent of mystical experiences may be that there are other kinds of intense experience which are regarded by some as religious. One group consists of 'psychic' experiences of several kinds, such as reports of 'pre-cognition', out-of-the-body experiences, contact with the dead, 'telepathy', *déjà vu*, coincidences, near death experiences, and miracles. Here is an example:

> In 1952 when out at work on a polio patient – my mind entirely taken up with work in hand – suddenly my mind seemed to go blank and I then saw 'in my mind' my son lying in the road run over – it was quite impossible to remove this from my mind so I excused myself . . . I insisted on going directly, very quickly, my husband being very annoyed but realizing something was upsetting me – we arrived home in 25 minutes, but on arrival I said 'No, not here, take me to the market place' – as we drew up – the school bus drove into the market place and my young son (who was standing by the door) opened the door and fell out of the bus, it hitting him and he lay *exactly* as I had seen him – How did I see something before it happened?
>
> (Hardy, 1979, p. 45)

Greeley (1975) asked about experience of several 'psychic' phenomena, and the findings are shown in Table 5.2. In the Hay and Heald survey (1987) in Britain, shown in Table 5.3, it was found that of the 29 per cent who reported experience of 'synchronicity' only 32 per cent regarded this as religious; and of the 18 per cent who reported contact with the dead, 35 per cent thought this was religious. That a substantial minority regard these 'psychic' experiences as religious is a very interesting finding.

Wuthnow (1978) also asked about 'psychic' experiences, and found that in his sample of California students 44 per cent claimed to have experienced 'telepathy', usually with close friends or relatives who were ill or dying,

Table 5.2   'Psychic' experiences reported (percentages)

Type of experience	Never	Once or twice	Several times	Often
Déjà vu	38	29	24	6
ESP (thought you were in touch with someone when they were far away)	40	26	24	8
Clairvoyance (have seen events that happened at a great distance as if they were happening)	72	14	8	2
Have felt that you were really in touch with someone who had died	70	16	8	3

Source: Greeley (1975)

42 per cent reported precognition, mostly of danger or disaster, some in dreams, 3 per cent apparitions, 2 per cent clairvoyance and 1 per cent psychokinesis. He also found that more of his subjects believed in these occult phenomena than believed in basic religious beliefs. Out-of-the-body experiences have been reported by as many as 15–50 per cent in different surveys (McCreery, 1993).

Other American surveys have found an increase in the number of 'psychic' experiences reported; Levin (1993) found an increase between 1973 and 1988 in *déjà vu* from 50 per cent to 67 per cent, and of ESP from 58 per cent to 65 per cent. McClemon (1988) repeated these surveys in China and found slightly higher percentages of such experiences there. Again we are not concerned with whether or not such things really happen. The main point of interest to us is that some people give a religious interpretation to them. The origins and effects of 'psychic' experiences were found by Wuthnow (1978) to be different from those of REs proper. He found that experiences of *déjà vu*, ESP, and 'clairvoyance' occurred to the young and black among the males, to people from unhappy homes, with unhappy marriages, and that there was no correlation with life satisfaction. Mystical experiences, on the other hand, were reported by older, more educated, religious believers, from happy homes, and this was strongly correlated with positive affect and life satisfaction. Those who reported talking to the dead were mostly widowed, and many were female and black.

Another variation is peak experiences which are aesthetic, for example brought on by music or the beauty of nature. These are often experienced as religious, as we shall see, but they may also be experienced purely as aesthetic. This may again reflect differences in background and education. In Wuthnow's California survey (1978) subjects were asked, 'Have you experienced the beauty of nature in a deeply moving way?' Forty-nine per cent said that they had and that this had a lasting effect on their life, and another 33 per cent had but without such lasting effects. In Hay and Heald's (1987) British survey (see Table 5.3), 16 per cent reported awareness of a sacred presence in nature and 61 per cent of them interpreted this in a religious way.

Table 5.3 Religious experience in Britain

Type of experience	(1) % reporting this	(2) % interpreting religiously	% religious experience (1×2)
Awareness of the presence of God	27	80	21.6
Awareness of receiving help in answer to prayer	25	79	19.8
Awareness of a guiding presence not called God	22	58	12.8
Awareness of a sacred presence in nature	16	61	9.8
Awareness of patterning in synchronicity	29	32	9.3
Awareness of the presence of someone who has died	18	35	6.3
Awareness of an evil presence	12	38	4.6
Experiencing that all things are one	5	55	2.75

Source: Hay and Heald (1987)

In the Gallup poll reported by Hay and Heald, the first three categories of RE, which are the most common, all reflect transcendent experiences. The last one on the list is the most clearly mystical or immanent, and is quite rare; the fourth could also be interpreted in this way. There was no analysis of aesthetic experiences here, though the sacred presence in nature could be interpreted in this way. Reported awareness of 'synchronicity' and of the presence of the dead were also quite common. The remaining one, awareness of evil, has not been widely reported in other studies, but could be important as the basis of belief in evil and the devil.

What seem to be missing from these lists so far are any specifically Christian experiences. Visions of the Virgin Mary are probably rare, but evangelical Christians who claim to 'know Jesus' or to 'be a friend of Jesus' are very common. Perhaps they do not reply to social surveys, or perhaps the researchers have not looked for such reports.

DEMOGRAPHIC VARIATIONS IN RELIGIOUS EXPERIENCES

Gender

As we show in Chapter 8, women report more REs than men; 41 per cent compared with 31 per cent (Hay, 1982). They feel closer to God, which is found when they are as young as nine or ten, and their REs are more 'receptive' than males, supporting a possible sexual theory. As Hood and Hall (1980) suggested, it is possible that male God-images have an inhibitory effect on mystical experiences reported by males.

Age

In Chapter 8 we describe how children aged six report their feeling that God had been close to them, especially girls, and especially when they were in trouble. National sample surveys show a gradual increase in the frequency of REs with age, for example 29 per cent in adolescence rising to 47 per cent for those aged 60 and over in Britain (Hay, 1990).

Education

We will show in Chapter 9 that educated individuals are more active in some aspects of religion, and the same is found for REs. In Britain 56 per cent of those educated to age 20 or over answer 'yes' to the Hardy question, compared with 37 per cent of those educated only to age 13–14 (Hay, 1990).

Table 5.4   Denominations and REs: response to the question, 'Have you ever been aware of or influenced by a presence or a power?'

Denominations	Positive response %
Anglicans	33
Nonconformists	44
Roman Catholics	41
Other Christians	68
Jewish	39
Other non-Christians	60
Agnostics	23
Atheists	24
Don't Know	23

Source: Hay (1982)

Social class

The effects are similar to those of education; in Britain 47 per cent of the upper-middle class and 32 per cent of unskilled workers reported REs (Hay and Morisy, 1978).

Denominational membership

REs occur to members of all denominations and none, as Table 5.4 shows. Perhaps the most interesting finding here is the quite high rate of REs among agnostics, atheists and 'don't knows'. There is a higher rate for church members, and especially for 'other Christians', who will be members of sect-type groups.

TRADITIONAL METHODS OF AROUSING RELIGIOUS EXPERIENCES

There are several ways of inducing REs which have been used in most religions for a long time. On p. 85 we shall consider other methods, such as drugs and sensory deprivation, which have also been used to induce REs. A variety of situations seem to act as triggers for REs. The frequencies found by Greeley (1975) are shown in Table 5.5. This is a very interesting list, with one or two surprising items such as childbirth and lovemaking, but we will look first at some of the familiar and traditional sources of REs.

Table 5.5 Triggers of REs

Trigger of RE	Percentage reporting such trigger, out of those reporting one or more REs
Listening to music	49
Prayer	48
Beauties of nature such as sunset	45
Moments of quiet reflection	42
Attending services	41
Listening to sermon	40
Watching little children	34
Reading the Bible	31
Being alone in church	30
Reading a poem or novel	21
Childbirth	20
Sexual activity	18
Your own creative work	17
Looking at a painting	15
Physical exercise	1
Drugs	0

Source: Greeley (1975)

Music

In Chapter 4 we traced the long history of the use of music in religion, from the use of frenzied drumming in Voodoo, celestial harmony in Greece, and the creation of elevated religious feelings in classical masses and requiems, to the emotional hymns in charismatic and evangelical churches today. Music was at the top of the Greeley list (Table 5.5). It seems likely that there is quite a close connection between REs and some states induced by music; they are similar mental states, both depend on right hemisphere activity, both are non-verbal and non-rational. Another important similarity is that both are commonly performed, with tight synchrony, in a group, leading to a special kind of communal experience, a special kind of social cohesion (Spickard, 1991).

Prayer and meditation

There are several kinds of prayer; Heiler (1932) distinguished nine varieties, and Poloma and Pendleton (1991) carried out a factor analysis and found four kinds. These were: colloquial prayer, 'conversations with God'; meditative prayer; petitionary prayer, regarded by Heiler as the most basic; and ritual, or set prayers. The percentages of respondents in the Poloma and Pendleton (1991) sample who reported engaging in these kinds of prayer 'often' were: colloquial 30.9, meditative 4.6, petitionary 5.3 and ritual 6.9. Heiler regarded contemplative and mystical prayers as leading most often to REs; Poloma and Pendleton (1991) found that meditative prayer led most often to REs. The meditative prayer factor consisted of items such as 'spending time just "feeling" or "being" in the presence of God', 'spending time worshipping and adoring God', 'asking God to speak and then trying to listen for His answer'.

Prayers are often said while adopting certain postures, such as kneeling, standing with head bowed, prostrating; members of 'charismatic' groups raise one hand or both. As with other non-verbal signals these postures may be able to arouse religious feelings: 'those who deliberately kneel are rewarded by an increase in worshipping love' (Underhill, 1911). These postures have a universal connotation of humility and supplication, a search for union, but they also reflect historical traditions of practice within particular groups, and have an added meaning of signifying group membership.

More individuals pray every day (or claim to do so) than claim to go to church weekly. In Britain over 40 per cent claim to pray daily, and they are more likely to come from the working class. In the USA over 60 per cent say that they pray daily, 76 per cent say that prayer is an important part of their daily lives, and 19 per cent say that they pray three times a day or more (Poloma and Gallup, 1991).

The main goal of meditation in most traditions is to obtain some kind of RE, though different kinds are sought in Buddhist, Hindu or Christian traditions. Buddhists seek the loss of self, while Christians seek union with God. Prayer came second in the Greeley list (Table 5.5), and there are other related items lower down. We have seen that the contents of REs depend on religious training and tradition, but secular meditation can bring about quite similar experiences. Deikman (1963) asked eight subjects to meditate on a blue vase for a series of 15-minute sessions. These subjects all experienced: more vivid perception of the vase, such as increased colour saturation; personal attachment to the vase; increased ability to keep out distracting stimuli; and time shortening. Some saw the vase radiating or transfigured, or saw a merging of self and object. They all felt that the experience was pleasant and valuable. This has several similarities to the core RE.

There has been much research into the practices known under the names of Yoga and Zen, which comprise hundreds of techniques. These are primarily aimed at an immanent, mystical, state of trance and loss of self, but Yoga aims for transcendence and union with God (Puhakka, 1995). There has been research into the physiological effects of these practices, which seem to be reduction of heart rate, blood pressure, and anxiety, and some changes in brain rhythms. However, the same can also be claimed for entirely secular forms of relaxation. Some of the effects of meditation may be due to breath-holding through deep breathing, and in some other traditions there is very rapid breathing. The effect of this is hyperventilation, with increased concentration of carbon dioxide. Experiments on breathing carbon dioxide find that there can be cosmic experiences, ecstasy, sometimes horrifying hallucinations (Wulff, 1991).

Group worship

Attending services and listening to sermons came high on the Greeley list (Table 5.5). It is familiar that emotional REs are very common in religious services; these may be quite mild but they can also be extreme, as in charismatic groups. These services seem designed to generate emotions. At charismatic services the aim seems to be to create a high level of excitement, by means of the music and the verbal message. The intensity of emotional arousal is shown by people collapsing on the floor or speaking in tongues at some charismatic and Pentecostal churches.

Part of the experience of high arousal worship is an enhanced feeling of union with the others, which Turner described as 'communitas' (Chapter 4), and which is much the same as the 'ego loss' of the classic RE. Feeling close to God is apparently related to feeling close to other worshippers. This is recognized in accounts of the Jewish experience of worship: 'Davening (praying together)...is...a social experience as well as a religious experience. It makes me feel very connected, very close towards Jews, and gives me a warm feeling' (Davidman and Greil, 1993).

As well as producing powerful emotional experiences, worship probably has a direct impact on the content of REs, by suggesting very forcibly what those present should be experiencing. This is done by the contents of hymns, pictures, and by prayers.

Experience of nature

Experiencing the beauty of nature is a common source of REs. This came third in the Greeley list (Table 5.5) and was also very common in Wuthnow's survey (1978). Traditional writing on mysticism has often mentioned mountains and deserts as sources of REs, for example the experiences of the desert fathers. Their effect could be due to the obvious grandeur of these features of the environment, 'proclaiming the glory of God'. However, environmental psychology finds that the most pleasing environments are those which have water, greenness, depth of vision, and probably sun (Altman and Wohlwill, 1983), which are important for survival, suggesting an evolutionary explanation.

Rosegrant (1976) studied the effects of wilderness experiences. More mystical experiences were reported under low stress conditions, but were not significantly higher for those reporting a communal experience. Comparing mountain versus creek, the mountain experience was more meaningful, and experienced as more communal, but not more mystical. Hood (1977) replicated this study with schoolboys who went white water rafting, rock climbing or on a night walk alone. He found that there were higher scores for both of his two mysticism factors when less stress was anticipated, and when there was incongruity between actual and antici-pated stress. This was confirmed in a later study (Hood, 1978) which made use of an unanticipated thunderstorm: again there was greater reported mystical experience when anticipated and actual stress were in conflict, whether the stress was greater or less than expected. The explanation offered for this finding is that such incongruities in nature lead people to look at reality differently.

Distress

Some have maintained that REs are precipitated by states of distress, low self-esteem, or 'existential crisis' (e.g. Batson *et al.* 1993). Some support for this theory was provided by Brown, Spilka and Cassidy (1978, cited by Batson *et al.* 1993). They studied 192 Christians who reported having had one or more REs. These subjects rated what their state of self-dissatisfaction had been before the experience, and this was found to correlate 0.18 with 'enlightenment and new knowledge', 0.22 with 'unity-completeness' and 0.31 with 'sensory stimulation', which are, however, low correlations. Hay (1982) with a sample of 172 British adults, of whom 100 reported an RE, found that as many as 50 per cent had been 'distressed and ill at ease' and another 6 per cent 'confused' before their experiences. What they had mostly been worried about was the possibly impending death of self or a close relative, damage to the body, or loss of job. However for 34 per cent there was 'nothing special' about their state of mind at the time of the RE. Alister Hardy (1979) found a smaller rate among his 3,000 cases: 18.4 per cent had been in a state of depression or despair, 8 per cent were ill, 3.7 per cent had crises in personal relations, and a few worried about death.

EXPERIMENTAL INDUCTION OF RELIGIOUS EXPERIENCES

Drugs

There is a long history of the effects of drugs on REs. Mescaline, found in the cactus peyote, was used by the Aztecs in 300 BC and is still used today by members of the Native American Church (Boire, 1994). Psilocybin has been used for centuries in Siberia, and is used today in Mexico. Marihuana is used in parts of India (and by Rastafarians) for religious purposes, and LSD was claimed as a sacrament in the USA in the 1960s. Alcohol is not a psychedelic drug but it too has been used for religious purposes (Aaronson and Osmond, 1970).

There are many studies of the effects of the psychedelic drugs LSD, mescaline and psilocybin. They produce striking visual sensations, of intensified light and colour, objects may seem alive, there can be distortion of time and space, objects change in size or shape or become two-dimensional, there may be depersonalization, and experience of union with the surrounding world. There may be experiences of great bliss or great terror, of love and forgiveness or sacrifice and execution (Wulff, 1991). Often the experience is reported to be religious, but the percentage of subjects who describe it in this way has varied from 5 per cent to 90 per cent, more typically 35–50 per cent. We shall see below how this depends on both the setting and the religious background of the subjects.

The best-known study of the effects of drugs on REs was carried out by Pahnke (1966) with 20 theological students taking part in a 2½-hour Good Friday meditation in their chapel. Half were given a psilocybin pill, half were given a placebo. The subjects were given a 147-item questionnaire afterwards and an interview; on the basis of these they were given scores on dimensions mainly derived from Stace. Table 5.6 shows high scores for members of the experimental group on the classic dimensions of religious experience. No measures of imagery were obtained. This study was later

Table 5.6 The Marsh Chapel miracle: the effects of psilocybin on mystical experience

Category	Percentage of maximum possible score for 10 subjects		
	Exp.	Control	p*
1 Unity	62	7	0.001
(a) Internal	70	8	0.001
(b) External	38	2	0.008
2 Transcendence of time and space	84	6	0.001
3 Deeply felt positive mood	57	23	0.020
(a) Joy, blessedness and peace	51	13	0.020
(b) Love	57	33	0.055
4 Sacredness	53	28	0.020
5 Objectivity and reality	63	18	0.011
6 Paradoxicality	61	13	0.001
7 Alleged ineffability	66	18	0.001
8 Transiency	79	8	0.001
9 Persisting positive changes in attitude and behaviour	51	8	0.001
(a) towards self	57	3	0.001
(b) towards others	40	20	0.002
(c) towards life	54	6	0.011
(d) towards the experience	57	31	0.055

* Probability that the difference between experimental and control scores was due to chance.

Source: Pahnke (1966)

replicated by Pahnke (1967) with 40 older professionals, not in a religious setting this time, and the control group were given a drug with a lower dose of psilocybin. This time 7 out of 20 of the experimental group and 1 out of 20 of the control group reported mystical experiences (taken as over 60 per cent of the maximum score).

Masters and Houston (1966) found a high level of religious imagery in their 206 subjects, who were given LSD, as shown in Table 5.7.

From our description of drug experiences above, the majority of them not said to be religious, it is clear that these have a number of clear similarities with the classic RE: timelessness, depersonalization, being in touch with basic reality, and vivid visual sensations, for example. There are also some differences: REs do not include the horrors and terrors sometimes reported with these drugs, there is no distortion of objects, indeed visual effects are less common, and it is often hard to say which sense is involved.

Table 5.7 Religious imagery during psychedelic (LSD) experience

Traditional religious imagery	Percentage reporting imagery during psychedelic experience
Religious architecture	91
Religious art	43
Religious symbols	34
Religious persons	58
Devil, demons	49
Angels	7

Source: Masters and Houston (1966)

There are more REs after taking drugs when those involved are in a religious setting, as were the subjects in Pahnke's first study, but not in his second. Masters and Houston (1966) also found that this made a great difference (Table 5.8).

Table 5.8 Religious experiences under LSD

Reported experience	Non-religious setting % (N = 74)	Some religious stimuli % (N = 96)
Felt it (LSD) was the greatest thing that ever happened to me	49	85
A religious experience	32	83
A greater awareness of God or a Higher Power, or an Ultimate Reality	40	90

Source: Masters and Houston (1966)

Those who have a strong religious background are more likely to give a religious interpretation to their drug experiences. Religious background and training also affect the contents of the experience. The effects of peyote (containing mescaline) on Mexican and American Indians depends on whether they belong to the Native American Church, in which case they have theistic experiences, or if they are Catholics, in which case they may have visions of the Virgin Mary (La Barre, 1938).

Schachter (1967) found that the same drug, in this case adrenaline, could produce either euphoria or aggression, depending on the environmental setting – that is, a confederate who was in one of these emotional states. In the same way, the basic physiological state produced by psychedelic drugs can be interpreted in different ways, depending on the environmental setting and the past religious training of those taking the drug. From a non-religious point of view the drug produces a vivid set of stimuli needing interpretation. From a religious point of view the drug can be said 'to open the doors of perception of the spiritual world'; what is seen depends in part on tradition and training, but there is a central core of shared experience.

Isolation and sensory deprivation

The explanation of the effect of wilderness experiences on REs may not be the beauty of nature but the isolation. There has been a long history of holy men living in the desert, up trees, on pillars, or shut up in small cells. Psychologists devised the sensory deprivation tank for other research purposes. The subject floats in a solution which is at skin temperature; the tank is circular, 7.5 feet across, 4 feet high, and has water 10 inches deep, there is no light and no sound. Hood and Morris (1981) put subjects in one of these tanks and asked them to try to imagine either religious figures or cartoon figures. They later reported the frequency of religious imagery. Subjects selected as very high in intrinsic religiosity reported more religious imagery than those very high in extrinsic, for the religious instructions only; neither reported much for the cartoon set; neither the religious nor the cartoon set produced much religious imagery when the experiment was repeated out of the tank. In a second study Hood (1995) asked subjects while in the tank to attain 'as total silence as possible of heart and mind. Having attained it you will expose yourself to whatever *religious revelation/ insight* it brings.' There were two alternative wordings here. Subjects were interviewed while in the tank with a short form of the Hood mysticism scale; the high intrinsics had higher scores on Hood's second (transcendent) factor, but not on the first (general) mysticism factor. There was no such effect for the extrinsics. The conclusion is that sensory isolation, combined with a religious set or suggestion, produces REs in those who are high in intrinsic religiosity. The reason that sensory deprivation works in this way is probably that sensory images are formed more readily in the absence of external stimulation (Spilka, Hood and Gorsuch, 1985).

Hypnosis and other techniques

Aaronson (e.g. 1968) has experimented with the effects of hypnosis on 'religious-type' experiences. His method was to hypnotize subjects and give them post-hypnotic suggestions. He succeeded in producing perceptions of increased depth, enhanced colour and contour, distortions of time in the direction of timelessness, cosmic unity, loss of self, knowledge of ultimate reality – all on Stace's list (see p. 74).

Houston and Masters (1972) have experimented with ways of inducing REs in the laboratory. In the 'cradle of creativity', subjects are blindfolded and stand in a swinging platform, which responds to the subject's movements. This regularly produced states of trance, ecstasy and 'religious type' experiences. The same authors devised a series of 'mind games' involving trance states, enhanced by initiation rites, fasting, meditation, and isolation out of doors at night. This is said to produce REs, though no controlled data are reported. It would be interesting to know whether such methods work with all subjects, or only those with the right religious orientation.

THE EFFECT OF RELIGIOUS EXPERIENCES

Here individuals are asked to report whether their behaviour has been changed by the experience. In several of these studies it was found that the effects lasted for six months, or were described as 'long-lasting' effects.

Happiness

Happiness, or subjective well-being, has often been found to be associated with REs. Pahnke (see Table 5.6) found that six months after the experiment the experimental group reported 'persisting and positive changes' in their attitudes to life, compared with the control group. Hay (1982) found that 61 per cent of his Nottingham sample said that they were 'At peace or restored, happy/elated, or uplifted/awestruck'. Greeley (1975) modelled the prediction of scores on the Bradburn affect balance scales and found that these were predicted by classic mystical experience, such as 'being bathed in light', at 0.60, regular REs predicted at 0.39, and 'psychic' experiences had no effect at all. Poloma and Pendleton (1991) found that while REs had strong positive correlations with subjective well-being, 'occult' experiences had small negative correlations.

Prayer produces a number of benefits, according to self-reports. Poloma and Pendleton (1991), in a survey of 627 adults in Dayton, Ohio, found that prayer was reported as having greater benefits than other aspects of religiosity. The greatest benefits were reported by those who had REs during prayer, which occurred during meditative prayer in those who prayed most often. REs during prayer were the strongest correlates of happiness, and existential well-being. In another study Poloma and Gallup (1991) found that prayer was the strongest factor in explaining forgiveness. Prayer was rated as an effective way of dealing with the diagnosis of cancer, bereavement, and danger in battle, events over which there is no control (Brown, 1994).

Moral values, attitudes to other people

Pahnke (Table 5.6) found that his experimental group had another 'persistent and positive change', of more positive attitudes to others, six months later. Hardy (1979) found that 18.4 per cent of his 3,000 cases reported a sense of purpose or new meaning to life, and 7.7 per cent reported changes in attitudes to others. In Wuthnow's (1978) survey, those who had a number of peak experiences, religious and otherwise, valued having a highly paid job, job security or a beautiful house less (11 per cent) than those who had not had peak experiences (49 per cent). More of the peak experience group (79 per cent) valued working for social change, social problems or people in need, than the others (52 per cent). The peak experience group also claimed to be less concerned with social status, fame or having a lot of friends.

Religious life

It is not surprising that REs result in more religious activity. Poloma and Pendleton (1989) modelled the predictors of evangelistic activities in the Assemblies of God movement, and found that ecstatic charismatic experiences were one of the predictors. Spilka et al. (1992) studied 192 people who had Christian REs and found that afterwards they had a greater sense of unification with God. Hay (1982) found that 24 per cent said the experience had 'Confirmed or intensified my beliefs', and Downing and Wygand (1964) found that the effect was to deepen commitment.

Attitudes to the self

Sometimes people are in a state of low self-esteem before they have an RE. Pahnke found that 57 per cent of his experimental group and almost none of the control group had more positive attitudes towards themselves. And Spilka et al. (1992) found that after their REs his subjects felt more at one with themselves.

BACKGROUND AND PERSONALITY FACTORS

Religious activity

The first and least surprising finding is that REs are more common among those who are religious in other ways. Hay and Heald (1987) found that 56 per cent of those who attended church at least occasionally in their British sample reported REs compared with 26 per cent of those who never went. Perhaps it is more surprising that so many non-attenders reported them. Hood (1976) found a correlation between attendance and both of his mysticism scales, but non-attenders also had high scores. Hood (1995), in his isolation tank experiments, found that the intrinsically religious had REs in the tank, on his transcendent factor 2, while extrinsics did not.

Cognitive structures

Hood (1975) found that subjects with high scores on his mysticism scale had high scores on Taft's scale of Ego Permissiveness, which is intended to measure openness to experience, including unconscious and illogical aspects of experience. Hoffelt and Batson (1971, cited by Batson *et al.* 1993) found that subjects who reported REs had higher scores on the Repression–Sensitization scale, which is intended to measure openness to unusual, reality-threatening aspects of experience. We shall see on p. 92 that there is a relation between REs and schizotypy, which is also about openness to non-logical aspects of experience. Hood (1974) found that those who report REs had higher ego-strength as measured by Stark's Index of Personal Inadequacy; he argued that while those who have REs may experience loss of self this is as part of a larger whole, and they are in fact psychologically healthy and have 'psychological strength'.

There is an interesting pattern of attribution in connection with REs. We saw on p. 84 that individuals are often in a state of stress or despair before their experiences. This gives a feeling of loss of personal mastery, which has been found to be inversely correlated with attributing control to God, which relieves them of their burden and opens the way to conversion or other REs. Identifying or cooperating with God in 'religious coping' enables them to feel in control (Spilka and McIntosh, 1995). We shall consider attribution theory on p. 95 as a way of interpreting REs, of understanding religious thinking in this area.

Self-actualizers

Maslow (1970) proposed his well-known theory of a hierarchy of needs, in which when all other needs have been satisfied a fifth level of motivation takes over, for 'self-actualization'. Here individuals want to realize their potentialities, know themselves and become more integrated. He reports that it was common for his self-actualizing subjects to report what he called 'peak experiences'. Wuthnow (1978) found that those who had such peak experiences as contact with the sacred, the beauty of nature or harmony with the universe, also found life very meaningful, thought often about the purpose of life, and they were more self-assured than others. However it is not clear which is cause and which is effect here.

We showed on p. 90 that one of the reported effects of REs is greater self-acceptance and integration. Those who were in a state of despair or distress feel much better afterwards, and have a more positive view of themselves; they had perhaps moved towards self-actualizing. Shostrom (1966) developed a measure of self-actualization (POI). Does it predict REs? Hood (1977) found a small correlation of 0.22 with the first, general mysticism factor of his mysticism scale. High scorers had different kinds of

RE, which were triggered by sex or drugs, rather than by religion or nature, as with the low scorers. Lindskoog and Kirk (1975) with 45 theological students found no relationship between self-actualization and REs. Other studies have found little relationship with measures of religiosity, and conflicting results on the effects of meditation. It seems likely that the POI has a bias towards unconventional attitudes, and against traditional religion, as is suggested by Hood's findings. It has been found to be correlated with being assertive, happy-go-lucky, and venturesome, which is not the same as self-actualization (Wulff, 1991).

Schizotypy

Claridge (1985) proposed that there is a personality dimension that he called 'schizotypy', which is a latent form of or disposition to have schizophrenia. It is quite different from schizophrenia itself, which is partly due to high levels of this trait, but also involves a breakdown, in the same way that high blood pressure predisposes to strokes. The trait consists of a tendency to hallucinate and have other anomalous perceptual or cognitive experiences, but also enables those who have it to be creative in art or literature, and to be religious.

Jackson (1991) used a schizotypy scale with 208 subjects from a twins subject panel, 28 per cent of whom reported REs, and found that this scale correlated with a measure of numinous experience and also with the Hardy question, accounting for about 25 per cent of the variance. There were smaller correlations with two other measures of REs, a mysticism scale, and one for negative REs. The schizotypy items with the strongest correlations were 'Do things sometimes feel as though they were not real?' (0.43), 'Do you believe in telepathy?' (0.40), and 'Do you believe that dreams can come true?'(0.30). These 208 subjects were compared with 44 schizophrenic outpatients who belonged to a self-help 'voices' group. The patients had much higher RE scores, especially on the mysticism and negative experience scales. The greatest differences from the twins group were on the schizotypy items 'Hearing something unusual' (twins 12.3%, voices sample 57.1%, rho = 0.44), 'Being aware of tremendous peril or threat' (0.40), and 'A feeling of being controlled by something outside of yourself' (0.35).

McCreery (1993) carried out a related study on the personalities of people who report out-of-the-body experiences (OBEs). The schizotypy scale discriminated between the OBE subjects and controls, especially for part of the scale dealing with dreams, hallucinations and delusions; they were also somewhat hypomanic and low on anxiety, and he called them 'happy schizophrenics'. He then carried out an experiment using the 'ganzfeld' technique, where subjects wear goggles made with half ping-pong balls, a form of sensory deprivation. They were asked to relax and imagine themselves out of their bodies. The OBE subjects had more visual images, and there was more EEG activity in their right hemispheres while they were in the experiment.

EXPLANATIONS OF RELIGIOUS EXPERIENCE

Physiological theories

We have seen that several physiological states have been found to be connected with REs. Intense arousal, produced by ecstatic dancing and singing, is one trigger for REs, though equally high arousal from sport or exercise has no such effect. Very low arousal, produced by meditation, is another, though it can also send people to sleep. Drugs can produce REs in some individuals, though they need to be believers. Childbirth and sex have been reported as triggers for REs, especially in self-actualizers. But what is the common physiological final path here? Activation of the right brain hemisphere may be one, as found by McCreery and others, and it is known to be associated with certain relevant psychological processes. It is well established that the left hemisphere is the main locus of language, number, and logic, though this lateralization is less for women and for left-handed men. The right hemisphere is weaker on these, but stronger on vision and space, music, emotions, and holistic perceptions. It seems likely that this is where religion belongs. Clearly these physiological states cannot produce REs by themselves, and they need the right religious context and training which enable people to interpret these experiences in a religious way.

One interpretation is that a variety of events, physiological and others, produce unusual experiences, which go beyond the limits of normal understanding, and may be given a transcendental interpretation (Spilka, Hood and Gorsuch, 1985; Hood, 1995). This could explain why apparently 'psychic' phenomena are sometimes given a religious explanation. Physiological states can do more than this however, they can produce visions, as experiments with drugs have shown. So is there a biology of mysticism? The main contribution of religion to survival, as we shall suggest later, is in the creation of group cohesion and social support. And REs have a strong prosocial component. REs are also very rewarding, and personal problems are often solved; the good mood produced lasts for months. There may be physiological mechanisms for bringing about these effects, and they may reside in the right hemisphere.

It has long been believed that there is a connection between epilepsy and having REs. It has been reported that some patients have REs during their attacks, and others present may think that they have been possessed by a spirit, in shamanism for example. This has not been confirmed by analysis of samples of epileptics in general, but Dewhurst and Beard (1970) studied 69 patients with temporal lobe epilepsy; they found that only 8 had been involved with religion before their illness, but 26 out of the 69 were interested in religion afterwards, and 6 had a conversion experience. Since many more individuals have REs than have epilepsy this cannot take us very far in explaining the general phenomenon. Persinger (1987) proposed that the temporal lobes are the locus of mystical experience. In one of several studies by this group, Makarec and Persinger (1985) related EEG measures to a questionnaire on RE. There was a strong correlation between the presence of EEG spikes in the temporal lobes and reported religious beliefs, paranormal and mystical experience, and sense of presence. Meditation also leads to more right hemisphere brain activity, probably by suppressing left hemisphere activity (Fenwick, 1987).

Reaction to distress

We have seen that a proportion of REs occur to individuals who were in a state of distress of some kind, though many other REs took place as far as we know without such distress. One of the general psychological theories of religion which we shall discuss on p. 235ff. is that deprivation leads to a projective religious solution, and there is evidence that religious conversion often takes place when people are in a state of conflict or anxiety. The same is true of glossolalia. Stress in general does not seem to produce REs; Hood (1995) found with his stressful Outward Bound experiments that there was more mysticism under low stress. The kinds of stress which have been reported to produce REs are different – a sense of sin, depression and sadness, fear and dread, and crises of meaning (Spilka and McIntosh, 1995). The RE may take the form of a conversion experience and new way of looking at things, such as feeling forgiven or that God is in charge. We have seen that the usual outcome of REs is increased happiness, suggesting that a problem has been solved, but also more positive attitudes to other people.

We looked at individual differences in the propensity to have REs, and this suggests that there is a certain kind of person who can deal with distress in a religious way. REs are more common in those with an open kind of cognitive structure, which is open in particular to images and intuitions of a non-rational nature, perhaps emanating from the right hemisphere. Those high on 'schizotypy' are also prone to REs; these are individuals with a tendency to hallucinate but who are also creative, and who have been called 'happy schizophrenics'.

Two-factor theories

A number of psychologists have favoured two-factor theories, in the tradition of Schachter's (1967) theory of emotion. Here an emotion is produced by the combination of a physiological state of arousal and cognitions suggesting how this should be interpreted. We saw how certain drugs can produce REs in some individuals and in some settings. We have just seen, however, that several rather different physiological states, and a variety of other triggers, can produce REs, so perhaps the first factor can be extended to include all of these.

The second factor can be seen as 'attribution', the way in which people interpret events. It is now emphasized by psychologists that the perceiver brings a lot to the situation that he or she is perceiving; his or her language and ideas contribute to what is perceived, and cognitive structures such as beliefs and ideologies contribute to the perception and understanding of what is going on (L. B. Brown, personal communication).

We can extend the second factor too in four ways. First, religious people, as we have seen, are more likely to have REs in exactly the same situations, especially those high in intrinsic religiosity. Second, religious interpretations are more likely when there is a religious setting to suggest it. The first Pahnke experiment (1966), where there was a high percentage of REs, took place in a chapel and the subjects were theological students. Religious stimuli include such non-verbal signals as bells, chanting, incense, stained-glass windows and dim illumination, candles, pointed gothic windows and tall steeples pointing to heaven, sacred areas kept apart, altars, crosses and other religious symbols, even the characteristic smell of many places of worship. Third, people may be asked or encouraged to think about religious images, as they are during worship; this made a difference in Hood's isolation tank experiments.

Fourth, people are brought up in a culture which has a tradition of religious thinking, and they will be exposed to this in greater or lesser degree. We noted on p. 87 how the use of peyote by Mexican Indians produced different REs depending on their faith. This applies to all religions. Thus, in Hinduism there is a quest for transcendence, by contemplation of God and by spiritual disciplines such as Yoga (Puhakka, 1995), while in Buddhism there is a mystical search for nirvana through a state of emptiness and loss of self (Hong, 1995).

THE SOCIAL ASPECT OF RELIGIOUS EXPERIENCES

The theories which we have discussed so far do not do justice to the social aspects of REs which we have encountered. REs often have a social content, a feeling of unity with other people, and a determination to behave more kindly and altruistically towards them. How do groups help in the generation of REs? We have just looked at the build up of religious traditions, whereby there is a gradual growth of cognitions which enable religious attributions to be made. Groups are a source of heightened emotions in more or less ecstatic services. There is the group performance of ritual, that is, the acting out of beliefs in more or less dramatic group situations, where the actions are tightly shared and coordinated.

CONCLUSIONS AND FINAL COMMENTS

Religious experiences convey, to those who have them, that they have been in contact with a very powerful being or force, 'whether they call this God or not', that there is a unity in the whole of creation; they feel united and have love towards other people; they feel more integrated, perhaps 'forgiven'; they are happier; they have had experience of timelessness, perhaps eternity; and they believe that they have been in contact with some kind of reality. We know which are the situations which arouse REs most often, and which kinds of people are most likely to have them.

The cultural training aspect of REs cannot be overemphasized. We have seen that ecstasy can be secular, and induced by music, sex, or nature. Spilka *et al.* (1996) showed that the content of religious experiences reported in a US sample was highly predictable, and that cultural expectations determined that content (cf. Spanos and Hewitt, 1979). From a psychological point of view there has been a cultural elaboration of attributions.

We should keep in mind that most of the systematic surveys, discussed in this chapter, were done in Britain and the USA, and dealt with a wide variety of reported experiences. If we look at the descriptors listed in Table 5.1, it becomes clear that many of them (A feeling of deep and profound peace, A certainty that all things would work out for the good, Sense of my own need to contribute to others) would not be considered religious in many cultures.

When the same questions used in these surveys were used in surveys with (nominally) Jewish Israelis and Moslem Palestinians in 1995–6, only 9 per cent of Israelis and 4 per cent of Palestinians reported ever having had such experiences (Beit-Hallahmi, 1996a). Kedem (1991) summarized earlier findings with Israeli samples which were quite different from those reported in the USA or Britain. When asked about 'religious emotion', individuals mentioned historical, collective events they had experienced, such as military triumphs and great disasters. No one reported any such experiences when being alone. Even among Orthodox Jews in Israel, the experiences reported were radically different from those included in the Stace (1960) list, and reported in other countries. This is a clear effect of cultural traditions. It seems that Jewish and Moslem traditions lead to totally different conceptions and expectations of REs.

Chapter 6

Acquiring religious beliefs
Socialization and continuity

RELIGIOUS SOCIALIZATION: SOCIAL AND INTERPERSONAL INFLUENCES

The plausibility, legitimacy, and coherence of belief systems are created by culture and socialization, as the individual responds to, and assimilates, cultural givens. To most believers religion appears as a total ideology with a sense of the 'natural' and the 'real', without which it is impossible to conceive the world they inhabit. Religion appears 'not as a set of beliefs capable of correction by perceiving properly, but the very terms in which we perceive the world, almost . . . the condition and grounds of consciousness itself' (Dollimore, 1984, p. 9). Religious socialization is not just about learning a particular belief system, but is an introduction to the supernatural premise shared by all religions.

Our examination of religious socialization is an extension and articulation of the social learning explanation for religiosity (see p. 24). 'Belief systems persist because they and/or the social vehicles that carry them are able to generate and maintain commitment' (Borhek and Curtis, 1975, p. 85). If socialization is to be defined as the mechanism creating plausibility for a meaning system, then connecting it to primary relationships is likely to make it more effective. Socialization into religious continuity relies first on natural groups and affinities, as the young learn from parents and authority figures in the community, in established structures and socially given hierarchies. This leads to the strongest commitments. Socialization of the young is done by 'significant others', those with whom they have emotional ties and on whom they feel a natural dependence. As Miller (1963) pointed out, 'People do not internalize abstract norms, but images of themselves in concrete relationships with specific people or groups' (p. 666). The centrality of the family in religious training, and especially the role of the mother, has often been noted: 'traditional practices *must* be recreated by individuals if they are to remain plausible. But that seems easier to do . . . within a family, especially when the mother is religiously active' (Brown, 1988, p. 67).

Adolescents, who are at the stage of developing their personal identity, are a special focus of social attention, because of their perceived rebellious potential. They seem to be influenced by peers and develop their own culture. The role of peers in religious socialization has not often been studied. Some psychological functions are extensions of the interactions with parents and some are introduced by peers. The literature on peers' roles in socialization has emphasized two aspects of peer influence. Hunter and Youniss (1982) claim that peer influence is positive and complements that of the parents, while Bronfenbrenner (1979) emphasized that peer influence may be anti-adult and anti-social. It is likely that peer influence may take over when parental influence is weakened.

When society is traditional and one religion has a monopoly, there is no real choice of identity, as religion equals identity, and all education is religious education. Religion 'persists on the basis of a constant rehearsal of its complicated dramas, woven as they are into the whole rhythm of social and cultural life' (Geertz, 1960, p. 177). In societies where religion is integrated with the culture and plays a central role in it, there is no need for formal training of children in religious beliefs and customs, as religion is lived directly. The child knows what religion is about and what is expected. Still, in some major world religions there is formal training (Islam, Buddhism, Judaism, Catholicism, and many Protestant denominations).

FAMILY INFLUENCES

Two little boys, Sammy and Marty, both seven, are having a discussion, over milk and cookies, about God. Sammy says he believes in God and Marty replies he isn't quite sure there is a God. Sammy says that everybody believes differently about God – some people believe there is a God and some don't. 'But', Sammy adds,' it doesn't matter what you believe as long as it's the same thing your Daddy believes. So I'll go on believing there is a God.' 'Yes,' Marty nods in agreement, 'you're supposed to believe what your Daddy believes. So I'll go on believing that maybe there is and maybe there isn't a God.'

(Rokeach, 1981, p. 192)

Intergenerational transmission is the major factor in the formation of beliefs, because it is the major factor in the formation of identity. Significant others, and particularly parents, influence the development of all cognitions. Most religious individuals have been born into a particular identity. Children become aware of their group affiliations (religion, class, or ethnicity) before they acquire a particular set of beliefs. First they find out that they are Roman Catholic, a Baptist, or a Moslem, and only then will they learn that, as a Roman Catholic, as a Baptist, or as a Moslem, they are supposed to espouse certain beliefs. Later on these beliefs seem as natural as the ascribed identity.

Parental beliefs are deliberately and consciously transmitted, as part of the transmission of identity. Within-family transmission is more important than other factors, such as formal teaching, campaigns, or peers. Fichter (1961) reported that two-thirds of the candidates for religious vocations in the Roman Catholic church in the USA had at least one close relative (sibling, cousin, uncle, aunt) already serving as a priest, a nun, or a member or candidate in a religious order.

The parents are the most significant others, and have a monopoly on forming children's habits and beliefs, if not personality. Learning from the parents is tied to:

1 The parents' real power over their children, and the children's dependence.
2 The parents' perceived authority.
3 Love of the parents, and conscious or unconscious identification with them.

The parents are also in a good position to influence the child's social contacts with peers and others.

Parental attitudes

There can be no doubt that the attitudes of parents are among the most important factors in the formation of religious attitudes. Francis and Carter (1980), in a study of students in religious and secular schools in Britain, found that parents' religious behaviour correlated +0.49 with their child's behaviour. Greeley *et al.* (1976) similarly reported major effects of religious training within the family on religiosity in later life. Hunsberger and Brown (1984) found that religious teaching in the family, especially by the mother, had a positive impact on preserving one's religiosity as a young adult. Gibson *et al.* (1990) surveyed 2,717 British children aged 14–15 and found that the correlations with the church attendance of mothers and fathers respectively were, for child's attitudes to Christianity, 0.40 and 0.59, and, for child's church attendance, 0.65 and 0.56.

Although the similarity with parents falls with age, when the 'children' are of university age there is still a correlation of up to 0.60 between measures of their religious activities and those of their parents. When the children are in their forties there is still a substantial correlation (Glass *et al.* 1986), and the same was found by Hoge and Keeter (1976) for a sample of university teachers.

The similarity is greater for church attendance than for prayer; at age 16 the correlations were 0.67 and 0.59 for the church attendance of mothers and fathers and their children; for frequency of prayers the correlations were 0.35 and 0.30 (Francis and Brown, 1991). The similarity with parents is greater for religion than for other attitudes or kinds of behaviour. Cavalli-

Sforza *et al.* (1982) studied 203 Stanford students and their parents and friends, and found the pattern of correlations shown in Table 6.1.

Table 6.1 Effect on behaviour or attitude of US students of that of their parents or friends

Issue	Parent–child	Friend–child
Religious behaviour	0.57	0.20
Political behaviour	0.32	0.16
Sports played	0.13	0.16
Entertainment	0.16	0.10
Food habits	0.07	0.05
Miscellaneous beliefs (ESP)	0.09	0.12

Source: Cavalli-Sforza *et al.* (1982)

There is no question of the similarity between parents and their children in matters of religion, but it does not follow that this is primarily due to parents influencing their children; there are several other reasons for this similarity, to which we now turn.

The causes of parent–child similarity

One possibility is that children resemble their parents through heredity, not of church-going habits or particular beliefs, but of those underlying features of personality which, as we will see (Chapter 9), are associated with religion. The findings on genetic factors in religion are reported in Chapter 9. A second possible explanation of the similarity of parents and children is that they share the same environment. Glass *et al.* (1986) surveyed 2,044 subjects, in three-generation families, and assessed the influence of eight demographic variables, such as income and education. Shared 'status inheritance' was found to account for part of the parent–child similarity, but there was also a substantial effect of socialization. The path analysis by Francis and Brown (1991) similarly shows reduced similarities between parents and children when a number of other factors have been controlled.

A third factor is 'reciprocal influence' of children on their parents. In the three-generation study by Glass *et al.* there was evidence for this taking place, from the use of cross-lagged correlations, but only when the children were of student age and their parents in their forties, not when the children were in their forties and the parents in their sixties.

If we assume that genetics has a fairly small influence, after common environment and reciprocal influence have been taken into account, there is still a real effect of parents on children, and this is an important part of the explanation for parent–child similarity.

Factors affecting parental influence

The effects of parental attitudes and beliefs on those of their children vary with a number of factors. Parents have much more influence under some conditions than others, and we will now spell out what these conditions are.

Close relations between parents and children

Children who like, identify with, or have a close relationship with their parents are more likely to adopt their attitudes. Erickson (1992) found that the religiosity of children was a joint effect of parental religiosity and identification with parents. First-born children have on average a closer relationship with their parents, and MacDonald (1969) found that first-born children were more often religious, compared with later-born children. Weigert and Thomas (1972) found that a high degree of parental support was associated with conformity and religiosity in adolescents and that Catholic American adolescents reported attending church to satisfy parental expectations.

Close relations have often been found to be an important determinant of parental influence, for example by Hoge *et al.* (1982) in a study of 254 families. A number of studies have found that there is more similarity when parents give their children emotional support (Herzbrun, 1993). Findings regarding children's alienation from parental tradition, which is clearly linked to relations with parents, are discussed in Chapter 7.

Living at home

Young people, for example of student age, who are still living at home are more similar to their parents in religion than those who have left, and those who have got married are also less similar (e.g. Chesser, 1956). This presumably reflects the influence of friends or of a changed environment, though there may be some reverse causation here, in that children who disagree with their parents over religion may be more likely to leave home. However, as the study by Cavalli-Sforza *et al.* (1982) shows (see Table 6.1), parents overall have a greater influence than friends in matters of religion.

Influence of mother v. father

It is possible that each parent contributes to the development of religious beliefs in different ways. For example, nurturing and caring are typical characteristics of mother–infant interactions, while play is usually considered a typical characteristic of father–infant interactions.

One may generalize and describe the particular role of the father. The father brings the outside world into the closed, all encompassing, dyad of the mother and child. In traditional families, the disciplinary role is often relegated to the father (Parsons, 1964). The father's role is often to mediate to the child the values, expectations and demands of the external outside society. Since the father represents these social conceptions and values, he is the one who helps the child to accept societal values (Lamb and Oppenheim, 1989).

Many studies have found that there is more similarity with mothers than with fathers; this is the case for zero order correlations, and for weights in multiple regressions. Francis and Brown (1991) found that at age 16 child church attendance correlated with mother's church attendance 0.50, and with father's 0.26, after sex, class and the other parent's attendance had been controlled. However, Acock and Bengtson (1978) found that mothers resembled their children more in traditional religious beliefs, but fathers resembled them more in religious behaviour and self-rated religiosity. Clark *et al.* (1988) also found that fathers had more effect on child attendance and mothers on beliefs; perhaps this is because children discuss religion more with their mothers, and simply go to church or have to go to church with fathers. The greater influence of mothers may be expected to change now that more women are working and as a result spending less time in the home talking to the children (Spilka, Hood and Gorsuch, 1985).

Parental agreement

The effect of parents is greater if both father and mother hold the same religious beliefs, as Hoge and Petrillo (1982) and others (Lenski, 1953; Putney and Middleton, 1961) have found. When parents differ in their religious loyalties, the children are more likely to rebel in this sphere, and more likely to follow the mother than the father (Bell, 1938), as would be expected from the findings about the greater influence of the mother.

Age

Similarity with parents over religion is greater for younger children, for example at age 11 compared with 16 (Francis and Brown, 1991). However there is still a lot of similarity when the children are in their forties (Glass *et al.* 1986). There is also more similarity when the *parents* are younger, as Hoge *et al.* (1982) found.

Influencing children via child-rearing

Parents influence the religious outlook of their children in a second quite different way, through their methods of child-rearing. There appears to be some evidence for a direct connection between child-rearing and beliefs. Alwin (1986) analysed a number of American surveys which asked people whether they valued obedience and conformity or autonomy more in their children. In earlier studies there was a clear Catholic–Protestant difference, the Protestants valuing autonomy more, but in recent surveys this difference has disappeared. Several other differences are still found: Jews value autonomy most highly, fundamentalist Protestants value it less than non-fundamentalists, and blacks value it less than whites. In a later study Ellison and Sherkat (1993a) found that conservative American Protestants valued obedience if they held certain other beliefs, in literalism and in original sin, and had a punitive attitude to sinners; however Catholics in this study also valued obedience highly, and for them this was independent of such beliefs.

If Catholics and conservative Protestants value obedience, it is likely that they will try to coerce their children to follow their own religious practices; we saw earlier that there is more similarity between Catholic and Baptist parents and their children than is the case for other denominations. Nelsen (1981) found that when parents had frequent fights or arguments they also used more physical punishment on their sons, and both variables led to the latter having reduced religiosity.

In some cases, references to divine authority are used by parents to bolster their authority in disciplining their children. Thus, the parents become allied with divine authority. Examples can be found in all cultures (Geertz, 1960; Nunn, 1964). Nunn (1964) found that this 'coalition' with divinity was prevalent among parents who were ineffectual and powerless.

How parents influence children

We have seen that parents do have some influence on the religion of their children, though this is a lot more modest than the correlations of 0.6 or so with which we started. Nevertheless parents have more impact on the religious views of their children than on their political attitudes or their sporting or leisure activities. Parents also have more influence than friends do, at least up to adolescence. And they have a lot more influence on their children's religion than special religious schooling.

The most important way in which parents influence their children in religion is by involving them in religion at home, and by taking them to church, temple, or synagogue, perhaps participating in services and rituals. Erickson (1992) studied 900 16–18 year olds, using statistical modelling. The results are shown in Figure 6.1. The finding is that adolescents' religious activity in the home, for example taking part in prayers and Bible reading, was a crucial variable which was affected by the parents' reported level of religious activity and their reported religiosity.

Bibby (1978) found that in mainstream Protestant churches 27 per cent of children went to church with their parents, but in conservative churches 68 per cent did. However Hoge *et al.* (1982) found that it was only girls who

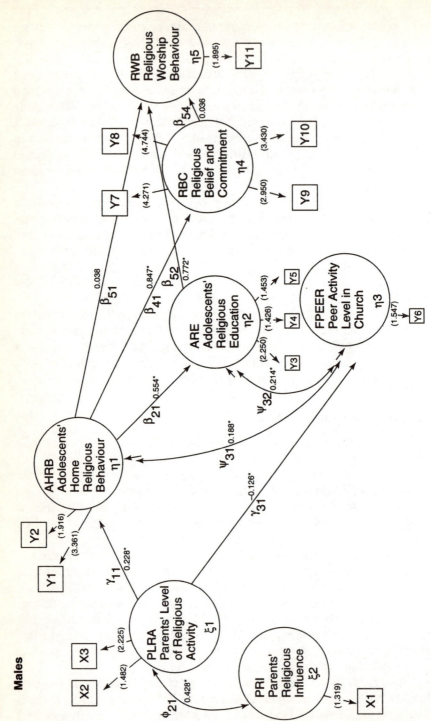

Males

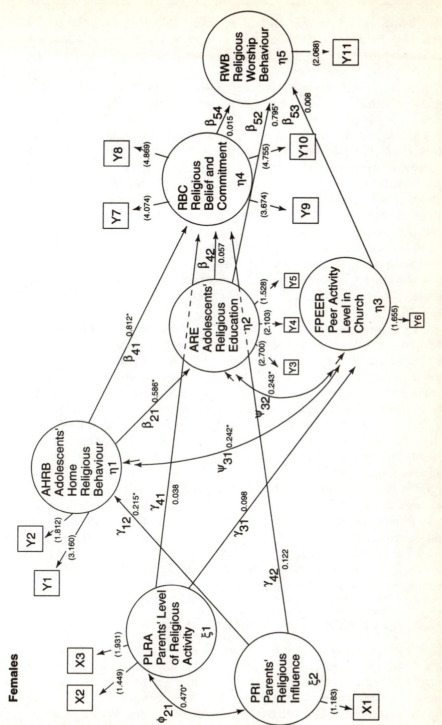

Figure 6.1 Models of male and female adolescent religious belief and commitment (subjects are 16–18 year olds who have been at a particular church for two or more years; standardized solution, *significant at $p < 0.05$)
Source: Erickson (1992)

were influenced in this way. It is often found that girls are influenced a little more by their parents than boys are, but not much more. There are really two processes here, the effects of participating in religious activities, and modelling of parental behaviour. The effects of participation will be dealt with again in the next section, and the effects of parental religious behaviour, which we can assume works via modelling, have been found by Kieren and Munro (1987).

A second way in which parents influence children is by talking to them. Hoge *et al.* (1982) found that for girls only there was more parent–child agreement when parents talked to the children a lot about religion. Herzbrun (1993) found that, amongst Jewish children, girls and the sons of liberal fathers agreed more with their parents over religion when they talked to them a lot about it. Frequent conversation has been found to have the same effect for political attitudes (Jennings and Niemi, 1968). It is curious that such conversation has less of an effect for boys; it follows that they must be influenced in other ways.

A third means of social influence is that parents may send their children to special religious schools, to be taught by someone else; we turn to these on p. 109ff.

We can link the impact of families to the stages in the religious life of children. As we shall see in more detail in Chapter 8, children at ages 3–12 usually accept the religion of the home without question. From age 13 onwards they try to work out their faith in collaboration with the peer group. There are many conversions and changes during adolescence, and the different influence of home, friends and education may pull in different directions. Final beliefs are often crystallized at age 14–15 or a little later. The fact that there is still quite a lot of similarity at student age shows that overall young people do not move very far away from the beliefs of their families.

Even in some cases of nonconformist, radical religious youth groups, research has shown much continuity with parents. Research has shown that most members of the 'Jesus Movement' in the USA in the 1970s came from fundamentalist Christian families (Richardson *et al.* 1979). They were rebelling against their parents by internalizing their parents' religious beliefs, but then acting on them in a more radical way. This phenomenon will be discussed further in Chapter 7.

PARENTAL IMAGES AND THE DEITIES

The intimate connection between parenting and religion is reflected in a basic and central aspect of religious beliefs: the similarity between the images of the gods and of the parents. Since parental-like (paternal or maternal) descriptions of deities are part of religious traditions, we can assume that in many individuals they are simply learned. We may suppose that the similarity between parental images and deity images is the result of interaction between cultural tradition and the individual's own experiences, a result of universal family situations. An added factor is the observation that religious traditions themselves are learned from the parents.

What we are dealing with, then, is an interaction between a cultural belief system and an individual personality system. Borrowing from Spiro and D'Andrade (1958), we can state two assumptions: that belief systems are not created anew by each individual as he or she grows up, but are transmitted from generation to generation; and that belief systems endure because the private fantasies and images of individuals correspond to these cultural traditions. Kirkpatrick (1992) stated that God was the ideal parent or attachment figure. Freud (1927) stated that objective childhood helplessness leads to the need for protection, which is met by the powerful figure of the father. The God image is an extension of the strong, protective father. This hypothesis is the starting point for most of the research on this question.

Numerous empirical studies have tested the hypothesis of similarity between parental images and deity images. The findings can be summarized as follows:

1 The main finding is that God is described as more similar to father (De Neuter, 1981; Pasqualli, 1981; Vergote and Aubert, 1972). Especially if a descriptive, cognitive measure is used, rather than attitudes, God is seen as primarily paternal (Vergote *et al.* 1969): father–God correlations for 180 American students, of both sexes, were 0.70, mother–God correlations were 0.37. Vergote and Tamayo (1980), using a cross-cultural sample, noted that both males and females overwhelmingly used paternal images. Roof and Roof (1984), with a representative US sample obtained the same results.

2 Sometimes, God is seen as similar to both mother and father (Birky and Ball, 1987; Strunk, 1959; Tamayo and Desjardins, 1976), but more recent research has noted similarity to mother (Gorsuch, 1968; Nelson and Jones, 1957; Tamayo and Dugas, 1977; Vergote and Tamayo, 1980).

3 Attitudes towards God are closer to attitudes towards the opposite sex parent (Godin and Hallez, 1964; Strunk, 1959). Attitudes towards God and father were most similar for nuns (r = 0.65), followed by unmarried girls, followed by older women (Godin and Hallez, 1964). Later studies failed to reach this finding.

4 God is described as, and attitudes towards God are similar to those towards, the preferred parent (Nelson, 1971; Godin and Hallez, 1964). Two studies (Godin and Hallez, 1964; Nelson, 1971) found that with respondents reporting no preference for one parent, the correlations between the deity image and the images of both parents are very similar.

This has been interpreted as supporting Alfred Adler's theories of parent–child relationships, and his notions of religion. Adler stated that the idea of God is a concretization of the human ideal of the sublime and the perfect, and the preferred parent is closer to this ideal (Rattner, 1983). Spilka *et al.* (1975) tested both Adlerian and Freudian notions, and found both sides wanting.

5 Results vary according to the cultural and educational background of the respondents (Tamayo and Dugas, 1977). Thus, there is some evidence that Catholics see God as more similar to mother than Protestants (Rees, 1967).

6 Potvin (1977) found that adolescents who describe their parents as exercising control over their lives are more likely to portray God's image as punishing. Kirkpatrick and Shaver (1990) reported that adult respondents with avoidant attachments to their mothers were most likely to be highly religious, when the mother herself was low on religiosity. Direct parallels between parenting styles and God images in a sample of 3,400 mother–father–youth triads were reported by Hertel and Donahue (1995).

There are some relevant findings on the concept of the deity in young children. Using interviews with children, Heller (1986, p. 118) concluded that 'God and father are fused and cause confusion in the child'. In a study of kindergarten children in Japan, the god image was viewed as part of the family for children from Roman Catholic families, and closer to the teacher in other children (Saski and Nagasaki, 1989). Deconchy (1967), in a study of 4,660 French Catholic children aged 8 to 16, obtained descriptions of God. Among boys, the percentage describing God as like their fathers varied with age, showing a general upward trend. The lowest point for girls (9 per cent) was at age 10, and the highest point (39 per cent) at age 15. In a further analysis of the same data, Deconchy (1968) reported that the image of God in boys was more often connected with the maternal image of the Virgin Mary and less often with the image of Christ, while for girls the opposite connection was found.

The relative importance of mother and father as sources of the God image evidently varies among different groups. At the same time the tendency to indicate similarity between the deity and opposite-sex parent or preferred parent can be related to Jones' (1951) formulation and to Freud's more general view of religion as a consequence of the Oedipal situation. However, respondents may report images of God which contained conventional paternal elements, but which were unlike their conceptions of their own fathers (Vergote *et al.* 1969). Cross-cultural findings from eleven countries show the paternal image dominance effect quite clearly (Vergote and Tamayo, 1980). Looking at these findings together, it seems possible that the paternal image of God varies with the culture while the affective attitude towards God is derived from relations with parents.

Thus, parents are not only the bearers of religious traditions, but determine more directly the particular content of images and the attitude towards them.

FORMAL RELIGIOUS EDUCATION

All groups seek to create loyalty to identity and ideology, and an immunity to frequent attitude changes. While so far we have observed the enormous influence of the parents in the transmission of religiosity to the children, their success is far from assured. Religious communities do not leave this assignment just in the hands of the parents. Religion is an ideology, and transmitting it requires action and effort. While all religious traditions emphasize the importance of free will and human agency in making free choices about religious commitments, they all make sure to create structures which lead to only particular outcomes, namely religious commitment, on the part of children born into a tradition.

All religious groups are aware of the power of social learning, and that is why so much effort is put into religious education within the community, and proselytizing outside of it. In all cultures a serious effort is made in educating the young in matters of religion. This may be to ensure the survival of society, or of the cosmic order, or for the good of the souls of the young and to guarantee that they will prosper in the next life. The methods used are much the same everywhere – the study of sacred books, instruction in myths and theology, and taking part in rituals. This instruction may be part of the job of regular teachers, or it may be done by priests, or by special experts in religious training. In traditional, preliterate societies adolescents are given religious secrets at the time of adolescent puberty rites and other rituals (see Chapter 4).

Religious authorities often try to maintain belief monopoly through the control of communications reaching their communities. Most traditions make sure that children are not exposed to competing traditions or identities. Social segregation in itself means enhanced learning. This is a major tool of socializing, and it is easier to do in smaller communities and uniform societies. When individuals know that beliefs and behaviours are expected, supported, and likely to be reinforced within their social group, and among their peers, they are more likely to conform (Fishbein and Ajzen, 1975).

The effects of religious education seem to be quite weak, when other variables are taken into account. For example, Francis (1987a, b) surveyed nearly 5,000 11-year-olds in one English county, and found that going to a Catholic school had a predictive power (i.e. a beta weight) in predicting attitudes to Christianity of 0.04, going to a Church of England controlled school had a weight of –0.05 (i.e. had a negative effect), while going to a Church of England aided school was no different from ordinary state schools. In similar studies in another English county Francis (1979) had also found that Roman Catholic schools had a small positive effect, and all Church of England schools had a small negative effect. In a replication of this study with 15–16 year olds (Francis, 1984), the path analysis shown in Figure 6.2 was obtained.

This analysis was directed to finding the predictors of attitudes to Christianity, not church attendance; there would have been causal arrows in a different direction if church attendance were being predicted. Francis and Brown (1991) studied 711 16-year-olds to find the predictors of praying. The findings were very similar to those for the 11-year-olds; the strongest predictor of prayer was church attendance, and this was much stronger than religious education in the schools, or parental religiosity. It should be noted that in these studies a number of important variables were held constant – parental church attendance and social class, school size, and size of town.

Several studies have been made of the effects of parochial schools in the USA. Johnstone (1966), in a study of Lutheran schools, found that these schools had little effect on religious knowledge and behaviour, if parental attitudes were held constant. However, the schools did have some effect in the case of parents who had little contact with the church. On the other hand, Greeley and Rossi (1966) found that Roman Catholic schools did have an effect independent of that of the parents.

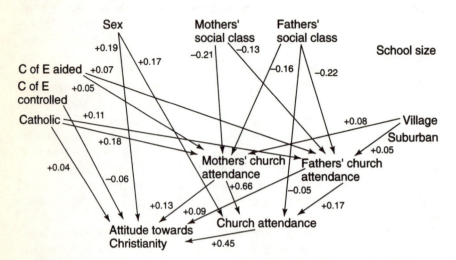

Figure 6.2 Path analysis of the predictors of attitudes to Christianity of 15–16 year olds
Source: Francis (1984)

Looking at Sunday schools, US studies have obtained similar results. For example, Hoge and Petrillo (1982) found that while parents had a massive effect on the religion of their children, Sunday school did not. However it has been found consistently that going to a Catholic school does have a definite effect on religious beliefs, attitudes and later church attendance, especially when this was supported by parental influence. This was first found by Greeley and Rossi (1966); they found that the effects were strongest for males attending parochial schools and Catholic colleges. These effects of American Catholic education have been replicated several times (Hyde, 1990). Similar effects have been found for fundamentalist schools, and for Jewish schools, inducing feelings of Jewish identity (Hyde, 1990). However Cohen (1974), in a study of 626 American Jewish students found very little effect of religious schools or Saturday schools; the main effect was on knowledge of Hebrew. The effect for mainstream Protestant schools is weaker: Erickson (1992) surveyed 900 16–18 year olds, and found a definite though modest effect of formal religious education.

We shall see in Chapter 8 that many children have some kind of religious experience at an early age. Francis and Greer (1993) found that those children who reported having had such experiences at ages 8–10 also had more positive attitudes to Christianity and accepted Christian moral values more.

The implication for teachers of religion is presumably that children should be put in situations where they have religious experiences. One possible way is through ritual. Sociologists of religion have emphasized the importance of ritual, some giving it priority over beliefs. This may be correct; Garrison (1976) found that when children took part in church services, in churches where there was a lot of 'division of labour', they went to church more often when at college; this was still true when earlier frequency of attendance was held constant.

Finally, religious schools and part-time religious schools ('Sunday schools') have positive effects, partly through social influence rather than education proper. Belonging to a group with certain norms, in this case about religion, or being impressed by and forming attachments to teachers, are major forms of social influence. We have seen (Chapter 4) that young men go into the Catholic priesthood partly as the result of the influence of their priest, and the same is probably the case with other traditions too.

DIFFERENCES IN DENOMINATIONS AND TRADITIONS

We should expect differences in socialization policies and strategies, based on the history and social situation of any religious tradition. Minority groups would tend to enforce selective contacts or minimal contacts with the wider society around them. They would carefully control social interaction. When a group is smaller and more distant culturally, as compared to the majority, the more the limitations it puts on young members. Restricting social interaction with non-members by creating clubs and summer camps means keeping children and adolescents busy in activities with other members only. Minority religions are more likely to employ social barriers and close control of adolescents.

Differences in strategy should be related to differences in resulting loyalties. There are clear differences among denominations in the effectiveness of religious training. We can measure this effectiveness by looking at the endurance of beliefs, or the percentage of those who are still loyal to their religion when they come of age. It has often been found that there is more agreement with parents in Catholic families, and Cavalli-Sforza *et al.* (1982) found a correlation of 0.92 for the religious behaviour of Catholic students and their parents. Many studies have shown that Catholic religious training seems to be the most successful in terms of endurance, and Jewish training the least successful. Conservative Protestants are similar to Roman Catholics in their ability to transmit their beliefs to their children (Bruce, 1983).

The Mennonites, a conservative Protestant group, have been found to have even more influence than Catholics (Hunsberger, 1976), and Baptists have been found to have nearly as much similarity (Hoge *et al.* 1982). We saw on p. 103 above that conservative Protestant families make their children go to church with them. The apparent power of Catholic parents may have another explanation; for Catholics being brought up in the church makes one a member, but for Protestants, and especially for Evangelicals and Pentecostalists, an individual decision for salvation by faith, being born again, is required.

CONCLUSIONS

Continuity in religious identity between generations is the rule rather than the exception, and is the result of deliberate effort within the family and in formal educational settings. Normal religious socialization, even today, creates identity, not conviction or choice. For any individual, the reality of religion is always learned as part of the acquisition of identity, family attachments, and group culture. This involves the development of a sense of kin loyalty, which may explain some of the social consequences of religious affiliation. Religious socialization is part of the continuing formation of collective and individual consciousness. Socializing the young in any social system aims at creating social and cultural continuity by enlisting them to collective assignments. Social learning takes place through identification and modelling, conscious as well as unconscious. Religious involvement in later life can be predicted, for most individuals, from knowledge of the religious background of their family of origin. The force of tradition is the force of identifying with one's parents. The psychoanalytic idea of identification is highly relevant here, as it is the basis of social processes and group membership. Identification is the psychological mechanism through which religious continuity in socialization is created. It is natural and almost automatic.

For most of human history, individual religious identity was ascribed and immutable. Together with language and cultural heritage, it was part of the attachment to a 'tribe' (real or metaphorical). In many cultures today, religious identity is still determined by kinship, and considered immutable, like 'race'. It is a matter of birth within a certain family. Thus, many Moslems around the world consider Salman Rushdie a Moslem, which to them implies clear loyalties. In traditional cultures, it is the parents' duty, and in modern cultures their right, to socialize their children into religious faith, as part of the parental role. Children then become a captive audience, whose religion and religiosity is a matter of destiny, not decision. In Chapter 8 we discuss further how children accept and digest religious ideas. Discontinuity in religiosity and religious identity, even while being the exception, raises interesting psychological questions, and will be discussed in Chapter 7.

Changing beliefs and identities

Conversion, religious movements, and defection

If in the last chapter we have seen how intergenerational transmission seems to be the rule in the development of religious identity, this chapter will deal with changes in religious identity through conversion, defection, and apostasy. Such acts, however unlikely, are a constant challenge to theories of religiosity.

Discontinuity could be measured in distance (change from previous score) and direction (more or less religious in comparison to parents or self). It is significant that when we speak of discontinuity, we most often mean it to be discontinuity in comparison to parents, because continuity with parents is such a strong and obvious norm. The majority of religious believers carry the exact same religious labels as their parents before them. Very few have changed labels, and this tiny minority gets our well-deserved theoretical attention. Discontinuity is sometimes considered a failure or an error in socialization.

We should note that there are two kinds of discontinuity, one in which the person becomes less religious than his or her parents (apostasy, defection), and the other in which the person usually becomes more religious (conversion). The first kind appears to be much less dramatic, and has attracted much less scholarly attention, compared to the second kind (Shaffir, 1991). It seems that individual secularization, as we might call apostasy, is accepted as needing fewer explanations, while conversion is examined with a sceptical gaze.

CONVERSION

Conversion can be defined as a perceptible change in one's religious identity, a conscious self-transformation, which is often discussed and proclaimed for all to see. This may take the form of a change from one formal faith to another or a re-commitment to a nominal existing faith. In the majority of cases, it is a re-affirmation of the tradition in which the person has been raised. Conversion is a miracle, claim the converts and their brethren in faith. We can see why, because it is sometimes accompanied by truly dramatic changes. The rarity of this phenomenon has been in inverse proportion to the interest it has generated in students of religious behaviour. Conversion has been *the* classical topic in the psychology of religion, and has been studied earlier and more extensively than many of its students today realize (Leuba, 1912; Pratt, 1920; Starbuck, 1899; Thouless, 1923). As Allport (1950, p. 37) attested, 'no subject within the psychology of religion has been more extensively studied than conversion'.

This preoccupation, or seeming obsession, with converts may be understood in terms of theoretical concerns. The topic has been so attractive to psychologists because it highlights, so it has been believed, as if by a magnifying glass, the dynamics of religious faith. What characterizes the convert is the high level of displayed commitment, emotion, and activity tied to the religious transformation. While we can claim that most nominal religious believers do not have much of an ego-involvement in their faith, which is only a matter of heritage and social learning, in the convert we have a person who has invested much in a conscious (and possibly unconscious) search for a binding belief system. In the search for 'pure' religiosity (see Chapter 3), conversions seem to provide ideal cases of religious motivation. If conversion involves joining a majority, it is suspect. When it means joining a minority and losing status or power, or a persecuted minority, we are likely to perceive purity of motives. 'Pure' conversions do not seem to involve gains in status or power.

Theoretical approaches

There are four theoretical approaches to the phenomenon of dramatic transformation in religious identity.

Identity and cognitive quest

The quest leading to conversion has been regarded as the model of an adolescent identity crisis and its resolution. Since the nineteenth century, when psychologists such as G. Stanley Hall, William James, and Edwin D. Starbuck turned their attention to this matter (Hall, 1904; James, 1958; Starbuck, 1899), religious conversion has been rightly considered an adolescent phenomenon, or even an essential part of adolescence. Developmental psychologists described adolescents as not only capable of abstract thought, but also having a desire for a rational (or an irrational) explanation of everything. 'The adolescent is an individual who begins to build "systems" or "theories" in the largest sense of the term' (Inhelder and Piaget, 1958, p. 339). Some political ideologies and religion offer such explanations (Elkind, 1971). Giving up one's autonomy in return for absolute ideological security is a powerful motive (Deconchy, 1980), sometimes called an 'Escape from Freedom' (Fromm, 1941). 'The search for the strong, supportive, and protective figure who conveys absolute sureness fits into the magical thinking and messianic wishes of hundreds of thousands of people' (Liff, 1975, p. 116). Such individuals join an intensive group situation, offering collective identity, charismatic leadership, and messianic hopes.

Adolescence is characterized by conversions that are most commonly experiences of personal re-commitment to a familiar religious tradition, and less often involve the change from one religious tradition to another. Often the new framework is more demanding than the religious tradition to which the parents belong, so that adolescents can adopt a 'holier than thou' attitude towards the apparently superficial religiosity of their families.

Ordinary conversions are rare after age 30, but 'second conversions' (known in Christianity as being 'born again') do occur. A few individuals have 'mystical conversions' in which an already religious person begins to have religious experiences of a stronger and more continuous nature, in some cases leading to taking up a contemplative life. Bucke (1901) describes 43 such cases, which include some of famous historical saints and mystics; almost all had their mystical conversions in their thirties, often at about the age of 33. The famous 'midlife crisis', supposedly common in modern individuals after age 40, does not seem to lead to many conversions. However, midlife conversions have been known to occur in various non-Western traditions, and they take place once an individual has completed the task of having and raising children (Bilu, 1990).

Interpretations of changes in religious identity as the result of a search for meaning have to account for the fact that while alienation and meaninglessness may be experienced by many, only a few choose a religious answer to their quest (cf. p. 12). Batson *et al.* (1993) interpret conversion as the re-organization of cognitive structures, on the model of figure–ground reversals in perception. The stimulus for such a change is an initial discontent, a dissatisfaction with the self, or an 'existential crisis', the loss of meaning in life. The restructuring process is a kind of creative problem solving, leading to a new way of looking at things. This must be tested to see if the new outlook works, that is, if it solves the initial problem. Batson *et al.* (1993) speculate that the initial preparation and incubation of the problem take place in the left hemisphere, while the re-structuring takes place in the right one.

Powerful defensive solution to an unconscious conflict

The psychodynamic view of conversion, starting with Freud's *tour de force* on religious experience (1928), delineates an unconscious conflict, which finds a defensive solution through a reorganization of impulses and attachments. The specific content of religious beliefs and commitments is secondary to the real process (Christensen, 1963; Kligerman, 1957; Salzman, 1953).

To use the psychoanalytic terminology, what happens to the ego in the process of conversion is a revitalization through a new, totally positive, internalized love object. We should consider the possibility that the most efficient model we can use to understand the intensity and suddenness of the conversion experience is that of any intense emotional attachment, which may be just as sudden and dramatic. This attachment is accompanied by a rise in self-esteem and general well-being.

If we adopt the psychoanalytic view, a major hypothesis would be that the relationship with parents, and more specifically father, would play a major role in religious beliefs and activities. More specifically, good parental relations or bad relations, or losing a parent would lead to varying levels of religiosity (for a Victorian case study, see Goss, 1907).

For young people (sometimes for older ones) joining a deviant group and choosing a new identity is an act of rebellion against their parents and parental authority: 'the inner struggle with the problem of hatred toward the father or toward father symbols – that is, toward authority – results in overwhelming anxiety and can result in the conversion experience' (Salzman, 1953, p. 186). In terms of individual and family dynamics, every identity change is a rebellion against one's parents, who usually created a former identity, and against one's past. When a young European, who grew up in an average family, turns into a 'born-again' Christian or joins a new religion, he or she is declaring a revolt against his or her parents. Whether or not the individual will remain in the group for long seems to be affected by relations with the parents (Wright and Piper, 1986).

Personality predispositions

While conscious reports focus on precipitating incidents, some of which seem miraculous, the psychological viewpoint searches for a predisposing character. The picture that emerges from the literature is one of a certain weakness or vulnerability:

> we would characterize the period before religious conversion as one of severe demoralization . . . the person becomes confused and attributes inner experiences to the outer world, entering a state of transient psychosis. Dominant affects include despair, hatred, resentment, and helpless fury, often directed . . . toward a parent or parent-substitute . . . The person . . . longs to submit to an all-powerful, benevolent figure who can give absolution and restore order.
>
> (Frank and Frank, 1991, p. 81)

Psychological readiness, or vulnerability, or psychopathology, may be called upon to explain why particular individuals, and not others in similar social situations, have chosen, or have grown into, conversion experiences.

Disturbed individuals are more likely to experience such sudden trans-formations, which in themselves are evidence of severe pathology (Linn and Schwartz, 1958). The enthusiastic believers who tell us about their conversion may be covering up a deep depression. Schimel (1973) stated that 'the quest for identity and meaning can be seen as an index of pathology. It is the continuous preoccupation with, rather than the fact of, a concern with identity that is the index of difficulty' (p. 407). What James (1902) suggested is that a profound personal crisis is always the prelude to the dramatic personality change which is observed in converts. He described a number of well-known converts, such as Bunyan, Tolstoy and St Augustine, who showed marked signs of melancholia. And we hear about profound crisis in the contemporary conversion testimonials. This loss of self-confidence, the restlessness which leads to the search for an answer, is the *sine qua non* for the transformation of the self through conversion. 'Perhaps the strongest qualitative characterization of tension supportable by the data is that pre-converts felt themselves frustrated in their various aspirations and *experienced* the tension rather more acutely and over longer periods that most do' (Lofland, 1978, p. 41). Pruyser (1968) suggested that sudden religious conversion is an indication of a severe psychological crisis, and, at the same time, a way of warding off a total breakdown (cf. Meissner, 1988; Olsson, 1983; Spero, 1982).

This vulnerability is tied not only to low self-esteem and depression, but to a limited network of social support. Vulnerability can be defined as 'neuroticism' or anxiety, and it can be defined as stemming from low social status, economic deprivation, and other factors leading to insecurity (Weimann, 1987). A general social-psychological explanation for the open-ness of certain individuals to new modes of experiencing the self and the world has to do with their immediate social relations. Individuals who are in the midst of transitional social situations are more open (or vulnerable) to new self-definitions and new groups. Examples of such individuals include adolescents and people without family attachments. Personal loneliness is a major factor in personal vulnerability, and converts can be compared to other individuals likely to experience dramatic life changes.

A remarkably similar set of social circumstances characterizes people who develop tuberculosis and schizophrenia, become alcoholic, are victims of multiple accidents, or commit suicide. Common to all these people is a marginal status in society. They are individuals who for a variety of reasons . . . have been deprived of meaningful social contacts.

(Cassel, 1973, p. 110)

Individuals who have few personal ties to others and a weak sense of identification with family and friends are more likely to develop salvation careers. Social isolation means that individuals are detached from struc-tures that would channel them into conventional activities. In a situation of crisis and social disintegration, individuals with weaker personalities and borderline functioning will be more sensitive and will react with symptoms, with psychological breakdowns, or by finding new solutions.

When social support is so weak, those friends that one is forced to rely on become crucial, and they may be followed on the road to conversion. Those who do not feel a sense of belonging to any immediate, primary social groups are likely to feel detached from wider ideologies and to be open to new ideas.

Recruitment and persuasion

Hypotheses and findings related to this explanation, focusing on the process rather than on personlaity dynamics, are discussed on p. 123.

Research findings on converts and conversion

Most studies of converts are retrospective, i.e. members of new religious movements (NRMs) or 'born again' individuals are administered various self-report measures. The sampling process is unclear, and usually reflects only willingness to cooperate with researchers. There are almost no prospective studies of conversion and recruitment, which would include measures taken before the conversion. Ideally, what we need is a prospective research design, in which individuals are assessed before changing their religious identity during their time of active membership, and possibly afterwards (if they leave). Such studies would be, of course, quite expensive and complicated, but could answer some important questions. Another problem is that very few studies have used control groups. The reliance on self-report measures in most studies is quite problematic, because of the tendency of converts to exaggerate the benefits of recent transformations. Because of this, data on converts must be approached with caution. Biographical research, which relies not on reported feelings but on life events, can provide more reliable data. Objective events are those that are externally verifiable, and observers can agree as to whether these have occurred. Examples include such events as deaths in the family, illness, divorce, and financial gains or losses. If we can obtain information about objective life events preceding conversion, some of the hypotheses can be tested.

The few studies using controls and biographical data with converts indicated that these individuals had experienced a personal crisis prior to achieving conversion and their relations with their parents were more problematic, compared to controls. Ullman (1982, 1989), in a comparative study of converts and individuals with a stable religious identity, showed that converts' perceptions of their parents were more negative, and the incidence of father absence was much higher in their life histories. Converts were more likely to have had fathers who were absent, passive or hostile, and mothers who were hostile, unstable or overprotective. Converts described their childhood and adolescence as unhappy, and recalled more traumatic childhood events. Personal stress was reported as characterizing the two-year period preceding the conversion. Beit-Hallahmi and Nevo (1987) compared 59 male converts to Orthodox Judaism in Israel with matched controls. The converts were higher on authoritarianism (see Chapter 9), reported significantly lower identification with their parents, fewer relationships with women, and more readiness to ask other people for help when faced with personal problems. The converts were also lower on two different measures of self-esteem, and lower in their level of aspirations. In a group of 23 converts studied by Kirkpatrick and Shaver (1990), almost all reported an intense emotional crisis or trauma preceding the conversion. Biographical information on members of ISKCON (the International Society for Krishna Consciousness) in the USA showed an identical pattern of parental loss or absence, and an identity crisis preceding conversion (Poling and Kenney, 1986). Individuals who have 'sudden' conversions are also found to have had less close relations with their parents (Kirkpatrick and Shaver, 1990). In a study of modern US televangelists, both an absent father and an admiration for the mother were uniformly reported in their conversion autobiographies (Lienesch, 1993). After performing a meta-analysis of 25 studies covering 4,513 converts, Oksanen (1994) concluded that conversion should be viewed as a fantasy compensation for an attachment deficit (cf. Kirkpatrick, 1992). These findings seem to lend clear support to the psychodynamic view of conversion.

Christensen (1963), Linn and Schwartz (1958), and Saltzman (1953) offer evidence showing that religious conversion is often preceded by psychopathological states. Manic depressive patients were found to have a higher incidence of religious experiences, described as 'conversion' or 'salvation', compared to a control group (Gallenmore *et al.* 1969). Among the patients, 52 per cent reported such experiences, while among the control only 20 per cent did. The results were interpreted in terms of the general emotional reactivity of these patients, which is expressed in both psychiatric symptoms and religious experiences.

Using the Minnesota Multiphasic Personality Inventory (MMPI), Spellman *et al.* (1971) found that converts scored higher than controls on the hysteria scale, reflecting more anxiety and denial. Wuthnow (1978) found that converts are more likely to be restless, unhappy, and uncertain about their identity and life goals. Cavenar and Spaulding (1977) state that religious conversion occurs when the defence mechanism of isolation fails in seriously disturbed individuals. They found a correlation between conversion and depression following ambivalence about the death of close relatives. Galanter (1982) found that among members of the Divine Light Mission and the Unification Church, 30–40 per cent had sought professional help before joining and 6–9 per cent had been hospitalized (cf. Levine and Salter, 1976). In a survey of 103 members of ISKCON ('Hare Krishna'), 48 per cent admitted to 'feeling discouraged and/or anxious about life' before joining the group, while 37 per cent had some kind of psychological treatment (Rochford *et al.* 1989). A report on members of the US Jesus Movement in the early 1970s also showed that many of them had been in various forms of treatment before their conversions (Richardson *et al.* 1979), and data from a community clinic in Israel clearly demonstrate that converts show much higher rates of psychiatric illness of a serious nature (Witztum *et al.* 1990). In a follow-up study of 520 mental patients, hospitalized in the New York State Psychiatric Institute between 1963 and 1976, and diagnosed as borderline or psychotic, it was found that 32 (6 per cent) had conversions by 1985, which is far more than expected for the general population (Stone, 1992).

While converts seem to be more vulnerable before conversion, the process of adopting religious faith seems to have positive consequences for many of them. It has been found, supporting the notion proposed by Batson *et al.* (1993), that the extent of self-dissatisfaction before conversion correlates with reports of positive and fundamental change, enlightenment and new knowledge (Brown, Spilka and Cassidy, 1978, cited by Batson *et al.* 1993). For many individuals, especially adolescents, functioning improves following a conversion (Allison, 1968, 1969; Apprey, 1981), which supports the notion of a defensive solution. The most immediate improvement is in having a subjective feeling of meaning and purpose in life. In a study using converts and controls, Paloutzian (1981) found that Purpose in Life scores were significantly higher following conversion. In some cases, the effect of joining a group and being a member could be clearly therapeutic. Joining a group often provides structure and support, and often improves individual functioning significantly. Severely disturbed individuals are held together by group support and group practices.

> Religious communities can also provide a haven for those who are disturbed or do not cope well with the world, and they can have a therapeutic value because of that. While religious institutions could carry those influences uniquely, religious (and other group) participation is itself linked to psychological well-being and social integration, simply because it offers social involvement rather than isolation.
>
> (Brown, 1988, p. 57)

Several studies report that joining NRMs did enhance self-confidence in many converts (Frank and Frank, 1991; Freemesser and Kaplan, 1976; Galanter, 1980, 1982; Galanter *et al.* 1979). Levine and Salter (1976) report both subjective and objective improvements, but for specific measures of mental health the results are more ambiguous (Weiss and Mendoza, 1990).

Levine (1981) found that of 57 disturbed converts, only 15 had decompensated while in the groups being observed. He concluded that the incidence of psychological casualties in NRMs is no greater than that caused by any intense group experience. There is little doubt that conversion, especially with group support, helps the individual to rebuild his or her ego and to function better. It is also possible that the same process of rehabilitation operates for group leaders themselves, and other individuals who serve in leadership roles in salvation moments.

Religious conversion seems to be helpful as a treatment for certain self-destructive behaviours, such as drug abuse, gambling, and sexual orientation difficulties. By invoking belief in and reliance on a higher power and by mobilizing strong group pressure, religious groups may create a motivation strong enough to put an end to the use of drugs, especially alcohol (Galanter, 1982), or to ego-dystonic sexual behaviour (Pattison and Pattison, 1980). They may also provide the continuing support needed to maintain the improvement in the recovering addict or the habitual user (Robbins, 1969; Robbins and Anthony, 1972; Simmonds, 1977; Volinn, 1985).

We have stated that those likely to report dramatic conversions are also likely to be socially isolated. Research has shown that, as predicted, the lack of constraining attachments and commitments or fewer other competing commitments will lead to conversion. Individuals are more likely to join groups when they have few other social obligations, and when they have close relationships with group members. This personal exposure to the group's beliefs allows potential members to check whether these beliefs match their own quest. The data on adolescents are relevant here as the young people are in a stage of non-attachment, confusion, and identity diffusion. Many studies show that those likely to adhere to new religious groups are overwhelmingly unattached (Argyle and Beit-Hallahmi, 1975; J.F.C. Harrison, 1979; M.I. Harrison, 1974). Data on those who joined NRMs in the USA in the 1960s and 1970s show them typically to be unmarried adolescents (Richardson et al. 1979). This has been found in other cultures. In a representative Japanese sample, those who joined NRMs had weak social ties; were younger, unmarried, and of little education; and had unskilled jobs (Miller, 1992). In describing one Japanese NRM, Hashimoto and McPherson (1976, p. 83) state that 'In both the United States and Japan, membership data suggest that members of the Sokagakkai are marginal in social and economic characteristics.' A change in religious affiliation in North America has been found to be related to personal deficiencies (Wallace, 1975). These deficiencies could be in social rewards (occupation, income, education) or in coping with a crisis situation. Identical findings were reported in a study of Protestant converts in Guatemala (Roberts, 1968). The converts turned out to be newcomers to big cities, lacking a network of social and economic relationships (cf. Flora, 1973, 1976).

All forms of individual conversion are rather precarious. Religious identity change will also be susceptible to reversals. Personality transformation under dramatic conditions is notoriously unstable (Levine, 1984). The individual is always in danger of reverting to his or her old self, because of internal (psychological) or external reasons. Whether this will happen or not depends on both personality and social circumstances.

Following the dramatic events surrounding conversion, there must be a decline in excitement and gratification, and the new doctrines may be seen as no longer attractive (Seggar and Blake, 1970). Dramatic conversions and successful charismatic recruitment seem to be just as hard to achieve for traditional religions as for NRMs. 'While there are dramatic saints from sinners conversions, the amount of attention given to these shows their rarity' (Bruce, 1983, p. 402).

Another variety of identity discontinuity includes 'switching'. 'Switchers' are those who change their religious affiliation, but do it for a variety of 'extrinsic' reasons, mostly marriage to a partner of another religious group (Roof, 1989). Switching, or 'circumstantial' conversion, may occur with migration or geographic mobility, where the newly acquired identity helps social integration (Lewis *et al.* 1988). Even in the case of those changing affiliation because of marriage, it has been found by Wallace (1975), that various social deficits, such as low income and education, had a strong effect on the likelihood of 'switching'.

Bibby and Brinkerhoff (1973) found that recruits to conservative churches in Canada were in most cases switching from one conservative church to another, the product of childhood socialization, or were individuals accommodating themselves to the religion of their spouses. 'Evangelicals are in the main produced by evangelical parents, Sunday schools, youth fellowships, seaside missions and camps, Christian Unions in universities and colleges, and membership in one or more of the many inter-denominational evangelical organizations' (Bruce, 1983, p. 402).

RECRUITMENT

If we said in Chapter 6 that socialization of the young is done by 'significant others', natural authorities with whom they have emotional ties and on whom they feel a natural dependence, recruiters have the task of becoming 'significant others' for those they want to recruit. In recruitment into discontinuity there is an attempt to establish a new authority or source of teaching. Socialization for discontinuity involves models outside the family and the community, as well as peers. The major challenge for recruiters is creating identification and gaining plausibility or authority. Here socialization is 'unnatural', because the identity offered is deviant or stigmatized, and a disengagement from the previous identity is hard to achieve. Even when what is involved is a re-commitment to a nominal 'old' identity, a rejection of social learning, parental teaching and parental authority is often involved.

Recruitment models in the literature can be divided into three categories, differing in the importance they accord to the recruiters or to the individual.

'Mind control', coercion, and manipulation vs. normal persuasion

Such terms are most often used in the mass media (Nordheimer, 1974), but really have little conceptual meaning in psychology. They are never used when a person joins an old religion, only when he or she joins a new one. What has developed, especially in the mass media, is the myth of a remarkable technique of persuasion, ascribed to small and marginal groups, because of their deviant image. Many popular explanations of the rise of new religions, and even some of the questions raised in academic articles, are merely expressions of prejudices about minorities and other cultures. Joining a small, deviant group arouses opposition and calls for an explanation. From the observer's point of view, it just does not make sense. When a young German joins ISKCON ('Hare Krishna'), the identity change involved is so dramatic that many observers will react with horror and prejudice.

Those using the term 'mind control' usually mean a powerful system of persuasion based on deception, group pressure, and coercion (Galanter, 1989; Scanlon, 1966; Ungerleider and Wellisch, 1979). The whole 'mind control' approach is predicated on the notion that deviant groups have been amazingly successful in their recruiting efforts. Magical prowess in recruiting new members is often attributed to new religions, while in reality they remain small, and usually fail in their attempts to recruit new members. A look at the history of these groups (see p. 133) shows that NRMs have not been any more successful than other new social movements, and have been much less successful than most secular movements. Actually, new religions have been quite unsuccessful in both recruiting and keeping members, which explains their limited impact and their limited rate of survival.

If we want to examine seriously the recruitment practices of new religions, what we discover are normal attempts by true believers to persuade others to follow them, which mostly fail miserably, and possibly a special readiness or openness among those who are ready to accept the new message. Barker (1984) showed that out of 1,000 individuals persuaded by the Unification Church to attend one of its overnight programmes in 1979, only 8 per cent joined for more than one week, and less than 4 per cent remained members by 1981, only two years later. Out of any 1,000 who had visited any of the Unification Church centres, less than one would be a member five years later. Attrition rates are thus extremely high, and are similar to what we know about the effectiveness of all conversion campaigns (see p. 129).

In social-psychological terms we can speak of an attempt at persuasion by a source without authority, but it seems that peers take the place of parents and other authorities. Despite the dramatic nature of conversion accounts, there must be a preparation stage before the actual conversion (Rambo, 1993). The preparatory stage functions because the converts have role models, and know earlier cases. We can use here the differential association model, used by criminologists and sociologists: 'The probability that a person will become a member of the Watch Tower movement will vary directly with the intensity and frequency of interaction with members of the sect' (Beckford, 1975, p. 161).

The central role played by peers in recruitment and conversion has not received adequate attention. Findings on the recruitment process underline the importance of friendship and peer influence (Harrison, 1974; Nelson, 1972). Actually, this was the light-hearted view of conversion offered by Sapir (1937): 'Certainly one may allow oneself to be converted to Catholicism or Christian Science in exactly the same spirit in which one invests in pewter or follows the latest Parisian models in dress' (Sapir, 1937, p. 143). Emphasizing the concepts of persuasion, attitude change and group membership to describe recruitment misses one essential component in the process, that of personal attachments which create new, committed relationships. The cognitive overemphasis, often expressed, leads to assuming that recruitment means accepting certain beliefs, while in reality primary group attachments play a major role in recruitment (Snow *et al.* 1980). The literature tends to underestimate the impact of friendship. People often follow their close friends on their salvation trek. Recruitment is often by personal friends, and not by unknown recruiters. Still, the group may have a strong hold on them, because what they do have is attachment to another person, rather than a conviction in some abstract faith. The attachment may not be to a charismatic leader, but to a close friend who introduced them to the group and now stands by them (see Ebaugh and Vaughan, 1984; Rochford, 1982; Snow *et al.* 1980; Stark and Bainbridge, 1980). Primary relationships do have an effect on commitment in traditional congregations as well (Welch, 1981).

Recruitment by a spouse or a close friend does not constitute a real conversion, because it is mediated through personal relationships, with no religious motivation. Very often, individuals join religious groups as a cluster of relatives or friends, and identification with the group is formed through belonging to this cluster of intimates (Harrison, 1974). According to Davidman and Greil (1993), women are more likely to become converts through a social network, while men were more independent seekers. The effect of intimate relations is demonstrated when looking at defections from NRMs. It has been found that when one partner in an intimate dyad leaves, the other may also leave, though having no problem with the group itself (Wright, 1986).

Commitment is formed through devotion to the group, which is often warm and supportive, compared to other groups the recruit has known. The personal past is erased, including past sins and errors. In communal religious groups it is anti-materialism, sincerity in interpersonal relations, dependence on leaders and close guidance in all details of everyday living, that create the strong group bonding. The sources of commitment include not only changes in self-image and cognitive restructuring, but also overt 'bridge burning' acts that mark these changes (Hine, 1970). In research on Roman Catholic 'charismatics' in the USA, it has been found that glossolalia served as a commitment symbol, but a testimonial was the central commitment mechanism (McGuire, 1977).

We tend to forget that there must be differences in the involvement and commitment among group members. Some are passionately and totally committed, while others are merely curious. An unexamined assumption is that members of deviant ideological groups all support and hold the group's ideology. Knowledge of beliefs, in the case of some members, may be quite superficial. Researchers may be more knowledgeable than members about elaborate belief systems, and there are cases where presumed members do not really understand what they are supposed to believe. Not all members of NRMs or the newly committed to old religions have experienced conversion, as described here, and not all have the same degree of involvement in their new identity. Some, despite outward appearances, are not fully committed (Pittard-Payne, 1980). While only a relative minority has experienced conversion, a larger minority has experimented with various salvation modes, and has adopted part of their ideology. Some conversions may be rather undramatic (Lynch, 1977).

> The typical adherent of these ... movements established a peripheral, transitory relationship to one of these groups and then drops out ... It is possible to distinguish two forms of participation. In one form, persons' ... memberships become a major source of meaning, values, and norms for individuals involved ... Such 'committed members' provide the core or central cadre for these movements ... Other persons, however, may have a more peripheral or transitory form of affiliation.
>
> (Bird and Reimer, 1982, p. 4)

The recruit as an active seeker

The emphasis on recruitment views the new member as passive, subject to more or less sophisticated recruitment techniques, which determine his or her future course of behaviour. The recruit is often far from passive, and may be an active seeker, who plays an important role in the process (Balch and Taylor, 1977; Richardson, 1985a; Straus, 1979). He or she may be a vulnerable and needy individual, who translates his or her inner hunger for meaning and belonging into active seekership, or at least an openness to new messages. An openness to the religious frame of reference is the *sine qua non* of joining the new religions. There may be in modern societies a population of seekers, individuals in crisis, who are open (or vulnerable) to accepting new self-definitions or, at least, new ways of looking at the self (Lofland and Stark, 1965). We can list their social background characteristics, which explain why they have become seekers or converts (Straus, 1976). Beyond the social background, what all these individuals share is, at the psychological level, an openness to new ways of defining themselves and their potential happiness (cf. Neal, 1970).

The seekers may be those who are more sensitive to contradiction, ambiguity, and lack of structure. We can find serial, or habitual, converts, who switch from one group to another within one lifetime, or within just a few years. Seekers combine a self-definition of stress and distress with an active search for personal change. Thus, among those who 'take refuge in otherworldliness' in one anthropological study is Zachary, a young South African. He

> has studied Hinduism and other Oriental mysticisms. He has been an adept of an Indian guru and once thought seriously of joining a Zen monastery in England . . . involved in several spiritualist groups . . . and has more recently been attending the services of a neognostic society whose members come from the wealthiest strata of Johannesburg's spiritually enlightened.
>
> (Crapanzano, 1985, p. 174)

The initial openness to religious salvation messages is the crucial factor in recruitment. Defining problems in religious terms is what the old and the new religions share. This perspective of problem-definition (and solution) is crucial for joining both old and new religious groups (cf. Lofland and Stark, 1965). Frank and Frank (1991) make clear that the individual must experience a sense of dissatisfaction which lends itself to a religious solution. Openness to new ideas means a heightened responsiveness or suggestibility, as opposed to resistance and critical reception (see Chapter 9). Some individuals are so susceptible to the new message that no great deal of persuasion and no great efforts at recruiting them are necessary.

'Charisma'

Some of the active recruiters into religious movements and leaders in these groups fit Weber's description of the charismatic actors:

> All *extraordinary* needs, i.e. those which *transcend* the sphere of everyday economic routines, have always been satisfied in an entirely

heterogeneous manner: on a charismatic basis. It means the following: that the 'natural' leaders in moments of distress – whether psychic, physical, economic, ethical, religious, or political – were neither appointed officeholders nor 'professionals' in the present-day sense, but rather the bearers of specific gifts of body and mind that were considered 'supernatural'.

(Weber, 1968, pp. 1111–12)

Charisma is always in the eye of the follower: 'Charismatic authority exists only as long as it "proves" itself, and such "proof" is either believed or not' (Bendix, 1977, p. 418). It is felt and held by convinced clients, who are ready to offer testimonials and payments. Conger and Kanungu (1987) suggested that leaders are perceived as charismatic when they form and articulate an ideological vision that is discrepant from the majority view, employ unconventional means for achieving a vision, and are ready to take personal risks. This description would fit well many leaders in new religious movements. But it is possible that the leader develops his or her ideas not alone, but perhaps in relation with the group, through trying to solve the group's problems. And one cannot be a charismatic leader without a suitable group of followers, so that the charisma of religious leaders is situation-specific (Wallis, 1982).

RECRUITMENT CAMPAIGNS

We know from the literature on attitude change that making a formal, public, commitment in front of a group increases the likelihood of living up to that commitment, as compared to cases of private commitment. Revivalism is a tradition of periodic campaigns of recommitment (of believers) or recruitment (of non-believers), including public meetings, public confessions of faith, or 'conversions', and an emotional style of preaching. Historians have described four large waves of revivalism, or 'great awakenings' in the USA, 1725–50, 1795–1835, 1875–1915, and 1945–70, as well as the US, Irish, and Welsh revivals of 1857–9, and the Welsh revival of 1905–6 (McLoughlin, 1959). It is easy to point out that this is essentially a Protestant phenomenon, in line with Protestant religious traditions. Such traditions have emphasized flexibility of religious commitment, which can be renewed or 'regenerated' as the person is 'reborn' (Smelser, 1962).

These same traditions have enabled the institution of organized revivals to continue flourishing, especially in the USA, where its manifestations include both old-style revival-tent meetings (Sims, 1991) and television evangelism, which reaches tens of millions on any given Sunday (Martz and Carroll, 1988). The twentieth century has seen the rise of mass media evangelists, who use mass meetings and the media in order to reach the general public and recruit 'converts'. The best known among them has been Billy Graham of the USA. Mass campaigns aim at using the power of public, mass charisma, together with the effects used in normal ritual (music, prayers, 'healings').

Despite the dramatic nature of modern recruitment campaigns, their effectiveness seems limited in terms of reaching uncommitted segments of the population. Table 7.1 presents data on Billy Graham's campaigns in Britian in the 1950s.

Table 7.1 Percentages of audiences responding at Billy Graham's meetings in Britain, 1954–5

	Average size of meeting	Number of meetings	Percentage making decisions
Graham's Harringay meetings, London, 1954: first four weeks	11,600	33	2.30
Relay services during 1954 campaign	930	430	0.44
Meetings addressed by members of Graham's team, 1954	410	425	1.15
Graham's Glasgow meetings, 1955	16,000	16	2.39
Graham's Wembley meetings, London, 1955	56,000	8	5.30

Source: Computed from various figures given in Colquhoun (1955) and from figures released by the campaign organization

Graham's campaign in New York in 1957 was similar. About 2 million people came to his meetings in Madison Square Garden, which had 19,000 seats; 56,246 (2.8 per cent) made decisions (Lang and Lang, 1960). Most surveys of such efforts have shown that the audiences reached in these 'crusades' contain many individuals who are already members of various churches. Only Herron (1955), in a survey of British participants in the Billy Graham 1954–5 campaigns, found that almost 50 per cent were genuine non-churchgoers. Analysis of samples of those who came forward in the USA (e.g. Whitam, 1968a, b) showed that those who made decisions mainly came from middle-class homes and were of white Anglo-Saxon or European origin. They belonged to the main Protestant churches, and 75 per cent were already regular church attenders. There were few African-Americans, Jews, or other minorities. In all, about 50 per cent of British 'converts' and about 75 per cent of the Americans were already going to church regularly. Whitam concludes that most of those 'making decisions' were not being converted at all but merely engaging in a religious ritual. It turns out that attending these events is actually an indication of prior commitment (Bruce, 1983). Research in the USA shows that Billy Graham rallies are attended by members of local congregations, mobilized by their ministers (Johnson *et al.* 1984), and that participation meant reaffirmation, not conversion (Clelland *et al.* 1974). Thus, evangelistic activities may reinforce existing commitments for those who attend or watch the event on television. It seems that revival campaigns of the past century have not been more effective. Carefully documented research on the renowned 1876 Moody Evangelical campaign in Chicago, a three-month effort involving thousands, shows that about 50 per cent of those who joined later dropped out completely, while 32 per cent changed affiliations (Robertson, 1989).

Joining high-involvement groups does not seem to result from any mass campaigns, but follows normal primary group attachments. However, the proportion of long-term conversions achieved by religious movements and at revival meetings is an inadequate measure of their effects. Such a criterion ignores evidence that many people regard participation in a revival meeting or sect-type group as a rewarding personal experience in its own right, however temporary. As Glock (1962) points out, they may have shifted to a deeper level of emotional commitment, or to a changed set of beliefs. Even believers (in both religious and secular causes) need strengthening in their faith, and dramatic mass rallies provide just that. The feeling of unity and conviction on such occasions may be ritualized, but still effective.

RELIGIOUS MOVEMENTS

Over the past 200 years, since 1800, the world has seen the appearance of perhaps 20,000 new religious movements (NRMs), which are a uniquely modern phenomenon, possibly tied to secularization and the decline of religious authority (Beit-Hallahmi, 1993b). In recent years, such movements have been examined under the rubrics of religious experimentation, marginal religions, or oppositionist religions. Only with the decline of religious authority and uniformity can NRMs develop to such an extent.

We are using the term new religious movement (NRM) throughout this book, rather than sect or cult, commonly used in everyday speech and the media. These latter terms have become derogatory, even stigmatic, in many countries. We are using the term sect-type, referring to an innovative, small, high-involvement religious group, following the sociological distinction between church and sect. While not using derogatory terms, we should pay attention to the special situation of NRMs as belief minorities in modern society, which dictate certain behaviours to the groups and their members. This means that NRMs are sometimes not completely truthful about their doctrines or practices, out of concern for possible majority reactions. At other times, deception in fund-raising, practised by some groups, may be justified in religious terms. NRMs are groups in which membership in most cases is achieved, rather than ascribed, through voluntary conversion and recruitment, as described above. Many of these groups promise their followers immediate and true salvation by means of changes in themselves and in the world around them.

Social science studies and explanations of religious awakenings point to their association with deprivation and suffering in both traditional and modern societies (Wilson, 1961, 1967, 1970, 1973, 1975, 1976; Eister, 1974). Millenarian movements are likely to appear under conditions of social upheaval:

> Following a disaster such as an epidemic, famine, revolution or war, people feel vulnerable, confused and full of anxiety, and they turn to millennial beliefs in order to account for the otherwise meaningless events. The disaster is given meaning as a prelude to the messianic period so that the deepest despair gives way to the greatest hope.
>
> (Sharot, 1980, p. 401)

Smelser (1962) suggested that different kinds of stresses evoke anxieties and arouse beliefs of hysterical wish-fulfilment, and hostile types, with social panics, crazes, and riots, and proposed social strain, caused by social discontinuities, as a general explanation for religious movements. Smelser stated that 'a common pattern of strain seems to make its appearance before revivals, and to conform to the general picture of structural strains underlying crazes in general' (p. 199).

These social processes may lead to the formation of religious movements, which emerge because of

> Change in the economic position of a particular group . . . disturbance of normal social relations . . . industrialization and urbanization; the failure of the social system to accommodate particular age, sex and status groups . . . Particular groups are rendered marginal by some process of social change . . . Insecurity, differential status anxiety, cultural neglect, prompt a need for readjustment.
>
> (Wilson, 1967, p. 31).

In pre-industrial societies, NRMs in recent times have been known as 'crisis cults', including so-called Cargo Cults (Barber, 1941; Worsley, 1968) and Ghost Dances (La Barre, 1970; Mooney, 1965; Thornton, 1986). Cargo cults and ghost dances represent desperate efforts to cope with terrible realities (Wilson, 1973; Wallace, 1956). Referring to the Navaho peyote movement, Douglas (1973) describes

> the new Navaho, impoverished . . . inadequately involved in the . . . economy . . . could not count on his kinsmen. He was alone. Eating peyote gave him a sense of greatly enhanced personal worth and a sense of direct communion with the supernatural. Notice that his God has become like himself.
>
> (Douglas, 1973, p. 33)

A crisis may lead to a complete surrender, and religious movements may express resignation and hopelessness (Vidal, 1983). Some religious movements are attempts to respond to crises by revitalizing collective faiths. An example of a successful revitalization movement is described by Wallace (1970), who shows how the Seneca tribe in North America, suffering every possible disaster since 1650 and a total disintegration at the end of the eighteenth century, was reborn in the nineteenth century thanks to a religious vision.

Under particular circumstances, changing religious affiliation may be an attempt to cope with deprivation whose source is religious identity. Thus, groups of 'untouchables' and other low-status groups in India have converted to Islam, Christianity, or Buddhism, trying to shake off a stigma created by the Hindu caste system (Fiske, 1969; Bopegamage, 1979). There have been recent cases of conversion movements among native tribes in South America which are connected to economic development, rather than deprivation (Kanagy, 1990; Lewellen, 1979). It seems that in these cases the conversion to Protestantism, originating in North America, is tied to the desire to adjust to the market economy and become 'modern'.

In both individuals and social groups we can show that religious awakening (or conversion) as well as the appearance of new religious ideas are tied to crises and anxieties. Wuthnow (1980), after reviewing the histories of revitalization movements, from Anabaptists in Europe in the sixteenth century to 'Cargo cults' in twentieth century Melanesia (Cochrane, 1970), concluded that they were all responses to the destruction of traditional social and economic patterns, and that they 'provide hopes that transcend immediate deprivations' (p. 62).

Numerous examples of millennial movements which followed on the heels of social dislocations, catastrophes, plagues, famines, and massacres are provided by Thrupp (1962), Cohn (1957), and Barkun (1974). Countless case studies of religious movements appearing in response to various social and economic frustrations are available, covering numerous cultures and historical periods (e.g. Baer, 1988; Fernandez, 1982). The Sabbatian movement in the seventeenth century is a well-known example. It was a messianic upheaval unprecedented in Jewish history, which engulfed the whole Jewish world at the time (Scholem, 1973; Sharot, 1980). A recent example can be found in the Ukraine, where economic and political upheavals since 1990 have led to the appearance of numerous messianic movements.

Among historical cases of crisis religions are those in the USA in the nineteenth century, with a wealth of private and collective salvation movements, the rise of Spiritualism, and the founding of so many new religions (e.g. Christian Science, Mormonism, Seventh Day Adventists, Theosophy), and in the USA in the 1960s there was another Great Awakening of salvation movements.

Examples of modern conversion movements in times of crisis abound. Beit-Hallahmi (1992) described the astounding development of NRMs and an awakening of old traditions in Israel, following the unprecedented crisis of the 1973 October War. The situation of whites in apartheid South Africa in the 1980s led to a multifaceted religious revival (Crapanzano, 1985). Many South African whites were, in the 1980s, engaged in 'religious renewal', seeking 'to escape through a transcendental religious language ... through Oriental mysticism and pointillist word games' (Crapanzano, 1985, p. 30). Still others joined charismatic, 'enthusiastic', churches:

> many members of the Christian Renewal remove themselves from active political engagement and concern ... Members of the renewal ... tell stories of extraordinary conversions, miraculous healings, and 'groups overcome mightily by the spirit of the Lord' ... Trances, praying in tongues, visions, and extraordinary auditory phenomena are understood as the inflowing of the Spirit of the Lord.
>
> (Crapanzano, 1985, p. 211)

When religious renewal movements appear in modern societies, and attract individuals who are sometimes quite well off, their growth has been interpreted as a response to what Glock (1962) called ethical and psychic deprivations (Johnson and Weigert 1978).

In discussing NRMs, we have to explain not only recruitment and growth, but also disaffection and failure, which are quite common. NRMs in modern societies receive much attention, which is out of all proportion to their success in recruiting members or their overall growth (see p. 124). In a study of 417 NRMs in the USA, Stark and Bainbridge (1985) found that only 6 per cent were growing rapidly, while 53 per cent were declining. Twenty-one per cent started their decline in membership on the day they were founded. The reason for that is that many religious movements are started through schisms in existing groups. Many religious groups fail to grow because of their opposition to society around them, which leads to their encapsulation. They are able to survive, but not to grow. Another problem that NRMs face is that the number of seekers, motivated or open to identity change in any society, is limited, for social and psychological reasons. The tension between NRMs and society is typical of all orthodox ideologies, as described by Deconchy (1980). In such cases of an orthodox system 'the rational fragility of information is functionally counter-balanced by the strictness of social control' (1980, p. 176). This characterizes most belief minorities, not just NRMs. Under these conditions, a challenge to the group is met by an affirmation of ideological loyalty.

Some groups experience a direct disproof of predictions made by the leaders. The best known case in this century was described by Festinger *et al.* (1956). The group leader, named Marian Keech in the study, claimed to have received messages from a space being named Sananda, warning her about a flood that would destroy most of North America at a later date. This date was announced (December 1953), and group members expected the end of the world, and their own salvation by a spaceship sent by Sananda. After the prophecy failed, some of the group members maintained their faith. Mrs Keech claimed that the world was saved by their full faith. She also made additional predictions about various disasters, which also failed to materialize. These events took place in Chicago in late 1953, but the leader continued her activities into the 1980s.

Such prophetic failures may have a serious impact on the fate of any group. It has been suggested that such failures may increase fervour among group members, but this happens only in a few well-specified cases (Festinger et al. 1956). There are other cases where prophecy failures have not led to a visible crisis or collapse, possibly because the prophecies are only subject to disconfirmation in terms of timing. Thus, a prediction about the coming end of the world in 1984 may be re-interpreted as true in principle, and only temporarily delayed by other events. A belief system may be flexible enough to accommodate such failures (Singelenberg, 1989; Weiser, 1974; Zygmunt, 1970, 1972). Some groups have survived disconfirmation through some effort, but in other cases a direct disconfirmation of claims leads to crisis and sometimes decline or disintegration (Hazani, 1986; Palmer and Finn, 1992; van Fossen, 1988).

A notion derived from Festinger et al. (1956) is that disconfirmation leads to increased proselytising, as a way of increasing social support and so reducing members' cognitive dissonance. This proselytising hypothesis has not been confirmed in other studies (Balch et al. 1983; Hardyck and Braden, 1962; Sanada, 1979).

New religions in Western societies, often subject to external opposition, are mostly unstable groups with unstable members, which need extra-ordinary luck and leadership to survive and prosper (Pittard-Payne, 1980). NRMs suffer from high rates of defection (Barker, 1984; Bird and Reimer, 1982; Wright, 1988). Kanter (1972) found a relationship between sacrifice, commitment and survival in nineteenth-century religious communes in the USA. Groups that made more intense demands on their members tended to survive longer than groups that were more lenient. Kanter (1972) suggested that demands for sacrifices are correlated with the structural qualities of clearer role definitions for members, and clear goals for the group.

The impact of NRMs is much smaller than often perceived. They are small and marginal, and touch the lives of fewer than 1 per cent of religious believers (Wilson, 1975). Many are so unstable as to be ephemeral. A look at the history of twentieth-century NRMs is quite sobering in this respect. Movements that once seemed on the verge of becoming global powers are now remembered only by historians. Moral Rearmament (the 'Oxford Group Movement'), the best-known NRM of the 1930s in Britain and the USA (Eister, 1950), is totally forgotten. The Jesus Movement of the early

1970s in the USA (Richardson, Stewart, and Simmonds, 1979), with its hundreds of communes in major US cities, has similarly disappeared. It seems that high utopian excitement cannot be maintained for long, and that adolescence is more of a factor than is often realized. When enthusiastic members get older, commitment wanes in favour of more conventional pursuits (cf. Beit-Hallahmi, 1977). Nevertheless, like the phenomenon of conversion, NRMs deserve and do get attention, because of their rarity and intensity.

As we reported above, there are cases where joining an NRM will lead to improved individual functioning, and the group environment is clearly therapeutic. There are also opposite cases of deterioration and pathology in individuals and groups where there is clear evidence of destructive and self-destructive behaviour. The victims often include dependents, not just members. This was the case with the People's Temple mass suicide in Jonestown, Guyana on 18 November 1978, when minors and the elderly comprised the majority. Of the 912 victims, 199 were aged over 65; 300 were under age 16; and 137 were under age 11. In the Branch Davidians case (Texas, April 1993), there were 17 children among 86 victims (Beit-Hallahmi, 1993b). In other groups, withholding medical care from mothers and children has been known to cause high mortality rates in mothers giving birth and their infants, sometimes classified as 'infanticide' (Hughes, 1990). Other deviant and destructive groups such Aum Shinrykio and the Order of the Solar Temple must be viewed against a background of severe personal and social pathology. These are extreme forms of the typical variables of vulnerability and deprivation (Pozzi, 1982).

APOSTASY, ATHEISM, AND DISBELIEF

By looking at individuals at the low end of the belief continuum, apostates and atheists, we can learn something about religion and religiosity. This is, in a way, a validation of the findings about committed believers. Apostasy is not just having doubts or deviating from official doctrine. Most believers have doubts and differ in their commitments; that is why we find such variance on measures of religiosity within the same group. Apostasy is defined as alienation, and disaffiliation from a religious group. It means leaving behind a tradition, a group identity, or even a recently acquired membership in a religious group. Defection from NRMs is less of a challenge theoretically, because of the instability inherent in members and groups, and the inherent instability of the conversion to NRMs. Apostasy means not merely not switching to another group, but declaring no allegiance to any religious tradition (Caplovitz and Sherrow, 1977). Thus, it is a general disillusionment with religion, a private secularization. Caplovitz and Sherrow (1977) stated that 'Apostasy indicates not only loss of religious faith, but rejection of a particular ascriptive community as a basis for self-identification' (p. 31). The process of reducing religious commitment is especially stressful in the case of members of the clergy or of religious orders (San Giovanni, 1978). Disengagement is long and painful, and in the case of Roman Catholic nuns, the process of reaching a decision to leave takes between two and a half and four years (Ebaugh, 1988).

Continuity and discontinuity in any identity may be a function of inter-personal networks (Kotre, 1971), especially involving intimate relations (see p. 125). Apostasy and conversion can both be seen as a rebellion against one's parents (see p. 117). In both cases there is a rejection of parental identity and parental beliefs. It 'might well be symptomatic of familial strain and dissociation from parents . . . apostasy is to be viewed as a form of rebellion against parents' (Caplovitz and Sherrow, 1977, p. 50). The alienation may be not just from the parents, but from the community of origin. Ferenczi (1926) stated that disillusionment about the omnipotence and perfection of one's parents and significant others leads to scepticism.

Findings regarding those who come from religious homes and then give up religion show that they have had more distant relations with their parents (Hunsberger, 1980, 1983; Hunsberger and Brown, 1984). Caplovitz and Sherrow (1977) found that the quality of relations with parents was a crucial variable, as well as a commitment to intellectualism. Hunsberger and Brown (1984) found that lesser emphasis placed on religion in the home, especially by the mother, and self-reported intellectual orientation had a positive impact on rejecting the family's religiosity as a young adult. Dudley (1987) found that alienation from religion in Seventh-Day Adventist adolescents was correlated (0.72) with the quality of their relationship with their parents and other authority figures. Alienation was tied to authoritarianism and harshness on the part of the parents.

Reaffiliation, that is, coming back to the family's religious tradition, is related to the influence of the family of origin (cf. Chapter 6) and to becoming a parent (Wilson and Sherkat, 1994). In a survey of US 'baby boomers', born between 1946 and 1982, Roof (1993) found that 67 per cent dropped out of their parents' religious denominations, but 37 per cent of the drop-outs later reaffiliated in their middle and late twenties. Again, becoming parents was a major factor in reaffiliation. From a psychoanalytic perspective, it has been stated that individuals past their adolescence (or in post-adolescence) experience a 'super-ego victory' which means moving closer to their parents in significant ways (Wittenberg, 1968; Beit-Hallahmi, 1977).

What about adult atheists and secularists? In modern society, we can find two groups of secularists: first, ideological, self-defined individuals whose lack of religiosity is part of a pattern of action and belief (Campbell, 1971), and, second, secularists by default, those who stay away from religious activities without being committed secularists. Are committed (or even behavioural) secularists the mirror image of devout believers?

Most of the findings we have come from surveys which included a broad distribution of religiosity levels. Individuals not affiliated with any religious denominations, who made up only 0.049 per cent of the US population in the 1970s, were found to be much better educated than affiliated individuals. More than 55 per cent of them had at least some college education, as compared to 32.6 per cent of the affiliates (Welsh, 1978). Similar findings were reported by Tamney *et al.* (1989), showing that of those in the US population with a complete university education, 11 per cent were unaffiliated. Data on secularists in Australia show them to be much better educated than the rest of the population, socially liberal, independent, self-assertive, and cosmopolitan (Hogan, 1979). In Canada, census data and national surveys show that those reporting 'no religion' are younger, urban, male (Veevers and Cousineau, 1980), as well as upwardly mobile (Ley and Martin, 1993). In representative surveys of the US population in the 1970s and 1980s, the unaffiliated were found to be younger, mostly male, with higher levels of education and income, more liberal, but also more unhappy and more alienated in terms of the larger society (Feigelman *et al.* 1992; Hadaway and Roof, 1988).

As can be expected, the least religious are also the most liberal in social and political attitudes. In a classical study of ethnocentrism and anti-Semitism, the scores of those respondents reporting no religious affiliation were found to be lower than members of most religious groups (Adorno *et al.* 1950). The authors summarized the findings as follows: 'it appears that those who reject religion have less ethnocentrism than those who seem to accept it' (1950, p. 213). These findings have been confirmed many times since. The correlation between rejection of religious beliefs and radical political views has been demonstrated in several studies (e.g. Demerath, 1969). Spray and Marx (1960) showed that the degree of political radicalism was directly related to the degree of irreligiosity. Self-identified atheists were more radical than self-identified agnostics.

Nelson (1988a) found that, in surveys using representative samples of the US population between 1973 and 1985, disaffiliation from churches contributed to greater political liberalism. Using a representative sample of the US population between 1973 and 1977, Hadaway and Roof (1979) found that individuals raised as 'nones' who remained unaffiliated were more liberal in politics and morals than those who became religiously affiliated. In a study of 532 US Roman Catholic adolescents and their parents, it was found that those described as 'indiscriminately antireligious' were the lowest on dogmatism, compared to all others (Thompson, 1974). One psychoanalytic view has been that atheism represents realism, but also sublimated sadism (Bonaparte, 1958). Ross (1990) reported that individuals with no religious affiliation in the USA enjoyed low levels of psychological distress, just like highly religious individuals, despite their marginal status in society. Maslow (1970) reported that of the 57 individuals he judged to be self-actualized, that is, having achieved the highest level of personality development, very few were religious.

In light of findings presented below in Chapters 9–11, we can state that secularists are less prejudiced, less authoritarian, less dogmatic, and less suggestible, compared to religious individuals. This could be predicted from looking at data for lower levels of religiosity, such as the findings about the Quest dimension.

CONCLUSIONS

The idea of individual choice and voluntary change in religious identity is in itself a relatively novel idea, tied to secularization and individualism. We have seen that, even within modern culture, converts stand out in being more vulnerable and less stable than controls. This instability is also typical of NRMs.

Chapter 8

Religion as a dependent variable
Gender, age, class, and community

In this chapter we look at the effects of the three main 'demographic' variables on religiosity: gender, age, and social situation (class and community size). It is well-known that women are on average more religious than men. Which aspects of religion are most affected? Above all what is the explanation? Is it because the personality of women is more compatible with religious ideas and values? Is religiosity partly a matter of age? What is the religion of very young children like? Are there differences due to social class?

GENDER DIFFERENCES

The differences between men and women in religiosity are considerable, and this is a major field of empirical enquiry for us. We will look first at the differences on different measures of religiosity, then at the findings for different denominations, and then try to explain these results.

Gender differences on different criteria

We shall use the ratio of females to males as our main measure of gender differences, so that 1.50 for example means that there are 50 per cent more women than men. The main trouble with this index is that it will be smaller if the percentages being compared are very large; the ratios for American data tend to be smaller than British ones, since Americans are more active in religion than the British. We will start with those aspects of religion where the greatest gender differences have been reported, and work downwards.

High involvement rituals

The largest differences have been reported for Catholics going to confession (1.93; Fichter, 1952) and for people being converted by Billy Graham (1.8; Colquhoun, 1955). Women in a black American sect were much more likely to go into a trance in services (Alland, 1962), and the sex ratio for members of Pentecostal and similar groups is about 2.0.

Daily prayer

The sex ratio is higher here than for any other common form of religious activity. Gallup (1980) found a ratio of 1.57 for reading the Bible, and 1.36 for prayer, in the USA, and Gorer (1955) found a ratio of 1.87 for English adults.

Beliefs

Women are more 'conservative' or orthodox in religion, that is, they more often say that they hold the central and traditional beliefs, in God and in the after-life, and, for Christians, that Jesus was the Son of God. In British surveys the ratio is about 1.50, in American surveys it is lower, about 1.2, because of the larger percentages of believers. In addition, women hold different images of God. For them God is seen more as a healer, as supportive rather than instrumental (Nelsen *et al.* 1985), and as loving, comforting and forgiving, whereas males see him as a supreme power, a driving force, a planner and controller (Wright and Cox, 1967). Yeaman (1987) in a study of members of a radical Roman Catholic association found that 73 per cent of the women had a 'sex-inclusive' image of God, i.e. as neither male nor female, compared to 58 per cent of the men.

Religious experience

Differences here are smaller, the ratios are 1.32 in Britain (Hay, 1982), and 1.20 in the USA (Back and Bourque, 1970), although the percentages are much the same in both countries, about 33 per cent. Feltey and Poloma (1991) found that women felt 'closer to God'; this was not affected by feminine self-image. The gender difference is found in early childhood; at age 9–10 more girls say that they have experienced 'God's closeness' (Tamminen, 1994). Hood and Hall (1980) tested a sex-related theory of religious experience with 220 students. They found that the females described both their sexual and their mystical experiences, when they had them, in 'receptive' terms; the males described their sexual experiences in 'agentic' terms but not their mystical ones. The sexual model was therefore supported for females but not for males.

Ritual attendance

This is the most visible and obvious source of sex differences, though the differences are lower here. In the USA the ratio is typically about 1.20, in Britain it is higher at 1.50, reflecting the lower percentages overall.

Overall religiosity measures

In the British Values Survey (Gerard, 1985), factor analysis produced two factors, and the scores on each were combined to give a single index of religious commitment. One factor consisted of items about basic beliefs, and reported religious experience, the second was about ritual attendance and positive attitudes to the church. Fifteen per cent of men, 20 per cent of working women, and 26 per cent of non-working women had high scores, a ratio of 1.53 if the two groups of women are combined. The ratio for the medium to high group was 1.61. The American Gallup ratio for 'being a religious person' was 1.45.

Overall membership in all religious groups

This is an unsatisfactory index since the criteria for membership vary with denominations and from time to time. The total ratio in the 1936 American Census of Religious Bodies was 1.32 (Census, 1936).

Self-reported membership in different denominations

In all Christian denominations there are more women than men, but the proportion varies. Table 8.1 shows the ratios found in a recent survey of 310,000 Australian church-goers (Kaldor, 1994) and in US Gallup polls (Gallup and Castelli, 1989).

Table 8.1 Proportion of women and men in different Christian denominations in Australia and the USA

Denomination	Ratio of women to men
Australia	
Anglicans	2.02
Uniting church	1.86
Baptists	1.38
Pentecostalists	1.33
USA	
Episcopalians	1.39
Charismatics	1.35
Evangelicals	1.28
Mormons	1.28
Methodists	1.23
Baptists	1.00
Lutherans	1.00
Catholics	0.96
Nones	0.59

Sources: Australia – Kaldor (1994), USA – Gallup and Castelli (1989)

In British studies the Church of England again has a high sex ratio, and the Roman Catholic church a low one, but there are also very high ratios for NRMs, often 2.0–4.0 (e.g. Wilson, 1961). There is one aspect of religious activity where men predominate, and that is in the ministry (Yinger, 1970), as the clergy is open for men only in most religions around the world. Weber (1963) thought that religious movements of the underprivileged gave equality to women at first but then, as they became established, withdrew it. This theory has been found to be true of American Pentecostal sects in the early twentieth century, some of them Afro-American. At first they had many charismatic women preachers, sometimes the founders of sects, but their numbers then fell (Barfoot and Sheppard, 1980).

Parareligious beliefs

Women are also higher in parareligious beliefs, such as astrology, 'telepathy', and fortune-telling, as well as readier to believe in various 'miracle drugs' (Emmons and Sobal, 1981; Markle *et al.* 1978; Wuthnow, 1976; Zeidner and Beit-Hallahmi, 1988).

Explanations

The greater religiosity of women must be one of the oldest, and clearest, findings in the psychology of religion. Here are some of its most likely explanations.

Gender differences in personality

Historians have explained women's religiosity as related to personality factors. Thus, the prominence of women in nineteenth-century US revivalism was explained by Cross (1965) as due to their being 'less educated, more superstitious, and more zealous than men' (p. 178). There is plenty of evidence for personality differences between men and women; some of these may be relevant to the differences in religious activity. Some of them may be innate, such as greater male aggressiveness (Gray, 1971). Males tend to be more aggressive and dominance oriented than females in most mammalian species, including humans (e.g. Daly and Wilson, 1983; Pratto *et al.* 1993). Sex differences in dominance emerge early in the preschool years and at about the same age in all cultures (Maccoby 1988). Human males are verbally and physically more aggressive than females across cultures (Eibl-Eibesfeldt, 1989; Rohner, 1976).

As children, boys are observed to be competitive and aggressive. Girls are sociable and helpful, and enjoy social contact for its own sake (Opie, 1993). In most cultures males are less nurturant and less emotionally expressive (D'Andrade, 1966). Research on sex differences finds that women are more submissive and passive, anxious and dependent (Garai and Scheinfeld, 1968). 'Women tend to manifest behaviors that can be described as socially sensitive, friendly, and concerned with others' welfare, whereas men . . . can be described as dominant, controlling, and independent' (Eagly, 1995, p. 154). Females 'express more fear, are more susceptible to anxiety, are more lacking in task confidence, seek more help and reassurance, maintain greater proximity to friends, score higher on social desirability, and at the younger ages at which compliance has been studied, are more compliant with adults' (Block, 1976, p. 307). On standard personality inventories, such as the Edwards Personal Preference Schedule (EPPS), consistent differences are found, with women higher on Affiliation, and Nurturance, and men higher on Dominance and Aggression.

As we report in Chapter 9, there is much evidence showing that women have stronger guilt feelings, and are more intro-punitive than men (Wright, 1971; Bernard, 1949). Miller (1986) suggested that the subjective experiences of women are affected by two major factors. The first is the permanent inequality of women in social relationships, under which women are encouraged to be submissive, dependent, and passive. The second is the relational self which is the core of self-structure in women and so they assume more responsibility for relationship maintenance and social support (Turner, 1994; Belle, 1982). Boys' groups tend to be larger, forming 'gangs', while girls organize themselves into smaller groups or pairs (Thorne, 1993). Eibl-Eibesfeldt (1989) suggested that throughout human evolution the social style of females provided the basis for maintaining the long-term stability of social groups. 'Women throughout the world are perceived to be the nurturant sex' (Maccoby and Jacklin, 1974, p. 215). Males are more object oriented, and females more people oriented (McGuinness 1993).

It has been stated that women experience higher rates of childhood abuse, especially sexual abuse, which is a predictor of later depression, and may have depressions related to hormonal changes and to sex role conditioning that encourages patterns of negative thinking and passivity (McGrath *et al.* 1990). In the USA, it has been estimated that between 2.3 per cent and 3.2 per cent of men, and between 4.5 per cent and 9.3 per cent of women meet the diagnostic criteria for major depressive disorder at any given moment (Depression Guideline Panel, 1993). Kaplan (1983) showed that women were more commonly diagnosed as suffering from disorders of internalized conflict, such as depression and phobia, while men were more often diagnosed as suffering from acting-out disorders, such as substance abuse and antisocial personality.

Many of the 'female' traits could well lead to greater religiosity. Dependence, on gods and saints, is part of the religious attitude. Nurturance is a basic religious value. Guilt feelings are often appealed to in sermons and revivals, which then offer relief from them. Miller and

Hoffmann (1995) found that males' risk preference and females' risk aversion were related to religiosity. Thompson (1991) found that both men and women who had a feminine self-image, on the Bem Sex Role Inventory, were more religious, especially as measured by prayer and other devotional activities. Suziedalis and Potvin (1981), with a large sample of children aged 12–17, found that religiosity was related quite differently to the self-images of boys and girls. For the girls religion was related to aspects of extraversion such as help-seeking and sociability, and to being rule-bound rather than rebellious, interpreted as needing external guidance. For the boys religion was related to an activity cluster (adventurous and ambitious), but not to a potency cluster of 'macho' scales, and was also related to a socialized cluster (nurturance, trusting and tolerant), interpreted as inner harmony. We shall see in the next section that religious attitudes are crystallized during adolescence, and it seems likely that sex differences in religion are fixed at this age too.

The effect of employment

Luckmann (1967) suggested that the most active in religion are women, especially those not at work, together with the old and young, who are also not at work. There are a number of reasons why women who are not at work should be more active in religion – they have more time, may feel that they are not filling a valued social role, or feel socially isolated, they have narrower social contacts so are under less secular pressure, and have less conflict with worldly instrumental activities (de Vaus, 1984). It is indeed the case that women at work are less active in religion, though not very much less, as Table 8.2 shows. But how about men, should not some or all of these processes affect them equally?

Table 8.2 The effect of employment on ritual attendance in the USA and Canada

	Men %	Women %	Ratio
USA (n = 12,120)			
Employed full-time	41	51	1.24
Employed part-time	33	56	1.70
Not working	30	54	1.80
Canada (n = 11,000)			
Employed full-time	53.5	62.0	1.16
Employed part-time	45.7	62.3	1.36
Not working	58.9	67.6	1.48

Sources: USA – de Vaus (1984), Canada – Gee (1991)

From these two large surveys, actually combinations of several national surveys, in the USA and Canada, it can be seen that non-working women were a little more active. This is a universal finding, though often the effect of work for women is greater. In an Australian study, de Vaus and McAllister (1987) found that employment was a powerful explanatory variable for female ritual attendance; it explained a little over half of the variance. However, this does not explain the other half of sex differences in religion.

The main problem, however, concerns men. In the American study in Table 8.2 the men were less religious the less they worked, as was also found by Hertel (1988) with data from 14,900 people, though in the Canadian study the part-time workers were the least religious. The opposite effects of work on attendance for men and women may be because those who play the usual gender roles also play conventional religious ones (Steggarda, 1993). Perhaps women who are independent and assertive enough to go to work are by temperament less attracted to religion. Perhaps men who are out of work are too demoralized to attend religious services. Part of the explanation is simpler – unemployed men are less educated and of lower social class, two groups which are less religious (Hertel, 1988). According to deprivation–frustration theories of religion they should attend religious services more often, but they do not.

A closely related explanation is that women will be more religious when involved in child-rearing. However, careful analysis in an Australian survey, comparing otherwise similar females with and without children, has found that children have no such effect (de Vaus and McAllister, 1987). The greatest gender difference in this study was found for single individuals; the difference declined during the life cycle and was least after children had left home. However, in a study of 2,384 subjects in the Netherlands, Steggarda (1993) found that *men* engaged in child rearing were more religious, but not women, so that there was no gender difference when they both shared this task.

Differences in socialization

More important may be the different ways in which boys and girls are socialized. Barry *et al.* (1957) found that nearly all cultures emphasize nurturance, obedience and responsibility for girls, while boys are trained for self-reliance and independence. It has sometimes been suggested that female socialization includes the expectation of being active in the religious congregation, doing 'religious work', supporting and nurturing others, being subordinate to the clergy. There have been massive changes in the role of women in recent years, so it would be expected that women will be less willing to take this kind of role. Pilkington *et al.* (1976) repeated a British student survey carried out eleven years earlier, and found a much greater fall in the religiosity of women than of men over this period, i.e. a reduction in sex differences. Since there are now many more women at work, it would be expected that religious gender differences would have become smaller; however the respondents in the earlier study were students, so these changes in the religious sex ratio may be due to more general changes.

Women are better socialized

This explanation, connected to the second explanation on p. 142ff., suggests that women are on the whole much better socialized than men, as they conform much more to most social norms. But women are not only well socialized; they are also the main socializers. They are the main transmitters and guardians of cultural norms and traditions, including religion, in their maternal role (see Chapter 6 on parental influences).

Parental projection

None of the theories discussed so far throws any light on the greater sex differences found in Protestant groups. However, Freud's notions of paternal projection (see Chapters 2, 6, 12) can provide an explanation. According to psychoanalytic conceptions of the Oedipal period (age 3–6), girls should have a positive attachment to fathers but boys should feel ambivalent about them. Freud then proposed that God is a fantasy and substitute father figure. The main evidence in support of this hypothesis is the finding that images of God are similar to images of parents, particularly to opposite sex parents (see Chapter 6). For women the image of God, and attitudes to God, are more similar to those towards father, and for men for those towards mother. We saw that for women God is seen more often as a healer; He is also seen more often as benevolent rather than punitive. If the culture carries an image of God as male, as a father, this image should therefore appeal more to women. It is also found that Catholics experience God as more like a mother (Rees, 1967); in addition the Virgin Mary and some female saints are very prominent in Catholic worship. This could produce a stronger religious response from males. For Protestants the main object of worship is Jesus, and this should do the same for women. Deconchy (1968) indeed found, in a large study of Roman Catholic children, that for boys the image of God was connected more often with the Virgin Mary, while for girls it was linked more often to Jesus. Also relevant is the maleness of most of the clergy, who are addressed as 'father' in many religious traditions. The attraction for women may be repeated here.

Women are more deprived

This explanation looks at women's social status and power. It is easy to conclude that women are deprived and oppressed in many social situations. Religion in this case functions as it does with other oppressed groups.

Women are not allowed to express their sexuality

Explanations of religiosity as related to sexuality (see pp. 24 and 240) are especially relevant to women, who have always been less free to express their sexual impulses. Some religious experiences, especially in women, seem to reflect diverted sexual energy (see Chapter 5).

AGE AND RELIGIOSITY

Age greatly affects the incidence of religious behaviour and religious experience. We suggest viewing it in terms of the life cycle.

Children: 3–12 years

Children are found to be 'very disposed towards religion' (Vergote, 1969) – if they are exposed to it, that is. Attitudes towards politics in contrast are formed much later.

Beliefs

Harms (1944) asked several thousand children to draw their idea of God and to give written or spoken comments. While no statistical analysis was done, Harms concluded that there were three stages in developing an idea of God:

1 The 3–6 fairy-tale stage, when God is regarded as in the same category as giants and dragons, but bigger and wearing flowing robes.
2 The 7–12 realistic stage, when God is seen as a father, like a real person; many orthodox ideas are accepted.
3 The 12+ individualistic stage, when there are a variety of interpretations, mystical or conventional.

Petrovich (1988) tested 60 children aged 4, and found that most of them could distinguish between man-made and natural objects. When asked who made the natural objects, such as the sky, ground, rocks and animals, many said 'God', especially for the sky (68 per cent), rocks (53 per cent) and animals (43 per cent). When asked what God was like, 41 per cent said 'a real man', 25 per cent 'a person without a body' and 21 per cent 'air or gas'. When asked where this knowledge came from, 30 per cent said a book or TV and the rest did not know.

Goldman (1964) interviewed 200 children aged between 6 and 15+ about five biblical episodes, such as Moses and the burning bush, and three pictures of religious scenes. He found that the accounts given at different ages followed the Piagetian developmental sequence. The younger children were thought to be in the 'intuitive' stage, of literal interpretations, for example the burning bush was put out by water but some bad men came and lit it again. After age 6:6 to 8:10 the children were thought to be in the 'concrete' stage, and made logical but limited interpretations, for example that the bush was lit from an electric torch. After the age 13:5 to 14:2 they were said to be in the 'formal operational' stage, and now capable of more abstract and symbolic interpretations, for example that God was appearing in the fire. The younger children, aged 6–8, had a sense of awe and dread about God, and older children associated God with guilt feelings. The question of cultural tradition is ignored here, because what some may consider 'concrete' interpretations are part of cultural traditions found among many adults in a given culture.

Vergote (1969) reports the findings of a number of studies of children among the Catholic population of Belgium. He and his colleagues find that the early family is very important for the religion of children, since the idea of God is based on the parents; like them God is all-powerful and all-knowing, and a source of protection and punishment. By age 5–7 children begin to distinguish between God and parents, as the limitations of the latter appear. Jesus is seen as the perfect child. Children have a strong sense of awe, and a growing sense of religious fear. Between ages 6 and 11 the image of God becomes less anthropomorphic, and by the age of 12 God is regarded as invisible and everywhere.

Childhood experience of religion may be important for another reason. Pratt (1923) argued that the emotional associations of religious symbols are acquired by immersion in a religious community, so that adult converts will always be lacking the 'emotional and volitional significance' of religion.

Prayer

Children pray from an early age, if they have been taught to do so. Long *et al.* (1967) interviewed children of different ages, factor analysed the results and found the following stages:

1 Age 5–7   Vague understanding, linked with verbal formulae.
2 Age 7–9   Verbal requests
3 Age 10–12 Private conversations with God, sharing of confidences, less egocentric.

Children often pray for new toys, and they believe that prayer works. Goldman (1964) found that most of his children believed that prayer worked; the younger ones thought that this happened in a magical way, after age 9 they were aware of other causal factors, and after age 12 they thought that it was through human agency by a change of attitude or motivation. Brown and Thouless (1964) found that 35 per cent of 12-year-olds believed in it, but this belief fell off during adolescence.

Religious experience

Goldman (1964) found that children think that God is present everywhere, can hear prayers and see everything. God was associated with awe and dread, but for 12-year-olds with guilt feelings. Tamminen (1994) questioned 3,000 Finnish young people aged 7–20, 95 per cent of them Lutherans, about their experiences. Some of them were asked, 'Have you at times felt that God is particularly close to you?' At grade 1 (age 6) 84 per cent of the children said 'yes', and at grade 3 (age 8) 42 per cent said this had been very often, and 30 per cent a few times. These percentages fell off with age, as shown in Figure 8.1.

The percentages were similar for 'Have you at times felt that God is guiding, directing your life?' The occasions when they felt that God was near were when they were afraid or in trouble, but also quite often in happy situations, for the younger children, and in emergencies and devotion for the older ones. God's guidance was reported most for danger and

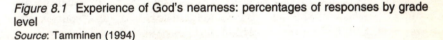

Grade-level (N)		I (183)	III (184)	V (238)	VII (280)	IX (229)	XI (405)
Yes (grade I)	▦	84					
Very often	▨		42	17	10	10	8
A few times	◺		30	40	33	31	27
Maybe once	⊠		18	12	15	14	13
No	▢	16	10	31	43	44	53

Figure 8.1 Experience of God's nearness: percentages of responses by grade level
Source: Tamminen (1994)

difficulties, but the next most common situation was categorized as 'success and happy guidance'. There were substantial gender differences; girls experienced God's nearness and guidance more than boys did, and these gender differences were greater than the differences in believing in God. These findings about the pervasiveness of early religious experience, its subsequent decline, and the gender differences in these, have also been obtained in European studies (e.g. Thun, 1963), as well as in earlier American ones.

Adolescents and youth: 13–23

Children in the period of early adolescence, at 12–14, have a high level of religious beliefs and activity. Loukes (1961) interviewed British 14-year-olds and found them very concerned about religion and other goals and values. During adolescence there is an overall fall in religious activities and beliefs. Typically there is a drop of about 25 per cent in the number who go to services or report religious affiliation (Wadsworth and Freeman, 1983). This is not due to historical changes since it is found when the same individuals are compared at different ages (Willits and Crider, 1989). Religious beliefs also decline; Francis (1987c) found a linear fall during the years 9–17. However, Sloane and Potvin (1986) found an increase in faith with age during adolescence in sect-type groups, while finding a decrease in mainstream US denominations.

Part of the reason for this decline in religiosity is that there is more questioning of the faith, reaching a peak at age 16 (Ozorak, 1989). There is some evidence that the awakening of intellectual interest in religion, and the ensuing doubts, takes place earlier for more intelligent children (Hollingworth, 1933); Ozorak also found more questioning and more change of beliefs among students with better grades. Religious doubts and questioning occur at this age in different social settings, for example among Catholic adolescents in Belgium (Hutsebaut, 1972). The main impact is on some traditional but not very central beliefs. Kuhlen and Arnold (1944) found that the percentage of adolescents who held some of these beliefs fell with age, as shown in Table 8.3. However on other items, such as 'I know there is a God' and 'There is a Heaven', the decline was much less.

Some of this decline may be the result of conflict with parents. Allport et al. (1948) asked 500 Harvard students if they had ever reacted against the beliefs taught by their parents; 73 per cent of the Protestants and Jews, and 62 per cent of the Catholics said that they had, at a median age of 15½ for men, 14½ for women. Ozorak (1989) also found that the peak age for acquiring new religious beliefs was at 14½.

Most religious traditions recognize this fact by having some ceremony, a rite of passage, at this age (see Chapter 4). Those who finally move towards religion have often discarded parts of it, such as the beliefs listed

Table 8.3 Percentage of adolescents holding traditional beliefs

Belief	Age		
	12 %	15 %	18 %
Only good people go to heaven	72	45	33
Every word in the Bible is true	79	51	34
People who go to church are better than people who do not go to church	46	26	15
It is sinful to doubt the Bible	62	42	27
I know there is a God	94	80	79
There is a Heaven	82	78	74

Source: Kuhlen and Arnold (1944)

at the top of Table 8.3, but keep those at the bottom. Ozorak (1989) found that those who had rated themselves as more religious when at school became more religious when at college, and vice versa.

Having shown that there is an overall decline in religion during adolescence we now have to take account of research on conversion, which shows that the peak age for conversions is also at just over 15 years (Spilka, Hood and Gorsuch, 1985). This is a well-established finding, from US revivalism to Billy Graham's campaigns in Britain. How do we reconcile the two findings?

Why do religious beliefs become crystallized at age 14–15, or a little later? Adolescent conversions were once thought to be related in some way to puberty, but the physical changes of puberty are now earlier than age 15. It might be related to the development of intelligence, or to stages of cognitive development, but no clear relation has been found here either for this age group (Slugoski et al. 1984). What does happen at precisely this time of life is the formation of an integrated identity, a consistent self-image (Chapter 7) and polarization, some moving towards religion, some moving away.

Identity formation goes through several stages, in the areas of occupational choice, sexual orientation, politics, and religion. McAdams et al. (1981) studied the religious identity of 56 students in depth, and distinguished between those at different levels of identity achievement. Those who were at the higher levels of identity in the religious sphere were also at higher levels on measures of complexity of ego-development, and had higher scores on measures of formation of a coherent identity. They also had higher scores on intimacy motivation, seeing God as an intimate companion, and appreciating communal rituals.

Adults: 23–60

In some of the earlier literature (Argyle and Beit-Hallahmi, 1975) the evidence seemed clear – there was an apparent decline in religious belief and activity between ages 18–30 followed by a rise to old age. There was always some doubt that what looked like effects of age might be partly or wholly due to historical, cohort effects, such as secularization or revival. Various attempts have now been made to separate the effects of age and history. Stark (1973) examined the results of a US survey, and found no increase with age for religious belief and behaviour; there was, however, a break between those who grew up before and after the Second World War – those from the earlier period being more devout. On two measures there was still an increase with age – belief in an after-life and private prayer (see below). Ploch and Hastings (1994) used data from successive US surveys carried out between 1972 and 1991. Some of their findings are shown in Figure 8.2.

Over this relatively short period only one historical change is evident, with Catholic women attending church less frequently, possibly because of discontent with official Roman Catholic views, on contraception for example. Otherwise no historical trends appeared, but there were some small age changes. In this and other studies there is a modest low point at age 25, and a modest increase up to the age of 60. Another, and better, way of tackling this issue is to carry out longitudinal studies, in which the same individuals are followed up over a number of years; we shall report such studies when discussing old age.

Intrinsic religiosity increases with age ($r = 0.29$, Watson, Howard *et al.* 1988). Others, however, may have doubts in middle life. Fowler (1981) interviewed 359 individuals aged up to 84, and found that his 40–50 year olds often became concerned about the relativity of their inherited religious views, engaged in critical questioning like adolescents, and experienced some demythologizing. The next stage, after 50, found the subjects more accepting of religion and more affected by symbolism.

Old age: 60 onwards

It used to be thought by psychologists that religious activity increased over the life-span up to old age; however, as we have seen, this was partly the result of confusing age changes with historical ones – older people had acquired their faith at a more religious period.

Church attendance

As we saw in Figure 8.2, Ploch and Hastings (1994) found that in the USA ritual attendance rises slowly to the age of 60, and falls after 70 or 75 for

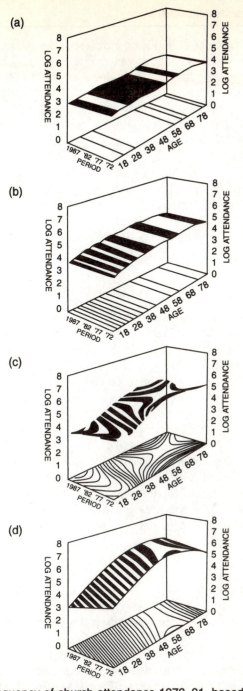

Figure 8.2 Frequency of church attendance 1972–91, based on US General Social Survey data, for ages 18–88, of (a) male white Protestants, (b) female white Protestants, (c) male white Catholics, (d) female white Catholics

Source: Ploch and Hastings (1994)

different groups. Markides (1983) used a different design, and followed up elderly subjects for a period of four years. There was no change in ritual attendance. Other studies have found a decrease in church attendance in the elderly, and also retirement from positions of leadership. This decline is presumably due to physical disability and increasing difficulty in moving around, and needs no further explanation. It can be seen as an example of the 'disengagement' theory of ageing, except that the disengagement takes place quite late, after 75.

Kingsbury (1937) found that the reasons given for going to services changed with advancing age. There was an increase in the number who said that they went to church 'for reassurance of immortality' (80 per cent at 50+), but fewer went 'to gain new friends' or 'to formulate a philosophy of life'. This last change is quite interesting in relation to theories about the wisdom of the old.

Beliefs

One of the classical theories of religion is that it helps to remove fear of death, and as we will show (Chapter 9) it is successful in doing this. The main index of religiosity which certainly increases with age is belief in the after-life. In a study by Cavan *et al.* (1949) 100 per cent of individuals over the age of 90 said that they were certain of an after-life. Old people usually believe that their going to heaven is automatic (Gorer, 1955).

Some eminent thinkers have believed that old people develop a kind of timeless wisdom. Thun (1963) carried out depth interviews with 65 people aged between 60 and 87. Some reported an unbroken religious faith since childhood, without crisis, some had changed within the same faith, some had moved to a different faith, and some had no religion at all. As Wulff (1991) suggests, the image of the long-lived 'elder', possessing wisdom and dignity, may be out of date. Many people live to a great age now, not all of them showing signs of great wisdom.

Other religious activities

Markides (1983) found that over a four-year period his Anglo-American subjects increased in self-rated religiosity; the Mexican–Americans did not. Although the old get to services less often, they do other things more. Many more listen to religious services on radio or television (e.g. Mindel and Vaughan, 1978). There is also a large increase in private prayer; Stark (1973) found that those with high scores for private devotionalism increased from 40 per cent for moderate Protestants in their twenties to 81 per cent at 70 and over, with similar increases for other denominations.

The benefits of religion for older individuals

As we show in Chapter 10, religion produces great benefits in terms of individual happiness. The religious congregation is the most important social group for old people, a source of close friends. Belief in an after-life is another source of well-being. Congregation membership also affects health, partly through social support, and partly through encouraging better health behaviour. All these benefits are greater for the old. When growing old many individuals experience loss of physical, social, and financial power, as well as kin and friends. Religion can not only serve as a source of human support but also provides much psychic solace.

SOCIAL CLASS AND COMMUNITY SIZE

Social class

Social status factors, often examined by sociologists and historians, do affect religiosity. According to Stark and Bainbridge (1987) the lower classes are more in need of compensators, and the upper classes would need fewer compensators, while enjoying the power to maintain successful religious organizations. Class differences in religiosity are both quantitative and qualitative, expressed in both style and substance. The determining factors of social class, namely economic power and social status, are assumed to be reflected in different patterns of religious behaviours. In a Canadian study comparing Protestants and Roman Catholics, it was found that class differences were more important than denomination in determining belief patterns (Northover, 1974). In various societies, religious sanctions define social classes (castes in India) and social barriers.

Religious activities reflect the complex of norms and roles which make up 'middle class' or 'lower class' culture in various societies. The church–sect dichotomy in type of religious organization parallels the class division between middle and lower. The stability and regularity of middle class existence, founded on economic advantage, are reflected in a pattern of stability and regularity in religious activity. We find that middle class individuals, in most countries, are more involved in formal activities. The difficulties and instability inherent in the life of the poor are going to be reflected in their ways of expressing religiosity (cf. Wilson and Clow, 1981).

Differences between middle class and lower class religious groups can be assessed along the dimensions of belief (orthodox or liberal), organizational quality (whether formal hierarchy or informal charismatic leadership), affective style, and consequences in the secular world. The general finding is that there is a positive correlation between social status and religious participation, that is, middle class and upper class individuals are more active in attending rituals. At the same time, lower-class members of small and new religious movements are more active than any other group.

The fact that members of religious denominations often have in common not only faith but also similar socio-economic status has been observed, especially in the case of American multi-denominational Protestantism (e.g. Niebuhr, 1929; Pope, 1948; Lazerwitz, 1961). In the USA, class correlations with religious style are reflected in the common reference to 'whispering Episcopalians, murmuring Presbyterians, shouting Methodists, and screaming Baptists'. The close relationship between social and church affiliation in the USA was expressed by Winter (1962) as follows: 'The Church is now a reflection of the economic ladder. Ascent on this ladder is validated by escalation to congregations of higher social and economic rank. For every rung on the ladder there is an appropriate congregation.' (p. 77). It should be recalled that social class definitions vary between the ones used by sociologists and those used in everyday language. Most North Americans, and indeed most members of modern societies, regard themselves as middle class, and the term is often used rather loosely. 'Sister' Aimee Semple McPherson (1890–1944), the founder of the International Church of Foursquare Gospel, an Adventist group, is reported to have said: 'I bring consolation to the great middle class, leaving those below to the Salvation Army, and those above to themselves' (Epstein, 1993).

In the USA, some religious groups are considered upper class, and their members have been over-represented among the élites (Baltzell, 1964, 1979, 1991). Class differences in the USA were commented on by Lynd and Lynd (1929): 'Members of the working class show a disposition to believe their religion more ardently and to accumulate more emotionally charged values around their beliefs. Religion appears . . . more prominently as an active agency of support and encouragement.' (p. 329). Gerard (1985) found that lower class individuals in Britain had higher scores on an index of religious commitment. Using a measure of religious attitudes, Almquist (1966) found that social class was the best predictor of religiosity. When respondents were divided into upper middle class, lower middle class, and lower class, the lower class members scored higher than the other two groups. The most recent survey in the USA, done in 1990, showed that the old stereotypes were still quite true (Kosmin and Lachman, 1993). The poorest in the USA were (in ascending order) self-identified members of Holiness churches, Brethren, Pentecostal, Baptist, Jehovah's Witnesses, and Seventh Day Adventists. The wealthiest were self-identified Jews, Unitarians, Agnostics, and Episcopalians. The least well-educated were Jehovah's Witnesses, Holiness, Pentecostals, Baptists, and Brethren. The best educated were Unitarians, Jews, members of NRMs, and agnostics.

One way of looking at the difference in style of religious activity between classes in industrialized countries is that of seeing higher status individuals as involved with a religion of 'doing', while those with lower status are involved in a religion of 'feeling'. Thus, we should predict a greater frequency of religious experiences among the lower classes, and indeed, in three US surveys asking respondents about them, those with lower incomes more frequently reported such experiences. Thus, in a 1967 poll in the USA, 51.0 per cent of respondents with incomes below $3,000 and only 39.7 per cent of those with incomes above $3,000 reported mystical experiences (Back and Bourque, 1970). In Britain the findings regarding religious experience seem to be reversed. More recent surveys in the USA, Britain, and Australia show that more educated people and those with better jobs report greater frequencies of REs; for example, 50 per cent of college graduates and only 37 per cent of those with no high school education in a US survey in 1985 (Hay, 1990).

Sectarianism as a form of religious organization and expression is typical of the lower class. As opposed to the church-type organization, characterized by an adaptive stance towards the society around it, birth-based membership, and universalism, sect-type groups are characterized by high commitment, a converted membership, and separatism towards the larger society. They are really a subset of NRMs, discussed in Chapter 7. These groups, found in certain rural regions or neighbourhoods of large cities (Gerrard, 1970), are characterized by radical faith and intense emotionality. Rituals are described by such terms as fervour and ecstasy. Members of sect-type groups are poorer and less educated, and they display a pattern of membership characterized by higher levels of attendance, more money contributed, holding stronger beliefs, more likely to choose their closest friends from the congregation, and being less involved in groups other than the religious congregation (Iannaccone, 1990, 1994). That religious organizations of the sect type represent attempts to deal with various kinds of deprivation was suggested quite early on by Gillin (1910), who described them as protest groups of the poor in the USA (cf. Glock, 1964; Wilson, 1961). Clark (1965) summarized the common characteristics of 200 American sects and concludes that their beliefs are compensatory and that none of these bodies is interested in social reform. In some cases, sect-type movements have led to social mobility and integration. Moore (1986) stated that dissenting religious movements have provided millions of ordinary Americans with 'badges of respectability and . . . a path to upward social mobility' (p. 46). But this is not always true (Schwartz, 1970). Pentecostals historically have come from the poor and working class. Researchers have seen the movement as a form of symbolic compensation (Anderson, 1979; Hollenweger, 1972; Schwartz, 1970; Willems, 1967) or protest (Willems, 1967). Pentecostal rituals, known for their intensity, are viewed as a way of reconciling Pentecostals to their social and economic deprivation.

The lower class and minority group origins of sect-type movements in the USA (Yinger, 1957; Barkun, 1986; Boisen, 1939, 1955; Gerrard, 1968,

1970; Holt, 1940; Hoult, 1958) and elsewhere (Dodson, 1992; Walker, 1985) have been well documented. Goldschmidt (1944) saw Protestant denominationalism in the USA as a reflection of the class structure and social segregation based on class, and stated that while traditional churches meet the needs of the upper classes, evangelical groups meet working class needs by offering them a fantasy world. The Jehovah's Witnesses movement has attracted lower class individuals in countries all over the world, who seem to react to the complexity and pace of social changes (Bram, 1956; Cohn, 1955). Dynes (1955, 1956) reported that sectarianism as a social attitude, i.e. preference for sect-type religious activities, was correlated with lower socio-economic status. A study of a snake-handling group in the USA (La Barre, 1962) showed that members of this group came from among the poorest whites, described as the rural proletariat of southern USA. Poblete and O'Dea (1960), in a study of Puerto Rican immigrants in New York, described the formation of NRMs as the reaction to anomie and an attempt to redevelop a sense of community. Kaplan (1965) described sect-type religiosity among the lower class in the USA as 'religious escapism' (cf. Boisen, 1945). Recent findings show that

> sects tend to attract individuals with limited secular opportunities . . . classes of people experiencing relatively limited secular opportunities (such as minorities, women, and the young) are more likely than others to choose sect membership over mainline church membership . . . a general decline in secular opportunities, such as that which occurs during recessions, will make sectarian groups more attractive.
>
> (Iannaccone, 1994, p. 1201)

What are the psychological mechanisms underlying sectarian involvement? Photiadis and Schweiker (1970) showed that powerlessness was related to joining authoritarian organizations and sectarian movements, and suggested that in a period of fast social change membership in authoritarian groups will rise. Sales (1972) suggested that only certain churches become more attractive in times of insecurity, such as the great depression of the 1930s in the USA. In a test of this hypothesis religious conversion rates during the period 1920–30 in four authoritarian and four non-authoritarian churches were compared. These rates were correlated with changes in personal disposable income, and the results are presented in Table 8.4.

Caste and minority group membership

Differences in ethnic origin or caste are similar to social class differences, except that in these cases the barriers are almost impossible to cross. Many small sect-types draw their members from among the very poor and members of minority groups and this seems to be true in many countries.

Table 8.4 Correlations (r) between estimated per caput disposable income and estimated conversion ratios in four authoritarian and four non-authoritarian denominations

Denomination	r *between estimated per caput disposable income and estimated conversion ratio*
Authoritarian	
Church of Jesus Christ of Latter Day Saints	−0.460[d]
Roman Catholic Church	−0.456[d]
Seventh-Day Adventist Church	−0.67[c]
Southern Baptist Convention	−0.193
Non-Authoritarian	
Congregational Christian Church	0.503[d]
Northern Baptist Convention	0.403[b]
Presbyterian Church in the USA	0.533[c]
Protestant Episcopal Church	−0.312[a]

Notes: (a) $p < 0.10$, (b) $p < 0.05$, (c) $p < 0.01$, (d) $p < 0.015$
Source: Sales (1972)

Most findings on the connection between minority ethnicity and religious behaviour are from the USA, comparing whites and African-Americans. All aspects of religious activity are much higher for African-Americans, compared with American whites. In general, African-Americans in the USA show higher rates of religious affiliation, as compared to whites (Glenn and Gotard, 1977). In terms of their beliefs, African-Americans are consistently found to be more traditional, and in this respect they parallel lower class whites. In population surveys dealing with REs, African-Americans reported such experiences more often than whites (Back and Borque, 1970).

A major characteristic of Afro-American religion is the existence of small sects, often organized around a charismatic leader (Glenn, 1964; Dollard, 1949). Boling (1975) showed that when African-Americans and whites were compared within the same lower class group, lower class African-Americans were more likely to have sect orientations than their white counterparts. Some of these groups, however, move members closer to the values and practices of the majority and so help them to adjust (Edwards, 1968). Worship in these sects provides outlets for frustrated personal and group needs, through emotionality and cohesiveness. The prevalence of sectarianism and intense REs among African-Americans have most often been explained on the basis of their lower social status and many frustrations. Spiritualist churches among African-Americans were described by Baer (1984) as a magical reaction to their position in society. Cameron (1971), adopting the Marxian position (cf. Chapter 2), simply asserts that 'their social situation in the USA requires more "opiate"' (p. 73).

A notorious example in the USA was the People's Temple, which became the subject of worldwide horror when over 900 of its members committed suicide in Jonestown, Guyana. It started as a typical locally organized, lower class US congregation, founded in 1956 in Indiana as the Community National Church by Jim Jones. Jones was very active in racial integration when the idea was quite unpopular, and he was always very popular with African-Americans. In the late 1950s, Jones started developing an integrated church. Later the group moved to California. In 1974 the group started gradually moving its members to Guyana, in South America, and in 1977 Jones himself and several hundred followers moved there. On 18 November 1978, 912 members died in a mass suicide on orders from Jones, who was among them. It should be noted that most of the members who died with Jones were African-American females, a fact which faithfully reflects the composition of the membership (Beit-Hallahmi, 1993b).

Community size

Urbanization is tied to secularization (Ley and Martin, 1993; Veevers and Cousineau, 1980). Brown (1988) offered a psychological explanation for that, suggesting that socialization within the rural setting is more effective: 'traditional practices *must* be recreated by individuals if they are to remain plausible. But that seems easier to do in rural than urban settings' (Brown, 1988, p. 67). Many studies found more religious activity among those living in communities with a population of fewer than 50,000. Glock and Stark (1966) found in a nationwide US survey that residence in a small community was positively correlated with holding traditional beliefs. Similarly, an analysis of Gallup polls showed that rural residents showed more conservatism in religious beliefs (Nelsen *et al.* 1971). More residents of cities with populations below 50,000 reported having had mystical experiences than residents of larger cities (Back and Bourque, 1970).

When differences in religious activity and religious beliefs between farmers and non-farmers in the USA have been studied, the data 'indicate that the popular stereotypes and the impressions of social scientists are surprisingly accurate' (Glenn and Alston, 1967, p. 384). Farmers appear to be more traditional and fundamentalist in their beliefs than any other occupational group, despite the fact that they are less likely to be active congregation members. In many respects they appear to be most similar to the group of lower manual workers.

Living in a rural setting is viewed as being further away from modernity, and as a form of deprivation, tied to higher levels of religiosity (Hunter, 1983). Glenn and Alston (1967) explained the persistence of urban–rural differences as being due to the 'time lag' factor in the diffusion of innovation and change to the rural areas. These include changes in religious beliefs and traditions, and in general social attitudes. Support for this explanation is given by findings which show farmers to be more ethnocentric and isolationalist.

Nationwide public opinion polls in the USA indicate that respondents from large cities report less orthodox religious activity and beliefs compared with those from smaller cities and rural areas (Marty *et al.* 1968). Surveys have shown that non-affiliation is higher in the urban areas of Finland, Norway, and the USA (Mol, 1972; Tamney *et al.* 1989). Education and social class differences probably account for much of these findings. In the Third World today the picture may be different (cf. Arjomand, 1986). The exploding urban centres of the Third World may be the seedbeds for religious movements in the next century (cf. Dodson, 1992, and findings on Latin America in Chapter 7).

Social status factors: summary and explanation

Predictions, derived from Marxian ideas, lead us to expect two things: first, more religiosity in oppressed groups, and second, more emotion in the religiosity of the oppressed. Sect-type movements look like reactions to various kinds of deprivation, whether economic or social (Hill, 1971a, b).

We can summarize the American findings by stating that they reveal a difference in the nature of religious involvement in different classes in the USA. Most middle class religiosity in the USA is described as a rather formal and secularized affair, compared to the intensely emotional religiosity of the lower classes and minority groups. Members of the middle class score higher on measures of institutional participation: church attendance and church membership. Members of the lower class score higher on measures of traditional beliefs and reported REs. They are also more likely to become sect members, with a subsequent intense psychological and social involvement.

While class differences in religious style vary in different countries, the religious style of sectarianism is found in most countries today (Campbell and Fukuyama, 1970). Goode (1968) has also suggested a deprivation explanation of social-class differences in religious participation, since religious styles seem to be related to the felt needs and tensions in the life of various classes. Lower class people who are more frustrated will opt for a more involved religious style.

Another motive for socially underprivileged people to join sectarian religions is the felt increase in status; not only are they accepted as equals but they become part of a spiritual élite (Stark, 1967). It is important to remember that both the lower and the upper classes have other means of satisfying their respective needs and relieving their respective frustrations.

This may explain why more members of the lower classes do not join sect-type groups.

CONCLUSIONS

Basic demographic and social background variables seem to have important effects on religiosity, and should be taken into consideration ahead of other variables in accounting for religiosity. From looking at the evidence in this chapter we conclude that, worldwide, religious individuals are more likely to be female, over the age of 50, and of a lower social class. These findings, replicated many times in specific studies (e.g. Glock *et al*. 1967; Hunter, 1983) are most often discussed in the context of deprivation–compensation explanations of religiosity (see Chapter 12). It should be pointed out that gender has the strongest and widest impact on religiosity across societies. The role of women in maintaining religion as a living tradition and as an institution often does not get the attention it deserves.

Chapter 9

The effect of individual differences in personality and ability

It is still an open question why, under the same circumstances and with the same background characteristics, some people are more religious than others. This chapter examines whether differences in religiosity can be further accounted for by differences in personality. Here we use a variety of measurable traits and settings, most of which have been developed by researchers. Unlike the 'natural' (age and sex) and social categories used in Chapter 8, here most categories are derived from psychological theories and research.

Personality is defined by psychologists as a core of relatively stable traits, which are responsible for consistencies in behaviour. This idea implies the existence of particular styles of reacting to external and internal stimuli, of coping with stresses, and of interpersonal behaviour. Is there a 'religious personality'? Do religious people have a special kind of personality, or a 'religious temperament'? There has been no clear evidence in the past that they do, and we shall have to look at some fairly narrow traits, and at specific religious groups, to see if we can find any effects of personality.

THE EFFECTS OF HEREDITY

Is being religious in some sense inherited? One way to find out is by twin studies. Loehlin and Nichols (1977) studied 850 pairs of twins, aged 17, and found correlations for a scale of religious activities: 0.73 for male and 0.78 for female identical twins, and 0.55 for male and 0.71 for female fraternal twins. These results show a quite small genetic factor here, apparently stronger for males, for whom there is a greater difference between the similarity of identical and fraternal twins.

More recent research in genetics has used other methods of genetic modelling. The results of these studies have not been consistent, and have given differing estimates of the importance of inheritance (Martin et al. 1986; Plomin, 1989; Waller et al. 1990). However, the largest study was by Truett et al. (1992) who used 3,810 pairs of twins and found that about 16 per cent of the variance in their religious attitudes factor was due to heredity. What exactly is inherited? It cannot be the habit of ritual attendance, but must be some more basic features of personality which are associated with religiosity.

GENERAL PERSONALITY TRAITS

The two most general traits found in the literature are introversion–extraversion and neuroticism, most often measured by the Eysenck Personality Questionnaire (EPQ). Early studies found small correlations between religious variables and introversion, but with the revised extraversion scale of the Eysenck Personality Questionnaire there is no correlation. This is probably because the revised extraversion scale has been purified of impulsiveness, and it was the low impulsiveness which correlated with religion (Francis and Pearson, 1985). This negative result has been found with adults and children, and with different measures of both extraversion and religiosity. However, Costa *et al.* (1981), with a sample of 557 American men of different ages, did find a small correlation with 'thinking introversion', a measure of restraint and thoughtfulness, rather than of social withdrawal, again more an index of non-impulsiveness. It may be the case that members of some special religious populations are more introverted.

The other general trait is neuroticism. Again, it has been consistently found that there is no relationship with religiosity at all. For the third dimension of the EPQ, psychoticism, there *is* a connection with religiosity – it is consistently found that religiosity variables correlate between –0.25 and –0.35 with this dimension (e.g. Francis, 1993). An exception was the study by Kay (1981) of 779 British boys and 638 girls, aged 11–15; psychoticism was negatively related to religiosity in boys but not in girls. Psychoticism is a less general trait than either extraversion or neuroticism, and furthermore its exact meaning is less clear. It does not mean suffering from psychosis; what it does mean is a kind of tough-minded ruthlessness, and lack of empathy. We see in Chapter 10 that religious individuals score higher on empathy, and this is a closely related dimension.

There is a fourth scale on the EPQ, the lie scale, and here consistent findings show that religious people score higher than others. It is not clear how this should be interpreted. It is possible that the lie scale is tapping a tendency to be acquiescent and obedient, and that this is true of religious individuals too; it is possible that subjects with high scores are not being truthful when filling in scales about their religious beliefs. It is also possible that religiosity is tied to a general tendency towards denial in the psycho-dynamic sense. Crandall and Gozali (1969) found that religious children were more prone to socially desirable responses and suggested that a religious upbringing would lead to a greater use of repression and denial.

So far we have been using the EPQ as a source of notions about general traits, but another source is the 'big five', of Extraversion, Agreeableness,

Conscientiousness, Emotional stability and Culture (Norman, 1963). Two of these, Extraversion and Emotional stability, we have just dealt with. There has been some debate over the fifth dimension, and McCrae and Costa (1985) want to reinterpret it as Openness, that is, openness to experience, having artistic and intellectual interests, being strong in creativity and imagination. This is the only one of the five to have any link with religion, and it may be the other end of a psychoticism factor (Hampson, 1988). In Chapter 5 above we discussed schizotypy, which consists of a tendency to have anomalous perceptual or cognitive experiences. In a survey of 1,512 US university students, it was found that those scoring highest on a magical thinking scale (including ideas about contacts with the dead or 'telepathy') were also likely to have psychotic and schizotypal experiences (Eckblad and Chapman, 1983).

SELF-ESTEEM

Most studies show a positive association between religiosity and self-esteem, while only a few studies reported no association (e.g. Bahr and Martin, 1983). Results from a 1979–80 national survey of African-Americans show that religious involvement correlated with self-esteem (Ellison, 1993). A clearly positive correlation between religiosity and self-esteem has been found in a study of Roman Catholic adolescents from five different cultures (Smith *et al.* 1979). Benson and Spilka (1973), and Spilka *et al.* (1975) found a correlation between self-esteem and a positive image of God among believers.

AUTHORITARIANISM

Adorno *et al.* (1950) found that church members of all kinds in the USA were more ethnocentric than those with no religion, and later studies have found that authoritarianism is on average greater for individuals with the most orthodox beliefs, and is highest for Catholics and fundamentalists (e.g. Putney and Middleton, 1961; Brown, 1962). It was also found to hold for Moslem fundamentalists, in a study of 599 students at Kuwait University (Al-Thakeb and Scott, 1982), and to Moslem, Hindu and Jewish fundamentalists in Canada (Hunsberger, 1996). It has been suggested that religious individuals are authoritarian because they have been willing to accept parental views, but Putney and Middleton (1961) in a study of 1,088 students found that the believers were more authoritarian, whether they had followed parental beliefs or rebelled against them (cf. Brown, 1962).

If we look at different aspects of authoritarianism, it is found that only certain parts of it are related to religion. Kahoe (1977) found that 11 of the 30 items on the F-scale were correlated with intrinsic religiosity, corresponding to the dimensions which had been labelled Conventionalism and

Superstition/Stereotypy, but not with Cynicism, Aggressiveness, Projectivity, or the belief that there are good or bad people.

One problem with authoritarianism is that it is highly correlated with lack of education, typically –0.50 to –0.60 (Christie and Jahoda, 1954). This may explain some of the apparent authoritarianism of Catholics and fundamentalists in US studies. The explanation may also lie in different styles of child-rearing. A number of studies have found that Catholic parents use more physical punishment, and have more autocratic relations with their children (e.g. Elder, 1968), though again this may be partly due to differences in social class. A later study by Ellison and Sherkat (1993a) controlled for such variables, and found that Catholics and conservative Protestants valued obedience in children more than others. For the Protestants valuing obedience was mediated by beliefs in literalism, original sin and a punitive attitude to sinners, but this was not the case for Catholics, that is, they all valued obedience regardless of such beliefs. For conservative Protestants a causal chain was found (shown in Figure 9.1) from Conservative religious beliefs to beliefs in literalism, in human nature being corrupt (i.e. in original sin), and in punishment of sinners being desirable, leading to thinking corporal punishment was desirable.

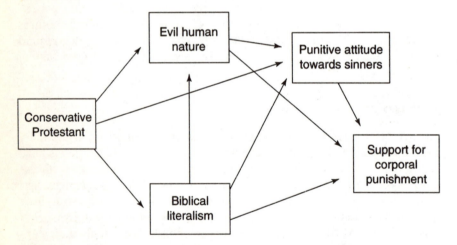

Figure 9.1 Theoretical model of religion and support for corporal punishment
Source: Ellison and Sherkat (1993b)

It must be concluded that many religious individuals do have some of the features of authoritarianism, such as being acquiescent to authority and accepting conventional views. And several studies have found some positive features in religious authoritarians, such as being cooperative and idealistic (Wulff, 1991).

DOGMATISM AND COGNITIVE COMPLEXITY

Rokeach (1960) located a dimension of personality which he called 'dogmatism', or the 'closed mind'. This has something in common with authoritarianism, except that it reflects the rigidity of both the political right and left, while authoritarianism is associated only with right-wing, or fascist, kinds of ideology. Individuals who scored high on his dogmatism scale were found in experiments to be rigid in their thinking, intolerant of ambiguity, and unable to deal with new information. Rokeach found among American students that Roman Catholics had the highest dogmatism scores, followed by Protestants, while non-believers had the lowest scores. This was confirmed in later studies, except that Protestants in the American South had higher scores than Catholics (Kilpatrick *et al.* 1970; Seaman *et al.* 1971). In a study of 532 US Roman Catholic adolescents and their parents, it was found that those described as 'indiscriminately antireligious' were the lowest on dogmatism, compared to all others (Thompson, 1974).

Rokeach found that dogmatic individuals showed a stronger tendency to reject members of other religions. Clergy from six religious denominations were asked to rank the similarity of the other religions to their own; students from all six groups then reported their social distance from the other groups (e.g. whether they would make friends with one). It was found that rejection was greater for the more dissimilar religions, but that dogmatic subjects rejected the other groups more (Figure 9.2). It can be seen that dogmatism has the strongest effect on the rejection of other denominations by Catholics and Baptists.

A related variable is 'cognitive complexity'; one way of measuring this is to ask subjects to finish paragraphs dealing with conflicting points of view, and to score what is written for variables such as ability to deal with opposing viewpoints. It is possible to use this method to obtain a measure of religious cognitive complexity. Batson and Raynor-Prince (1983) did this with 35 subjects, and found that it was less for those with high scores on a scale of doctrinal orthodoxy ($r = -0.37$), and for intrinsics ($r = -0.30$), even after controlling for general cognitive complexity; those high in Quest on the other hand were higher ($r = 0.37$). The paragraphs were scored on scales such as 'openness to alternative points of view', and 'ability to incorporate disparate views'. It is no surprise that orthodoxy had a negative correlation with complexity. Nor is it any surprise that Quest had a positive one, since the scoring scheme is closely attuned to the Quest position, of doubt and indecision over problems of belief. Pratt *et al.* (1992) carried out a similar study, with 60 subjects, in which they were interviewed about their solutions to three religious dilemmas, such as the conflict between religion and evolution, the answers being rated for taking account of two or more perspectives and being able to integrate them. Three age groups were studied, and the older scored lower ($r = -0.47$); complexity was again lower for those with orthodox beliefs ($r = -0.22$, -0.30 after controls), and higher

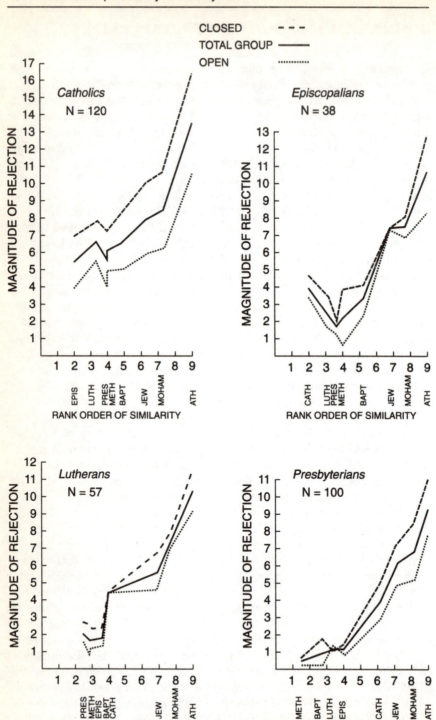

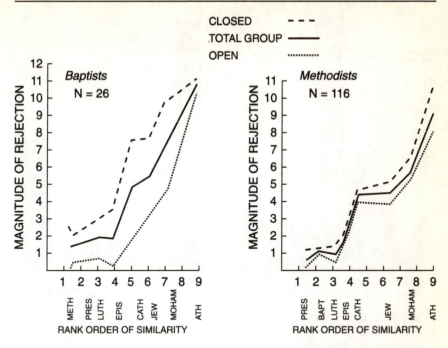

Figure 9.2 The effect of 'dogmatism' on the tendency to reject members of other religions
Source: Rokeach (1960)

for those with more education (r = 0.33) and who were more intelligent (r = 0.26). Hunsberger *et al.* (1993) found a positive correlation between self-reported religious doubt and cognitive complexity, measured in eight areas of religious faith.

Despite our doubts about the relation between complexity and Quest, it looks as if religious individuals are *less* cognitively complex than others, in the religious realm at least; this is strongest for fundamentalists and authoritarians, but also for orthodox believers. The relation with age is illuminating here; we have seen that religious complexity is higher for the young, as the Quest orientation may be. Elkind (1971) argues that it is normal for increasingly difficult and abstract questions to be asked by the young, who hope to find rational (or irrational) explanations of everything. For older people scores of religious complexity are lower, as they grow in commitment and orthodoxy.

Several other studies have been carried out on the nature of religious thinking. Thouless (1935), in an early and experimental study, asked subjects how certain they were of the truth of factual propositions of the kind 'Tigers are found in some parts of China' and of religious ones such as 'Jesus Christ was God the Son'. As Figure 9.3 shows, many were uncertain

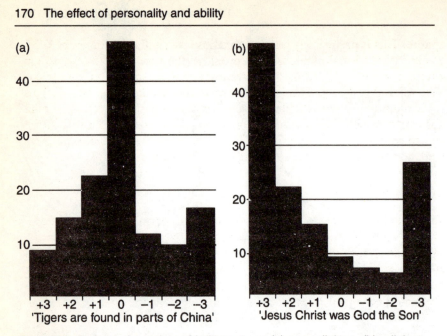

Figure 9.3 Degree of certainty of judgments on (a) non-religious, (b) religious propositions
Source: Thouless (1935)

about tigers in China, but most of his subjects were certain one way or the other about Jesus.

Feather (1964) presented syllogisms, some of them invalid, to devout and non-devout subjects in Australia. The devout subjects were more likely to accept invalid syllogisms which had a pro-religious conclusion. Batson (1975) carried out a study in which subjects were first given a questionnaire on religious beliefs. They then read a fake magazine article on a new discovery from the Dead Sea Scrolls which cast serious doubt on Christian traditions. The beliefs of believers who also believed this story were strengthened.

No doubt some professors of theology have very complex cognitive structures about religion, but this may not be typical of religious believers. Indeed surveys of the religious knowledge, or rather lack of it, of church members in the USA, suggest that many of them know almost nothing about their nominal faith (see Chapter 3). There is laboratory evidence that cognitive complexity may not always be desirable (Tetlock and Boettger, 1989). Religion may be one of the areas in which complexity is not helpful, in that it involves making a decision in the absence of conclusive evidence and trying to make it work, rather like choosing a partner in marriage, which is often used as an analogy.

The overall picture seems to be that many religious individuals have closed minds and are low in cognitive complexity, especially in the religious sphere. This is particularly marked for those we shall describe on p. 173ff. as extrinsics. Closed-mindedness is probably the normal state of a person who is committed to a religious faith; there may be some degree of open-ness when it comes to details but not regarding fundamental beliefs. This is the nature of religious faith – there is a non-rational 'leap of faith', in the absence of conclusive evidence, producing a commitment to a way of life and to some extent a closed mind. As Batson *et al.* (1993) point out, this leads to some kinds of freedom, but a loss of freedom to think.

SUGGESTIBILITY

Suggestibility assumes a 'tendency to respond uncritically to suggestions' (Turner and Killian, 1957, p. 84). This covers a variety of social influences. Schumaker (1990, 1995) offers evidence to support the view that religion is an induced form of irrationality. This induction process is carried out through various means of hypnotic suggestion, including music (a universal element in religious behaviour), dance, and sometimes drugs.

Research with laboratory measures of certain kinds of suggestion have found that there are consistent personality differences, and that there is not one personality factor but at least two. Eysenck and Furneaux (1945) found a clear factor which they called 'primary suggestibility', consisting of scores on the body sway test, in which blind-folded subjects were ordered, 'You are falling forward, you are falling forward now', and similar items. A second factor was found, 'secondary suggestibility', which was quite independent of the first, though with smaller correlations between its component tests. Here subjects were persuaded that weights were getting heavier or wires were getting hotter. These two factors have been found in other studies, though some investigators have found a wider range of kinds of social influence in the second factor (Stukat, 1968). It is primary suggestibility which is correlated with ease of being hypnotized, while the secondary kind is unrelated.

It has often been thought that what happens at revivals and evangelical meetings can be interpreted as suggestion. At early revivals it was often reported that some of those present engaged in twitching and jerking before finally collapsing. Coe (1916) found that of 14 individuals who had experienced dramatic conversions, 13 could be easily hypnotized, while 9 out of 12 who had expected to be converted, but were not, could not be hypnotized. Howells (1928) gave five tests of primary suggestibility to 50 religious conservatives and 50 radicals; the conservatives had higher scores on all of the tests. Gibbons and de Jarnette (1972) studied 185 students for hypnotic susceptibility. The 23 most and 26 least susceptible were compared; the highly susceptible were more likely to say they had been 'saved', and if they had been converted to have experienced powerful experiential changes.

Religious experience might be expected to be related to secondary suggestibility, since it produces changes of sensation and imagery. Such experiences can be produced in normal social conditions as well, as we reported in Chapter 5. Suggestibility may also be involved in religious 'healing' (cf. Chapter 4). Lasagna *et al.* (1954) found in a group of hospital patients that responding positively to placebo treatment was correlated with frequency of ritual attendance, and this result has been replicated several times. Cantril (1941) reported that among those who panicked following the famous 'Invasion from Mars' broadcast in 1938, individuals who tended to accept the programme literally were characterized by religiosity and ritual attendance as compared to those who did not.

Christian church attenders, and especially members of conservative Protestant bodies, score higher on tests of acquiescence, dependence on the group, and related measures. Symington (1935) studied 612 individuals and found that those with high scores on orthodoxy were more dependent on group opinion, while the liberals disliked being told what to do. Graff and Ladd (1971) with 152 male students found that the religious ones were more dependent on others, less inner-directed and less self-accepting.

The findings on suggestibility could be explained at two different levels. There may be basic physiological differences between those who can be easily hypnotized, or who are readily affected by placebo treatments, and others. Hysterics have been found to be easily hypnotized. In traditional cultures it is common for some of those attending religious rituals to go into trances, or be 'possessed' by spirits; sometimes they have skewers passed through their bodies or undergo other ordeals (Ward and Kemp, 1991). We saw earlier how shamans may be possessed in this way. In European religious history the stigmata have been reported, following the example of Saint Francis. Reports on the personalities of those concerned suggest that they have usually been hysterics (Thurston, 1951). On the other hand, such dramatic events may be part of a normal continuum, and be due to intense concentration and narrowing of attention, where rival stimuli are ignored. A quite different kind of social influence is found in those personalities who are dependent on others, submissive, less inner-directed and less self-accepting, though as we saw earlier this is a minor factor compared with situational ones.

There is no need for suggestibility to have just a negative connotation: human beings are basically social, and an important part of sociability is mutual influence. Forms of less critical social influence make possible bonding to groups, the influence of leaders, and the acceptance of religion and myths, which bring about powerful benefits, such as happiness and reduced fear of death, as we shall see in Chapter 10.

LOCUS OF CONTROL

This concept is based on the distinction between those individuals who have a generalized expectancy that they can control things that happen to them ('internals'), and those ('externals') who think that events around them are mainly due to chance, fate or powerful others (Rotter, 1966). This dimension of personality has been found to correlate with many aspects of behaviour. Does it also relate to religion?

Some large-scale studies with students reported contradictory results (Scheidt, 1973), while Rasmussen and Charman (1995) reported that religiosity correlated 0.70 with a revised Locus of Control scale. The Intrinsic–Extrinsic distinction has proved useful here, since Intrinsics score higher on Internal control, while Extrinsics score higher on External (e.g. Kahoe, 1977). In a later study Kivett (1979), with 301 adult church members, found that Internal control predicted a measure similar to Intrinsic religiosity, after a number of controls had been applied, and was one of the strongest predictors. Locus of control is relevant to some other beliefs too. Externals are more likely to believe in 'psychic' phenomena and the 'paranormal' (Haraldsson, 1981; Tobacyk et al. 1988).

No very consistent differences have been found between denominations. However, Levin and Schiller (1986) with 909 American adults found that the highest scorers on the Health Locus of Control Scale were Mormons, Episcopalians and Catholics, in that order, while Presbyterians were highest on part of External, Powerful Others. Jackson and Coursey (1988) carried out an interesting study of 98 Black American Baptists, using a measure of God control as a sub-division of External. God control correlated (0.26) with Internal, showing that it is possible to be both, perhaps an example of collaborative coping, though Internal was a better predictor of coping than God control. Moslems in India have been found to score higher on the External dimension than Christians (Rao and Murthy, 1984).

INTRINSIC AND EXTRINSIC RELIGIOSITY

Intrinsic and extrinsic religiosity scales have different and sometimes opposite correlates with behaviour and personality measures. Thus, Kahoe (1974) in a study with 518 US students found the correlations shown in Table 9.1.

On cognitive complexity, if different studies are averaged, intrinsic religiosity has a small relationship with complexity (0.06), extrinsic has a negative relation (–0.36), and Quest a small positive relationship (Donahue, 1985).

The average of 34 studies shows that the average correlation between intrinsic and extrinsic is –0.06 (Donahue, 1985), so there are good grounds for treating the two kinds of religiosity separately.

Table 9.1 Personality traits correlated with intrinsic and extrinsic religiosity

Personality traits	Religiosity	
	Intrinsic	Extrinsic
Authoritarianism	0.03	0.33
Dogmatism	0.04	0.30
Internal control	0.24	−0.25
Responsibility	0.29	−0.40
Intrinsic motivation	0.45	−0.25
Average grades	0.45	−0.25

Extrinsic religiosity

1 The study by Kahoe (1974) and many later ones have shown that there is a positive, though not large, correlation with authoritarianism, as there is with prejudice. Extrinsics score high on acquiescence; for example, they are 'yea-sayers' on scales.
2 There is a similar relation with dogmatism, closed-mindedness.
3 There have been a number of studies which have found that extrinsics are lower in internal control, and in related variables such as self-control and ego-strength.
4 Extrinsics score lower on measures of 'social responsibility' (from the California Personality Inventory) and 'social interest', measures of positive concern for others (e.g. Bergin *et al.* 1987).
5 Extrinsics score much higher on fear of death and anxiety of other kinds (Batson *et al.* 1993). This makes up a coherent kind of personality, though it does not correspond to any traditional major personality dimensions.

Intrinsic religiosity

The pattern here is in some ways the opposite of that for extrinsics. Most studies find no relationship with authoritarianism; in Kahoe's (1974) study it was 0.03, after controlling for acquiescence. The findings for dogmatism are similar. Intrinsics are stronger in responsibility and social interest, and they have less fear of death and less anxiety. On the other hand they have more guilt feelings (Watson *et al.* 1987).

This too makes up a coherent kind of personality, though again not a very familiar one. This is what Barron (1968) called 'believing for oneself', developing one's own beliefs and values together with other inner-directed processes. It is interesting that while there is less anxiety, there is more guilt. Watson, Hood *et al.* (1988) found that intrinsic was consistently correlated with guilt feelings, and with acceptance of the ideas of sin and grace, but was also associated with low depression, and with self-acceptance. This is all within a Christian context, where many churches preach sin and salvation.

PERSONALITY AND INTENSE FORMS OF RELIGIOSITY

It is possible that those who are intensely involved with religion in other ways may also have some special personality characteristics.

The clergy

We discussed the clergy, and members of religious orders in Chapter 4, where we saw that they were high in some 'feminine' traits if they were male, and in some traits more often found in males if they were female, that is, the males tended to be less aggressive and assertive.

Converts

Converts, especially those who have sudden or dramatic conversions, were discussed in Chapter 7, where we saw that they were usually in a state of anxiety and depression before the event, and in a more positive mood afterwards. We considered how far this relates to personality disposition or pathology.

Fundamentalists

This attitude complex was described in Chapter 3. It was further validated when Wiggins (1966) extracted a fundamentalism scale from the MMPI. We know that fundamentalism is associated with prejudice (see Chapter 11); twin studies have found that it is partly inherited (Waller et al. 1990); Sethi and Seligman (1993) found that fundamentalism is quite strongly associated with optimism, hope, and absence of self-blame, when comparisons are made with more liberal groups. This is an interesting example of a narrow personality trait which is characteristic of a particular religious group.

Those who have intense religious experiences

As we saw in Chapter 5, this is a very widespread phenomenon, but those who have them most often tend to be high on 'schizotypy', and on scales of cognitive openness. We also discussed how far having these experiences changes people. No differences in personality have been found for glossolalics (Lovekin and Malony, 1977), except for some interpersonal problems (Kirkpatrick, 1992).

Members of NRMs

As we have seen in Chapter 7, the evidence points to some degree of vulnerability and a history of psychological difficulties, apparently related to relations with parents.

DYNAMICS OF HANDLING GUILT AND ANGER

On p. 22 we discussed hypotheses regarding the role of super-ego projection and guilt relief in individual religiosity. One prediction from explanations emphasizing the role of guilt in religion is that people with guilt feelings should be attracted to religions which preach a doctrine of sin and forgiveness. Starbuck (1899) obtained some evidence that young people converted at a revival often had strong guilt feelings before this happened. If religion succeeded in relieving guilt feelings, there would be no difference between religious people and others. In fact, as we have seen, religious people do have stronger guilt feelings, as a number of studies have found. They also have stronger self–ideal self conflicts. In a study of 2,775 children and youth aged 11–14 in Minnesota, Nelsen and Kroliczak (1984) found that the belief in the statement 'God punishes youths who are bad' is positively associated with self-blame and obedience. Intrinsic religiosity has also been found to correlate with more guilt feelings (Watson *et al.* 1987).

Another question is whether religious cultures form, or affect, styles of interpersonal behaviour or personality dynamics. The emphasis on guilt should affect methods of handling anger. The subjective experience of guilt may also be tied to the suppression of anger among religious individuals, especially Protestants. Balswick and Balkwell (1978) found that Protestant religious orthodoxy was related to lowered expression of hate, while Pruyser (1968) stated that the suppression and repression of anger was a typical consequence of Protestant pietism.

The Protestant concern with sin suggests the hypothesis that Protestants are more intro-punitive, i.e. direct anger inwards, while others may be more extra-punitive, i.e. direct anger outwards. King and Funkenstein (1957), using physiological measures, found that religious conservatives had an extra-punitive cardiovascular response. Brown (1965), using the Rosenzweig Picture-Frustration test with Australian students, found that Roman Catholics were more extra-punitive than Protestants, and Protestant females more intro-punitive than Catholic females. Protestant males were more intro-punitive. Argyle and Delin (1965), in a study of 700 schoolchildren, found that guilt feelings (which can be equated conceptually with inner-directed anger) correlated with church attendance 0.30, for Protestant females only. Bateman and Jensen (1958) with 33 Protestant males found that religious background correlated 0.66 with intro-punitiveness, and –0.33

with extra-punitiveness on the Rosenzweig test; present religious belief showed much lower correlations in the same direction.

There seems to be some evidence showing that Protestants have stronger guilt feelings, and direct their anger inwards. The explanation may be in the content of Protestant teaching which increases guilt and discourages outward aggression. Or people with strong guilt feelings may be attracted by the Protestant emphasis on forgiveness and salvation, and are more likely to become converts (Starbuck, 1899). We should expect this to apply particularly to more orthodox Protestant groups, since they place more emphasis on sin and salvation. One of the implications of this hypothesis leads us to look at sex differences.

There is fairly extensive evidence that women have stronger guilt feelings, and are more intro-punitive, than men (Wright, 1971). This may provide an explanation for the greater religiosity of women. Taken together with the previous point, it leads to the prediction that there should be an increasing proportion of female members along the Catholic–Protestant dimension. We have seen that this is the case.

It may be that this mechanism operates in the young rather than the old, as the young are given to conflicts over sexuality and career choices. At evangelical meetings, where conversions are largely brought about by arousal of guilt feelings, it is mostly younger people who are converted.

INTELLIGENCE AND OTHER ABILITIES

Are religious individuals more or less intelligent than non-believers? The answer seems to be that there is probably no difference. Poythress (1975) reviewed a number of early studies with American students; some found a small difference in one direction, some found a small difference in the opposite direction. We shall see later that more intelligent university students have more religious doubts and are more likely to change their religious outlook. There has not so far been a large scale study with the demographic variables controlled, or any studies which make clear what the direction of causation is, if there is any effect at all.

A number of early studies in the USA found that religious conservatism, i.e. fundamentalism, was negatively correlated with intelligence. Thus, Symington (1935) used 300 adult subjects and found that this correlation was higher for students from liberal homes (–0.42 to –0.55) than for those from conservative backgrounds (–0.13 to 0.19). He argued that those from a liberal background were freer to use their brains to discard orthodox ideas. Hoge (1974) reported a negative correlation between Scholastic Aptitude Test scores and orthodoxy among university students in the USA.

Protestants usually score on average higher than Catholics in intelligence. Lynn *et al.* (1983), for example, with a sample of 701 15-year-olds in Northern Ireland found a biserial correlation of 0.14 between intelligence and being Protestant vs. Roman Catholic. We shall see in Chapter 11 that Protestants put more effort into education, and as a result get better jobs. Perhaps the greater exposure to education stimulates intelligence. Perhaps Protestant parents, more ambitious for their children's academic success, give greater intellectual stimulation. And in the past, though less so in the present, Protestant families have been smaller than Catholic ones, and large families are associated with lower intelligence and lower educational success (Zajonc, 1976).

Denominational differences in intelligence have often been found. Jews (mostly secular) and Episcopalians come out highest in American studies, Baptists, Catholics, and small Protestant sects lowest (e.g. Pratt, 1937). The high intelligence of Jews may be because, even more than Protestants, Jewish tradition puts a high value on education, so that the environmental sources of intelligence become enhanced. Another possibility is that there are differences in 'intellectualism'. Nelsen (1973) put together a scale, based on reported reading of books and magazines, going to lectures and other cultural events, and found a correlation of –0.07 with ritual attendance. There were denominational differences in both, and if these were controlled there was no effect of ritual attendance. Jews scored highest on this scale, 49.0, followed by Protestants (42.2), and Catholics (23.0); African-Americans scored 25.7. University education usually brings about more sceptical attitudes to traditional or irrational ideas. Rhodes and Nam (1970) arranged religious groups according to degrees of fundamentalism and anti-intellectualism; Baptists were at the top and Jews at the bottom. Position on this scale correlated with IQ at –0.17. Rigney and Hoffman (1993) surveyed 1,469 subjects and used eight measures of anti-intellectualism – valuing obedience, not valuing tolerance, education, and so on. The denominational means are shown in Table 9.2. Roman Catholics scored near the population means on these items; they were more tolerant and pro-intellectual than fundamentalist Protestants, but less so than liberal Protestants, Jews or nones. Younger and more educated individuals also scored higher. Related data showed that Catholics valued education not only for its material benefits but also for its non-material benefits.

THE RELIGIOSITY OF ACADEMICS AND PROFESSIONALS

It is often assumed that individuals who devote their lives to research would be less religious than the general population. This is because scientists are expected to excel in critical thinking. As we are going to see, the picture is more complex. We shall see in Chapter 11 that there are large denominational differences in the average number of years of education received; we give data for the USA in 1987. Jews and Episcopalians had the most education, Baptists and Roman Catholics the least, and this

Table 9.2 Religious affiliation and selected measures of intellectual orientation

Religious affiliation	Percentage of total sample	Value of obedience (% 'most important')	Value of thinking for oneself (% 'most important')	Priority of education (% 'too little emphasis')	Freedom of scientific inquiry (% 'disagree')	Tolerance (mean on 0–15 scale)	Newspaper (% read daily)	Literary membership (% yes)	Professional membership (% yes)
Catholic	26.2	21.2	49.8	64.0	66.0	8.88	54.2	4.9	11.0
Non-Catholic	73.8	23.8	49.1	66.7	64.8	8.63	49.2	9.7[a]	14.6
Fund. Prot.	(34.4)	(28.9)[a]	(43.1)	(66.1)	(54.6)[b]	(7.20)[a]	(43.2)[b]	(7.2)	(9.9)
Non-Fund. Prot.	(26.5)	(20.8)	(52.1)	(61.2)	(73.1)[a]	(9.30)	(58.1)	(9.2)	(18.9)[a]
Jewish	(2.0)	(4.5)[b]	(77.3)	(82.4)	(79.3)	(12.41)	(70.0)	(27.3)[b]	(31.8)[b]
Other	(2.9)	(29.0)	(45.2)	(78.6)	(75.6)	(10.29)	(45.8)	(19.4)[b]	(22.6)
None	(8.0)	(15.3)[b]	(57.6)	(76.9)	(76.1)[a]	(11.57)[a]	(42.4)	(12.8)[a]	(14.0)
Total sample	100.0	23.2	49.3	66.0	65.1	8.69	50.6	8.5	13.7
(N =)	(1,468)	(976)	(976)	(688)	(1,445)	(976)	(987)	(984)	(983)

Notes
(a) Difference between Catholic and non-Catholic comparison group is significant at $p \leq 0.05$ (chi-square, except one-way Anova on Tolerance).
(b) Difference between Catholic and non-Catholic comparison group is significant at $p \leq 0.01$.

Source: Rigney and Hoffman (1993)

seemed to be due to different values being placed on education in differing traditions, and to secularization levels.

As recently as the 1950s large differences have been found between the religious and non-religious, and between denominations, in the numbers of scientists. Bello (1954) found massive over-representation of nones and secularized Jews, and under-representation of Roman Catholics among American scientists (see Table 9.3). Lenski (1963) found that Roman Catholics produced only one-sixth of the proportion of scientists that Protestants or Jews did.

Table 9.3 Religious affiliation of American scientists (1954), their parents, and US population (1957)

Religious affiliation	% of scientists	% of their parents	% of US population
Protestant	23	53	66.3
Catholic	<1	5	26.2
Jewish	9	23	3.0
None	45	8	2.1
Other and no affiliation	23	5	1.9

Source: Lenski (1963)

This shows that these denominational differences are not much due to parental influence; for example, 45 per cent of scientists were nones, but only 8 per cent of their parents were.

A number of US studies earlier in this century found that the more eminent scientists were less religious than others. For example, Leuba (1934) found that only 32 per cent of 'greater' scientists believed in God, compared with 48 per cent of 'lesser' ones; the figures for belief in immortality were 37 per cent and 59 per cent. Beit-Hallahmi (1988) found that among Nobel Prize laureates in the sciences, as well as those in literature, there was a remarkable degree of irreligiosity, as compared to the populations they came from.

There is no doubt that a number of scientists and other academics have experienced conflict between their academic work and religion. This was not always so; in the early days of science, in the seventeenth century, Protestants at least were strongly in favour of science, as a way to finding out more about the glories of God's creation. The trouble arose later, when science seemed to be disagreeing with Genesis about the origins of the world and evolution. In addition, some religious traditions (e.g. Roman Catholic) are quite hierarchical and authoritarian, and in the past at least have required obedience rather than critical thinking, and taught that innovation and independence were not welcome; those so taught would not be likely to do well in scientific research. Lenski (1963) found that 32 per cent of Catholic graduates saw a serious conflict between science and religion, for example over evolution; for Protestants this figure was only 17 per cent. But a little later Greeley and Rossi (1972) found no evidence of conflict between academic work and religion for Catholic or Protestant graduate students. Conflict between religion and secular knowledge does not always lead to abandoning religion. De Jong and Faulkner (1972) gave in-depth interviews to 56 faculty members. Of these 71 per cent were church members, and 43 per cent attended twice a month or more; however they deviated a lot from traditional beliefs, and instead had a non-literal, demythologized faith. In a study of 2,842 graduate students in the USA, Stark (1963) found that church attendance was negatively associated with self-identification as an intellectual, and with positive attitudes towards creativity, occupational freedom and professional ambition. Thus, those who were religiously more conforming appeared to place less value on scientific and intellectual achievement. It has often been shown that universities in the USA which are dominated by religious organizations have a lower quality of students, faculty, and educational programmes (e.g. Hassenger, 1967). A study by Lehman (1972) showed that faculty members committed to a scholarly orientation were less involved in traditional religious activities than faculty members who were less scholarly.

A finding which goes against the common-sense view and calls for an explanation is the greater degree of religiosity among physical scientists, as compared with social scientists, especially psychologists. Several studies have found that there is some difference in religiosity between scientists and non-scientists, but physical scientists are (relatively) more religious, social scientists less so. Lehman and Shriver (1968) studied a sample of 99 faculty members, and found support for the 'scholarly distance' hypothesis: those in subjects remote from the study of religion, such as physics, were more religious than those whose academic fields studied religion, such as psychology and sociology. Subjects such as education and economics were scored as intermediate. Those at a greater distance were more religious in ideology, ritual and experience, but knew less about it. Parental religiosity had a small correlation with academic field, so there was some evidence that they chose subjects which would be consistent with their religious views. The low religiosity of social scientists, as compared to natural scientists, can be explained by the 'scholarly distance' hypothesis. The reason, in psychological terms, is that natural sciences apply critical thinking to nature; the human sciences ask critical questions about culture, traditions, and beliefs. The mere fact of choosing human society or behaviour as the object of study reflects a curiosity about basic social beliefs and conventions and a readiness to reject them. Physical scientists, who are at a greater scholarly distance, may be able to compartmentalize their science and religion more easily.

One factor may be that of self-selection in terms of unconventionality.

Social scientists are members of young, 'unconventional', disciplines and tend to deviate from many social norms. Studying cultures and societies leads to relativism regarding one's own society. Among physical scientists a compartmentalizing of scientific attitudes and religious attitudes is easier. Social scientists, who examine beliefs critically, may find it harder to compartmentalize their scientific attitudes.

It has been found that scholars in the natural sciences and technology are more conservative politically, while those in the human sciences tend to be more radical. Thus, the main factor seems to be the application of critical thinking. A related issue is whether individuals change their views as a result of training in natural or human sciences. These differences among fields of study appear even among undergraduate students, as the following studies show. Bereiter and Freedman (1962) found that social science majors take a more liberal and less conventional stand on most issues, while students in the applied fields are more conservative in their attitudes. Jones (1970) also found that among university freshmen those majoring in natural science were the most favourable to religion, those doing psychology the least. Hoge (1974) found natural sciences university students to be higher on orthodoxy. It seems likely that individuals choose their fields in terms of their own curiosity, whether about nature or about culture. This curiosity, in turn, may be related to personality factors and early experiences.

The gap between academics and professionals in science and technology compared to the humanities has been noted in Islamic countries and in recent Islamic revival movements. In Iran and in other Islamic countries, such as Egypt, it is estimated that Islamic activists constitute 25 per cent of humanities students, but 60–80 per cent of students in medicine, engineering and science (Arjomand, 1986).

As we saw earlier, social scientists are among the least religious, most often with an over-representation of 'nones' or Jews (who are highly secularized), together with some liberal Protestants, but rarely Catholics (Glenn and Weiner, 1969). Psychologists are also irreligious. Ragan *et al.* (1980) studied a random sample including 555 members of the American Psychological Association. There were 34 per cent atheists, compared with 2 per cent in the US general population; the least religious were the experimental psychologists, the most religious were in counselling and personality. In medicine psychiatrists are by far the least religious (Kosa, 1969).

Counsellors of various kinds are often close to the clergy in terms of their social role and background (Beit-Hallahmi, 1976), which explains the findings above about specialties in psychology. A study of 113 ageing (over 50) psychoanalysts in the USA reported that 42 per cent of the group were of Jewish background, and the group as a whole showed a high degree of irreligiosity, with most respondents listing no religious affiliation

(Tallmer, 1992). Weintraub and Aronson (1974) found that among individuals undergoing psychoanalysis in the USA, those of Jewish origin were over-represented (42 per cent) while Roman Catholics were under-represented (16 per cent). Psychotherapists remain less religious than the general population. Henry *et al.* (1971) found that out of 1,387 American clinical psychologists, 50 per cent came from Jewish families, but only 30 per cent described themselves as currently Jewish. Only 20 per cent of the clinical psychologists described themselves as Protestant, 8 per cent as Catholic, and 42 per cent were unaffiliated.

CONCLUSIONS

We can say in light of the above findings that religious individuals tend to be on average more authoritarian and suggestible, though this is more true of some religious groups than others. Some groups are also high in dogmatism, and having a fairly closed mind may be said to be a normal part of religious commitment. However, there are considerable differences between different kinds of religious persons, such as those between the intrinsically and the extrinsically religious. There are no great differences in intelligence between the religious and non-religious, though fundamentalists score a little lower, and there are some denomination differences which reflect their class differences. Academics are less religious the closer their subject lies to the study of religion; greater 'scholarly distance' leads to less conflict.

Chapter 10

The effects of religiosity
Individual level

In Chapters 10 and 11 we will look at religiosity as an independent variable, assessing its effects on individual and social functioning. There are a number of clear expectations here. It is expected that religion would enhance well-being, otherwise it would have been unlikely to survive so long. So we shall ask whether religious people are happier, in better physical or mental health, and if they are, what psychological processes are involved.

HAPPINESS AND THE QUALITY OF LIFE

Several social surveys have found that members of religious congregations are more satisfied with their life as a whole compared to non-members. In a survey of 160,000 individuals in 14 European countries 85 per cent of those who went to church once a week or more were very satisfied, compared with 77 per cent of those who never went (Inglehart, 1990). Sometimes a curvilinear relation has been found, with the most and least religious being happiest (Shaver *et al.* 1980). But both religion and well-being vary with age, social class, and other variables, and these need to be held constant to find the true relation between them. This was done by Campbell *et al.* (1976); when reanalysed by Hadaway (1978) the religious variables all correlated with well-being, for example church attendance 0.17 with subjective well-being.

Moberg and Taves (1965) used an extensive measure of subjective well-being with a sample of 1,343 elderly people in Minnesota, and found that belonging to churches was associated with greater well-being, as shown in Table 10.1. Witter *et al.* (1985) carried out a meta-analysis of 56 studies on the relation between religion and happiness. Overall there was a positive effect, of 0.16 standard deviation. The effect was stronger for older samples, and for religious activity rather than religiosity. The former affected happiness, life satisfaction, morale, and quality of life, and all aspects of well-being were affected, including happiness, marital relations, and job satisfaction (Willits and Crider, 1988). There is a particularly strong effect on having a sense of meaning and purpose in life (Chamberlain and Zika, 1988).

The data in Table 10.1 suggest a simple explanation of the benefits of religious involvement – that it provides social support for those who are socially isolated, as the elderly often are. Cutler (1976) found that the congregation was the only one out of 17 different kinds of groups which affected the well-being of the elderly, and it did so with income, occupation and health controlled. It has been found that 37 per cent of church members in a British sample rated their church friendships as closer than other ones, so it looks as if church can provide an especially powerful kind of social support. This could be because worship generates shared emotions, because the religious community offers certain love and acceptance, or because sharing important beliefs has a special power (Argyle, 1996). One of the main processes involved is the social cohesion and social support provided by the local religious community, leading to enhanced happiness and mental health, and reduced risk of suicide. This effect is possibly related to the more purely social side of congregational life. The result is that many close friendships involve other members of the worshipping group. In the study of 310,000 church attenders in Australia by Kaldor (1994) it was found that overall 24 per cent said that their closest friends were in their church, and another 46 per cent had some close friends in it. The figures were higher for Pentecostalists of whom 33 per cent had their closest

Table 10.1 Scores on an index of adjustment, and church membership

	Church leaders	Other church members	Non-church members
Married	15	15	12
Widowed	15	11	7
Single	12	8	5
65–70	18	14	10
71–79	15	12	7
80+	13	8	6
Fully employed	18	18	17
Partly employed	16	16	13
Fully retired	15	12	7
Health (self-rated)			
Excellent	17	14	13
Good	15	14	11
Fair	17	6	8
More active in religious organizations than in fifties	16	13	9
Less active	14	11	7

Source: Moberg and Taves (1965)

friends in the church, and for other small Protestant bodies such as the Seventh Day Adventists (38 per cent), and the Foursquare Gospel (38 per cent). This is not limited to a particular religious tradition. Identical effects were found in the case of unemployed Moslem men in Britain. Mosque membership and the social support of the community enabled individuals under stress to cope much better with their situation (Shams and Jackson, 1993).

Recent research has shown that religion can affect well-being in other ways apart from social support. This has been shown by carrying out multiple regressions to examine the separate effect of different aspects of religion. Pollner (1989) found that reported 'closeness to God' correlated (0.16) with happiness and satisfaction, independently of church attendance, and with demographic variables held constant. It has been suggested that prayer, religious experience and other private devotions are experienced as a kind of social relationship which gives similar benefits to human social support (Kirkpatrick, 1992). We saw in Chapter 5 that religious experiences produce enhanced happiness in those who report them, and the design of these studies makes a causal interpretation possible.

Beliefs have been found to offer a third, and independent, source of well-being. Ellison (1991) used data from an American national survey and found that firm beliefs, 'existential certainty', correlated with life satisfaction independently of church attendance and private devotion, especially for older and less educated people. Multiple regressions supported a causal model in which church attendance and private devotions cause beliefs, which in turn cause well-being. Another study (Ellison et al. 1989) found that all three religious variables affected life satisfaction, and that members of American Baptist churches, who are mostly fundamentalists, were more satisfied than members of other churches. This could explain the finding by Shaver et al. (1980) that the slightly religious are the least happy – because they are the least certain.

The contents of beliefs are also relevant here. Steinitz (1980) found that the strongest religious predictor of well-being in the elderly was belief in an after-life. It has been found that religion reduces loneliness, but only for those who believe in a supportive, caring and helpful God, not a wrathful one (Schwab and Petersen, 1990). Fazel and Young (1988) found that Tibetan Buddhists had a higher reported quality of life than Hindus, probably because they have a less fatalistic outlook, believe that they could improve their lot, and value home and friendship more than material things. Religious beliefs, and prayer, can increase optimism and a sense of control; these are routes to happiness (Dull and Skokan, 1995).

We have explained why the old benefit most from religion – it is because they tend to be isolated and are worried about death. However, few of these studies have demonstrated a causal relation of religion to well-being, though all have assumed it. We might expect, for example, that those in distress would pray more, which is the reverse direction of causation. Lowenthal has pointed out (1993) that strictly following religious commandments may be a source of distress for some individuals. This is possibly balanced by the benefits reported in this chapter.

HEALTH

There is a positive correlation between religiosity and subjective (i.e. self-rated) health. Levin and Vanderpool (1987) analysed 28 such studies, and found a consistent, though small, relationship, with other variables controlled. Sometimes the relation has disappeared when physical capacity is introduced as a control, partly because only those who are well enough can get to church. However, Broyles and Drenovsky (1992) found a correlation of 0.09 for the elderly between attendance and subjective health among the able-bodied. But we know from other research that subjective health is not an accurate indicator of actual physical health. It is partly an indicator of subjective well-being, and people are often not aware of high blood pressure or high cholesterol levels, for example. So we turn to the effect of religion on objectively measured health.

Comstock and Partridge (1972) obtained death rates for a large sample of church goers and others, with the results shown in Table 10.2. It can be seen that those who went to church once a week or more had much lower death rates from heart disease and several other causes. The criticism made above has been made of this study – that physical inability might explain the results. This may be a valid point for a small proportion of the elderly. However, several studies are not open to this objection. Frankel and Hewitt (1994) found for Canadian students that inner commitment to church, followed by frequency of attendance, predicted a smaller number of visits to the doctor. There have been numerous studies of the relation between religion and morbidity, and effects have been found for all the major diseases, including heart disease, strokes, several kinds of cancer, colitis and enteritis (Levin, 1994). And Dwyer *et al.* (1990) compared rates of church membership in 3,060 American counties and found that there were lower rates of cancer, especially of the digestive and respiratory kinds, in counties with large numbers of church members.

If religion affects health it might be expected that the clergy would benefit at least as strongly as their flocks. As reported in Chapter 4 above, it has been found that the clergy of several faiths live longer and in better health than others. This effect is now weaker than it was, and has almost disappeared for Roman Catholic priests (Jarvis and Northcott, 1987; Levin, 1994). The most striking effects on health are to be found in the differences in life expectancy between denominations. It has been found that male American Seventh Day Adventists live for four years longer than average, and females for two years, and that there are similar effects for Mormons,

Table 10.2 Mortality rates of regular church-goers and others (per 1,000 over 3, 5 or 6 years)

Cause of death	Attendance	
	Once a week or more	*Less than once a week*
Heart disease (5 years)	38	89
Emphysema (3 years)	18	52
Cirrhosis (3 years)	5	25
Cancer of the rectum (5 years)	13	17
Suicide (6 years)	11	29

Source: Comstock and Partridge (1972)

Orthodox Jews, and the Amish (Jarvis and Northcott, 1987; Levin, 1994). Those denominations with the greatest longevity have the strictest rules about drinking, smoking, sex and diet, and some also prescribe exercise. On the other hand, within the mainstream Christian denominations, it has been found that members of the more conservative bodies are in worse health than the others (Ferraro and Albrecht, 1991).

It is clear that religion has some effect on health, including objective health and longevity, but what is this due to? The most obvious factor is the health behaviour of different religious groups – diet, avoiding alcohol and nicotine, regulated sexual behaviour, and exercise. In the Comstock and Partridge (1972) study there were lower rates of death from cirrhosis of the liver (due to alcohol), emphysema (due to smoking), cancer of the cervix (partly due to promiscuous sex), and heart disease (partly due to smoking and diet). However, Kune *et al.* (1993) in Australia found that self-reported religiosity was a protective factor for cancer of the rectum and colon, with diet and drinking held very carefully constant.

A second, very likely, explanation is in terms of the social support of the religious community, which we saw was important for happiness. It is known from many other studies that social support benefits health, and congregation membership has often been treated as one of these forms of support (Berkman and Syme, 1979; Ellison and George, 1994). Social support affects health in special ways and produces better health behaviour, since family members drink less and have better diets for example, and family members look after each other; this may happen to church members too. We saw earlier that for old people the congregation is the strongest form of group support.

However, effects of religion have been found even after social support has been controlled for (Broyles and Drenovsky, 1992), and in some studies private commitment or devotions have been found to be independent predictors of health (Frankel and Hewitt, 1994). Kass *et al.* (1991) found in a longitudinal study that scores on an index of spiritual experience predicted a reduced number of medical symptoms, whereas belief in God did not.

A possible explanation is that the beliefs induce a peace of mind which is beneficial to health, especially in times of crisis (Idler, 1994). We saw earlier that this is a factor in subjective well-being. Yates *et al.* (1981) found that religious cancer patients reported lower levels of pain. Worship and prayer are said to engender positive emotional experiences such as relaxation, hope, forgiveness, and empowerment (McFadden and Levin, 1996). These effects may operate by activating the immune system. It has been found that this is aroused by close relationships and by positive moods and relaxation; in one experiment simply watching a film about Mother Teresa was sufficient to produce a substantial increase in salivary immunoglobulin, while a film about Hitler did not (McClelland and Kirshnit, 1982).

At the other end of religion's impact on health, we should mention those cases in which religion is a cause of actual harm. This happens when physical punishment is advocated and practised, when violent 'exorcisms' are engaged in, and when medical help is withheld (for reasons of faith) from the sick. The victims in all of these cases tend to be children. The best known group to proscribe medical care is Christian Science, but there are smaller ones where the consequences are quite tragic. In the Faith Assembly World Wide Church of Christ, a small US group founded in 1963, there were at least 100 reported cases of death among members and their children as a result of medical neglect since 1976 (Beit-Hallahmi, 1993b).

MENTAL HEALTH

Are religious people in better or worse mental health than others? We will look first at measures of mental health in student or community samples, and later at mental patients. Batson *et al.* (1993) analysed the findings in 115 such studies, and the results were at first inconclusive. They found that 37 showed a positive relation with mental health, 47 a negative one, and 31 showed no relation. They then analysed separately the results for different belief orientations, intrinsic, extrinsic, and Quest measures of religiosity, with the results shown in Table 10.3. The results show that there is a

Table 10.3 Relation between mental health and three kinds of religiosity

Measures	Positive	Not clear	Negative
Intrinsic	49	30	14
Extrinsic	1	31	48
Quest	8	12	4

Source: Batson *et al.* (1993)

widespread tendency for intrinsically religious individuals to be in better mental health; the opposite is usually found for extrinsic, and for Quest there is no clear relationship. However, it is interesting that frequency of ritual attendance does not show any overall consistent relation here, as it did for happiness.

In a study of 2,811 elderly people in New Haven, Idler (1987) found that depression was reduced in men and women who went to church and also for men who worshipped in private; this held up after a number of variables have been controlled, including health behaviour. Other studies have found that in the USA, the non-religious tend to be in poor mental health (Schumaker, 1991).

Religion has been found to have a buffering effect for those who have experienced stressful life events. Park *et al.* (1990) found that intrinsic religiosity buffered the effect of uncontrollable life events on depression and anxiety for Protestants (Figure 10.1); there was a weaker effect for controllable life events for both Protestants and Catholics; the effect was slow to work, there was no immediate effect in cross-sectional analysis, only a delayed, longitudinal one.

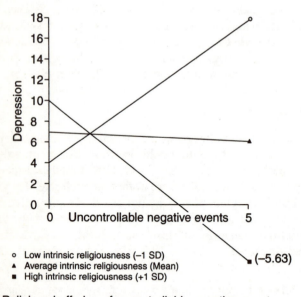

○ Low intrinsic religiousness (–1 SD)
▲ Average intrinsic religiousness (Mean)
■ High intrinsic religiousness (+1 SD)

Figure 10.1 Religious buffering of uncontrollable negative events
Source: Park *et al.* (1990)

The greater social support in smaller congregations (see Chapter 11) has been suggested to explain differences in psychopathology among Mexican–Americans in the USA (Meadow and Bronson, 1969). Williams *et al.* (1991) with a sample of 720 adults found that ritual attendance also buffered the effects of stress on mental health, and in a smaller sample Maton (1989) found that a self-report measure of 'spiritual support', through a felt 'relation with God', buffered the effect of major traumas, such as the death of a child, on depression, adjustment, and self-esteem; ritual attendance and orthodoxy of beliefs did not help those under such high stress (cf. McIntosh et al. 1993; Prudo et al. 1984). This may be achieved by religious forms of coping. When seven daily coping strategies were studied by looking at all life events for 60 married couples during 21 days, religion was the least used, mentioned in only 7 per cent of incidents (Porter and Stone, 1996). But apparently religious coping becomes more salient, and more helpful, in cases of real crisis. Pargament et al. (1988) located three factors in religious coping – collaborative (taking God as a partner, with joint responsibility), deferring (waiting, letting God decide) and self-directing (God gives freedom to take own responsibility). They found that collaborative coping, and to a lesser extent deferring, correlated with intrinsic religiosity and use of prayer, while self-directed was negatively related to both. In a later study Pargament et al. (1988) found that only collaborative coping led to positive mental health. Another process which can enhance the mental health of religious individuals is that they are able to interpret negative events in a positive way (Pargament and Park, 1995). Prayer can enable people to feel that they have more control, to face the future with optimism, greater self-confidence, self-esteem, and sense of purpose (Dull and Skokan, 1995).

Which ways of being religious are best for mental health? We have seen that intrinsic religiosity is a good predictor. Other measures of commitment also work; Ryan et al. (1993) found that a measure of the internalization of beliefs correlated with low depression, anxiety and GHQ scores, while superficial 'identification', where beliefs are to gain approval, had the opposite effect. This is like the negative effects of extrinsic religiosity. Ross (1990) found that the least distress was found in those who had either strong religious beliefs or none at all, it was those with weak beliefs who were most distressed.

RELIGIOUS IDEAS IN PSYCHIATRIC DISORDERS

The studies mentioned above were all of students or others in the community, and would not have included hospitalized schizophrenics, who are incapable of completing the questionnaires used. The occurrence of religious ideas and religious claims among psychotic patients is often noted. There have been a number of surveys of patients at various periods, and all have found a percentage with a definite religious content to the disorder, such as claiming to be famous religious figures, adopting religious postures, or having intense religious experiences. Surveys of psychotic patients showed that the content of their delusions was often taken from the dogmas of their respective religions, while the formation of the psychosis was a result of individual and social conditions.

Religious content has been found in neurotic and psychotic disturbances of all kinds, including obsessive-compulsive, phobic, depressive, and paranoid disturbances (Mailloux and Ancona, 1960). In the USA, the Group for the Advancement of Psychiatry (1968) stated that religion is more likely to play a part in affective disorders and cases of paranoid schizophrenia. After comparing the content of schizophrenic ideas over the past two centuries, Klaf and Hamilton (1961) made a convincing case for the argument that the religious content in psychotic delusions is a result of cultural factors. Patients in the mid-nineteenth century were more likely to express religious concerns, since religion was more influential as a social force. Religious delusions today are more common among members of the lower classes, where fundamentalist beliefs and intense religiosity are more common, as opposed to the more formal religion of the middle class. In earlier historical periods considerable numbers of people were classified as suffering from 'religious excitement' or 'exaltation' at the time of revival movements. Stone (1934) analysed admissions to the New Hampshire State Hospital for three months in 1842–3, during the height of the Millerite Second Adventist movement in New England. Out of 100 admissions, twenty-four were judged to have 'religious excitement' as a result of attending Miller's meetings. Of these, eighteen were diagnosed manic, three depressive and two catatonic. Religions of crisis (see Chapter 7) may be related to gross psychopathology. Group paranoia, created by paranoid leaders, characterizes some religious movements in Oceania, according to Burton-Bradley (1982). 'Revival hysteria', expressed through extremely violent and psychotic behaviours, has been reported in the 1970s around the activities of Evangelical preachers in Papua New Guinea (Robin, 1981). McDaniel (1989), studying religious ecstasy in four groups in Bengal, pointed out that divine madness is quite similar to ordinary madness in that culture. There have been reports about the higher prevalence of serious psychopathology among members of certain sect-type movements. Montague (1977) suggested that advanced age and socio-economic status were more important contributors to the high rate of mental illness among Jehovah's Witnesses than elements of the group's doctrines.

Certain religious beliefs are sometimes personalized by disturbed individuals. There are tragic cases when insane individuals, living in a religious community which believes in the reality of Satan, believe that they are possessed by the Devil, and as a result commit horrible crimes. Joy Senior, who had been brought up in the Seventh Day Adventist Church in Britain, killed her three children and then herself in May 1995, after believing that both the house she was living in and then she herself were possessed (Mullin, 1995). Here, as in other cases, personal psychopathology seems responsible, rather than any religious doctrine.

The evidence presented above points to the need for considering factors other than purely religious ones in determining the role of religious ideas in psychiatric disorders. The occurrence of religious ideas in individual delusional systems can be explained on the basis of exposure to religious ideas through social learning. It may be also related to the prominence of religion, *vis-à-vis* other belief systems, in the culture. Individual psycho-dynamics determine the appearance of symptoms, but their particular form will be the result of these background factors, one of which is religion.

Cases of more or less serious psychopathology in religious leaders have been reported and analysed. Biographical analysis of six English Messiahs led to the conclusion that three were suffering from paranoid schizo-phrenia, and one each from paranoia, hysteria and mania (Matthews, 1936). Such analyses are of great interest in understanding individual personalities, but have less value in explaining the religious movements which were started by some of these disturbed individuals. These leaders were more effective than mental patients, and their ideas had a wide appeal, but the mental status of their followers should be considered as well (cf. Gordon, 1987).

FEAR OF DEATH

Death is the most universal, and most negative, aspect of the human condition, and dealing with it is at the heart of all religions. There may be anxiety about dying, the loss of the good things of this world, the loss of personality, the possibility of going to hell if one believes in it, or the sheer uncertainty of what is going to happen. Religions provide an account of what will happen, though it is often very vague. It is commonly supposed that there are two processes: fear of death (FOD) leads to accepting reli-gious beliefs about the after-life, and this in turn reduces anxiety. Here we discuss whether religion is successful in reducing anxiety about death, and whether FOD enhances religious beliefs.

There are several ways of measuring FOD. There are elaborate scales assessing different factors of attitudes to death, such as that by Spilka *et al.* (1977) shown in Table 10.4. Most of the research on FOD has used scales measuring death denial and death avoidance (Nelson and Cantrell, 1980). Other investigators have elicited measures of 'unconscious' FOD, by recording physiological reactions to death words (Williams and Cole, 1968), or rate of response on word association tests and colour interference tests to religious and neutral words (Feifel, 1974).

From the results of studies with some thousands of mainly US respondents, it seems that there is little fear of death in the population at the conscious level, the majority saying that they are 'not afraid, it is inevitable', but there is more anxiety at an unconscious level, as shown by the delayed verbal responses to death words compared with neutral ones

Table 10.4 Correlations between death perspectives, modes of death transcendence, and intrinsic/extrinsic religiosity

	Religious Mode	Mysticism Mode	Biosocial Mode	Creative Mode	Nature Mode	Intrinsic	Extrinsic
Death as pain and loneliness	-0.31[b]	0.06	0.19	0.34[b]	-0.02	-0.11	0.32[b]
Death as an afterlife-of-reward	0.60[b]	0.08	0.24[a]	-0.14	-0.06	0.51[b]	0.03
Indifference toward death	-0.38[b]	-0.15	0.13	0.34[b]	-0.04	-0.33[b]	0.12
Death as unknown	-0.20[a]	-0.12	0.00	0.23[a]	0.23[a]	-0.35[b]	-0.35[b]
Death as forsaking dependents plus guilt	-0.17	0.03	0.47[b]	0.40[b]	-0.03	0.08	0.34[b]
Death as courage	0.34[b]	0.17	0.34[b]	0.29[b]	0.09	0.15	0.26[b]
Death as failure	-0.32[b]	-0.02	0.30[b]	0.45[b]	-0.14	-0.17	0.28[b]
Death as a natural end	0.18	-0.34[b]	0.00	-0.11	0.43[b]	-0.08	0.17

Notes
(a) $p < 0.05$ (two-tailed)
(b) $p < 0.01$ (two-tailed)
N = 105
Source: Spilka *et al.* (1977)

(e.g. Feifel, 1974). Death plays a central role in religious life. In a British survey respondents were asked which situations made them think about God: for 64 per cent 'death' made them think about God, compared with 2 per cent for making love, and 2 per cent for holidays. Forty-four per cent said that they would consult a priest or clergyman if they were afraid of death, compared with spouse 15 per cent, or doctor 8 per cent, and this was the main problem for which the clergy were said to be consulted (ITA, 1970). Gustafsson (1972) used free associations and semantic differential ratings and found that the 'cemetery' was 'a highly charged emotional symbol inspiring at times fear and sadness and at other times quiet reflection'. It was frequently used as a place for meditation by non-believers, more than by believers.

Many studies have looked at the correlation between FOD and measures of religiosity – testing the hypothesis that the more religious individuals will have lower FOD. Most studies have found, with a variety of measures of FOD, and of religiosity, that there is a negative relationship, though not a very large one. They have also found that while FOD has a negative correlation with intrinsic religiosity, as high as –0.4 or –0.5, it has a lower but positive correlation with extrinsic religiosity (Batson *et al.* 1993). The same is found for positive and negative images of death, as in the study by Hood and Morris (1983) shown in Table 10.5. However this finding may apply particularly to Christians; it did not work for Buddhists, for example (Patrick, 1979). Nelson and Cantrell (1980), with a representative sample of 1,279 from a mid-Atlantic American state, and Levy *et al.* (1985), with a sample of 856 from Quebec, found a curvilinear relationship, with the lowest FOD for the most and the least religious.

We will now look at cases where FOD has been aroused in some way, to see if this results in greater belief in the after-life, and if religious people are less upset than others. During the eighteenth and nineteenth centuries, and sometimes in this century, revivalists have used frightening images of hell to convert their listeners; it seems likely that the arousal of FOD was part of the persuasion process. But for more controlled findings we turn to some remarkable experiments. Osarchuk and Tate (1973) aroused FOD by telling subjects, who were either high or low in religious beliefs, about the dangers of dying from accidents and diseases, accompanied by dirge-like music and 42 slides of corpses and other death-related scenes. This rather strong manipulation produced substantial increases in reported belief in an after-life; FOD was reduced and subjects thought more positively of the after-life – but only if they were already believers. This result has not always been replicated. Ochsmann (1984) was restrained by ethical considerations from using such a strong FOD induction and the method he used, a 15–20 minute death questionnaire, did not produce the predicted results. From the laboratory evidence it looks as if the theory works only for strong FOD arousal and with strong believers.

There are some very strong cases of FOD arousal in real life so we now turn to these. Feifel (1974) studied carefully matched samples of healthy and terminally ill individuals and found little effect of religion on their FOD, either conscious or unconscious, though more of the religious (81 per cent) said that they were not afraid, compared with 70 per cent of the irreligious; there was no difference between the terminally ill and the others. Croog and Levine (1972) studied 324 men who had recently had a heart attack; there was no effect on their religious life. Feifel and Jones (1968) studied 371 individuals, 92 of them terminally ill; the latter engaged in denial and avoidance of this topic, and were less able to conceptualize death. A number of other studies have found that not only seriously ill individuals but also doctors, who have a lot of direct contact with death, often do not adopt a religious solution to this problem.

Another source of FOD in real life is war experience. Surveys in the American Army in the Second World War found that many said that they had been helped by prayer when things were very difficult, especially those who had been exposed to most stress in battle, such as seeing close friends killed. The percentage was higher for those who had been most frightened, 72 per cent, compared with 42 per cent for those who had been least frightened (Stouffer et al. 1949). However, there was no general lasting effect on religion after the war. Surveys of ex-servicemen who became students found that some had become more religious, some less, but the majority were unchanged (Allport et al. 1948). Entering a war situation with a previously adopted religiosity seems to help in avoiding high levels of FOD. Florian and Mikulincer (1993) studied Israeli soldiers and compared religious and non-religious ones, looking also at their exposure to actual battle. They found that religious soldiers showed lower levels of FOD even after experience in battle, and that in this case religious beliefs seemed to provide a defence against FOD.

Old age is another probable source of FOD. We have seen that old people believe more in the after-life than do younger ones; this is one of the main changes of religion with age. In one study 100 per cent of those over the age of 90 had this belief. We have also seen that one of the strongest predictors of happiness in the elderly is belief in an after-life. It looks as if the theory works for the old at least. Swenson (1961) studied 210 people aged over 60 and found that both ritual attendance and fundamentalism correlated with looking forward positively to death, as opposed to negative or evasive attitudes. The religious were more likely to say, 'it will be wonderful' or 'I look forward to death', and to associate it with 'glorious happy life'. Those in poor health looked forward to death more, and FOD was lowest for those living in homes for the aged or with their family, higher for those living alone.

When people overcome their FOD in a religious way how do they do it? Hood and Morris (1983) suggested that there are several ways of thinking about death which may enable people to 'transcend' it. These are:

1 Religious, by accepting religious ideas about immortality.
2 Biosocial, seeing the self as part of the family and children.
3 Creative, living on through one's continuing work and projects.
4 Nature, identification with natural processes.
5 Mystical, a means which is not cognitive, in which death transcendence is experienced directly.

Table 10.5 shows the relationship between these modes of thinking and FOD and other variables. It can be seen that the religious mode has the strongest correlations with FOD, and so is presumably the most successful. It is done by accepting, literally and not metaphorically, traditional teachings; we have seen how strongly some of the terminally ill are looking forward to the next world. Orbach and Florian (1992) found that the differences in attitudes to death between religious and non-religious individuals, due to religious teachings, appear as young as age 10. However, there is a second and quite different route to believing in an after-life. Although the mystical mode appears to be ineffective in reducing FOD, there is some evidence that those who have meditated a lot or taken psychedelic drugs have reduced FOD at both conscious and unconscious levels (Garfield, 1975).

Religion has traditionally played a role in helping the bereaved; the death of a spouse, a child, or a parent is extremely distressing, and can produce long-lasting emotional disturbance. The religious rites of passage for the dead are probably more use to those who are left, by the religious ceremony, the family gathering, and the period of mourning. The bereaved may also be helped to believe that they will meet their loved ones again, a belief which is most common for Spiritualists.

As we saw at the beginning of this section, religion is seen by many people primarily as a means of coping with death. All religions invest much in dealing with death, through rituals, and through descriptions of the hereafter, and these efforts seem to bear some fruit, individually and collectively.

SUICIDE

Durkheim (1897) proposed that suicide in modern society was either 'egoistic', due to lack of integration into social groups, or 'anomic', due to rapid social change and lack of regulation of individuals by society, resulting from industrialization. The prediction was that Roman Catholics would commit suicide less often, because they are more strongly integrated into the church by shared beliefs and rituals, compared with Protestants who could make individual interpretations of religion. Roman Catholic

Table 10.5 Death perspectives scales

Scale 1: Death as pain and loneliness

Death as . . .
1 A last agonizing moment
2 The conclusion to a time of isolation
3 The final misery
4 The fate of falling by the wayside
5 The ultimate anguish and torment
6 A lonely experience at the time of dying

Scale 2: Death as an after-life-of-reward

Death as . . .
1 Entrance to a place of ultimate satisfaction
2 Leading to a cleansing and rebirth of oneself
3 Leading to one's resurrection and reward
4 Union with God and eternal bliss
5 Opportunity to give up this life in favour of a better one
6 The doorway to heaven and ultimate happiness

Scale 3: Indifference toward death

Death as . . .
1 Unimportant in the scheme of things
2 Of little consequence
3 Something to be shrugged off and forgotten
4 Neither feared nor welcomed
5 Making no difference one way or another

Scale 4: Death as unknown

Death as . . .
1 The biggest uncertainty of all
2 The greatest mystery
3 The end of the known and the beginning of the unknown
4 Something about which one must say 'I don't know'
5 A question mark
6 The most ambiguous of life's perplexities

Scale 5: Death as forsaking dependents plus guilt

Death as . . .
1 Leaving one's dependents vulnerable to life's trials
2 A forsaking of loved others when one dies
3 Reason to feel guilty that one may not be adequately providing for future family necessities
4 A reason for feeling guilty
5 Leaving the family to fend for itself

Scale 6: Death as courage

Death as . . .
1 A chance to show that one has stood for something during life
2 An occasion to show how one can meet this last test of life
3 A great moment of truth for oneself
4 An opportunity for great accomplishment
5 A time to refuse humiliation or defeat
6 The test of commitment to one's life-values

Scale 7: Death as failure

Death as . . .
1 An event that prevents the realization of one's potentialities
2 The end to one's hopes
3 The final failure of one's search for the meaning of life
4 The destruction of any chance to realize oneself to the fullest
5 Defeat in the struggle to succeed and achieve

Scale 8: Death as a natural end

Death as . . .
1 An experience which comes to each of us because of the normal passage of time
2 The final act in harmony with existence
3 A natural aspect of life
4 Part of the cycle of life

Note: A 6 point Likert format was employed with respondents indicating degree of agreement or disagreement with each item; 1 = strongly disagree, 6 = strongly agree.
Source: Hood and Morris (1983)

countries in Europe did have lower suicide rates in the nineteenth century. We might also predict that congregation members would have lower suicide rates than non-members, especially for tightly integrated denominations. There is a problem with international comparisons, because in Roman Catholic areas there may be reluctance to report suicides, and it has been found that there are more cases of 'sudden death', 'death from unknown causes', and so on in these countries (Day, 1987).

Suicide rates are strongly affected by the divorce rate, by the level of industrialization or prosperity, and by social instability. Most studies have controlled for divorce rate and social class, though both of these are in turn affected by religion. There has been a large increase in the divorce rate during the present century, together with a decline in religion and an increase in prosperity. Stack (1991) suggests that the decline in religion and in collectivist family values have gone hand in hand, and that both are causes of suicide.

Level of religious commitment is found to be negatively correlated with suicide rates. Comstock and Partridge (1972) found that the suicide rate for those going to church once or more per week was 0.45 per 1,000, for those going less than once a week it was 0.95, and for others 2.1. Rates of church membership may also have a protecting effect for suicide. Bainbridge (1989) used data from 75 cities and found a correlation of –0.40, but also found that this could be explained by differences in divorce rates; some studies have found negative correlations after controlling for divorce (e.g. Stack, 1983). Earlier European studies found that Protestants had much higher suicide rates than Catholics or Jews, with ratios of two or three to one. However the difference has narrowed during this century. Pescosolido and Georgianna (1989) compared 404 American counties, and found that the suicide rates were somewhat lower for Catholics and fundamentalist Protestants, but higher for Episcopalians, Lutherans and other mainstream Protestants; the same has been found in other studies. Faupel *et al.* (1987) studied 3,108 American counties, and after applying controls for divorce rates and economic variables, found a beta weight for Catholicism of –0.08 for suicide.

Can these effects of religion be explained in terms of cohesiveness, as Durkheim suggested? Stack (1983) studied 214 American population areas, and found a correlation of –0.36 between church membership and suicide; suicide also correlated with rate of population change, an indirect measure of social cohesion, but this could not explain the effects of religion. A revised version of Durkheim's theory has been put forward, that it is not the shared beliefs or ritual that are important, but network support. Pescosolido and Georgianna (1989) found evidence that suicide rates were lowest in those churches which were already known to be most socially cohesive in terms of proportions of friends from the church, and frequency of attendance. Stack and Wasserman (1992) took this further, with a sample of 5,726, by showing that suicide rates were lowest for members of those groups known to promote network involvement, for example by having high attendance, and where there was tension between the group and society, features which it is argued make for closer network support. Fundamentalist groups are like this, and have very low suicide rates. In another study Stack *et al.* (1994) found support for a model in which religion leads to a lower degree of feminism, i.e. to a more traditional, nurturant family role for women, and this in turn leads to disapproval of suicide. Earlier Stack (1991) had shown using Swedish data that family individualism (women at work, high divorce rate) and religious activity have declined together, representing a fall in collective values, which jointly account for an increasing suicide rate.

It does not seem possible to explain these findings in terms of different religious belief systems. In an international study of 71 countries Simpson and Conklin (1989) found no relation between suicide rates and Christianity, but did find a correlation of –0.55 with Islam. It is suggested that this is because of the tight social cohesion due to frequent shared ritual, on the lines of Durkheim's ideas. Hinduism and Buddhism do not forbid suicide and Hinduism has been a factor in some cases of 'altruistic suicide', as Durkheim called it, that is, suicide out of duty to others (Adityanjee, 1986).

HELPING, COMPASSION, HONESTY, AND ALTRUISM

Religious teachings often contain explicit exhortations to love, be forgiving, be helpful, and so on (at least to members of the same community), but do the teachings have any effect? There are also other teachings, with possibly negative effects. It has been hypothesized that beliefs about humanity's essential depravity would be tied to a rather cynical, harsh view of real human beings. This has indeed been found, with Evangelical Christians in the USA being more cynical and negative about humanity (Sorenson, 1981; Wrightsman, 1974). Forbes *et al.* (1971) observed that persons attending conservative church services in the USA tend to lock their cars more often than those attending liberal churches. This was interpreted as an indication of suspiciousness. On the other hand Bahr and Martin (1983) found that church attendance was related to faith in people, and Ellison (1992) found that religiosity among African-Americans was related to friendliness, as rated by interviewers.

One way of looking at religiosity and altruism is to measure 'empathy', regarded as a good indicator of concern for others. Watson *et al.* (1984) found correlations of 0.26 and 0.31 with intrinsic religiosity, but negative relations with extrinsic religiosity. Other studies have found similar results for 'social interest', and 'humanitarian' values. However, Batson *et al.* (1993) object that this may be because intrinsics just want to appear to be compassionate. On the other hand there have been positive results from studies which have obtained ratings from others of how kind or helpful individuals are. For example Clark and Warner (1955) obtained such ratings from 14 community members for 72 individuals.

For firmer proof we turn to behavioural evidence for altruism and helping. Donating money is one such measure (see Figure 10.2). An American Gallup poll found that weekly attenders gave 3.8 per cent of their income to charity, those who went once or twice a month gave 1.5 per cent, while non-attenders gave 0.8 per cent (Myers, 1992). Hunsberger and Platonow (1986) found that Canadian students with strongly orthodox beliefs were more likely to give 10 per cent of their income. However this can be partly explained by the strong pressures to donate in North American churches. Another indicator is doing voluntary work. A US Gallup poll found that 46 per cent of the 'highly spiritually committed' said that they were working among the poor, infirm or elderly, compared with 22 per cent of the 'highly uncommitted' (Myers, 1992). Hunsberger and Platonow (1986) found that strong believers did more good works in a religious setting, but not outside; intrinsics said that they intended to do various good works, but this did not materialize. There are more problems with self-reported good works. Bernt (1989) found that intrinsic religiosity among students predicted how much voluntary work they did on campus; extrinsic religiosity was a negative predictor again. Quest did not predict good works, but did predict whether individuals applied to join the Peace Corps or similar (secular) bodies after graduation. Among those who do voluntary work in Britain, religion is given as one of the main reasons that they do it (Lynn and Smith, 1991).

We turn now to more experimental studies of the relation between religion and helping behaviour. Forbes *et al.* (1971) used the 'lost letter' technique, in which unmailed letters are left in public places to assess willingness of church members to help strangers. They left unstamped letters near 25 churches in an American city. By counting the number of letters which arrived at their destination they found that members of theologically conservative churches were less willing to make sacrifices for total strangers. We have already seen that there is evidence that intrinsic religiosity correlates with helping, while extrinsic has a negative correlation. This was also found by Bolt (1982) in experiments in which students were asked to read to blind students or help other students with projects. Again Batson *et al.* (1993) argue that while intrinsics do actually help this is because they simply want to appear helpful. It seems that intrinsics helped persistently (not significantly so) even when the help was not needed, while the high Quest individuals did not. It could be argued that the intrinsics were simply helping *more*, and similar doubts of interpretation arise with subsequent studies.

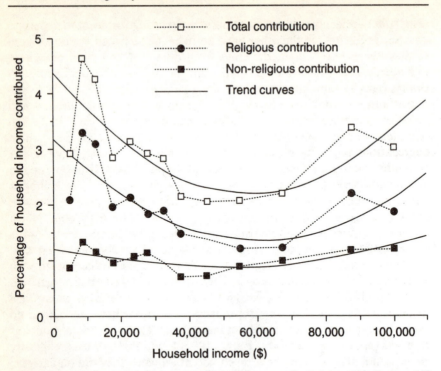

Figure 10.2 Percentage of household income contributed by contributing US households for total, religious, and non-religious contributions
Note: The upper curve is the trend for the total contribution as a percentage of income for households who reported non-zero contributions. The middle and lower curves are the trends for the percentage of income contributed to religious and to non-religious organizations, respectively, by these same households.
Source: Schverisch and Havens (1995)

Batson and Gray (1981) created a situation where subjects might help a lonely girl; the intrinsics helped whether or not she wanted it, the high Quests only if she wanted it. Again it could be that the intrinsics wanted to make sure that she was all right. Batson *et al.* (1993) created another situation where subjects would have to qualify on a stepping task in order to take part in a charity walkathon, but results were unclear. Finally, Batson and Flory (1990) asked people to volunteer to help someone in distress and gave them the Stroop test to assess word associations, via slower colour-naming. It was found that the high intrinsics thought about looking good, with words such as praise and merit, while the low intrinsics thought about looking bad. However, the Quests had only a non-significant tendency to think about victim-relevant words, such as care and tragic. It was concluded that intrinsics wanted to look good, and it was speculated that Quests were motivated by abstract principles of justice and fairness. We are not convinced by this, and think that the important point is the relation between intrinsic religiosity and helping; Quest is nearly always a weaker predictor. The finding that intrinsic is also related to empathy is evidence that it is based on concern for victims.

We saw in Chapter 5 that reported religious experiences lead to more positive attitudes towards others, and to the desire to help them; prayer led people to forgive those who had wronged them. Some of these studies were quasi-experimental, and make a causal interpretation possible.

In addition to altruistic acts by religious individuals, middle class congregations in Western countries have been active in various forms of community action, helping the poor and disabled. In nineteenth century Britain middle class congregations were active in helping the lower classes, including the provision of Sunday school education, which was instrumental in contributing to working class literacy. In the USA, such charitable activities with the poor and homeless have been important because of the limited provision of government welfare (Pargament and Maton, in press). The role of religion in creating unique and unusual patterns of altruism, which deserve to be known as saintly, in members of some religious orders and other selected groups should be noted here, even though such cases represent a very small minority of believers.

What happens in situations where altruism is literally hazardous to one's life? Oliner and Oliner (1988) claimed that religious faith was an important motive in the truly altruistic behaviour of individuals who risked their lives saving the lives of Jews in Europe during the Second World War. However, it was not the only motive, and there was an equal number of rescuers who had purely secular reasons for helping.

The effect of formal religious training on moral development has been rarely studied. A number of studies have found positive effects of formal religious education at school, especially for older children (e.g. Kedem and Cohen, 1987), although Dirks (1988) reports findings, using the Kohlberg stages, to the effect that evangelical religious training led to lower scores. It is suggested that this was because of the lack of discussion of difficult moral dilemmas.

Honesty and resisting temptation were studied by Hartshorne and May (1928) in a large number of Chicago children, using a variety of tests of cheating; there was no difference between regular church attenders and others. Among American college students several studies found no connection between religiosity and cheating (Goldsen et al. 1960; Garfield et al. 1967). Faulkner and De Jong (1968) reported that among Catholics the more religious reported more cheating. This may mean either that those who are more religious cheat more, or that they are more honest in reporting it. When college students in the USA, classified into four levels of religiosity, were given a chance to cheat and to perform an act of help-ing, there was no correlation between their eventual behaviour and their religiosity level (Smith et al. 1975).

SEXUAL BEHAVIOUR

In all religious traditions, it seems that sex is everywhere regarded as the forbidden impulse *par excellence*. It is the model for morality and self-restraint. In earlier work such as the Kinsey surveys (Kinsey *et al.* 1948, 1953) it had been found that religious people engaged in less sexual activity of every kind, including pre- and extramarital sex, but also marital sex. What is the situation after the 'sexual revolution'? Janus and Janus (1993) interviewed a sample of 2,765 Americans, and divided them into four levels of religiosity; some of their findings are given in Table 10.6. It can be seen that the most religious individuals reported less sex of several kinds, though the differences are mostly modest and were different for different activities.

Table 10.6 Religion and sex in the USA

	Very religious %	Religious %	Slightly religious %	Not religious %
I have had an abortion	18	21	27	32
I do use contraception	61	66	65	66
I have had extramarital affairs (at least once)	31	26	36	44
I have had sexual experience before marriage	71	85	98	93
Oral sex is very normal or all right	77	84	89	94
I consider myself to be sexually below average or inactive	25	22	16	15
	Protestants	Catholics	Jews	None
I have had an abortion	32	29	11	22
I do use contraception	64.5	66.5	69	74

Source: Janus and Janus (1993)

Premarital intercourse (PMI)

This is discouraged by all religions, but is nevertheless widespread in Western countries. Table 10.6 shows that as many as 71 per cent of the very religious had done it. Beck *et al.* (1991) report a longitudinal study of American youth, aged 14–22. Religious affiliation predicted PMI (or its absence) but mostly for Pentecostalists, Mormons, Jehovah's Witnesses, Baptists and other 'institutionalized sects'. Different churches proscribe sex to different degrees. In a British survey of nearly 19,000 subjects, Wellings *et al.* (1994) found that 20 per cent of men and 22 per cent of women in mainstream Christian churches were opposed to PMI, compared with 2.6 per cent and 3.8 per cent of the non-religious. Members of non-Christian religions were more strongly opposed, with 46 per cent of men and 41 per cent of the women believing that it was always or mostly wrong.

Extramarital intercourse (EMI)

This is proscribed much more strongly, as all religious groups are in favour of family values. Cochran and Beeghley (1991) combined a series of American surveys to give a sample of nearly 15,000, and found the percentages of members of various churches who believed that EMI was always wrong, and some of the results are given in Table 10.7. It can be seen that all groups thought that EMI was worse than PMI. These authors also analysed the effect of church attendance and other measures of religiosity on attitudes to EMI. The effect was greater for Baptists than for other churches.

Table 10.7 Attitudes to sexual acts

	No affil. %	Jews %	RC %	Episc. %	Baptists %	Total %
PMI always wrong	7	13	25	13	39	30
EMI always wrong	44	50	72	60	80	73
Homosexuality always wrong	42	37	71	57	86	74

Source: Cochran and Beeghley (1991)

Homosexuality

This shows a similar pattern to EMI, and again the Baptists were most opposed, followed by Catholics.

Contraception

This is strongly proscribed by Roman Catholics and some other traditions, but as Table 10.6 shows there is very little difference between them. The British survey however did find differences in the type of contraception used.

Abortion

There is a lower rate for church members (Table 10.6), an only slightly lower rate for Catholics, despite the strong official opposition, and a much lower rate for Jews.

Oral sex, and masturbation

Oral sex is now widely practised, in the USA at least, and regarded as normal by as many as 77 per cent of the very religious. Kinsey *et al.* (1948) and (1953) found earlier that masturbation was low, especially for the devout, low for Jews, and high for Catholics, especially non-practising ones.

Total sexual activity

In terms of orgasms per week, total sexual activity was considerably lower in the Kinsey surveys – the devout had about two-thirds of the rate for the non-religious, they experienced orgasm less often, and they started their sex life later. Table 10.6 shows a higher percentage of sexually inactive among the devout.

Comparing different churches in the USA, the strongest prohibition is by fundamentalist groups, followed by Southern Baptists, while the Presbyterians and Episcopalians are least proscriptive, showing a 'Protestant continuum' (Hertel and Hughes, 1987). This variation in attitudes is reflected in the effect upon sexual activity of belonging to these churches. Rate of attendance has more effect on sexual restraint for Baptists and fundamentalist Protestant bodies; for liberal Protestant churches it has a much smaller effect. This is for PMI and EMI, which all churches oppose. Baptists and Catholics are particularly opposed to abortion, but sometimes the views of churches do not seem to have much effect on behaviour, as in the case of Catholics regarding contraception and abortion.

We have seen that attendance and other measures of religiosity predict sexual behaviour. There is less premarital sex for those high in intrinsic religiosity, but more for those high in extrinsic religiosity. There is a high rate of PMI for low attenders (Haerich, 1992; Jensen *et al.* 1990).

The most likely explanation of the effect of church on sex is simply that traditions proscribe some sexual activities, and members obey if they are committed. Cochran and Beeghley (1991) found that the data fit this model for PMI, but not for EMI or homosexuality. And we have seen that attitudes to contraception and abortion do not follow official church teaching. The high rate of proscribed sexual activity for peripheral members is interesting; it has been suggested that these individuals see church as a source of pleasure, so take no notice of the other-worldly demands.

SUMMARY: INDIVIDUAL FUNCTIONING

We have seen in every section of this chapter that indicators of religiosity have a definite and in some cases a strong effect on people's lives. So religiosity affects happiness, health, mental health, suicide, altruism and sexual behaviour. The dimension of religion which has the strongest effect in some areas is intrinsic religiosity, which influences mental health and happiness, for example.

The benefits of religion for individuals apparently come from the beliefs which provide peace of mind, commandments which lead to a more disciplined life, and the explicit support for a stable family. Psychological theories of religion emphasize relief and support in terms of both the medium, social support, and the message of faith with assurance of overcoming death, and the provision of meaning and order in human existence.

Religious involvement may be an effective response to individual loneliness and social dislocation (cf. Burris *et al.* 1994; Paloutzian and Ellison, 1982). Throughout most of human history, and for large sections of humanity today, the local religious congregation is a major source of stability and support.

Chapter 11

The effects of religiosity

Group level

In the last chapter we looked at the effects of religion on those who practise it. In this chapter we will look at the effects of religion on social interactions and society as a whole.

FERTILITY

It would be expected that religious women would have more children, because of the link between religion and family values, and that Moslems, Roman Catholics, or Mormons would have most children. Fertility has been declining rapidly during this century, due to women's rising educational level and because of economic prosperity, so these factors need to be controlled for. In Europe the average number of children per family in 1970 was 2.4, it is now 1.5 (Social Trends, 1995).

In Western nations, women who belong to churches have more children than those with no church affiliation; Heaton and Cornwall (1989) found that non-affiliated women in Canada had an average of 1.84 children, compared with an overall average of 2.66. This is partly because many more non-affiliated women are childless; only 2 per cent of weekly attenders are voluntarily childless, compared with 5 per cent of those who do not go at all. Fertility is greater for women who are more committed to religion (Heaton *et al.* 1992), and this is particularly the case with Catholics; Sander (1992) found a correlation of 0.57 between family size and ritual attendance for Catholics, but this does not apply to Protestants.

The traditional finding is that Catholics have more children than Protestants, but in the USA there has been almost total convergence as shown in Figure 11.1.

There are some further denominational differences in North America. In Canada the most fertile groups are the Hutterites (5.28 children), Mennonites (3.31), Mormons (3.04) and the Salvation Army (2.80). Catholics are still above average (2.80), but this is the same as the Pentecostalists; Jews, most of whom are totally secular, score below average at 1.97 (Heaton and Cornwall, 1989). In a survey which controlled for

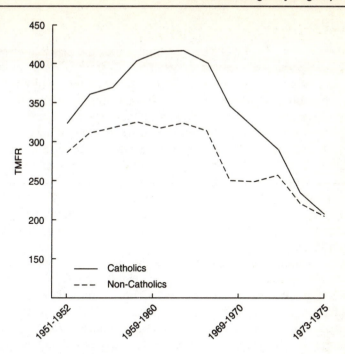

Figure 11.1 Total marital fertility rates (TMFR) for US Catholics and non-Catholics from survey data, 1951–75
Source: Westhoff and Jones (1979)

demographic variables, Marcum (1986) found that fertility correlated 0.09 with conservative religious attitudes, enough to give conservative couples half a child more.

The situation in European countries is less straightforward. Catholic Ireland has a relatively high rate (2.1), but Spain has 1.2 and Italy 1.3. France is higher (1.7), but so are Denmark and the UK (both 1.8) (Social Trends, 1995). There is no evidence of Catholic fertility here; can variations in prosperity explain the differences? Cutright *et al.* (1976) compared eighteen South American countries, controlled for modernization, and found that the more strongly Catholic ones had a higher birthrate (r= 0.16).

The explanation for the low fertility of irreligious Roman Catholic women may be that those who use contraception and limit their families may feel reluctant to go to church, while Protestants with large families may feel obliged to take them for religious education (Marcum, 1986). We saw in connection with divorce and contraception that Catholic attitudes on family values had changed a great deal during the twentieth century, in Europe and North America, though perhaps less so in South America. It is the Hutterites, Mennonites and Mormons who still maintain these values most strongly.

DIVORCE

There are several fairly obvious expectations about the possible effects of religiosity on divorce. We should expect that religious people would get divorced less often, in view of the value placed on the family by most traditions, that those traditions which emphasize family values more would have lower divorce rates, and that there would be fewer divorces when the partners share the same faith. The Roman Catholic church makes divorce very difficult, and it is found that there is an elevated rate for other kinds of marital dissolution or separation (Raschke, 1987). In cross-national studies the figures are suppressed for some Catholic countries (Trent and Scott, 1989). For Hindus too there are great obstacles to divorce. There has been a rapid increase in the rate of divorce in industrialized countries during the present century, so there will be age and regional effects which should be controlled for.

People who report no religious affiliation have much higher divorce rates than those who claim some affiliation; Heaton and Cornwall (1989), in a study of Canadian women, found that 12.7 per cent of the non-religious were divorced, compared with 7–8 per cent for the affiliated. Similar results have been found in Britain (Thornes and Collard, 1979). Frequency of attendance is also related to divorce; Heaton and Goodman (1985) combined several American surveys, applied a number of demographic controls, and found the divorce rates shown in Table 11.1. For each of the denominations, or groups of denominations, the divorce rate was considerably lower for those with higher rates of attendance. In addition to the figures in Table 11.1, Heaton and Goodman found that Mormons had a low overall rate of 16.6 per cent and those with no religion had the highest rate of 42.0 per cent. This was confirmed in a more recent study by Lehrer and Chiswick (1993), with a sample of 9,643 Americans, which used a lot of controls for education and social background. Five years after marriage those with no religion had the highest rate of dissolution, followed by Catholics; Mormons and Jews had the lowest rates. It is interesting that Catholics have such a relatively high rate. Thornton (1985) compared American surveys from 1962/3 to 1980 and found that the effect of being a Catholic on disapproval of marital dissolution declined, but the effect of being a fundamentalist Protestant had increased. A Canadian study by Heaton and Cornwall (1989) found that the lowest divorce rates were for Mennonites (3.2 per cent) and Hutterites (0.2 per cent).

Trent and Scott (1989) compared divorce rates in 66 countries, developed and underdeveloped, controlling for education and economic development, and found a small but not significant effect of Christianity, perhaps an underestimate since some Catholic countries did not report. There was a correlation of 0.11 with being Moslem, which was expected since that faith is more lenient about divorce.

Table 11.1 Divorce rates by church and attendance

	Catholic		Liberal Protestant		Conservative Protestant		Mormons	
				Attendance rate				
	High	Low	High	Low	High	Low	High	Low
Percentage divorced	13.3	30.4	24.0	32.3	20.3	37.4	12.7	23.9

Source: Heaton and Goodman (1985)

Many studies have found that divorce is more likely when the partners do not share the same faith, and this has sometimes been found to be one of the strongest predictors of an unsuccessful marriage. Bahr (1981) found that some combinations of faiths had nine times the divorce rates of others – the Catholic/Mormon combination was the worst, Mormon/Mormon the best in his data; Catholic/Protestant pairs were about twice as likely to break up as pairs of Protestants or pairs of Catholics. This was confirmed in the Lehrer and Chiswick (1993) study; all kinds of mixed marriages were less successful, but for Mormons to marry a non-Mormon made the greatest difference; mixed Jewish marriages were also very unpromising.

Religion clearly has an effect still on divorce, and is able to reduce the divorce rate of the religious to about a half of the overall rate. However the different denominations do not have the expected effect; it is Hutterites and Mennonites, and to a lesser extent American Mormons, not Catholics, who have the lowest rates, while the fundamentalist, conservative, Protestants have a high rate. Evidently, professed 'family values' are not strong enough to prevent divorce in the modern world; it requires the stricter controls of a uniquely organized community.

CRIME AND DEVIANCE

The claim that religion is an impulse control system is one of the most common made in its defence. There are several reasons for expecting that religious people would break the law less often, and show less deviance of all kinds. The most obvious reason is that religion constantly recommends behaving well and respecting social norms, and religious individuals are considered to be better socialized than others. In traditional societies, religion operates as a central part of the social control system, which closely watches individual behaviour. In such cases it is not a private, abstract, internalized system of rules, but has publicly defined and enforced norms, like the civil norms of modern society. It is observed that religion affects deviant behaviour more when it is condoned by civil society, as in the case of 'victimless crimes' such as drug abuse; religion promotes a more ascetic and controlled way of life (Burkett and White, 1974).

But does religiosity reduce criminal activity? Many earlier studies, in different countries, found that ritual attendance is negatively correlated with deviance of all kinds, as is belief in an after-life, though belief in God has had less consistent results (Ellis, 1985). However, crime is much more common for working class individuals, who are also less likely to attend rituals, so it is necessary to hold class constant. When this is done, the effect of religion is considerably weaker. Whether it is still there at all has been an open question. Jensen and Erickson (1979) studied 3,268 high school students in Arizona, and correlated 4 measures of religiosity with 18 kinds of offences. There were small negative correlations in nearly every case, but these were strongest for frequency of ritual attendance, and especially for using alcohol and marihuana. There were correlations of the order of –0.25 in these cases. The correlations for theft and violence were smaller, but there was no systematic relationship with seriousness of offence. These results were unaffected by social class.

We have seen that religion affects drug abuse (including alcohol) more than other kinds of deviance. Many large scale surveys have shown that the use of drugs is affected by ritual attendance and other measures of religiosity, for all denominations (e.g. Cochran *et al.* 1992). The effect is greater for illicit ones (Adlaf and Smart, 1985). In a study of 4,753 English teenagers, Francis and Mullen (1993) found that 69 per cent of the religious thought that marihuana use was wrong, compared with 52 per cent of the non-religious, with similar differences for alcohol and heroin. Some surveys of large samples of American adolescents find that after class has been removed the only remaining effect of religion is on drugs and sex – 'victimless offences' (Sloane and Potvin, 1986). Research on drugs has consistently found that religion is often the strongest correlate of non-abuse (Gorsuch and Butler, 1976). Summarizing numerous US studies of adolescents who are at risk because of their poverty and family history, Jessor (1992) showed that ritual attendance was a protective factor, reducing the probability of delinquency, drug use, and later maladjustment as adults. Large scale surveys of adults find that a wider range of offences and deviance is affected, including rape and other crimes of violence, property offences, but not suicide (Bainbridge, 1989).

The greatest source of influence in using alcohol or other drugs is the peer group, followed by the family. There is less use of drugs for young people who go to youth-oriented religious events (Dudley *et al.* 1987), and for older ones whose spouses belong to religious groups which disapprove of drug use (Cochran *et al.* 1992). Good behaviour may be mediated by social influences in the congregation, but Grasmick, Kinsey and Cochran (1991) found that shame, based on religious identification, had more effect than embarrassment, based on social bonds with the congregation, though frequent attendance activated both processes. However, the surrounding religious scene is important: Stark *et al.* (1982) found that religious commitment reduces delinquency when church membership is the norm, as in Utah, but not where it is unusual, as in West Coast schools, though being a Mormon has an equally strong effect in both high and low religious areas (Chadwick and Top, 1993). The effect of church is greater in small towns, probably because social influences are stronger (Jensen and Erickson, 1979).

Denominational differences have often been reported, with Jews offending least and Catholics most, especially violent offences. This can partly be explained in terms of class differences, and the cultural traditions of Italian and Irish immigrants. However, some studies found a difference with class held constant. Engs *et al.* (1990) studied 6,500 North American students and found that Catholics and mainstream Protestants drank and became drunk most, Jews and members of strict Protestant groups least. Jensen and Erickson (1979) found that (controlling for class) Catholics had the highest rates of breaking and entering, shoplifting, vandalism, robbery and drinking, Protestants the highest rate for truancy, while Mormons had low rates of smoking, drinking and drugs.

Denominational differences can be explained by the beliefs and practices of different bodies. For Mormons religious participation correlates negatively with smoking –0.54, drinking –0.77, and marihuana –0.49, far more than for members of other denominations (Jensen and Erickson, 1979). Jews have the lowest rate of alcoholism, though this does not extend to other drugs; the reason is that Jews have a tradition of moderate drinking and have ways of avoiding excess (Glassner and Berg, 1980). However, Jews at college are likely to move towards the same pattern of drinking as others (Perkins, 1987). Members of fundamentalist Protestant groups also have low rates of drinking; for them it is forbidden. And Grasmick, Bursik and Cochran (1991) found that tax cheating and littering were much less frequent for fundamentalist Christians in the USA.

We conclude that religiosity has modest overall effects on crime and deviance, but that these effects are stronger for drugs, especially alcohol, and that the effects are more marked when an act is strongly proscribed by a denomination but not by civil authorities, as in the case of the Mormons and smoking. It is remarkable that drug use should be so much affected by religion, since most traditions do not proscribe them at all clearly. One theory is that a supernatural sanction, the fear of hell, acts as a deterrent, but this has not been supported. Dudley *et al.* (1987) asked fundamentalists why they avoided drink, drugs and tobacco, and fear of hell was not given as a reason. Belief in an after-life or the devil is unrelated to deviance (Hirschi and Stark, 1969).

WORK AND ACHIEVEMENT

Max Weber (1904–5) observed that the rise of Protestantism and of capitalism coincided in several European countries, and that Protestant entrepreneurs did better than Catholic ones. He concluded that Protestantism produced a life-style which was conducive to capitalism. It is possible that Weber's original ideas have been over-interpreted, since he thought that the ascetic accumulation of wealth was a feature only of first generation capitalism (Hammond and Williams, 1976). This theory has been the source of much research and theorizing, as well as scathing criticisms (Samuelsson, 1993). Tawney (1966) stated that capitalism was not affected by any specific Protestant doctrines, but by its spirit of individualism. McClelland (1961) suggested a psychological theory of how it worked – Protestantism encourages self-reliance, and hence the early training of children to be independent, which in turn leads to higher levels of achievement motivation.

Several predictions have been thought to follow from the theory of the Protestant Work Ethic (PWE):

1 Religious individuals and countries should have positive attitudes to the value of work.
2 Protestants should have more positive attitudes to work than Catholics, or indeed others.
3 Religious individuals and countries should be more successful economically and in occupational status.
4 The same applies to Protestants compared to Catholics or others.

There is data which is relevant to these propositions both from the comparison of different countries and from comparing different individuals.

A number of different scales have been constructed to measure what has usually been called the 'Protestant Work Ethic'. Furnham (1990) factor analysed the items from seven such scales with over 1,000 subjects, and found a strong general factor with items such as 'If you work hard you will succeed'. The idea is perhaps better realized in an item from another scale: 'Hard work is fulfilling in itself' (Ho, 1984, cited by Furnham). These and many other studies make it clear that there really is a work ethic factor, though its meaning has varied between studies.

Do PWE scores lead to harder work? There is not a great deal of research here, but laboratory studies have found that the PWE predicts rate of work at laboratory tasks, and improvement of performance after negative evaluation (Greenberg, 1977), and in real work settings leads to more constant attendance at work and greater commitment to the organization (Furnham, 1990). How does PWE relate to religiosity? Several studies have found that there is a quite small but positive relationship, other studies have found none at all. Lenski (1963) found that Catholics and Protestants who were rated as high in devotionalism were more upwardly mobile and expressed more positive attitudes to work. Blackwood (1979), with an area sample in Detroit, found a regression slope of 0.17, and Furnham (1990) found a 'religious and moral beliefs' factor with a similar small positive correlation. Hammond and Williams (1976) found the stronger correlation of 0.29 between an other-worldly asceticism scale and a spirit of capitalism scale, and this was stronger, 0.48, for Mexican and African-Americans, compared to those in mainstream denominations. Blackwood (1979) found that African-Americans tended to have rather a low work ethic score, but those who believed in an after-life had much higher scores. Lenski (1963) found the same for active black church members.

The greatest research interest has been in the comparison of Protestants, Catholics, and others. Many surveys have been analysed to compare Protestant and Catholic individuals, and they have all found that the Protestants are a little stronger in work ethic scores than Catholics, but that (secular) Jews have higher scores still (Furnham, 1990), while some studies have found that atheists also have higher scores than Protestants (Giorgi and Marsh, 1990). Comparisons between countries produce larger differences. Giorgi and Marsh used data from ten European countries, with samples of 1,200 from most of them, and found the scores for intrinsic work ethic shown in Table 11.2. There are clear differences between Protestant and Catholic countries in Europe. While Protestant–Catholic differences within countries in work ethic scores were mainly due to Protestants receiving more years of education, this could not account for the differences between Protestant and Catholic countries.

The other predictions of the Protestant Work Ethic theory are about differences in achievement. There is no consistent evidence on whether

Table 11.2 Intrinsic work ethic scores by country

	Factor 1 scores				
	Low (0–3) %	Med. (4) %	High (5–8) %	Factor 1 means	
Catholic					
Spain	70	12	18	2.92	(N = 2,303)
Belgium	66	14	20	2.64	(N = 1,145)
Ireland	54	18	28	3.45	(N = 1,217)
Italy	46	19	35	3.77	(N = 1,348)
France	45	16	39	3.79	(N = 1,200)
Mixed					
The Netherlands	60	16	24	2.99	(N = 1,221)
Ulster	52	18	30	3.49	(N = 312)
Germany	50	16	34	3.75	(N = 1,303)
Protestant					
Denmark	41	19	40	3.65	(N = 1,182)
Britain	41	19	40	4.02	(N = 1,168)

Source: Giorgi and Marsh (1990)

religious people make more money or have better jobs. Most research has been directed to comparing the success of Protestants, Catholics and others. There are many American studies, following that of Lenksi in Detroit (1963), reviewed by Riccio (1979). The latest and most extensive is by Homola *et al.* (1987) who report data from several US surveys with a total sample size of 12,120. The average incomes, education and occupational status scores for several religious groups are shown in Table 11.3. It is interesting to note parallels with social class stereotypes of denominational membership, discussed in Chapter 8.

Table 11.3 Denomination and achievement in the USA

	Education (years)	Job status (av. scores)	Income ($)
Episcopalians	14.6	49.9	19,250
Jews	15.8	50.7	24,765
Baptists	11.9	40.2	13,424
Italian RC	12.9	43.2	14,779
Irish RC	13.8	45.8	16,217
Methodists	13.2	45.2	16,901

Source: Homola *et al.* (1987)

We will discuss income first, as Table 11.3 shows large differences in income, from $24,765 for Jews to $13,424 for Baptists. The authors succeeded in explaining some of these differences in terms of some groups having more years of education, smaller family sizes, and in the case of the Jews, living in New York. Table 11.4 shows the average incomes for 113 countries, again with the Protestant ones having the highest incomes.

Table 11.4 Median per caput income for groups of nations classified by dominant religious tradition, 1957

Type of nation (i.e. dominant religious tradition)	Median income ($)	No. of nations
Protestants	1,130	11
Mixed Protestant–Catholic	881	6
Eastern Orthodox	365	5
Roman Catholic	329	33
Moslem	137	20
Primitive religions	88	15
Eastern religions (Hinduism, Buddhism, etc.)	75	16
Others (including mixed types)	362	7
All nations	224	113

Source: Furnham (1990)

Table 11.3 shows the average scores on a scale of job status in the analysis by Homola *et al*. (1987). Again the Jews score highest, and the Baptists lowest; Episcopalians are higher than the Catholic groups, though the Baptists are lower. Homola *et al*. (1987) analysed these data to look at the difference between (secular) Jews and Methodists, and found that this could be mainly explained by differences in years of education, and in the education of fathers. In Lenski's area study of Detroit (1963) it was found that 43 per cent of Jews were upper middle class, compared with 19 per cent of white Protestants and 12 per cent of white Catholics. There was more vertical mobility for Protestants than Catholics, though black Protestants showed little mobility. Protestants were more likely to be self-employed, showing the entrepreneurial spirit. However, successive American studies have shown that the gap in occupational status between Protestants and Catholics has narrowed since 1930 (Argyle and Beit-Hallahmi, 1975). This all gives some support to the Protestant Ethic theory for the USA earlier in this century.

Table 11.3 also shows denominational differences in education. It can be seen that there are quite large differences in years of education in the USA, from 15.8 for Jews to 11.9 for Baptists. Again Episcopalians score higher than Catholics, though Methodists and Baptists do not. These differences in education can partly be accounted for by differences in parental education; this is less so for Jews since education is a widespread Jewish value. Featherman (1971) controlled for social origins but still found that (secular) Jews had the most education, followed by Anglo-Saxon Protestants, Catholics other than Italian or Mexican, Italian and Mexican Catholics, and lastly those with no religious preference. In a longitudinal study of the early careers of 4,309 American high school seniors, Stryker (1981) found similar differences, and these could be accounted for by differences in parental encouragement, peers' plans, and occupational aspirations. Lenski (1963) found similar differences in Detroit, and that this was because Catholics were much more likely to drop out of their courses in school or college than Protestants.

We have seen that there is quite a lot of evidence that Protestants are on average higher in work ethic and are more successful than Catholics, though Jews do even better, and some Protestant groups such as Baptists do not. We have also found that these effects can be explained to some extent by differences in amount of education. But how does religion lead to differences in education? We saw that McClelland (1961) proposed that Protestantism encourages self-reliance, and hence the early training of children to be independent, but recent studies have found little evidence for Protestant–Catholic differences here. Surveys of work ethic in countries which are mainly non-Christian in culture have found evidence for high scores in Japan, India and parts of Africa, which are presumably nothing to do with Protestantism, though they may reflect the ideas of other religions (Furnham, 1990).

PREJUDICE AND ETHNOCENTRISM

Ethnocentrism is the technical name for prejudice, a viewpoint 'in which one's own group is the center of everything, and all others are scaled and rated with reference to it' (Levine and Campbell, 1972, p. 13). Many religions teach their followers to love others, most often members of the same faith. Christianity and a few other religions have emphasized love for everyone, including enemies, of all races and creeds. On the other hand, religion has been implicated in wars such as the Crusades, and conflicts in India, Northern Ireland, and many other parts of the world. Research by psychologists has been concerned with how far religiosity increases or decreases prejudice towards other social groups.

Batson *et al.* (1993) analysed 47 American studies, some with students, others with population samples, and found that in 37 of them there was a clear positive relation between ritual attendance, religious attitudes, or orthodox beliefs, and racial prejudice; in 8 studies the results were unclear, and in only 2 was there a negative relation, both of them with young adolescents. This positive relation between religiosity and prejudice has also been found in Britain, Europe and Australia. The effect is often quite weak, and is weaker still when social class or other demographic variables have been held constant. It has been noted that in many Western countries there has been a gradual decline in prejudice, which is directly tied to secularization. This phenomenon again ties religiosity directly to prejudice.

Once we go beyond this general finding, the issue becomes that of explaining the psychological mechanisms responsible for the correlation. Research has shown differences related to patterns of religious commitment. If different church members are compared, a stronger but curvilinear relation is often found: those who go to church more often, or who are more committed, are *less* prejudiced than those who go less often (Figure 11.2). This is illustrated by the study by Eisinga *et al.* (1990) of the attitudes to Surinamese and other ethnic groups in a sample of 3,000 Dutch adults.

However, such a curvilinear effect has not always been found, and it has been pointed out that there is little difference in prejudice between the most religious and the totally irreligious (Hunsberger, 1995). There is evidence showing that extrinsic religiosity correlates with prejudice, while intrinsic religiosity has a low correlation with lack of prejudice; extrinsics are certainly more prejudiced than intrinsics (Gorsuch and Aleshire, 1974; Batson *et al.* 1993). However, these findings mainly come from studies of attitudes to Jews and Africans; Batson *et al.* (1993) review nine studies of attitudes to other groups not proscribed by tradition, and show that intrinsics are actually *more* prejudiced towards communists and homosexuals, and amongst West Indian respondents to Rastafarians. Respondents high

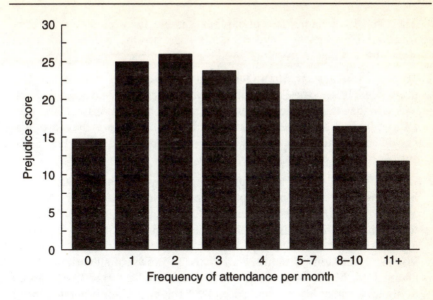

Figure 11.2 Prejudice and church attendance
Source: Struening (1963)

on Quest were *less* prejudiced towards such groups, but this may reflect the views of the radical young. And Ponton and Gorsuch (1988) found that Venezuelan student intrinsics were *less* prejudiced to other South American groups. The suggestion is not that intrinsics are unprejudiced, but that they only accept other groups when the tradition tells them to.

Batson *et al.* (1993) raise another doubt over whether intrinsics are really unprejudiced; they found that intrinsics said that they were less prejudiced on a questionnaire, but given a behavioural choice they preferred a white to a black interviewer; they had only been presenting themselves as unprejudiced. On the other hand, Brannon (1970) found that intrinsics were more likely to opt to stay with a church which was committed to desegregation. Gorsuch (1988) argues against the idea that intrinsics are expressing socially desirable attitudes, because they gave unprejudiced replies in parts of the USA, such as Texas, where it was socially desirable to be prejudiced.

There are differences between denominations in racial attitudes, the main finding being that members of fundamentalist churches such as American Southern Baptists are more prejudiced than others (Gorsuch and Aleshire, 1974). Fundamentalists are also prejudiced against women (Powell *et al.* 1982). And while the keener members of other churches are less prejudiced, keener fundamentalists are more prejudiced (Kirkpatrick, 1993). In studies reported so far, the most prejudiced have been members of African-American Protestant churches (Gay, 1993).

There have been a number of explanations for the prejudice–religiosity connection. They can be divided on the basis of emphasizing either the content of the religious message, social factors, or personality factors:

1 There is no mystery about why some of the more devout are less prejudiced. It is because of the official teachings to love and accept others. We saw that the keener members of most congregations are less prejudiced and that there is some doubt over whether they are less prejudiced towards groups on which there would be less clear teachings, such as homosexuals or women.

2 Religious hostility and competition, inspired by myth and doctrine, may be a factor in creating specific prejudices (cf. Griffin *et al.* 1987). Normal religious socialization then inculcates these ideas together with other teachings, creating religious chauvinism. This is especially so when groups compete over the idea of being the elect, and claim the same historical tradition. Moslems, Christians, and Jews, of all varieties, have claimed to be the truly elect within the Biblical tradition. Shared mythologies may lead to an especially virulent prejudice, while a total lack of commonality in beliefs may create a more general hostility. Glock and Stark (1966) suggested that American anti-Semitism was partly due to Christian teachings, and found that 86 per cent of Southern Baptists agreed that 'The Jews can never be forgiven for crucifying Christ', compared with 60 per cent of other Protestants and 46 per cent of Catholics. These findings were replicated for Protestant clergy (Stark *et al.* 1971), Lutherans (Kersten, 1971), and Mormons (Mauss, 1968) in the USA, and for Christians in The Netherlands (Eisinga *et al.* 1995). This approach, and these findings, cannot account for the findings of other prejudices, such as those of Southern Baptists towards African-Americans and women, unless we assume a more general tendency to prejudice in other cases.

3 Prejudice may be triggered by threats. According to terror-management theory (Greenberg *et al.* 1986), outsiders are easily perceived as threats to our established worldview, on which our death-transcendence illusion is based. They found that reminding Christians of their mortality leads to increased hostility towards Jews (Greenberg *et al.* 1990).

4 Conformity to social norms could produce both religious activity, of the extrinsic type, and prejudice, if both are local norms, as in the American South and formerly in South Africa. It has been suggested that conformity and membership in religious organizations are both related to authoritarianism.

5 The latest theory is in terms of 'localism', that is, attachment to the local small community; Roof (1974) found support for a causal model in which localism produces prejudice both directly and via religious orthodoxy;

Eisinga *et al.* (1990) found that the link between church membership and prejudice could be explained by localism and authoritarianism.

6 Congregations are very cohesive communities with great intimacy (Chapter 10), and it is well known that racial prejudice most affects situations of possible intimacy; the intimacy between members is probably based partly on shared beliefs, partly on personal compatibility, so that this can explain why both religious and ethnic out-groups are rejected. With a social reality of religious pluralism and competition, measurable social distances among different groups are maintained, and they will affect intimate social contacts across group boundaries (Cavan, 1971). Different churches reject the members of other churches to different degrees, as Brinkerhoff and MacKie (1986) found in a study of social distance.

POLITICAL INVOLVEMENT

The first issue is whether there is a general relationship between religiosity writ large and a basic political stance. Can we assume a relationship which holds true for both British and Indian politics? Is there an inherent connection between religiosity, or religious conservatism, and political conservatism? Does religion always side with the rich and the powerful, as McLeod (1981) claims? Are religious influences general or specific to explicit doctrinal issues? 'While some studies did not find a connection between religious orthodoxy and political attitudes (Lenski, 1963), no empirical study has ever found a relation between doctrinal orthodoxy and political liberalism or radicalism' (Argyle and Beit-Hallahmi, 1975, p. 107). This is the conclusion of an earlier survey, and it is still valid now.

One general hypothesis assumes that religiosity would be linked to support for non-democratic ideology, because religion has always been connected to tradition, authority, and hierarchy. Most religious organizations in history have been not only authority oriented but positively authoritarian, even totalitarian. Their tenets and structure are not likely to inspire equality or egalitarianism. 'Let every soul be subject unto the higher powers. For there is no power but of God: the powers that be are ordained of God' (Romans, 13, 1). This was the official Christian stance in the West for many generations. In the industrial revolution the early Protestants were on the side of the industrialists, and indeed cooperated with the owners of industry. The British Parliament's actions in the early nineteenth century to construct Church of England parishes in south-east England has been interpreted as a direct response to the French Revolution. To avoid revolution, official religion among the working classes had to be strengthened (Homan, 1986). Awareness of the powerful controlling functions of religion is indicated by the financial and public support given to churches by the American 'robber barons' of the nineteenth and twentieth centuries (Josephson, 1962).

However, religion has sometimes been the source of utopian visions of equality, brotherhood, and peace, but promised bliss has had to follow a violent apocalypse, trials and tribulations. The rise of the ideals of democracy, tolerance, equality, and individual rights has been tied to secularization and the declining power of religion. Nelson (1988a) found that, in surveys using representative samples of the US population between 1973 and 1985, disaffiliation from religious denominations contributed to greater political liberalism (cf. Wald *et al.* 1988).

Religious identity creates a special kind of group loyalty and identity, which may be the prototype of tribal and national loyalty. Findings on religiosity and prejudice (see p. 218) are relevant, as well as findings on authoritarianism (Adorno *et al.* 1950). These clearly indicate a connection between extreme right-wing views and religiosity. Eckhardt (1974), after reviewing research over the previous forty years on religious beliefs and practices in relation to peace and justice, reported that most studies found correlations between orthodoxy, militarism, and nationalism. Among Israeli Jews, Peres (1995) found a clear correlation between the level of religiosity and anti-democratic and nationalist attitudes. Nelson (1988b) found that foreign aid provision was inversely related to religious salience and religious diversity among economically advanced nations.

In modern times, political movements tied to conservatism, tradition, family, and nationalism, i.e. right-wing parties, have relied on the support of religious institutions. In a study of newly converted Pentecostalists in El Salvador, Martin-Baro (1990) found that the majority turned significantly conservative following their conversion. He further suggested that conservative governments in Latin America were aware of this effect, and so encouraged the spread of evangelical movements in their countries. It should be noted that Martin-Baro himself was assassinated by government agents in El Salvador in 1989.

If there is a relationship, how is it mediated? Bord and Faulkner (1975) found that Catholic Pentecostals in the USA were following church teachings on abortion (i.e. opposition), but were opposed to the US involvement in the Vietnam War, where the Roman Catholic Church did not take a clear stand. They concluded that religious beliefs will correlate with socio-political attitudes only when the issue is related to doctrine. However, findings below show that there are religious influences which are more general. One general explanation states that religion is involved in politics because of the different socio-economic composition of religious denominations (Lipset, 1964). If politics is the struggle for economic and social resources among competing groups, and if religion provides compensation for the losers in this struggle, then we can expect more religiosity in oppressed groups. More specific predictions can be derived from Marxian ideas, as follows: holding religious beliefs should be positively correlated with holding conservative social and political views and negatively correlated with holding radical political views. Tiryakian (1993) stated that the vitality of religion in the USA since the nineteenth century had a dampening effect on any socialist movement there. Similarly, Christiano (1988) showed that the level of religiosity in any US state in the 1920s was inversely related to the presence of radical labour unions.

It has often been stated that in modern societies, sect-type religiosity will be tied to a general lack of political involvement. This has been suggested to hold for both developed and developing societies: 'To the extent that a religious sect opts for . . . ideological purity over time . . . it will not take part in political developments . . . When sects opt for ideological purity they insure that the major cleavage between the dominant and subservient society will be reinforced' (Janosik, 1974, p. 171).

In the USA, Pentecostalism has been described as a movement that started as a protest against the whole social order, but then was transformed into a conservative force, which serves to perpetuate that order (Anderson, 1979). Small Protestant sects have long been described as the 'churches of the disinherited' (Niebuhr, 1929). Nelsen and Nelsen (1975) reported, as expected, that for African-Americans church-type religiosity was tied to militancy, while sect-type religiosity was tied to political passivity (cf. Chapter 8). Dearman (1974) reported similar findings regarding sect-type religious commitment. Baer (1988) and Baer and Singer (1993) stated that main African-American churches sustained a moderate critique of racial and class inequalities in the USA.

Religion has always offered consolation and promised success, thus aiding integration in the face of frustrations (Schneider and Dornbusch, 1950). Sectarian movements in modern society have contributed to political stability by diverting the attention of their impoverished members to rewards in heaven, and controlling them by the prospects of punishment in the hereafter (Hollenweger, 1972). 'In this way revivalistic religions may help their adherents maintain a sense of personal integration in the face of widespread and enduring frustrations' (Frank and Frank, 1991, p. 76). We saw above that members of Pentecostal and other sects are particularly closely bonded – to each other but not to the wider society. Pope (1942) showed how different types of religious organizations prevent radical social change and contribute to the maintenance of the status quo. It was shown that churches openly and directly cooperated with the industrial owners, who owned the church buildings and hired the preachers, while sects directed the concerns of the industrial workers from this world to the next. A 1960s follow-up study of the same US community which Pope (1942) studied in 1929 (Earle et al. 1976) showed a clear continuation of the same patterns.

Much research on religiosity and politics was done in the USA during the politically turbulent 1960s. The majority of church members in the USA in the 1960s were described as 'reactionary' (Glock and Siegelman,

1969), and political radicalism on the left should have been tied to low religiosity. In a 1966 sample of US students at nine midwest private colleges, an inverse relationship was found between religiosity and support for the civil rights movement active then (Eckhardt, 1970). One way of looking at the relationship between religious and political beliefs is to examine closely members of radical political groups. Grupp and Newman (1973) studied, in 1965, two well known groups in the USA: the John Birch Society, a radical right-wing group, and Americans for Democratic Action (ADA), a left-wing group within the Democratic Party. There were clearcut differences. Among the Birchers, 16 per cent belonged to liberal Protestant groups or had no affiliation, while among ADA members 80 per cent were in that category, or Jewish. Among the John Birch Society members, 25 per cent were Roman Catholic, while for the ADA the corresponding figure was 5 per cent. Nassi (1981) reported that radical students who were members of the students' Free Speech Movement at the University of California, Berkeley, in 1964 (starting the 1960s upheavals on US campuses), were more likely to come from families that were identified as Jewish, agnostic, or atheist. Fifteen years later, they were likely to report the same affiliations.

Studies in the USA showed that religious orthodoxy was tied to hawkish, pro-war, attitudes (Granberg and Campbell, 1973; Tygart, 1971). For Christians in the USA, those who considered themselves more devout were found to be most militaristic (McClelland, 1975; Russell, 1971). In a survey of 1,062 American students, Connors et al. (1968) found that Catholic students showed most acceptance of modern war, with the non-affiliated most opposed to it. Hamilton (1968) showed that in both 1952 and 1964, when the USA was involved in foreign wars, Protestants were most supportive of strong military actions, Catholics were less supportive, and Jews were the least supportive. In both cases, the non-affiliated were most opposed to military measures. Among participants in a demonstration against the Vietnam War, 61 per cent were non-affiliated (Parrott, 1970), and among American students in the 1960s, participation in protest demonstrations against the war was positively correlated to no affiliation or coming from a Jewish family. It was negatively correlated with the practice of praying (Astin, 1968).

Traditionally, political issues were defined in terms of political/economic justice debates over wealth and power in society. Rokeach (1969) carried out a survey of 1,400 adults in the USA. Concerning the poor, church attenders were less in favour of passing laws to help them, and more likely to agree that poverty is caused by lack of effort: however on nine out of eleven issues there were no differences in compassion towards the poor. Hartmann and Peterson (1968) studied 1,500 freshmen at 37 American colleges. A 'liberalism' factor was extracted, consisting of support for a welfare state, organized labour and social change towards greater equality.

The non-religious and Jews scored highest, Protestants lowest. Today, political discourse has changed in terms of extending the classical welfare debate, and of covering questions of individual and societal morals in new ways, such as concern about the environment. Public disagreements have arisen around attitudes towards 'outsiders' in general: minority groups; those who are deviant or suffering misfortunes, such as the handicapped and the mentally ill; immigrants; refugees; homosexuals; and drug-addicts. Do we support their rights to special consideration or equality? Do we support more or less public spending on welfare and unemployment insurance? Such questions frame the political debate in industrialized societies. Other issues looked at in the context of politics include punishment for criminals, abortion rights, pornography, and the teaching of 'creationism'.

Since the 1940s, numerous studies in the USA have investigated attitudes to deviants of various kinds. The results have shown that the more religious are less tolerant, Jews and the irreligious most tolerant. Kirkpatrick (1949) found that people who scored high on his 'religionism' factor had more punitive attitudes towards criminals, homosexuals, unmarried mothers and conscientious objectors, though the relationship was very weak. Stouffer (1955) found that churchgoers were more intolerant of political dissent than non-churchgoers and stated: 'There would appear to be something about people who go to church regularly that makes fewer of them, as compared with non-churchgoers, willing to accord civil rights to nonconformists' (p. 142). Jewish respondents, noted for secularity, were more tolerant than the others. Smidt and Penning (1982) found that in representative samples of the US population in 1974, 1977, and 1980, religious commitment was inversely related to political tolerance. Rooney and Gibbons (1966) found that Catholics were less tolerant of 'victimless' offences, such as homosexuality and drug addiction, compared with Protestants and Jews. Roof and McKinney (1987) found that members of mainline Protestant denominations, which are more liberal in terms of religious beliefs, tended to be more liberal on several social–political issues, such as civil rights for minorities, women's rights, and sexual morality, when compared to members of more conservative denominations.

Piazza and Glock (1979) reported that belief in a god who ordains social life as compared to one that affects personal life is correlated with conservative, racist, and anti-feminist political views. In a representative sample of the US population in 1988 it was found that moral rigidity (quest for certainties) and benign images of god were respectively correlated with environmental insensitivity and sensitivity in various denominations (Greeley, 1993). Eckberg and Blocker (1989) found that biblical literalism inversely related to environmental concerns. Peek and Brown (1980) found that, in a representative sample of the US population, white Protestants more than others opposed female participation in politics, and fundamentalist religiosity was correlated with such opposition. Ellison and Sherkat

(1993a), in a representative sample of the US population in 1988, found conservative Protestants supporting corporal punishment of children, with belief in biblical literalism and a sinful human nature emerging as causal factors. Similarly, fundamentalism was found to correlate with support for punishment as an end in itself in dealing with convicted criminals (Grasmick *et al.* 1992). And a survey of a representative sample of the US population showed that conservative Protestant denominations membership was related to negative attitudes towards AIDS patients (Greeley, 1991).

Young (1992) found that in a 1988 representative sample of the US population, fundamentalism correlated with support for the death penalty, but devotionalism and evangelism (trying to convert someone) with opposition to it. In a 1994 public opinion survey in the USA (NORC, 1994), it was found that opposition to the death penalty was highest (34 per cent) among those reporting no religious affiliation, and lowest (9 per cent) among Mormons. The overall figure was 25 per cent, and it was 26 per cent among Jews, 27 per cent among Protestants, and 25 per cent among Catholics.

Though most of the research reported here has been done in the English-speaking world, there is reason to believe that the findings hold true for the rest of the world. Extremism in politics seems to find support in various religious orthodoxies, whether in Japan, Egypt, Algeria, India, or Israel, to name just a few cases, and seems to be the norm, rather than the exception (Liebman, 1983). More findings related to this issue will be presented in the next section.

SOCIAL INTEGRATION OR SOCIAL EXCLUSION

How far are ideas about the contribution of religion to social integration confirmed by empirical data? Religiosity is learned and maintained through solidarity and group membership. Together with the promises of eternal life there are immediate rewards of affiliation. Within congregations there is a high degree of social cohesion. The experience of community is the most important function of tradition for most people. Being in a group in which they feel valued and accepted, even special, just because they belong is deeply rewarding. We saw on p. 185ff. that in a large survey of Australian churchgoers 24 per cent said that their closest friends were members of their church, while for Pentecostalists the percentages were even higher (Kaldor, 1994). Intimacy in the group may affect its survival. A study of commitment levels in Jehovah's Witness congregations showed that the smaller congregations were highest in commitment (Alston and Aguirre, 1979). Friendships in the congregation were found to be related to the strength of commitment, as expressed in belief orthodoxy and participation (Welch, 1981). One of the present authors recently carried out a survey in the Oxford area and found that 37 per cent said that their church friend-ships were closer than other friendships; this was a higher proportion than for any other kind of leisure or voluntary group; the next highest was mem-bership of groups doing voluntary work (Argyle, 1996).

We saw in Chapter 10 that religion provides benefits in health, mental health and happiness. These benefits are particularly related to participation in the religious community, and are strongest for those who are otherwise socially isolated, such as the retired and the single. We saw that the suicide rate is lower for congregation members, and especially members of congregations who have close social bonds, as predicted by Durkheim. Religion has 'identity functions' in being a source of legitima-tion for group identity and for individual self-esteem.

Social categorization is accompanied by evaluation, and intimately tied to the management of self-esteem. Individuals express an overvaluation of the in-group, thereby enhancing their self-esteem, and a parallel sys-tematic underevaluation of the out-group. Religion provides a perfect outlet for in-group frictions and aggression, by allowing hostility and aggression towards out-groups and non-believers. Guarding community and identity is a major effort, with both costs and gain for individuals, and being a member of a religious minority, just like being a member of any minority, may take its toll. One study in the USA in the late 1950s found that high school students who were members of local religious minorities showed lower self-esteem, and more symptoms of anxiety and depression (Rosenberg, 1962).

We looked earlier at preliterate cultures, and reported that religious rituals are able to enhance social cohesion among groups of men about to undertake dangerous hunting or fishing, where they would be much depen-dent on each other (Chapter 4). The effects of religion as an integrating force have been seen in other small communities. In a study of American utopian communities between 1776 and 1900 it was found that those with a single religious faith survived longer than those with several religious faiths or no religious orientation at all (Stephan and Stephan, 1973). In a national survey of 2,107 African-Americans, Taylor and Chatters (1988) found that 25 per cent reported that they often received help from congregation members, whether material, emotional or spiritual (for example, with food, clothing, advice, or help when ill), while 64 per cent received some such help; this shows a high level of integration within black church communities (cf. Winter, 1992; Levine, 1986). However, in these studies it has not been shown that the direction of causation is one way rather than the other. There is also some solidarity among members of different congregations who belong to the same denomination, as shown by the greater willingness to marry or make friends with members of the same denomination. That religions encourage in-group altruism and support is a positive contribution, even if limited to one group (cf. p. 200ff.).

What of social integration in the wider society outside the individual congregation? A number of US surveys have examined this issue. The findings have been rather mixed, but usually show that there is a weak tendency for religiously affiliated individuals to have lower feelings of anomie, and for them to feel that they are members of the community (Kanagy *et al.* 1990; Martinson *et al.* 1982). However, the other side of this is the prejudice towards out-groups, expressing social exclusion. We looked on p. 168ff. at the work by Rokeach (1960), who found that such prejudice was greater the more the belief systems differed, and was greater for more fundamentalist groups. Such divisions are likely to be added to differences in education, income or geographical region. So the existence of more than one congregation in the community may be a source of prejudice and social division. There has been a long and bitter history of conflict between Catholics and Protestants in Europe, though this has gradually diminished over the last three centuries, as tolerance has increased (Kamen, 1967). British Catholics recognize that while church schools may be very desirable this leads to segregation (Hickman, 1993). And while rituals and dietary rules in Orthodox Judaism enhance community cohesion, they also result in (deliberate) separation from the rest of society.

Many members of sect-type groups are impoverished or are members of ethnic minority groups, and this is true all over the world (cf. Chapters 7, 8). Such people may feel that they have been rejected by the wider society, but that they are accepted by their churches. In some cases the result may be that they become better integrated into the wider society, as these groups often help to resocialize their members in disciplined ways, and they become more prosperous as a result, and indeed the whole group may become upwardly mobile for the same reason. Brown and Gary (1991) surveyed 921 African-Americans and found that religious socialization led to increased educational attainment, which would have consequences for social mobility and integration (cf. Edwards, 1968).

Religion does have a considerable impact on solidarity and integration at the national level. In some countries there is a single, dominant, national religion, which may be the official state religion, whose doctrines are taught in school, and whose ceremonies are used on state occasions. It seems inevitable that religion would be a positive force for social integration in such cases. Religious uniformity in a community or nation, like ethnic uniformity, seems to aid cohesion.

What about social integration on the international, or inter-ethnic, scale? Conflicts between Arabs and Jews, Moslems and Hindus, Protestants and Catholics, among others, have been very bitter. It is generally agreed that in most modern conflicts religion may be dragged in, but is not really a causative factor (Beit-Hallahmi, 1993a). This seems to be the case in former Yugoslavia, where leaders of nationalist conflicts seek to use religions in order to obtain legitimacy (Vrcan, 1994). On the other hand, there seem to be a few cases, such as in Lebanon, where confessional boundaries sow the seeds for civil wars (Labaki, 1988). In other cases, such as in Northern Ireland, religious boundaries are tied to inequality and discrimination (Covello and Ashby, 1980).

While religion has been only one factor among others in many conflicts, it seems to have made things worse rather than better. Although religion *per se*, or religious identity, is not often the direct cause of large-scale conflict, religiosity does contribute to more aggressive attitudes once a conflict has started. The growth of religious nationalism in several countries is a negative factor from this point of view (Juergensmeyer, 1993).

CONCLUSIONS

At group level, religion does have an impact on crime, prejudice, fertility, divorce, work and achievement. Those who are actively religious have 50 per cent of the divorce rate of others, have lower rates of crime, work harder and are more socially integrated. In this respect, religion can be said to contribute to social cohesion and integration (cf. Stark, 1984). Most religious traditions have promoted 'family values', that is, keeping the family together, restricting sex to marriage, and producing a lot of children. These values have been undermined in the modern world, with the education and increased employment of women, and it is only the most conservative and tightly knit bodies, such as the Hutterites, Mennonites and Mormons, which strongly enforce them today. The differences between Catholics and Protestants, which had been noted at the beginning of the century, have now almost disappeared in the USA and Europe (e.g. divorce, fertility rates). The remaining differences between Catholics and Protestants are mainly due to differences in education. Some smaller religious movements have greater power over their members. What is observed here is that it is the specific content of religious beliefs and commandments that has an effect on behaviour.

The social harmony provided by religion is inherently limited by the nature of religious identity. Religion achieves its often positive effects through social cohesion and social support. All religious congregations are cohesive, and provide strong social support to their members, but at the cost of isolation from other bodies and risk of prejudice against those of other faiths and other ethnicities. The social harmony provided by religion is inherently limited by the nature of religious identity. NRMs are particularly prone to this combination of high cohesion and social isolation. On a more global scale, religion and large religious groupings are the source of conflicts which remain serious threats for all of us.

Chapter 12

Evidence, inferences, and interpretations

So far we have summarized research done, mostly over the past century, by hundreds of researchers in several disciplines, all looking for the origins and consequences of religion and religiosity. At this stage, after looking at much evidence, we are ready to pass judgment on causal notions, abstractions, and generalizations. The researchable propositions were presented in Chapter 2, and we promised to assess their success in gaining empirical support. Before we proceed, however, we should point out some limitations and constraints.

THE PROBLEM OF CROSS-CULTURAL GENERALIZATIONS

Our survey of findings from all over the world could be criticized as a wild brew of cultures and, especially, of meanings, which cannot be mixed. Just adding up measures and numbers does not make sense. Modern secularized societies cannot be combined with traditional ones. Can we put Bangladesh and France, or the USA and Japan, in the same basket? Even comparing Roman Catholics in Spain and in Canada today shows large differences (Northover and Gonzalez, 1993). The cultural meaning of religion differs in different nations, depending on their unique histories. Moreover, some may claim that outsiders will never appreciate the true meaning of another culture, be it the USA, Egypt, or India. The outsider's view is quite naturally affected by simple ignorance, biases, prejudices, and stereotypes. These are very common, and often dominant, factors in our perception of other cultures.

Most of the research reported in this book has been carried out in the English-speaking world. We have relied on the copious published behavioural science literature, mostly in English, and most of the studies we called upon were done in the USA, with a minority in Great Britain and Europe. We are well aware of this inherent limitation, and we should caution all our readers accordingly. Moreover, most of our data on traditional cultures come from anthropological research, while most research on industrialized societies is based on sociological surveys and psychological research. As we said in Chapter 3, it is easy to see that the best-controlled studies used US college students, while less elegant data collection involves the 'real world' (away from the US campus).

Since we are basing our conclusions on research in societies which are advanced, industrialized, relatively secular, but with a predominantly Christian heritage, it is not easy to generalize about more traditional, non-Christian societies. Can we generalize to the rest of the world? Is this another expression of Western imperialism?

We can generalize from our findings to the situation in other English-speaking countries, and with some certainty to other Western countries. We should recall that Western tradition, including Christianity and its cultural manifestations, dominates global culture today. Formally, Christianity (in various forms) is the world's leading religion, and together with Islam, a sister tradition, it reaches a clear majority of the world's population. Our findings are clearly relevant to the industrialized North civilization, covering today more than 20 per cent of humanity. We know that our basic generalizations hold quite well for the reality of religiosity in post-Communist Russia (White *et al.* 1994). Our awareness of the limits and the limitations of US-based research has led us to use so many reports by historians and anthropologists dealing with other societies. We find that religion everywhere is attenuated by society and culture. Individuals follow cultural scripts for religion, as for other behaviours. But we can still point to some generalizations or even universals. Despite the cross-cultural and historical evidence for the diversity of religious beliefs, there are also some universal features in terms of the common belief system: gods are envisaged as invisible spiritual forces with some of the properties of persons, who are good and powerful. They are usually thought of as male. Religion is universally claimed as the source of, and the authority for, moral codes, impulse control and social power arrangements. Women are everywhere more committed to religion, and the family is everywhere sacralized. It has often been noted that the same themes are found in religious myths all over the world. These include such themes as the creation of the world, the flood, slaying monsters, Oedipal stories, and hero myths (Brown, 1991; Kluckhohn, 1959). Are the psychological mechanisms involved in belief, ritual, and myth identical everywhere? We do find not only similar stories, but identical behaviours, and it stands to reason that the meaning of fasting or sacrifice must be similar in different places, just as the acts are similar.

OTHER PROBLEMS IN TESTING THEORETICAL EXPLANATIONS

One problem facing all researchers in this area is that some of the most provocative and insightful statements about religious behaviour are not actually taken from systematic theoretical presentations. There are very few systematic theories of religious behaviour, and many of those that exist are merely descriptive. As a result some interesting theoretical insights are hard to test empirically.

EVIDENCE FOR SPECIFIC PROPOSITIONS

Neural factors

Several areas of religious activities are relevant here. Some are common and non-dramatic, such as the involvement of music, dance, and other rhythmic actions. Others are dramatic and exceptional, such as glossolalia. Schumaker (1990, 1995) states that religious acts may be the result of an induction or hypnotic suggestion. The universality and centrality of music in so many religious rituals (see Chapter 4) must be related to a universal neuro-physiological and neuropsychological reaction in all humans (Schumaker, 1995). Findings about the effects of drugs in inducing religious moods and experiences, and evidence about specific regions of the brain related to some religious experiences (Chapter 5) support the notion of the neural substratum of religion (Davidson and Davidson, 1980). Distinctively religious or mystical experiences appear only in a minority of cases under the same chemical conditioning.

Research on the relative dominance of the two hemispheres of the brain may be relevant here. There is some evidence that the left hemisphere is dominant for verbal and allied cognitive activities, while the right is dominant for spatial, aesthetic, and non-verbal operations (for right-handed males at least). There has been a suggestion that religious people tend to be right hemisphere dominant (Bakan, 1971). This suggests that religious attitudes and ideas are connected to the non-verbal right hemispheres.

Cognitive need

Cognitive need explanations appear to be broadly correct, though there is not a great deal of detailed evidence. Some support may be provided by Thouless' classical finding (1935) reported in Chapter 9. Judgments of religious items showed a stronger tendency towards the two extremes of judgment, disbelief being as dogmatic as belief. This finding was replicated much later by Brown (1962). Sanai (1952) in a similar study of adult students found a W-shaped distribution for religious items, a normal distribution for factual items, and a U-shaped distribution for political items. Towler (1985) analysed 4,000 letters written to the Anglican Bishop of Woolwich in Britain, J. A. T. Robinson, following the publication in 1963 of his controversial book, *Honest to God*. The analysis led to two dimensions: the need for certainty and the wish to find meaning in the world.

Adolescents are commonly observed to move from one coherent set of beliefs, or disbeliefs, to another. During adolescence they are converted and deconverted. It is significant that there is a peak of interest in religion, especially in its ideological aspects, at or shortly before the age at which identity problems reach their height (see Chapters 6, 7).

Historical observations have shown clearly how particular sets of religious ideas have provided socially shared meanings and goals. It is not clear that majority religions at present do very much to affect individual behaviour, except in certain limited spheres (Chapters 10, 11), because of growing secularization. What they still are expected to do is to provide some kind of solution to the eternal problems of death and suffering.

The idea of a need for meaning is not universally accepted. Bainbridge and Stark (1981), among others, have challenged the view that humans always possess a worldview, a 'value-orientation', or a meaning system. Bibby (1983) stated that many Canadians, possibly a majority, achieve integration in their lives in the absence of identifiable meaning systems. Some of the findings reported in Chapter 7 show that cognitive needs are not the primary motives for conversion.

Cognitive styles: evolutionary optimism

We may conclude that the optimistic view of existence, characteristic of most religions, may have much to do with the considerable benefits to believers in terms of health and happiness (Chapter 10). As reported in Chapter 9, Sethi and Seligman (1993) found that fundamentalism is quite strongly associated with optimism, hope, and absence of self-blame, when comparisons are made with more liberal groups.

While the benefits of optimism are significant, and it may have real evolutionary value, it may sometimes reach levels that are too high to be useful. Schumaker (1990, 1995) offers evidence to support the view that religion is both an inevitable part of our evolutionary heritage, and an induced form of irrationality. It is easy to point out that many religious beliefs (e.g. transubstantiation in the Roman Catholic church) may be construed as delusions. The findings reported in Chapter 9 regarding suggestibility also support this hypothesis.

Cognitive styles: religion as art

As predicted, findings show a similarity in the nature of the audience for both art and religion. In most societies the audience for both religion and art is largely made up of women, while the creators of both art and religion are men (see Chapter 8). Looking at art and related processes leads to insights about one of the persistent questions in the contemporary research on religion: the question of effects or consequences. The effects of religious rituals and beliefs can be compared to the effects of art. There is an obviously satisfying quality about art, but we would not expect this to affect one's behaviour outside the specific artistic setting, such as a theatre or a museum (Beit-Hallahmi, 1989). There should be only minimal behavioural consequences to artistic experience, because it provides only an imaginary solution to behavioural problems. Religion and art turn out to be similarly expressive, not instrumental.

Response to anxiety

The claim that religious faith is an anxiety-reducing mechanism seems to be sustained by the findings, as it seems to provide humans with a feeling of security (McCrae, 1984). Much of the data reported above on personality and religiosity, on deprivation and its effects, and on individual and social integration is relevant to this explanation (Chapters 9–11). The evidence presented in Chapter 7 on converts is directly relevant, as conversion seems to reduce anxiety and provide confidence.

Fear of death

The predictions and findings may be summarized as follows (see Chapter 10):

1 All religious traditions are preoccupied with death and the denial of death through ideas about the eternal soul, survival following physical death, resurrection, and the Millennium, when death will be abolished. Most religious texts, prayers and rituals mention death and the next world, or reincarnation. The energy invested in these beliefs and activities can be interpreted as an attempt to relieve anxiety.
2 It would be expected that people would become progressively more religious as they get older. As has been shown, there is an increasing amount of religious concern from the age of sixty onwards; there is also increasing belief in an after-life.
3 We have seen that older people (over 60) who are religious, and believe in an after-life, are also better adjusted and happier. They are less apprehensive about death, and even look forward to it.
4 It would be expected that the after-life to which people look forward would be a pleasant one. Most of those who do believe in an after-life think that it will either be like this one, or will be a pleasanter version of life. On the other hand, some religious individuals say that they believe in hell, which would not be expected at all on the present theory. Belief of hell requires some further explanation. Life is manifestly unfair, so that punishments as well as rewards are needed in the after-life, and hell is usually reserved for other people. A second explanation

of hell would be that some people have such strong guilt feelings that they feel in need of further punishment. If this mechanism operates at all it probably applies to a minority of people.

5 It would be predicted that people exposed to great danger would become more religious, and there is some evidence supporting this notion.

Childhood effects

Much of the findings summarized below on the projection and on social learning hypotheses is relevant to the question of childhood effects. The effects of parental beliefs have been found to be more important than any other factor in determining individual religiosity (Chapter 6). In general, early learning and socialization may be more important than any other variable.

Conversion (see Chapter 7), while representing a rebellion, is still determined by parenting (Ullman, 1982). Moreover, findings show that the images of god are similar to images of parents, particularly to opposite sex parents. The quality and content of early bonding to the parents affect both individual religiosity levels and religious mythology. Thus, Kirkpatrick and Shaver (1990) found a connection between avoidant attachments to the mother and religiosity. Jacobs (1989) considered new religions as surrogates for the idealized nuclear family, which often fail. In one of the most original studies in the psychology of religion (see Chapter 3), Hood *et al.* (1991) tested Carroll's (1986) hypothesis about the origin of the Catholic cult of the Virgin Mary. Early maternal bonding was related to a preference for the images of both a suffering Christ and an erotic/nurturing Virgin Mary.

The projection hypothesis

We have described (Chapter 2) two major traditions of theorizing about projection, one emphasizing the projection of social realities and the other the projection of individual personality dynamics. Reflective (consonance) theories find their evidence in historical, sociological, and anthropological data, where the correspondence between social structure and symbolic systems is found. Psychological research attempts to find projection on the personality level, looking at individuals as the locus of interaction.

Historical, sociological, and anthropological evidence

It was Durkheim who said that any deity was a reflection of the whole society. And this observation started a tradition, consisting of literally hundreds of studies. The variety and quantity of cases, presented by historians, anthropologists, and sociologists, is quite striking in the constitency of its conclusions. Only a few of those could be cited here, by way of illustration. Cultural belief systems are found to match and reflect a view of the whole social system, or individuals' social class positions. Thus,

> It might be said of the Brethren, that . . . their worship of God is worship of the community . . . the assembly appears as a form of the Deity . . . The community . . . has a sense of special sanctity from which individual and household sanctity is derived.
>
> (Wilson, 1967, p. 336)

Swanson (1960, 1967) showed that spiritual beings worshipped in any society were related to the socio-political structure of that society. Monotheism was mostly found in societies 'where . . . there are three or more types of sovereign groups ranked in hierarchical order' (Swanson, 1960, p. 64–5). Economic complexity was found to be correlated with the presence of high gods (Underhill, 1975), and so both economic and political complexity were causal in the creation of high gods (cf. Lemert, 1974; Sheils, 1980; Simpson, 1984).

In ancient Greece, the gods reflected actual social structures (Harrison, 1927), and in ancient Egypt the after-life was imagined as a perfect copy of daily life. In ancient China, the spirit world followed government structures:

> Already by the Han (206 BC–AD 220) the netherworld was thought of as a 'subterranean spirit administration' governed by bureaucratic strictures. The pantheon of Taoist transcendence (*hsien*) . . . that took form centuries after the fall of the Han was modeled after the Han bureaucracy.
>
> (Gregory and Ebrey, 1993, p. 9)

In a study of 19th century US revivalism, Thomas (1989) states that the notion of individual responsibility for one's salvation did correspond to a general cultural myth of individualism, and to the reality of 'rugged individualism' in the developing capitalist marketplace.

Moffatt (1979) found exact parallels between the human hierarchy of the caste system in India and the imaginary divine hierarchy of gods and goddesses. The Rastafari movement in Jamaica was interpreted as a fantasy compensation by Kitzinger (1969). This movement is male-dominated, and this comes as a reaction to the practically matriarchal lower class Jamaican society that members came from. They create a world which denies their past experience. In the Ethiopian Orthodox tradition heaven is imagined as a hierarchical order, much like their social world in reality (Hoben, 1970). Looking at the African Tallensi religion, Fortes (1959, p. 78) concluded that its beliefs are 'extrapolations of the experiences generated in the relationship between parents and children'.

The literature on social class differences in religiosity may also be interpreted as demonstrating isomorphic projection of social conditions, reflecting the complex of norms and roles which make up 'middle class' or 'lower class' culture in various societies (see Chapter 8). Lewis (1966) found that in cases of spirit possession, individuals whose social status is marginal (women, serfs) are possessed by spirits marginal to the main pantheon. This is interpreted as a compensation, but Douglas (1973) suggests that it may be better understood as an accurate projection of their situation. This replication theory of religious action was used by Wilson and Clow (1981) to explain the main Pentecostal ritual of possession as a way of dealing with the lack of control experienced by the lower class believers in their daily lives.

Psychological evidence

The basic similarity underlying world mythologies, together with cultural variations in myth and ritual, support isomorphic notions of projection. According to Kurtz (1992), Hindu believers regard all goddesses as the multiple identities of a single Mother Goddess, reflecting the early experiences of being raised by many 'mothers' in the Indian family, a social–psychological complex projected into religious beliefs (cf. Harlan, 1992). The notion of religious beliefs and objects as projections of family and personality dynamics, not just as isomorphic reflections but as fantasy solutions, has not been tested directly very often. There is an inherent difficulty in testing a mechanism which is defined as unconscious and cannot be directly observed. Most studies measure the perception of religious objects by respondents, not direct projection. The latter is inferred from similarities in description.

Looking at the proliferation of religious images in world religions, we find a majority of anthropomorphisms, using humanlike images of fathers, mothers, and brothers, and a minority of zoomorphisms, where animals, such as monkeys, cows, and elephants, are addressed in worship. In all religions gods (even when zoomorphic) are so obviously humanlike that little formal testing is needed. References to 'Our Father in heaven','Holy Mother' and 'the Holy Family' are frequent in prayers and sermons (Warner, 1961). It might be argued that these references in themselves lend support to the family projection hypothesis, even without any further psychological findings. The idea of authority is expressed through a father-figure. A look at world religions shows clearly that a majority of religious objects are father figures or male authority figures, with plenty of cultural references to them in this way (cf. Foster and Keating, 1992).

If Jones (1926) is correct, then family issues will play a major role in religious mythology and ritual. This is indeed the case (Brown, 1991; Kluckhohn, 1959). Stories about religious heroes are quite similar everywhere; they often start with a miraculous birth (Rank, 1914). Buddha, Krishna, Moses, Jesus all share similar biographies in these myths (Dundes, 1981). Psychoanalytic studies of specific myths and belief systems claim that Oedipal guilt is central to religion and is expressed in the Garden of Eden story, where opposition to the father and knowledge of the primal scene are followed by shame and punishment. Not everybody is ready to adopt the psychoanalytic framework, but the evidence for the recurrence and repetition of certain themes all over the world is uncontrovertible (Beit-Hallahmi, 1996b; Caldwell, 1989; Campbell, 1981; Carroll, 1986, 1989; Obeyesekere, 1991; Rank, 1914).

Cross-cultural studies show consonance between cultural activities, child-rearing, parenting, and images of deities. Support for psychoanalytic formulations of parental and family projections are found in such studies as those by Spiro and D'Andrade (1958), using cross-cultural data, and by Larsen and Knapp (1964), using semantic differential ratings of symbolic stimuli. Larsen and Knapp found that the deity image as rated by females was more benevolent, while males rated it as more punitive; they interpreted the difference as supporting the Oedipal theory of the origin of the deity image.

Cross-cultural studies also found that when parents are punitive religion includes punitive gods, while where parents are kinder they believe in loving gods (Lambert *et al.* 1959; Rohner, 1975; Spiro and D'Andrade, 1958). Terry (1971) found that monotheistic beliefs were associated with strong independence training. However, it is not clear from these studies which is the direction of causation; child-rearing does not necessarily generate the beliefs. The most obvious derivations of the parental projection hypothesis would lead us to examine supernatural beliefs in children and their developmental sequence. Findings by Deconchy (1967) show a clear and general upward trend.

The findings reported in Chapter 6 seem to offer additional corroboration of the earlier ones for adults, and are quite consistent with the parental-projection hypothesis. While only one study gives clear support to the paternal-projection hypothesis in its original form, other studies indicate a considerable degree of maternal projection as well. We can conclude that the evidence presented so far does lend support to the hypothesis that parental projections play a part in the religious ideas of adolescents and adults in Western societies.

The findings which seem to indicate a general parental projection, rather than a specific paternal projection, bring us back to the original psycho-analytic formulations. How do these stand now in the light of the findings? The empirical findings can be summarized by saying that they give definite support to ideas about the impact of family relationships on religious ideas. Vergote *et al.* concluded: 'we may acknowledge an extraordinary analogy between the Oedipus structure and the structuring of the religious attitude'

(1969, p. 87). Freud's hypothesis regarding the special impact of the father image received only limited support, but broader notions such as those of Jones (1926) and Spiro and D'Andrade (1958) were closely supported.

The observed similarity between the image of god and the image of the opposite-sex or preferred parent lends support to the notion of the deity as a projected love-object, with positive qualities projected more than negative ones. Freud emphasized the ambivalence towards both father and god, while the respondents in most studies project a relatively positive picture.

Projection of maternal attributes seems to be another bit of evidence which goes against the original formulations. Freud himself admitted being 'at a loss to indicate the place of great maternal deities who perhaps everywhere preceded the paternal deities' (1913, p. 247). Maternal projections do provide partial, but significant, support for psychoanalytic object relations theory, which implies that early contacts with the mother contribute to the image of the imaginary love object in religion.

The validity of Freud's theory of the ultimate origin of religion will not be established by psychological studies of contemporary individuals. They only suggest that psychological mechanisms similar to those involved in a historical creation of religion can be shown to exist and operate (cf. Freeman, 1968). The findings support the Kardiner and Linton theory (1939) of religion as a 'projective system'. At the same time, perceptions of oneself may also play a role. As reported in Chapter 9, positive attitudes towards the self are correlated with positive attitudes towards the image of god (Benson and Spilka *et al.* 1975).

The father-projection hypothesis can be tested in the real world due to recent developments in which the Great Mother image, or neuter images of gods, are adopted by feminist groups. The prediction derived from this hypothesis is that such images will be unattractive to believers, and are destined to remain minority options. Another prediction, backed by findings (Chapter 8), is that Great Mother images will be more attractive to men, rather than to their target audience.

Super-ego projection and guilt

A direct test of the super-ego projection hypothesis was carried out by Rasmussen and Charman (1995). A questionnaire measure of super-ego strength correlated 0.60 with religiosity, and the hypothesis was clearly supported. If indeed the super-ego is projected heavenward, and if the instincts are opposed by the super-ego in religious people, this should result in a decrease of the forbidden instinctual activity. Indeed we find much data connecting religiosity to impulse control. Religiosity is negatively correlated with sexual activity, which is lower for the devout, whether Catholics, Protestants or Jews. Religion is widely recognized as an effective impulse control system, based on the conscious use of guilt. Guilt feelings are strongest in those whose parents use strict discipline and are stronger in females than in males (Wright, 1971). They have often been interpreted as the direction of aggression towards the self, and there is evidence that it is connected with internal conflicts (Flugel, 1945; Rosenzweig, 1945).

Confirmation of another kind is provided by Unwin's study (1934) of 80 preliterate societies: he rated each society for the degree of restriction on sexual behaviour and for the development of religion; the two variables were found to be highly correlated with each other. Aggressive behaviour too would be expected to be lower in religious people: research shows that regular ritual attenders are less delinquent, though this is not true of those who merely hold orthodox beliefs.

If religious behaviour is derived from the super-ego, religion should have an irrational, implacable, super-ego quality about it. There are several ways in which this proves to be true. Gods are often perceived as forbidding, punishing figures. Funk (1956) discovered that a majority of students thought that they were not as strict in their religion as they ought to be, and wished that they were perfectly sure that religion was true, while Wright and Cox (1967) found that religiosity correlated with severity of moral judgments. Secondly, religion always has an ethical flavour, in which powerful moral demands are made, and sin is condemned. In most human cultures, morality is perceived and experienced as closely tied to religiosity, even though the relationship is complex (Chapter 10).

The effects of the hypothesized super-ego projection and guilt feelings could be tested by looking at religious practices, and there we find that mortifying the body and controlling the impulses are central to most religions. Self-blame is found in all religions, in prayers and confessions, and considered a virtue. An individual feeling of sinfulness and worthlessness is pervasive and even recommended in most religious traditions. Sacrifice (see Chapter 4) is another way of placating the super-ego. It is clear that sin, guilt, punishment, atonement, right and wrong, good and evil, and forgiveness are major themes in religious discourse everywhere. For many, these themes make up the essence of religion, thus validating human morality. Beliefs in the devil and in demons, common to most religious traditions, offer reduction of guilt by projecting blame on external agents, which is sanctioned by the religious community (cf. Bilu and Beit-Hallahmi, 1989; Ward and Beaubrun, 1980). The role of the projection of guilt in religious rituals was presented in Chapter 4.

Sexuality and religion

There is evidence, mainly from case studies and observation, regarding the role of sexual impulses in various forms of religious ritual and religious experience. Scenes of sexual excitement during religious rituals are rare today, but by no means non-existent. La Barre (1962) reports sexual responses displayed by women members of a snake-handling cult during services. More sublimated forms of sexual expression can be observed in more reserved groups of believers. The clearest instance of a sexual content to religious activities is provided by some of the testimonies of classical saints and mystics. As demonstrated by Leuba (1925) and Thouless (1923), many of the writings are full of scarcely disguised sexual symbolism. When we consider that these people had no overt sexual satisfaction at all, it seems very likely that frustration is partly responsible for their religious activities. Thouless (1923) regards the great emphasis placed on chastity as evidence of the sexual basis of religion.

Religious literature throughout history has been filled with descriptions of love, devotion and yearning, which must be regarded as related to human experiences of intimacy and attachment. Not only the famous mystics but also common believers in every age have expressed erotic urges through their religious devotion. Observations offered by psychoanalytic object relations theory (Klauber, 1974) and attachment theory (Kirkpatrick, 1992) seem especially relevant here, as they refer to the general need for an object, rather than a purely sexual impulse.

The evidence presented on sex differences (Chapter 8) and on sex and marriage (Chapter 10) is relevant to the question of sexual motivation. We have seen the lower overall level of sexual activity in the devout. We have also seen that women, who are less free to express their sexual impulses, score higher than men on all measures of religiosity. Throughout history women have invested much energy in religious devotion, and this has sometimes reached what has been called hysterical frenzy. It seems possible that this devotion was motivated in part by diverted sexual energy, which otherwise could not be expressed.

On the basis of a study correlating sexual attitudes and religiosity, Mol (1970) suggested that religion and sex are alternative forms of commitment, and that sexual indulgence is a form of self-enhancement which is competitive with religious activities. Wallin (1957) and Wallin and Clark (1964) showed that religiosity decreased the impact of women's lack of sexual gratification on their reported satisfaction with marriage. This was interpreted as meaning that religious activity provided a substitute for sexual satisfaction in marriages, and more so for women than for men. We have seen that a higher level of religiosity is correlated with a lower level of sexual activity, which supports the hypothesis that religious activities and sexual activities may be alternative ways of satisfying similar needs. Sudden conversions during adolescence may be due to sexual guilt feelings which come to a height during this time. It should also be remembered that old age is the most religious time of life, when the sexual instinct is greatly weakened.

Social learning

To the question, 'Why do people believe in God?', the best answer remains: 'Because they have been taught to believe in God'.

Religious behaviour and beliefs are clearly and absolutely conditioned by culture and society. This may sound like a truism, but it is an important and elementary truth that tends to be quite often neglected. Social learning, despite its seeming simplicity (and maybe because of it), remains the best explanation for the overall prevalence of religion, for individual religiosity, and for the most varied and most dramatic of religious experiences (Spanos and Hewitt, 1979). Findings presented throughout this book provide direct evidence for the social learning theory, and show in detail how the learning takes place (Chapters 6, 7, 11). It is found, for example, that children acquire beliefs from their parents, particularly if they like them and continue to live at home. Religious attitudes and beliefs are modified by membership in educational and other social groups, in the same way that other attitudes are affected. The variety of religious traditions and the correspondence between the tradition of the social environment and the religious beliefs of the individual are the most obvious proofs to the validity of the social learning approach.

There is no religious behaviour without a prior exposure to specific religious ideas. Actually, as we look closer at more unusual and 'esoteric' religious actions it becomes clear that they are socially learned, just like the less esoteric ones (see Chapters 5, 7). We see that the contents of mystical visions, the most intense and personal of religious involvements, is wholly predictable from the exposure to certain ideas, which are always learned. Visions of the Holy Virgin occur exclusively among Roman Catholics or those exposed to Catholic ideas. It has never occurred among orthodox Moslems, and we understand why. There is much evidence to show that the content of mystical experiences depends on the beliefs which are held beforehand, and that the stigmata have occurred as a result of suggestion in hysterical personalities. No one experienced this before St Francis in the early thirteenth century, though several hundred have done so since that time (Whitelock and Hynes, 1978). Even in the most dramatic cases of religious conversion, there is no acceptance of new belief systems without prior exposure.

While there is a good deal of evidence in support of the social learning theory, its limitations are obvious. In the first place, it cannot account for any of the very considerable individual differences in religious activity within the culture, variations due to age or personality in particular. This is because the theory shows how religion is passed on but does not show the motivational forces maintaining it: behaviour is not learned unless a need is satisfied, though several different ways of satisfying the same need may be learned. The theory obviously provides one important postulate of a more complete account. Sex differences can be partly explained: females become better socialized during childhood than males. Personality effects in religion are not very great, as we have seen.

The other important limitation of the theory is that it predicts, if anything, that all religious movements will remain unchanged by time; it cannot account for the initiation of new movements or for the decline of old ones. New religious movements are of great interest today, because here we can observe new movements being born and we can then see them growing and changing.

Identity and self-esteem as factors

Much of the evidence presented above on socialization and social learning is relevant to the hypothesis of viewing religion as identity (Chapters 6, 7, 11). For most believers and most humans, identities are ascribed and prescribed, not chosen. As we have pointed out more than once, most believers are 'accidental': they have been born into a tradition. They do not have to do much to retain membership, and they do not have a choice or a chance to consider the content of their identity (Beit-Hallahmi, 1989). Religious identity, which prescribes many behaviours, has nothing to do with decision, choice, belief, or personality. This may be related to the paucity of findings relating personality and religion in the general population.

Under secularization, identity is much more persistent than any kind of religious practice (Winter and Short, 1993). Group loyalty and mutual assistance have an obvious survival value, and are expressed through group identity. Other identities are avoided and derided. Most humans during most of history have never known any identity or culture other than their own.

One essential feature of a living religion is the community, the feeling of partnership and belonging, which brings about real gratification to members. This collective aspect is often felt as the most powerful. Religion creates a real community, not just an imagined one, through rituals, identity definitions, life together, limitations on interactions. Much effort is put into behaviours which mark identity boundaries. Acts of exclusion determine the identity of large and small groups, and social categorization is highly effective in creating barriers and out-group under-valuation.

> a religion, even if it calls itself the religion of love, must be hard and unloving to those who do not belong to it. Fundamentally indeed every religion is in the same way a religion of love for all those whom it embraces; while cruelty and intolerance towards those who do not belong to it are natural to every religion.
>
> (Freud, 1921, p. 98).

We have seen that religiosity is tied indeed to ethnocentrism, discrimination, prejudice, and anti-democratic ideas.

The connection between identity and self-esteem, which may be responsible for some of the beneficial effects of religiosity for individuals (Chapter 10), is responsible also for some of the destructive effect of religion as a group phenomenon. Certain beliefs carry special power, such as being chosen and special, and are found everywhere, leading to great similarities in the content of religious and national mythologies. Belief in the group's superiority (and the consequent inflated self-esteem) is likely to be threatened and thus lead to violence (Baumeister *et al.* 1996). This seems highly relevant to numerous religious wars, conflicts, and prejudices, as well as to similar effects of secular identities and ideologies.

Deprivation hypotheses

The validity of the deprivation–compensation hypothesis can be tested by trying to locate those who are more deprived, those 'oppressed creatures', as Marx put it, and see if they are more religious, compared with others. Support for the deprivation–compensation view of religious activity has been offered in both individual context (religiosity and religious activity as reactions to individual frustration) and in the sociological–historical context (religious groups as organized attempts to deal with felt deprivation).

Historians tend to tie the appearance of religious fervour to preceding problems and difficulties:

> at the time of the First Crusade of 1095 the areas which were swept by mass enthusiasm had for ten years been afflicted by famine and drought and for five years by plague, while the crusades of 1146, 1309, and 1320 were all precluded by famines.
>
> (Cohn, 1962, p. 34)

And Trevor-Roper described

> that stock refuge of the oppressed: mysticism, the Messiah, the Millennium. . . . as the Anabaptists of the seventeenth century manipulated their Scriptural logarithms to hasten the Apocalypse, so also the Jews of the Dispersion deviated into mystical heresies, counted the days to the Millennium, or discovered the Messiah.
>
> (Trevor-Roper, 1963, pp. 148–9)

Apparitions of the Virgin Mary in Roman Catholic communities have also been tied to times of crisis in marginal regions of Europe (Blackbourn, 1994). The Voodoo religion of Haiti flourishes under the conditions of the worst possible deprivation, in one the world's poorest countries (Deren, 1953). Even in the most advanced economies in the world, this effect has been observed. Harris (1981) suggested that in the USA religious awakenings in the twentieth century were the result of frustration with the lack of worldly progress in society. The failure of the American Dream to become reality, has pushed Americans in the direction of magical and supernatural solutions. (cf. Smith, 1986; Anderson, 1979). Within US society, it is clear that religious fundamentalism is tied to low income and lower education in individuals (Kosmin and Lachman, 1993). On p. 130 we saw how the appearance of NRMs is tied to frustration.

Deprivation may lead to a certain type of religiosity. Marx described the projective element in religion not as a reflection of reality but as an 'inverse world', in which fantasy compensates for real suffering (Marx and Engels, 1957). From this claim we would predict that such fantasy gratification will be part of religious beliefs among deprived social groups (Chapters 8, 11). If we look at economic conditions worldwide, it is easy to see that religiosity is higher in less developed nations (a population of 3.2 billions and per caput income of $390 in 1994), as compared to the wealthy North (a population of 850 million, per caput income of $24,170). Higher per caput income is tied to higher life expectancy, lower infant mortality, no illiteracy, and secularization.

Turning to individuals, our findings (Chapters 7, 8, 11) demonstrate that there is a relationship between measures of deprivation and traditional beliefs in most populations studied. The effects of social deprivation in the case of individuals are quite clear. Findings reported in Chapter 7 about individuals (conversion) and groups (NRMs) are highly relevant.

Autobiographical accounts of converts (Beit-Hallahmi, 1992) tell of suffering and confusion which preceded their reported salvation. Glock *et al.* (1967) found that individuals who were older, female, unmarried, having a low income or less education were more likely to be religiously involved. Campbell and Fukuyama (1970) defined social deprivation on the basis of age, sex, education, socio-economic status, and place of residence (rural or urban). They found that traditional beliefs and devotional orientation (but not formal participation) were stronger among older people, females, less educated people, the poor, and the rural, and concluded that social deprivation was related to a style of religious activity emphasizing devotion and traditional beliefs. In a study of American Roman Catholics, Christopher *et al.* (1971) used a similar index of social deprivation, using measures of sex, age and education, which was found to be positively correlated with several measures of religiosity.

Consumers of religious services through the electronic media in Southern USA are more likely to be older, female, lower class, with less education (Stacey and Shupe, 1982), and a 1978 US Gallup Poll showed that unmarried females were more likely than others to believe in 'paranormal phenomena' (cf. Wuthnow, 1976). Hunter (1983) found that support for Christian doctrinal Orthodoxy in the USA was highest among women and retired men, with low education and income, living in rural areas of the South and Midwest. Religious involvement offers the frustrated and oppressed compensatory social status, definite norms, and an attractive set of values. Nottingham (1954) suggested that the beliefs associated with the Hindu caste system developed to ease its obvious stresses. It is believed that a position in the system is merited by performance in previous incarnations; social discontent is averted by these beliefs. The proposition that beliefs are generated to relieve the frustrations in the social–political order has some support. Kardiner (1945) traced the development of Jewish–Christian beliefs in these terms, and Pfister (1948) demonstrated that Jewish and Christian communities have always become ritualistic in times of stress.

Many people get adjusted to their economic and social status, and only experience frustration. Lenski (1953) found that people who had moved downwards in social status were more interested in religion than those who had kept the same position, or those who had moved upwards. According to the present hypothesis underprivileged minority groups should be more religious than other people. It is the case that African-Americans, for example, are considerably more religious than the majority population and it should be noted that their religion tends to be of the sect type (Chapter 8).

The greater level of membership and attendance among those with higher socio-economic status in some countries (especially in the USA and Great Britain) has been used as an argument against the validity of deprivation theories of religiosity. This argument can be countered on two grounds: first, the nature of middle class religious activity and, second, the possibility that it may still be a response to some kind of deprivation. As shown above, most middle class religiosity is a rather formal and secularized affair, compared to the intensely emotional religiosity of the lower classes and minority groups. Goode (1966), after studying class differences in religiosity in Great Britain, suggested that attendance should not be used as a measure of religious behaviour since it has become a totally secular activity, another voluntary group activity. If middle class ritual attendance is indeed a voluntary social activity, as many observers suggest, then it fits quite well with Glock's (1964) view of church-type organizations as responding to social deprivation (Table 2.3). Carlos (1970), in studying religious activities in the suburbs of large cities in the USA, suggested the satisfaction of social needs as explaining the higher rates of ritual attendance there. Spiritualist groups in the English-speaking world have been described as a response to specific middle class alienation experiences (Wagner, 1983).

Health problems, more prevalent among them, are likely to be one factor motivating African-Americans towards greater religious involvement (Ferraro and Koch, 1994). Another illustration of the role of organismic deprivation in religious activities is supplied by the case of Christian Science. This is a middle class group with branches in most Western nations, described by Wilson (1970) as manipulationist, offering its members relief for a specific problem. Since the problem which Christian Science deals with is illness, we can expect sect members to be suffering from health problems and other deprivation.

England (1954), in a study of Christian Science testimonial letters, found that most of the letters came from elderly females who suffered from a variety of physical and mental problems, some of which would be regarded as psychosomatic or hysterical. Table 12.1 shows two aspects of Christian Science membership: being female and concerned with health. A similar pattern of being female, older, and having health problems was found by Haywood (1983) in middle class Spiritualist groups in the USA (Nelson, 1972). Miller (1995) showed that in Japan age was positively related to belief in spirits and gods and chronic illness led to an increased belief in after-life. The greater religious activity of women everywhere may be due to general and specific frustrations. Women as a group are less educated, and wield much less economic and political power, thus being less able to satisfy personal needs and ambitions.

Table 12.1 Factors sustaining interest in Christian Science, by sex and problem

	Sex	
Problem	Male (%)	Female (%)
Health	75 (79.8)	392 (96.5)
Other	19 (20.2)	14 (3.5)
Total	94	406

Note: χ^2 = 33.85 significant at the 0.05 level
Source: England (1954)

Despite the mass of evidence which seems to support deprivation explanations, reservations about this approach should be mentioned. They raise two main issues: first, there are many cases where deprivations and frustrations are far from obvious, and then they are just assumed to exist, in a circular way; second, studies using deprivation as an explanation do not usually specify the pathways leading from the cause to the religious response. As we mentioned above, deprivation is used to explain secular responses as well, but only rarely can we find a description of what led to a specific response rather than another.

Personality factors

Brown (1962) in a study of 203 Australian students found that orthodox religious beliefs correlated with authoritarianism and positive attitudes to the church, but not with any familiar personality variables. It was concluded that it was social learning and attitudes, rather than personality, that were related to strength of belief. However, findings reported in Chapter 9 show that religiosity is related to several personality variables, such as suggestibility, authoritarianism, dogmatism, and self-esteem.

Differences in religious activity between men and women must be related to the evidence for personality differences between the sexes (Chapter 8). Research on sex differences finds that women are more submissive, passive, anxious and dependent. They are also more affiliative and nurturant, and guilt-prone. Such 'female' traits could well lead to greater religiosity. Thompson (1991) found that both men and women who had a feminine self-image were more religious. Attachment theory (Kirkpatrick, 1992) assumes a relationship between early bonding styles, which become stable personality traits, and religious involvements.

There is general agreement in the literature that personality predispositions play a role in the more dramatic and exceptional cases of religious behaviour (see Chapter 5). While they represent a statistical minority, their impact is out of proportion to their number, especially when they involve leaders and mobilize groups. As we have seen in Chapters 5 and 7, personality and psychopathology play some role in the great dramas and enigmas of religious life. High involvement religiosity means personalizing the religious message, which both energizes and is tied to pathology.

Individual integration

On the positive side there are several consistent findings (Chapter 10). Moderate, but positive, effects of religiosity on mental and physical health have been found. Church members and church attenders in the USA are better adjusted on measures of psychiatric impairment, and religious activity is positively related to adjustment in old age. Regular church attenders also enjoy better physical health and are less likely to commit suicide. They are less likely than the non-religious to abuse alcohol, and are better adjusted in marriage. Religious individuals may be able to face better some life crises and especially death. In addition, members of sect-type groups are probably helped by being given an identity as members of a spiritual élite, by an acceptable interpretation of their underprivileged position, and by cathartic group experiences. Members of low-involvement groups ('middle class' style, as described in Chapter 8) are possibly also supported in terms of individual identity and community feeling. On the whole, the religious message of hope and optimism seems to have a real impact. The belief in a supernatural sanction apparently creates a special effect in terms of comradeship, solidarity, and 'we-feeling'. Religious communities seem to create special bonds among members. Both Freud (1921) and Durkheim (1915) stated that a special kind of loyalty and commitment is created by the religious message, as it is expressed through a living community.

On the negative side (i.e. religion as related to deficient personality integration), there are the following findings. Religiosity has been found to be tied to narrowness of perspective, reflected in authoritarianism and dogmatism. Religious people have been found to be more suggestible and dependent. A high degree of religious orthodoxy is likely to interfere with scientific achievement and may be tied to some sex problems.

Social integration

Hypotheses regarding the positive effects of religion in social integration can be assessed at two levels, the communal and the societal. In the first case, we look at a congregation or community. In the second case, we look at whole societies. The effects of religion as an integrative force could be observed in cases of religious uniformity or plurality in small groups or small societies. Such minor societies are created, for example, when a utopian community separates from the larger society around it (Stephan and Stephan, 1973). The beneficial effects of membership in a congregation have been reported above (Chapters 9–11) and they are quite clear.

Deprivation–compensation explanations (see p. 244) state that religion contributes to overall societal and institutional integration by offering relief from various strains and tensions. To the challenge of cohesion and integration for both individuals and groups, religion responds by offering coherence and meaning. Religious innovations, rather than being disruptive, end up re-integrating potential deviants (e.g. Bord and Faulkner, 1983). While the positive findings are clear for small, well-defined groups, and could have been predicted on the basis of what we know about group dynamics, it has only a limited application to wider and larger societies.

Religious communities may maintain cohesion by directing all aggression towards out-groups and non-believers, but this may cause friction in a society which contains more than one such community. History provides many examples where religious differences have been the cause of divisions and conflicts. The potential of religion as a divisive factor was observed in the findings on ethnocentrism and politics (Chapter 11). One might say that religious uniformity in any society is a cohesive factor, which is certainly true, but societies where such a uniformity is possible are becoming rare. Religion as a force for social harmony is very much in evidence in traditional societies. Thus, research on the religious beliefs and behaviours of the Harijan ('untouchables') in India showed that they share the beliefs and religious ideals of the upper castes, though some of their rituals obviously must differ. This consensus enables the caste system, with its self-evident inequalities, to survive, and Indian society to function (Moffatt, 1979). In modern societies the integrative role of religion is clearly diminished. The extent of secularization in the industrialized world tends to cast doubt on the idea that modern societies are indeed integrated through a central religious value system. Eister (1957) showed that general theories about the integrative and supportive functions of religion do not lend themselves to easy confirmation in a complex secularized society, and that most of the evidence goes against them. Fenn (1978) made a convincing case for the argument that modern society is not held together by a common set of values; and that if there is such a set of values, it is not a religious one. While social control in secularized societies seems to be quite effective, other mechanisms, such as the mass media, have taken the place of religion as controller and as integrator.

If we regard individual and social conformity and conservatism as contributing to social integration and stability, the evidence is both plentiful and convincing to show that religiosity is related to both. Evidence presented above shows that religious people tend to be more conservative politically, and to support existing social arrangements. The evidence linking religiosity and conservative social attitudes extends across the areas of ethnocentrism, social issues and political attitudes.

We have seen that, among members of the lower class and of minority groups in modern societies, those who are more religious tend to accept their social and economic circumstances more easily. The kind of other-worldly religious activities that disadvantaged people engage in seems to be more committed and more psychologically involving. There is a great deal of emotionality, and Wilson (1966) suggested that 'the opportunity for emotional expression in the religious context might be seen as a deflection of concern from social inequalities' (p. 105).

While most of the findings indicate that religious involvement would tend to steer a person away from improving his or her situation in this world, religious involvement may lead to improvement via conformity and better adjustment. Schwartz (1970), for example, showed that in some instances religious reactions to deprivation may be instrumental in changing the real world. Moreover, several investigators have suggested that some 'deviant' religious movements socialize or resocialize their members in the direction of the central norms of society, and in this way contribute to an improved adjustment of their members (see p. 114). Johnson (1961) showed that some sect-type groups help to resocialize their members according to middle class values with their emphasis on 'clean living' and asceticism. This in turn helps members in their daily lives and improves their economic situation. Holt (1940) similarly described sects as helping in adjustment to the social environment.

Those who are more religious tend to be more conforming and less deviant, *vis-à-vis* society in general. We may also expect them to feel more integrated and less alienated. If we assume that religion helps social integration, then we should expect those who are better integrated in the society to exhibit a greater degree of religiosity. This hypothesis was tested by Swanson (1971) who found that to some extent those who were more socially involved (i.e. members of the racial majority and native-born Americans) were more likely to accept some religious beliefs.

In summary, we are able to state that despite the decline of religion as a common belief system and a meaningful mechanism for integration in modern societies, some of its social effects as an integrative force can still be seen. When competing religious identities co-exist, conflict is likely. When we look jointly now at the contribution of religiosity to both individual and social integration, we encounter a paradox. At the individual integration level there is a large contribution, as well as at the small group level; when we move on to relations with other groups at the denomination level, problems arise. This is apparently the cost tied to the benefits of religious identity.

The search for the 'religious personality'

Something which the layperson expects of the psychologist studying religion is a psychological description of the religious person, rather than information about any social background variables. Can we offer a profile of the typical, modal, believer worldwide? The obstacles to the completion of this task have been many. Numerous studies have tried to contribute to the hoped-for psychological profile (see Beit-Hallahmi, 1989; Brown, 1973b), but so far the results seem disappointing. What we are able to conclude about the modal believer or religious person in Western societies today is that such a person is probably more conventional, more likely to be a female, older rather than younger, unmarried, more likely to be happier and optimistic, as well as authoritarian, dogmatic and suggestible, compared to the non-religious (Chapters 8, 9). As we stated above, gender has the strongest impact on religiosity across societies. The role of women in maintaining religion as a living institution should lead us to more research on the personality characteristics involved.

Why have the attempts to relate personality variables and religiosity been unsuccessful? A major reason may be that religiosity and religion are indeed, in many cases, connected to the identity level of individual functioning, i.e. the level connecting individual and collectivity, and not the personality level (Beit-Hallahmi, 1989). Does religion really affect the personality level of functioning or does it just operate at the identity level? There are high-involvement religious acts, such as conversion, to which personality traits and dynamics may be more relevant (see Chapter 7), but in most forms of mass religiosity social forces are more important.

The question of consequences in individual behaviour

Discovering the consequences of religiosity in non-religious activities is one of the knottiest problems in the psychology of religion. As Paloutzian (1996, p. 222) put it: 'Does religion predict behaviour?' The Glock (1962) model, described on p. 40, was originally made up of five dimensions: ideology, belief, knowledge, experience, and consequences. The consequential dimension dealt with the hypothesized effects of religiosity on conduct in other spheres. Later on, as the result of further research, the consequential dimension was dropped, the reason given that such consequences in non-religious behaviour could not be found, and only four dimensions have remained, and are widely used (Stark, 1984). The main reason for the expectation of consequences is that religious traditions quite explicitly predict those consequences. Religion exists for many believers as a prescriptive behaviour system, containing specific should and should nots. For many believers, religion is a proscriptive, not a prescriptive, system, and at the psychological level it is tied mainly to impulse control. The findings indicate that religion does have a considerable effect on secular behaviour in two areas: sexual behaviour and the use of legal (nicotine, alcohol) or illegal drugs (Gorsuch, 1995). In the first area the effects are tied to specific proscriptions; in the second area, we may hypothesize a wider impact of the impulse control tradition in religion. Generalizing beyond these specific areas has been difficult.

It is possible to find evidence of consequences when looking at specific ideological issues on which the religious group has taken a clear stand. Then, committed members do indeed follow the teachings in secular matters. Sometimes the consequences of beliefs are only other beliefs and attitudes, which should have some social consequences, as in politics. Bord and Faulkner (1975, p. 258) proposed that 'religious beliefs and socio-political attitudes will covary to the degree that the attitude object is specifically included in ongoing doctrinal . . . considerations.' Similarly, Hoge and de Zulueta (1985) showed that increased salience of religious beliefs led to evidence of social consequences of religious commitment. In other words, when individuals are reminded of the implications of their identity labels, they will follow them. But that is exactly the issue; the consequences should be evident even when individuals are not so reminded.

The expectation that religiosity would lead to some kind of a general social attitude in response to the traditional moral exhortations of religious representatives has not been supported by research. Religious people are not more likely to engage in positive social actions, to be more honest, or to be more generous (Chapter 10), and the well known findings about the positive correlation between religiosity and prejudice have been mentioned in this context. Religious people tend to be conservative in their general world view and to support the traditional beliefs of their cultures in non-religious areas (Chapter 11). The question of consequences is related to the question of the religious personality, which is the search for consequences on an individual personality level. Secularization means on the psychological level that there is less detectable influence of religion on individual personality and behaviour.

Stark (1984) suggested that consequences of religiosity are found when we look at aggregate, rather than individual, data, but even in that case the findings are limited. As religion is losing its social control functions (Gerharz, 1970) in both public and private life, we are likely to find the specific influences mentioned above, but not much more than that. It might also be that consequences were always found at group level, even before modern times, and religion was always a matter of identity for most people. In high-involvement religiosity, consequences are easy to see, and often quite remarkable. In Chapter 7, the positive effects of some conversions were noted.

The proven benefits of religiosity in individual mental health, physical health, happiness, optimism, and self-esteem, reported in Chapter 10, are not usually mentioned when the consequential dimension is discussed, but they should be. Most research on consequences has looked for intentional, conscious, and deliberate behaviours. These positive benefits in terms of health and happiness are unexpected and unpredicted in many of the traditional approaches, but will have to be considered. They may explain much of the contribution of religion to individual and social integration.

The search for pure religious motives: one or two psychologies of religiosity?

This issue was presented in Chapter 3 as the most important issue for psychological studies of religion. The search for 'pure' religious motivation, and the various attempts to measure intrinsic, high-involvement religiosity stem from basic observations regarding the two kinds of religiosity encountered in the real world. The separation of believers into a low-involvement majority and a high-involvement minority is not a modern phenomenon, and is not the result of secularization. We find different levels of commitment in all historical periods, in all types of groups. Even inside sect-type groups and NRMs we can observe the hard core of committed members and around them others at various degrees of commitment and marginality (see Chapter 7).

Converts and sect-type religious groups are inherently attractive to students of religion, because they demonstrate the reality of heightened religious motivation and commitment. Conversion because of marriage is not pure, but conversion because of an 'experience' or a vision is. Where there is a price to be paid, and serious sacrifices are made, when a person joins a despised minority, we are rightly impressed. Such cases are fascinating, but far from representative, and constitute much less than 1 per cent of believers and activities.

The notion of religion as identity religion vs. religion as art (Beit-Hallahmi, 1989) reflects this recognition of differing religious styles, which parallels notions of church vs. sect in sociology. Are these distinctions just quantitative or qualitative? Is the high-involvement phenomenon (religion of art, instrinsics, sect-type group) just a stronger case of majority religiosity (religion of identity, extrinsics, church-type group) or are we dealing with a difference in kind?

Looking at the findings presented above in relation to the search for 'pure' motivation leads to two conclusions:

1 The extensive research done by psychologists on the Intrinsic, Extrinsic, and Quest dimensions tells us much about a small minority, but leaves behind the silent majority of believers. We end up again where we started, with the possibility of limiting psychological explanations to a minority of cases.

2 Social and historical factors, summarized above under social learning and identity (and discussed also in Chapter 7 and on p. 242), can account for most of the phenomena we observe. The subject matter for the psychology of religiosity should indeed be high-involvement phenomena, and there are plenty of those to investigate: lower class, sect-type groups, messiahs, mystics, 'Cargo cults', and converts. But even these phenomena may never be 'pure' in terms of motives, which are always mixed. Our search for purity in this area may reflect an idealization, our own fantasies about real saints and real saintliness. Nevertheless, our studies of religious movements, religious experiences, virtuosi, and converts show that their religiosity is indeed qualitatively different. There seems to be an implicit consensus, expressed in many ways in the research literature, about the two psychologies of religious behaviour.

The special role of psychoanalysis

There are several approaches to religious behaviour which have generated much writing and research. In the psychological literature Freud's psycho-analysis stands out. It has been the source and inspiration of so many ideas and hypotheses that its special position tends to be overlooked. The impact of psychoanalytic ideas is in evidence not only in cases of explicit theoretical debt (Beit-Hallahmi, 1996b), but in writings that represent all academic traditions. What is striking in the literature we surveyed is that terms such as father projection, identification, super-ego, or Oedipal solution have become part of the language of the human sciences when dealing with religion. Most of the different hypotheses discussed above as explanations for religion and religiosity can be found in one form or another in classical psychoanalytic writings.

Despite the criticism that has accompanied classical psychoanalysis since its inception one hundred years ago, it seems that its notions about religion still hold centre stage in scholarly writings, and its ideas about sources of projections and deprivations are supported by numerous findings.

Moreover, psychoanalytic insights about universal features of mythology and ritual remain central to all scholarly discussions of these phenomena.

Religiosity: the scholarly consensus

What emerges from the literature is a consensus first about the over-determination or multiple causation of religiosity. But when we examine the literature in terms of causal explanations there is a common human sciences approach, in the disciplines of history, sociology, anthropology, and psychology, focusing on two factors: deprivation and projection. As shown above, most of the research reflects a preference for these explanations. We have pointed out more than once that deprivation explanations are not limited to research on religiosity, but are used to account for most human behaviours (Smelser, 1962).

Research on the causes, correlates and consequences of religiosity over the past century has yielded some findings which are consistent and stable. The final product of this effort are some useful generalizations, if not axioms, about religiosity rather than religion. Although we find it impossible to trace the historical starting point of religion as a human institution, we can say much about its functions and consequences. We can also say something about individual religiosity (Table 12.2).

Table 12.2 Individual religiosity: a general model

Pre-cultural factors and universal sources: evolutionary heritage, including attachment; neural 'hard wiring'; cognitive mechanisms
Gender
Cultural transmission
Class and community
Family influence: father and mother effects
Personality variables
Situational variables (stress, security)

There are some counter-intuitive findings which are important, not because they are surprising but because they challenge us to provide causal explanations. The findings regarding the greater religiosity of natural scientists and engineers, as compared to scholars in the 'softer' humanities are an example, as well as the greater religiosity of women, and their enormous weight in preserving religion, as compared to men. Some of the negative findings are as important. The lack of clear connections to major personality characteristics and the lack of evidence for behavioural consequences are also counter-intuitive.

The general model which emerges from the literature and from this book is one that starts with pre-cultural factors, and then with the roots of religiosity in culture. These roots are transmitted through the family, and then grow (if they do) into a unique form through being processed by the individual personality. Pre-cultural factors create readiness, culture determines content, while social class, family socialization, and personality determine involvement. These are the mechanisms mediating the behavioural manifestations of religiosity.

References

Aaronson, B.S. (1968). Hypnotic alterations of space and time. *Parapsychology, 10,* 5–36.

Aaronson, B.S., and Osmond, H. (eds) (1970). *Psychedelics: The Uses and Implications for Hallucinogenic Drugs.* Garden City, NY: Anchor Books.

Acock, A.C., and Bengtson, V.L. (1978). On the relative influence of mothers and fathers: A covariance analysis of political and religious socialization. *Journal of Marriage and the Family, 40,* 519–530.

Adityanjee, X. (1986). Suicide attempts and suicides in India: cross-cultural aspects. *International Journal of Social Psychiatry, 32,* 64–73.

Adlaf, E.M., and Smart, R.B. (1985). Drug use and religious affiliation, feelings and behavior. *British Journal of Addiction, 80,* 163–171.

Adler, A. (1956). *The Individual Psychology of Alfred Adler.* New York: Basic Books.

Adorno, T.W., Frenkel-Brunswik, E., Levinson, D.J., and Sanford, R.N. (1950). *The Authoritarian Personality.* New York: Harper & Row.

Alland, A. (1962). Possession in a revivalistic Negro church. *Journal for the Scientific Study of Religion, 1,* 204–213.

Allison, J. (1968). Adaptive regression and intense religious experience. *Journal of Nervous and Mental Diseases, 145,* 452–463.

Allison, J. (1969). Religious conversion: Regression and progression in an adolescent experience. *Journal for the Scientific Study of Religion, 8,* 23–38.

Allport, G.W. (1950). *The Individual and his Religion.* New York: Macmillan.

Allport, G.W. and Ross, J.M. (1967). Personal religious orientation and prejudice. *Journal of Personality and Social Psychology, 5,* 432–443.

Allport, G.W., Gillespie, J.M., and Young, J. (1948). The religion of the post-war college student. *Journal of Psychology, 25,* 3–33.

Almquist, E.M. (1966). Social class and religiosity. *Kansas Journal of Sociology, 2,* 990–999.

Alston, J.P., and Aguirre, B.E. (1979). Congregational size and the decline of sectarian commitment: The case of Jehovah's Witnesses in South and North America. *Sociological Analysis, 40,* 63–70.

Altemeyer, B., and Hunsberger, B. (1993). Reply to Gorsuch. *International Journal for the Psychology of Religion, 3,* 33–37.

Al-Thakeb, F., and Scott, J.E. (1982). Islamic fundamentalism: A profile of its supporters. *International Review of Modern Sociology, 12,* 175–195.

Altman, I., and Wohlwill, J. F. (eds) (1983). *Behavior and the Natural Environment.* New York: Plenum.

Alwin, D.F. (1986). Religion and parental child-rearing orientations: Evidence of a Protestant–Catholic convergence. *American Journal of Sociology*, *92*, 412–440.

Anderson, R.M. (1979). *Vision of the Disinherited: The Making of American Pentecostalism*. New York: Oxford University Press.

Anderson, R.M. (1987). Pentecostal and charismatic Christianity. *The Encyclopedia of Religion*, *11*, 228–235.

Antonovsky, A. (1979). *Health, Stress and Coping*. San Francisco, CA: Jossey-Bass.

Apprey, M. (1981). Family, religion and separation: The effort to separate in the analysis of a pubertal adolescent boy. *Journal of Psychoanalytic Anthropology*, *4*, 137–155.

Argyle, M. (1988). *Bodily Communication*. London: Methuen.

Argyle, M. (1989). *The Social Psychology of Work* (2nd edn). Harmondsworth: Penguin.

Argyle, M. (1992). *The Social Psychology of Everyday Life*. London: Routledge.

Argyle, M. (1994). *The Psychology of Social Class*. London: Routledge.

Argyle, M. (1996). *The Social Psychology of Leisure*. Harmondsworth: Penguin.

Argyle, M. (in press). *Psychology and Leisure*. Harmondsworth: Penguin.

Argyle, M., and Beit-Hallahmi, B. (1975). *The social psychology of religion*. London: Routledge & Kegan Paul.

Argyle, M., and Delin, P. (1965). Non-universal laws of socialization. *Human Relations*, *18*, 77–86.

Arjomand, S.A. (1986). Social change and movements of revitalization in contemporary Islam. In J.A. Beckford (ed.) *New Religious Movements and Rapid Social Change*. Newbury Park, CA: Sage.

Aronson, E., and Mills, J. (1959). The effect of severe initiation on liking for a group. *Journal of Abnormal and Social Psychology*, *59*, 177–181.

Astin, A.W. (1968). Personal and environmental determinants of student activism. *Measurement and Evaluation in Guidance*, *1*, pp. 149–62.

Back, C.W., and Bourque, L.B. (1970). Can feelings be enumerated? *Behavioral Science*, *15*, 487–496.

Baer, H.A. (1984). *The Black Spiritual Movement: A Religious Response to Racism*. Knoxville: University of Tennessee Press.

Baer, H.A. (1988). Black mainstream churches: Emancipatory or accommodative responses to racism and social stratification in American society? *Review of Religious Research*, *30*, 162–176.

Baer, H.A. and Singer, M. (1993). *African–American Religion in the Twentieth Century: Varieties of Protest and Accommodation*. Knoxville: University of Tennessee Press.

Bahr, H.M. (1981). Religious intermarriage and divorce in Utah and the mountain states. *Journal for the Scientific Study of Religion*, *20*, 251–261.

Bahr, H.M., and Martin, T.K. (1983). 'And thy neighbor as thyself': Self-esteem and faith in people as correlates of religiosity and family solidarity among Middletown high school students. *Journal for the Scientific Study of Religion*, *22*, 132–144.

Bainbridge, W.S. (1989). The religious ecology of deviance. *American Sociological Review*, *54*, 288–295.

Bainbridge, W.S., and Stark, R. (1981). The 'consciousness reformation' reconsidered. *Journal for the Scientific Study of Religion*, *20*, 1–16.

Bakan, P. (1971). The eyes have it. *Psychology Today*, *4*, 64–67.

Balch, R.W., and Taylor, D. (1976). Salvation in a UFO. *Psychology Today*, *9*, October.

Balch, R.W., and Taylor, D. (1977). Seekers and saucers: The role of the cultic milieu in joining a UFO cult. *American Behavioral Scientist*, *20*, 839–860.

Balch, R.W., Farnsworth, G., and Wilkins, S. (1983). When the bombs drop: Reactions to disconfirmed prophecy in a millennial sect. *Sociological Perspectives, 26,* 137–158.

Ball, P. (1981). Dimensions of neopentecostal identity in the Church of England. *European Journal of Social Psychology, 11,* 349–363.

Balswick, J.O., and Balkwell, J. (1978). Religious orthodoxy and emotionality. *Review of Religious Research, 19,* 308–319.

Baltzell, E.D. (1964). *The Protestant Establishment. Aristocracy and Caste in America.* New York: Random House. (Revised edn 1987, New Haven, CT: Yale University Press).

Baltzell, E.D. (1979). *Puritan Boston and Quaker Philadelphia.* New York: Free Press.

Baltzell, E.D. (1991). *The Protestant Establishment Revisited.* New Brunswick, NJ: Transaction.

Barber, B. (1941). Acculturation and messianic movements. *American Sociological Review, 6,* 663–669.

Barfoot, C.H., and Sheppard, G.T. (1980). Prophetic vs. priestly religion: The changing role of women clergy in classical pentecostal churches. *Review of Religious Research, 22,* 2–17.

Barker, E. (1984). *The Making of a Moonie. Brainwashing or Choice?* Oxford: Basil Blackwell.

Barkun, M. (1974). *Disaster and the Millenium.* New Haven, CT: Yale University Press.

Barkun, M. (1986). *Crucible of the Millennium: The Burned-Over District of New York in the 1840's.* Syracuse, NY: Syracuse University Press.

Barron, F. (1968). *Creativity and Personal Freedom.* Princeton, NJ: Van Nostrand.

Barry, H., Bacon, M.K., and Child, I.L. (1957). A cross-cultural study of sex differences in socialization. *Journal of Abnormal and Social Psychology, 55,* 327–332.

Bateman, M.M., and Jensen, J.S. (1958). The effect of religious background on modes of handling anger. *Journal of Social Psychology, 47,* 133–141.

Batson, C.D. (1975). Rational processing or rationalization? The effect of disconfirming information on a stated religious belief. *Journal of Personality and Social Psychology, 32,* 176–184.

Batson, C.D. (1976). Religion as prosocial: Agent or double agent? *Journal for the Scientific Study of Religion, 15,* 29–45.

Batson, C.D., and Flory, J.D. (1990). Goal-relevant cognitions associated with helping by individuals high on intrinsic end religion. *Journal for the Scientific Study of Religion, 29,* 346–360.

Batson, C.D., and Gray, R.A. (1981). Religious orientation and helping behavior: Responding to one's own or the victim's need. *Journal of Personality and Social Psychology, 40,* 511–520.

Batson, C.D., and Raynor-Prince, L. (1983). Religious orientation and complexity of thought about existential concerns. *Journal for the Scientific Study of Religion, 22,* 38–50.

Batson, C.D., Schoenrade, P., and Ventis, W.L. (1993). *Religion and the Individual.* New York: Oxford University Press.

Baumeister, R., Boden, J.M., and Smart, L. (1996). Relation of threatened egotism to violence and aggression: The dark side of self-esteem. *Psychological Review, 103,* 5–33.

Beck, S.H., Cole, B.S., and Hammond, J.A. (1991). Religious heritage and premarital sex: Evidence from a national sample of young adults. *Journal for the Scientific Study of Religion, 30,* 173–180.

Becker, E. (1973). *The Denial of Death*. New York: Free Press.

Beckford, J. (1975). *The Trumpet Of Prophecy: A Sociological Study of Jehovah's Witnesses*. Oxford: Blackwell.

Beit-Hallahmi, B. (1973). *Research in religious behavior: Selected readings*. Belmont, CA: Brooks/Cole.

Beit-Hallahmi, B. (1976). On the 'religious' functions of the helping professions. *Archive für Religionpsychologie, 12*, 48–52.

Beit-Hallahmi, B. (1977). Identity integration, self-image crisis and 'Superego Victory' in postadolescent university students. *Adolescence, 12*, 57–69.

Beit-Hallahmi, B. (1979). Personal and social components of the Protestant ethic. *Journal of Social Psychology, 109*, 263–267.

Beit-Hallahmi, B. (1988). The religiosity and religious affiliation of Nobel prize winners. Unpublished data.

Beit-Hallahmi, B. (1989). *Prolegomena to the Psychological Study of Religion*. Lewisburg, PA: Bucknell University Press.

Beit-Hallahmi, B. (1992). *Despair and Deliverance: Private Salvation in Contemporary Israel*. Albany: State University of New York Press, 1992.

Beit-Hallahmi, B. (1993a). *Original Sins*. Brooklyn: Interlink.

Beit-Hallahmi, B. (1993b). *The Annotated Dictionary of Modern New Religions*. Danbury, CT: Grolier.

Beit-Hallahmi, B. (1996a). Unpublished data on reported religious experiences. University of Haifa.

Beit-Hallahmi, B. (1996b). *Psychoanalytic Studies of Religion: Critical Assessment and Annotated Bibliography*. Westport, CT: Greenwood Press.

Beit-Hallahmi, B., and Nevo, B. (1987). 'Born-again' Jews in Israel: The dynamics of an identity change. *International Journal of Psychology, 22*, 75–81.

Bell, H.M. (1938). *Youth Tell Their Story*. New York: American Council on Education.

Bellah, R.N. (1967). Civil religion in America, *Daedalus, 96*, 1–21.

Bellah, R.N. (1970). *Beyond Belief*. New York: Harper & Row.

Belle, D. (1982). The stress of caring: Women as providers of social support. In L. Goldberger and S. Breznitz (eds) *Handbook of Stress: Theoretical and Clinical Aspects*. New York: Free Press.

Bello, F. (1954). The young scientists. *Fortune, 49*, 142–143.

Bem, D.J. (1970). *Beliefs, Attitudes, and Human Affairs*. Belmont, CA: Brooks/Cole.

Bendix, R. (1977). *Max Weber: An Intellectual Portrait*. Berkeley: University of California Press.

Benson, P., and Spilka, B. (1973). God image as a function of self-esteem and locus of control. *Journal for the Scientific Study of Religion, 12*, 297–310.

Bereiter, C., and Freedman, M.B. (1962). Fields of study and the people in them. In N. Sanford (ed.) *The American College*. New York: Wiley.

Berger, P.L., and Luckmann, T. (1967). *The Social Construction of Reality*. New York: Doubleday.

Bergin, A.E., Masters, K.F., and Richards, P.S. (1987). Religiousness and mental health reconsidered: A study of an intrinsically religious sample. *Journal of Counselling Psychology, 34*, 197–204.

Berkman, L.F., and Syme, S.L. (1979). Social networks, host resistance, and mortality: A nine year follow up of Alameda county residents. *American Journal of Epidemiology, 109*, 186–204.

Bernard, J. (1949). The Rosenzweig picture frustration-study: I. Norms, reliability, and statistical evaluation, *Journal of Psychology, 28*, 325–332.

Bernt, F.M. (1989). Being religious and being altruistic: A study of college service volunteers. *Personality and Individual Differences, 10*, 663–669.

Berry, J. (1992). *Lead Us Not Into Temptation: Catholic Priests and the Sexual Abuse of Children*. New York: Doubleday.

Bibby, R.W. (1978). Gender differences in the effects of parental discord on pre-adolescent religiousness are growing: Kelley revisited. *Journal for the Scientific Study of Religion, 17*, 129–137.

Bibby, R.W. (1983). Searching for the invisible thread: Meaning systems in contemporary Canada. *Journal for the Scientific Study of Religion, 22*, 101–119.

Bibby, R., and Brinkerhoff, M. (1973). The circulation of the saints: A study of people who join conservative churches. *Journal for the Scientific Study of Religion, 12*, 273–285.

Bilu, Y. (1990). Jewish Moroccan 'Saint impresarios' in Israel: A stage-developmental perspective. *The Psychoanalytic Study of Society, 15*, 247–269.

Bilu, Y., and Beit-Hallahmi, B. (1989). Dybbuk possession as a hysterical symptom: Psychodynamic and social considerations. *Israel Journal of Psychiatry, 26*, 138–149.

Bird, F., and Reimer, B. (1982). Participation rates in new religious and para-religious movements. *Journal for the Scientific Study of Religion, 21*, 1–14.

Birky, I.T., and Ball, D. (1987). Parental trait influence on god as an object representation. *Journal of Psychology, 122*, 133–137.

Blackbourn, D. (1994). *Marpingen: Apparitions of the Virgin Mary in Nineteenth-Century Europe*. New York: Knopf.

Blacking, J. (1987). *A Commonsense View of all Music*. Cambridge: Cambridge University Press.

Blackwood, L. (1979). Social change and commitment to the work ethic. In R. Wuthnow (ed.) *The Religious Dimension*. New York: Academic Press.

Block, J.H. (1976). Issues, problems, and pitfalls in assessing sex differences. *Merrill-Palmer Quarterly, 22*, 283–308.

Bloom, H. (1992). *The American Religion: The Making of a Post-Christian Nation*. New York: Simon & Schuster.

Boire, R.G. (1994). Accommodating religious users of controlled substances: A model amendment to the Controlled Substances Act. *Journal of Drug Issues, 24*, 463–481.

Boisen, A.T. (1939). Economic distress and religious experience: A study of the Holy Rollers. *Psychiatry, 2*, 185–194.

Boisen, A.T. (1955). *Religion in Crisis and Custom*. New York: Harper.

Boling, T.E. (1975). Black and white religion: A comparison in the lower class. *Sociological Analysis, 36*, 73–80.

Bolt, M. (1982). Religious orientation, belief in a just world, and prosocial behavior. *Conference of the American Psychological Association*, Toronto.

Bonaparte, M. (1958). Psychoanalysis in relation to social, religious and natural forces. *International Journal of Psychoanalysis, 39*, 513–515.

Bopegamage, A. (1979). Status seekers in India: A sociological study of the neo-Buddhist movement. *Archives européennes de sociologie, 20*, 19–39.

Bord, R.J., and Faulkner, J.E. (1975). Religiosity and secular attitudes: The case of Catholic Pentecostals. *Journal for the Scientific Study of Religion, 14*, 257–270.

Bord, R.J., and Faulkner, J.E. (1983). *Catholic Charismatics: The Anatomy of a Modern Religious Movement*. University Park, PA: Penn State University Press.

Borhek, J.T., and Curtis, R.F. (1975). *A Sociology of Belief*. New York: Wiley.

Bouma, G.D. (1970). Assessing the impact of religion: A critical review. *Sociological Analysis, 31*, 172–179.

Bram, J. (1956). Jehovah's Witnesses and the values of American culture. *Transactions of the New York Academy of Sciences, 19*, 47–54.

Brandon, S.G.F.B. (1989). Rites of passage. *Encyclopedia Britannica, 26*, 844–856.

Brannon, R.C.L. (1970). Gimme that old-time racism. *Psychology Today, 3(11)*, 42–44.

Brinkerhoff, M.B., and MacKie, M.M. (1986). The applicability of social distance for religious research: An exploration. *Review of Religious Research, 28*, 151–167.

Bronfenbrenner, U. (1979). *The Ecology of Human Development*. Cambridge, MA: Harvard University Press.

Brown, D.E. (1991). *Human Universals*. Philadelphia, PA: Temple University Press.

Brown, D.R. and Gary, L.E. (1991). Religious socialization and educational attainment among African Americans: An empirical assessment. *Journal of Negro Education, 60*, 411–426.

Brown, L.B. (1962). A study of religious belief. *British Journal of Psychology, 53*, 259–272.

Brown, L.B. (1965). Aggression and denominational membership. *British Journal of Social and Clinical Psychology, 4*, 175–178.

Brown, L.B. (1973a). *Ideology*. Harmondsworth: Penguin.

Brown, L.B. (1973b). *Psychology and Religion*. Harmondsworth: Penguin.

Brown, L.B. (1988). *The Psychology of Religion: An Introduction*. London: SPCK.

Brown, L.B. (1994). *The Human Side of Prayer*. Birmingham, AL: Religious Education Press.

Brown, L.B., and Thouless, R.H. (1964). Petitionary prayer: Belief in its appropriateness and causal efficacy among adolescent girls. *Lumen Vitae, 3*, 123–136.

Broyles, P.A., and Drenovsky, C.K. (1992). Religious attendance and the subjective health of the elderly. *Review of Religious Research, 34*, 152–160.

Bruce, S. (1983). The persistence of religion: Conservative Protestantism in the United Kingdom. *Sociological Review, 31*, 453–470.

Bucke, R.M. (1901). *Cosmic Consciousness*. New York: Dutton.

Buckley, P., and Galanter, M. (1979). Mystical experience, spiritual knowledge, and a contemporary ecstatic religion. *British Journal of Medical Psychology, 52*, 281–289.

Burkett, S.R., and White, M. (1974). Hellfire and delinquency: Another look. *Journal for the Scientific Study of Religion, 13*, 455–462.

Burris, C.T. (1994). Curvilinearity and religious types: A second look at Intrinsic, Extrinsic, Quest Relations. *International Journal for the Psychology of Religion, 4*, 245–260.

Burris, C.T., Batson, C.D., Altstaedten, M., and Stephens, K. (1994). 'What a friend . . .': Loneliness as a motivator of intrinsic religion. *Journal for the Scientific Study of Religion, 33*, 326–334.

Burton, J. (1990). *Conflict: Basic Human Needs*. New York: St Martin's.

Burton-Bradley, B.G. (1982). Cargo cult syndromes. In C.T.H. Friedman and R.A. Fauget (eds) *Extraordinary Disorders of Human Behavior*. New York: Plenum Press.

Caldwell, R. (1989). *The Origin of the Gods*. New York: Oxford University Press.

Campbell, A., Converse, P.E., and Rodgers, W.L. (1976). *The Quality of American Life*. New York: Sage.

Campbell, C. (1971). *Toward a Sociology of Irreligion*. London: Macmillan.

Campbell, J. (1981). Bios and Mythos: Prolegomena to a science of mythology. In N. Wilbur and W. Muensterberger (eds) *Psychoanalysis and Culture*. New York: International Universities Press.

Cameron, P. (1971). Personality differences between typical urban Negroes and whites. *Journal of Negro Education, 40*, 66–75.

Campbell, T.C., and Fukuyama, Y. (1970). *The Fragmented Layman*, Philadelphia, PA: Pilgrim Press.

Cantril, H. (assisted by H. Gaudet and H. Hertzog) (1941). *The Invasion from Mars*. Princeton, NJ: Princeton University Press.

Caplovitz, D., and Sherrow, F. (1977). *The Religious Drop-Outs: Apostasy Among College Graduates*. Beverly Hills, CA: Sage.

Carlos, S. (1970). Religious participation and the urban–suburban continuum. *American Journal of Sociology, 75*, 742–759.

Carlton-Ford, S.L. (1992). Charisma, ritual, collective effervescence, and self-esteem. *Sociological Quarterly, 33*, 365–387.

Carroll, M.P. (1986). *The Cult of the Virgin Mary: Psychological Origins*. Princeton, NJ: Princeton University Press.

Carroll, M.P. (1989). *Catholic Cults and Devotions*. Montreal: McGill-Queens Press.

Cassel, J. (1973). The relation of the urban environment to health: Implications for prevention. *Mount Sinai Journal of Medicine, 40*, 539–550.

Cavalli-Sforza, L.L., Feldman, M.W., Chen, K.-H., and Dornbusch, S.M. (1982). Theory and observation in cultural transmission. *Science, 218*, 19–27.

Cavan, R.S. (1971). A dating–marriage scale of religious social distance. *Journal for the Scientific Study of Religion, 10*, 93–100.

Cavan, R.S., Burgess, E.W., Havighurst, R.J., and Goldhamer, H. (1949). *Personal Adjustment in Old Age*. Chicago, IL: Science Research Associates.

Cavenar, J.C., jr., and Spaulding, J.G. (1977). Depressive disorders and religious conversions. *Journal of Nervous and Mental Disease, 165*, 209–212.

Census. (1936). *Census of Religious Bodies*. Washington: US Department of Commerce, Bureau of the Census.

Chadwick, B.A., and Top, B.L. (1993). Religiosity and delinquency among LDS adolescents. *Journal for the Scientific Study of Religion, 32*, 51–67.

Chamberlain, K., and Zika, S. (1988). Religiosity, life meaning and well-being: Some relationships in a sample of women. *Journal for the Scientific Study of Religion, 27*, 411–420.

Charlton, J. (1987). Women in seminary. *Review of Religious Research, 28*, 305–318.

Chesser, E. (1956). *The Sexual, Marital and Family Relationships of the English Woman*. London: Hutchinson.

Christensen, C.W. (1963). Religious conversion. *Journal of Nervous and Mental Disease, 9*, 207–223.

Christensen, C.W. (1965). Religious conversion in adolescence. *Pastoral Psychology, 16*, 17–28.

Christiano, K.J. (1988). Religion and radical labor unionism: American states in the 1920s. *Journal for the Scientific Study of Religion, 27*, 378–388.

Christie, R., and Jahoda, M. (1954). *Studies in the Scope and Method of the 'Authoritarian Personality'*. Chicago, IL: Free Press.

Christopher, S., Fearon, J., McCoy, J., and Nobbe, C. (1971). Social deprivation and religiosity. *Journal for the Scientific Study of Religion, 10*, 385–393.

Claridge, G. (1985). *Origins of Mental Illness*. Oxford: Blackwell.

Clark, C.A., Worthington, E.L., and Danser, D. B. (1988). The transmission of religous beliefs and practices from parents to firstborn early adolescent sons. *Journal of Marriage and the Family, 50*, 463–472.

Clark, E.T. (1965). *The Small Sects in America*. New York: Abingdon Press.

Clark, W.H., and Warner, C.M. (1955). The relation of church attendance to honesty and kindness in a small community. *Religious Education, 50*, 340–342.

Clelland, D.A., Hood, T.C., Lipsey, C.M., and Wimberley, R.C. (1974). In the company of the converted: Characteristics of a Billy Graham crusade audience. *Sociological Analysis*, *35*, 45–56.

Cochran, J.K., and Beeghley, L. (1991). The influence of religion on attitudes toward nonmarital sexuality: A preliminary assessment of reference group theory. *Journal for the Scientific Study of Religion*, *30*, 45–62.

Cochran, J.K., Beeghley, L., and Bock, E.W. (1992). The influence of religious stability and homogamy on the relationship between religiosity and alcohol use among Protestants. *Journal for the Scientific Study of Religion*, *31*, 441–456.

Cochrane, G. (1970). *Big Men and Cargo Cults*. Oxford: Clarendon Press.

Coe, G.A. (1916). *The Psychology of Religion*. Chicago, IL: University of Chicago Press.

Cohen, S.M. (1974). The impact of Jewish education on religious identification and practice. *Jewish Social Studies*, *36*, 316–326.

Cohn, N. (1957). *The Pursuit of the Millenium*. London: Secker & Warburg.

Cohn, N. (1962). Medieval millenarism: Its bearings on the comparative study of millenarian movements. In S. Thrupp (ed.) *Millenial Dreams in Action*. The Hague: Mouton.

Cohn, W. (1955). Jehovah's Witnesses as a proletarian movement. *American Scholar*, *24*, 281–298.

Colquhoun, F. (1955). *Harringay Story*. London: Hodder & Stoughton.

Comstock, G.W., and Partridge, K.B. (1972). Church attendance and health. *Journal of Chronic Diseases*, *25*, 665–672.

Conger, J.A., and Kanungu, R.N. (1987). Toward a behavioral theory of charismatic leadership in organizations. *Academy of Management Review*, *12*, 637–647.

Connors, J.F., III, Leonard, R.C., and Burnham, K.E. (1968). Religion and opposition to war among college students. *Sociological Analysis*, *29*, 211–219.

Costa, P.T., McCrae, R.R., and Norris, A.H. (1981). Personal adjustment to aging: Longitudinal prediction from neuroticism and extraversion. *Journal of Gerontology*, *36*, 78–85.

Covello, V.T., and Ashby, J.A. (1980). Inequality in a divided society: An analysis of data from Northern Ireland. *Sociological Focus*, *13*, 87–98.

Crandall, V.C., and Gozali, J. (1969). Social desirability responses of children of four religious–cultural groups. *Child Development*, *40*, 751–762.

Cranston, R. (1957). *The Miracle of Lourdes*. New York: Popular Library.

Crapanzano, V. (1985). *Waiting: The Whites of South Africa*. New York: Random House.

Croog, S.H., and Levine, S. (1972). Religious identity and response to serious illness: A report on heart patients. *Social Science and Medicine*, *6*, 17–32.

Cross, W. (1965). *The Burned-Over District*. New York: Harper.

Csikszentmihalyi, M. (1975). *Beyond Boredom and Anxiety*. San Francisco, CA: Jossey-Bass.

Cutler, N.E. (1976). Membership in different kinds of voluntary association and psychological well-being. *Gerontologist*, *16*, 335–339.

Cutright, P., Hout, M., and Johnson, D.R. (1976). Structural determinants of fertility in Latin America 1800–1970. *American Sociological Review*, *41*, 511–527.

Daly, M., and Wilson, M. (1983). Sex, evolution, and behavior (2nd edn). Toronto: PWS Publishers.

D'Andrade, R. (1966). Sex differences and cultural institutions. In E. Maccoby (ed.) *The Development of Sex Differences*. Stanford, CA: Stanford University Press.

Darian, J.C. (1977). Social and economic factors in the rise of Buddhism. *Sociological Analysis*, *38*, 226–238.

Darley, J., and Batson, C.D. (1973). From Jerusalem to Jericho: A study of situtational and dispositional variables in helping behavior. *Journal of Personality and Social Psychology, 27,* 100–108.

Davidman, L., and Greil, A.L. (1993). Gender and the experience of conversion: The case of 'returnees' to modern Orthodox Judaism. *Sociology of Religion, 54,* 83–100.

Davidson, J.M., and Davidson, R.J. (1980). *The Psychobiology of Consciousness.* New York: Plenum.

Davis, K. (1948). *Human Society.* New York: Macmillan.

Day, L.H. (1987). Durkheim on religion and suicide – a demographic critique. *Sociology, 21,* 449–461.

Dearman, M. (1974). Christ and conformity: A study of Pentecostal values. *Journal for the Scientific Study of Religion, 13,* 437–453.

Deconchy, J.P. (1967). Structure genetique de l'idée de Dieu. Brussels: Lumen Vitae.

Deconchy, J.P. (1968). God and parental images: The masculine and feminine in religions free association. In A. Godin (ed.) *From Cry to Word.* Brussels: Lumen Vitae.

Deconchy, J.P. (1977). Regulation et signification dans un cas de 'compromis' idéologique (ecclésiastiques catholiques et propositions 'marxistes'). *Bulletin de Psycholgie, 30,* 436–450.

Deconchy, J.P. (1980). *Orthodoxie Religieuse et Sciences Humaines.* The Hague: Mouton.

Deconchy, J.P. (1985). Non-experimental and experimental methods in the psychology of religion. In L.B. Brown (ed.) *Advance in the Psychology of Religion.* Oxford: Pergamon.

Deikman, A.J. (1963). Experimental meditation. *Journal of Nervous and Mental Disease, 136,* 329–373.

De Jong, G.F., and Faulkner, J.F. (1972). Religion and intellectuals: Findings from a sample of university faculty. *Review of Religious Research, 14,* 15–24.

Demerath, N.J., III (1969). Irreligion, a-religion, and the case of the religionless church: Two case studies in organizational convergence. *Sociological Analysis, 30,* 191–203.

De Neuter, H. (1981). Maternal and paternal dimensions in the parental and divine figures. In A. Vergote and A. Tamayo (eds) *The Parental Figures and the Representation of God.* The Hague: Mouton.

Depression Guideline Panel. (1993). *Depression in Primary Care: Vol. 1. Diagnosis and Detection.* Rockville, MD: Department of Health and Human Services.

Deren, M. (1953). *Divine Horsemen: The Living Gods of Haiti.* London: Thames & Hudson.

de Vaus, D., and McAllister, I. (1987). Gender differences in religion: A test of the structural location theory. *American Sociological Review, 52,* 472–481.

de Vaus, D.A. (1984). Workforce participation and sex differences in church attendance. *Review of Religious Research, 25,* 247–256.

Dewe, P.J. (1987). New Zealand ministers of religion: Identifying sources of stress and coping processes. *Work and Stress, 1,* 351–364.

Dewhurst, K., and Beard, A.W. (1970). Sudden religious conversions in temporal lobe epilepsy. *British Journal of Psychiatry, 117,* 497–507.

Dirks, D.H. (1988). Moral development in Christian higher education. *Journal of Psychology and Theology, 16,* 324–331.

Dodson, M. (1992). Explaining Protestant fundamentalism in Central America. In B. Misztal and A.D. Shupe, jun. (eds) *Religion and Politics in Comparative Perspective. Revival of Religious Fundamentalism in East and West.* Westport, CT: Praeger.

Dollard, J. (1949). *Caste and Class in a Southern Town*. New York: Doubleday.

Dollimore, J. (1984). *Radical Tragedy*. Chicago, IL: University of Chicago Press.

Donahue, M.J. (1985). Intrinsic and extrinsic religiousness: Review and meta-analysis. *Journal of Personality and Social Psychology, 48*, 400–419.

Douglas, M. (1973). *Natural Symbols: Explorations in Cosmology*. London: Barrie & Jenkins.

Downing, J.J., and Wygant, W. (1964). Psychedelic experience and religious belief. In R. Blum (ed.) *Utopiates: The Uses and Users of LSD*. New York: Atherton.

Draper, E. (1969). Religion as an intropsychic experience. *Clinical Journal of Medicine, 19*, 111–119.

Dudley, R.L. (1987). Alienation from religion in adolescents from Fundamentalist religious homes. *Journal for the Scientific Study of Religion, 17*, 389–398.

Dudley, R.L., Mutch, P.B., and Cruise, R.J. (1987). Religious factors and drug usage among Seventh-Day Adventist youth in North America. *Journal for the Scientific Study of Religion, 26*, 218–233.

Dull, V.T., and Skokan, L.A. (1995). A cognitive model of religion's influence on health. *Journal of Social Issues, 51*, 49–64.

Dundes, A. (1981). The hero pattern and the life of Jesus. *Psychoanalytic Study of Society, 9*, 49–84.

Durkheim, E. (1897). *Suicide*. London: Routledge & Kegan Paul.

Durkheim, E. (1912/1976). *The Elementary Forms of the Religious Life*. London: Allen & Unwin.

Dwyer, J.W., Clark, L.L., and Miller, M.K. (1990). The effect of religious concentration and affiliation on county cancer mortality rates. *Journal of Health and Social Behavior, 31*, 185–202.

Dynes, R.R. (1955). Church-sect typology and socio-economic status. *American Sociological Review, 20*, 555–560.

Dynes, R.R. (1956). Rurality, migration and sectarianism. *Rural Sociology, 21*, 24–28.

Eagly, A.H. (1995). The science and politics of comparing women and men. *American Psychologist, 50*, 145–158.

Earle, J.R., Knudsen, D.D., and Shriver, D.W., jr. (1976). *Spindles and Spires: A Restudy of Religion and Social Change in Gastonia*. Atlanta, GA: John Knox Press.

Ebaugh, H.R.F. (1988). Leaving Catholic convents. In D.G. Bromley (ed.) *Falling from the Faith. Causes and Consequences of Religious Apostasy*. Newbury Park, CA: Sage.

Ebaugh, H.R.F. (1993). The growth and decline of Catholic religious orders of women worldwide: The impact of opportunity structures. *Journal for the Scientific Study of Religion, 32*, 68–75.

Ebaugh, H.R.F., and Vaughan, S.L. (1984). Ideology and recruitment in religious groups. *Review of Religious Research, 26*, 148–157.

Eckberg, D.L., and Blocker, T.J. (1989). Varieties of religious involvement and environmental concerns: Testing the Lynn White thesis. *Journal for the Scientific Study of Religion, 28*, 509–517.

Eckblad, M., and Capman, L.J. (1983). Magical ideation as an indicator of schizotypy. *Journal of Counseling and Clinical Psychology, 51*, 215–225.

Eckhardt, K.W. (1970). Religiosity and civil rights militancy. *Review of Religious Research, 11*, 197–203.

Eckhardt, W. (1974). Religious beliefs and practices in relation to peace and justice. *Social Compass, 21*, 463–472.

Edwards, H. (1968). Black Muslim and Negro Christian family relationships. *Journal of Marriage and the Family, 30*, 604–611.

Eibl-Eibesfeldt, I. (1989). *Human Ethology*. The Hague: Aldine de Gruyter.

Eisinga, R., Felling, A., and Peters, J. (1990). Church involvement, prejudice and nationalism: A research note on the curvilinear relationship between church involvement and ethnocentrism in the Netherlands. *Review of Religious Research, 31*, 417–433.

Eisinga, R., Konig, R., and Scheepers, P. (1995). Orthodox religious beliefs and anti-Semitism: A replication of Glock and Stark in the Netherlands. *Journal for the Scientific Study of Religion, 34*, 214–223.

Eister, A.W. (1950). *Drawing-Room Conversation: A Sociological Account of the Oxford Group Movement*. Durham, NC: Duke University Press.

Eister, A.W. (1957). Religious institutions in complex societies: Difficulties in the theoretic specification of functions. *American Sociological Review, 30*, 387–391.

Eister, A.W. (1974). Culture crises and new religious movements: A paradigmatic statement of a theory of cults. In I.I. Zaretsky and M.P. Leone (eds) *Religious Movements in Contemporary America*. Princeton, NJ: Princeton University Press.

Elder, G.H. (1968). Family structure and educational achievement. *American Sociological Review, 30*, 81–95.

Eliade, M. (1964). *Myth and Reality*. London: Allen & Unwin.

Elkind, D. (1971). The origins of religion in the child. *Review of Religious Research, 12*, 35–42.

Ellingson, T. (1987). Music and religion. *The Encyclopedia of Religion, 10*, 163–172.

Ellis, L. (1985). Religiosity and criminality: Evidence and explanations of complex relationships. *Sociological Perspectives, 28*, 501–520.

Ellison, C.G. (1991). Religious involvement and subjective well-being. *Journal of Health and Social Behavior, 32*, 80–99.

Ellison, C.G. (1992). Are religious people nice people? Evidence from the National Survey of Black Americans. *Social Forces, 71*, 411–430.

Ellison, C.G. (1993). Religious involvement and self-perception among black Americans. *Social Forces, 71*, 1027–1055.

Ellison, C.G., and George, L.K. (1994). Religious involvement, social ties, and social support in a Southeastern community. *Journal for the Scientific Study of Religion, 33*, 46–61.

Ellison, C.G., and Sherkat, D.E. (1993a). Conservative Protestantism and support for corporal punishment. *American Sociological Review, 58*, 131–144.

Ellison, C.G., and Sherkat, D.E. (1993b). Obedience and authority: Religion and parental values reconsidered. *Journal for the Scientific Study of Religion, 32*, 313–329.

Ellison, C.G., Gay, D.A., and Glass, T.A. (1989). Does religious commitment contribute to individual life satisfaction? *Social Forces, 68*, 100–123.

Emmons, C.F., and Sobal, J. (1981). Paranormal beliefs: Testing the marginality hypothesis. *Sociological Focus, 14*, 49–56.

England, R.W. (1954). Some aspects of Christian Science as reflected in letters of testimony. *American Journal of Sociology, 59*, 448–453.

Engs, R.C., Hanson, D.J., Gliksman, L., and Smythe, C. (1990). Influence of religion and culture on drinking behaviours: A test of hypotheses between Canada and the USA. *British Journal of Addiction, 85*, 1475–1482.

Epstein, D.M. (1993). *Sister Aimee: The Life of Aimee Semple McPherson*. New York: Harcourt Brace Jovanovich.

Erickson, J.A. (1992). Adolescent religious development and commitment: A structural equation model of the role of family, peer group, and educational influences. *Journal for the Scientific Study of Religion, 31*, 131–152.

Erikson, E.H. (1963). *Childhood and Society* (2nd edn). New York: Norton.

Eysenck, H.J., and Furneaux, W.D. (1945). Primary and secondary suggestibility: An experimental and statistical study. *Journal of Experimental Psychology, 35,* 485–503.

Faulkner, J.E., and De Jong, G.F. (1968). A note on religiosity and moral behavior of a sample of college students. *Social Compass, 15,* 37–44.

Faupel, C.E., Kowalsky, G.S., and Starr, P.D. (1987). Sociology's one law: Religion and suicide in the urban context. *Journal for the Scientific Study of Religion, 26,* 523–534.

Fazel, M.K., and Young, D.M. (1988). Life quality of Tibetans and Hindus: A function of religion. *Journal for the Scientific Study of Religion, 27,* 229–242.

Feather, N.T. (1964). Acceptance and rejection of arguments in relation to attitude strength, critical ability and intolerance of inconsistency. *Journal of Abnormal and Social Psychology, 69,* 127–136.

Featherman, D.L. (1971). The socio-economic achievement of white religio-ethnic sub-groups: Social and psychological explanations. *American Sociological Review, 36,* 207–222.

Feifel, H. (1974). Religious conviction and fear of death among the healthy and the terminally ill. *Journal for the Scientific Study of Religion, 13,* 353–360.

Feifel, H., and Jones, R.B. (1968). Perception of death as related to nearness of death. *Proceedings of American Psychological Association,* 545–546.

Feigelman, W., Gorman, B.S., and Varacalli, J.A. (1992). Americans who give up religion. *Sociology and Social Research, 76,* 138–144.

Feltey, K.M., and Poloma, M.M. (1991). From sex differences to gender role beliefs: Exploring effects on six dimensions of religiosity. *Sex Roles, 25,* 181–193.

Fenichel, O. (1945). *The Psychoanalytic Theory of Neurosis.* London: Routledge & Kegan Paul.

Fenn, R.K. (1978). *Toward a Theory of Secularization.* Storrs, CT: Society for the Scientific Study of Religion.

Fenwick, P. (1987). Meditation and the EEG. In M.A. West (ed.) *The Psychology of Meditation.* Oxford: Clarendon Press.

Ferenczi, S. (1926). Belief, disbelief, and conviction. In *Further Contributions to Psychoanalysis.* London: Hogarth Press.

Fernandez, J.W. (1982). *Bwiti: An Ethnography of the Religious Imagination in Africa.* Princeton, NJ: Princeton University Press.

Ferraro, K.F., and Albrecht, J.C.N. (1991). Does religion influence adult health? *Journal for the Scientific Study of Religion, 30,* 193–202.

Ferraro, K.F., and Koch, J.R. (1994). Religion and health among black and white adults: Examining social support and consolation. *Journal for the Scientific Study of Religion, 33,* 362–375.

Festinger, L., Riecken, H.W., and Schachter, S. (1956). *When Prophecy Fails.* Minneapolis: University of Minnesota Press.

Fichter, J.H. (1952). The profile of Catholic religious life. *American Journal of Sociology, 58,* 145–149.

Fichter, J.H. (1961). *Religion as an Occupation: A Study in the Sociology of Professions.* Notre Dame, IN: Notre Dame University Press.

Fiese, B.H., and Kline, C.A. (1993). Development of the family ritual questionnaire: Initial reliability and validation studies. *Journal of Family Psychology, 6,* 290–299.

Firth, R. (1981). Spiritual aroma: Religion and politics. *American Anthropologist, 83,* 582–601.

Fishbein, M., and Ajzen, I. (1974). Attitudes towards objects as predictors of single and multiple behavioral criteria. *Psychological Bulletin, 81,* 59–74.

Fishbein, M., and Ajzen, I. (1975). *Beliefs, Attitude, Intention, and Behavior: An Introduction to Theory and Research.* Reading, MA: Addison-Wesley.

Fisher, S., and Fisher, R.L. (1993). *The Psychology of Adaptation to Absurdity: Tactics of Make-Believe.* Hillsdale, NJ: Lawrence Erlbaum.

Fiske, A.M. (1969). Religion and Buddhism among India's new Buddhists. *Social Research, 36,* 123–137.

Fiske, S.T., and Taylor, S.E. (1991). *Social Cognition.* New York: McGraw-Hill.

Fletcher, B. (1990). *Clergy Under Stress.* London: Mowbray.

Flora, C.B. (1973). Social dislocation and Pentecostalism: A multivariate analysis. *Sociological Analysis, 34,* 296–307.

Flora, C.B. (1976). *Pentecostalism in Colombia: Baptism by Fire and Spirit.* Rutherford, NJ: Fairleigh Dickinson University Press.

Florian, V., and Mikulincer, M. (1993). The impact of death-risk experiences and religiosity on the fear of personal death: The case of Israeli soldiers in Lebanon. *Omega, 26,* 101–111.

Flugel, J.C. (1945). *Man, Morals and Society.* New York: International Universities Press.

Forbes, G.B., Tevault, R.K., and Gromoll, H.F. (1971). Willingness to help strangers as a function of liberal, conservative or Catholic church membership: A field study with the lost-letter technique. *Psychological Reports, 28,* 947–949.

Fortes, M. (1959). *Oedipus and Job in West Africa.* Cambridge: Cambridge University Press.

Foster, R.A., and Keating, J.P. (1992). Measuring androcentrism in the Western God-concept. *Journal for the Scientific Study of Religion, 31,* 366–375.

Fowler, J.W. (1981). *Stages of Faith.* San Francisco, CA: Harper & Row.

Francis, L. (1979). School influence and pupil attitude towards religion. *British Journal of Educational Psychology, 49,* 107–123.

Francis, L.J. (1984) *Monitoring the Christian Development of the Child.* Abingdon: Culham College Institute.

Francis, L.J. (1987a). Denominational schools and pupil attitudes towards Christianity. *British Educational Research Journal, 12,* 145–152.

Francis, L.J. (1987b). *Religion in the Primary School.* London: Collins.

Francis, L.J. (1987c). The decline in attitudes towards religion among 8–15 year olds. *Educational Studies, 13,* 125–134.

Francis, L.J. (1991a). Personality and attitude toward religion among adult church goers in England. *Psychological Reports, 69,* 791–794.

Francis, L.J. (1991b). The personality characteristics of Anglican ordinands: Feminine men and masculine women? *Personality and Individual Differences, 12,* 1133–1140.

Francis, L.J. (1993). Personality and religion among college students in the UK. *Personality and Individual Differences, 14,* 619–622.

Francis, L.J., and Brown, L.B. (1991). The influence of home, church and school on prayer among sixteen-year-old adolescents in England. *Review of Religious Research, 33,* 112–122.

Francis, L.J., and Carter, M. (1980). Church-aided secondary schools, religious education as an examination subject and pupil attitudes to religion. *British Journal of Educational Psychology, 50,* 297–300.

Francis, L.J., and Greer, J.E. (1993). The contribution of religious experience to Christian development. *British Journal of Religious Education, 15,* 38–43.

Francis, L.J., and Mullen, K. (1993). Religiosity and attitudes towards drug use among 13–15 year olds in England. *Addiction, 88,* 665–672.

Francis, L.J., and Pearson, P.R. (1985). Extraversion and religiosity. *Journal of Social Psychology, 1,* 25.

Frank, J.D. and Frank, J.B. (1991). *Persuasion and Healing: A Comparative Study of Psychotherapy.* Baltimore, MD: The Johns Hopkins University Press.

Frankel, B.G., and Hewitt, W.E. (1994). Religion and well-being among Canadian university students. *Journal for the Scientific Study of Religion*, *33*, 62–73.

Freeman, D. (1968). Thunder, blood, and the nicknaming of God's creatures. *Psychoanalytic Quarterly*, *37*, 353–399.

Freemesser, G.F., and Kaplan, H.B. (1976). Self-attitudes and deviant behavior: The case of the charismatic religious movement. *Journal of Youth and Adolescence*, *5*, 1–10.

Freud, S. (1953–1974). In J. Strachey (ed.) *The Standard Edition of the Complete Psychological Works of Sigmund Freud*. London: The Hogarth Press. Entries listed according to date of original writing and volume.

      (1907). Obsessive actions and religious practices. 9, 116–129, 1959.

      (1913). *Totem and Taboo*. 13, 1–164, 1955.

      (1915). Thoughts for the time on war and death. 14, 273–300, 1957.

      (1921). *Group Psychology and the Analysis of the Ego*. 18, 65–144, 1955.

      (1927). *The Future of an Illusion*. 21, 1–56, 1961.

      (1928). A religious experience. 21, 167–174, 1961.

      (1930). *Civilization and its Discontents*. 21, 57–146, 1961.

      (1939). *Moses and Monotheism*. 23, 1–138, 1964.

Fromm, E. (1941/1964). *Escape From Freedom*. New York: Avon.

Funk, R.A. (1956). Religious attitudes and manifest anxiety in a college population. *American Psychologist*, *11*, 375.

Furnham, A. (1990). *The Protestant Work Ethic*. London: Routledge.

Galanter, M. (1980). Psychological induction into the large group: Findings from a modern religious sect. *American Journal of Psychiatry*, *137*, 1574–1579.

Galanter, M. (1982). Charismatic religious sects and psychiatry: An overview. *American Journal of Psychiatry*, *139*, 1248–1253.

Galanter, M. (1989). *Cults, Faith Healing, and Coercion*. New York: Oxford University Press.

Galanter, M., Rabkin, R., Rabkin, F., and Deutsch, A. (1979). The 'Moonies': A psychological study of conversion and membership in a contemporary religious sect. *American Journal of Psychiatry*, *136*, 165–169.

Gallenmore, J.L. jr., Wilson, W.P., and Rhoads, J.M. (1969). The religious life of patients with affective disorders. *Diseases of the Nervous System*, *30*, 483–487.

Gallup, G.H. (1980). *Index to International Public Opinion*. Westport, CT: Greenwood Press.

Gallup, G., and Castelli, J. (1989). *The People's Religion*. London: Collier Macmillan.

Galton, F. (1883). *Inquiries into Human Faculties and Development*. New York: Macmillan.

Garai, J.E., and Scheinfeld, A. (1968). Sex differences in mental and behavioral traits. *Genetic Psychology Monographs*, *77*, 169–299.

Garfield, C.A. (1975). Consciousness alteration and fear of death. *Journal of Transpersonal Psychology*, *7*, 147–175.

Garfield, S.J., Cohen, H.A., and Roth, R.M. (1967). A correlative study of cheating in college students. *Journal of Educational Research*, *61*, 172–173.

Garrison, C.E. (1976). The effect of participation in congregational structures on church attendance. *Review of Religious Research*, *18*, 36–43.

Gay, D.A. (1993). Religious subcultures and political tolerance: Do denominations still matter? *Review of Religious Research*, *34*, 311–332.

Gee, E.M. (1991). Gender differences in church attendance in Canada: The role of labor force participation. *Review of Religious Research*, *32*, 267–273.

Geertz, C. (1960). *The Religion of Java*. New York: Free Press.

Geertz, C. (1964). Ideology as a cultural system. In D.E. Apter (ed.) *Ideology and Discontent*. New York: Free Press.

Geertz, C. (1966). Religion as a cultural system. In M. Banton (ed.) *Anthropological Approaches to the Study of Religion*. London: Tavistock.

Gerard, D. (1985). Religious attitudes and values. In M. Abrams, D. Gerard, and N. Timms (eds) *Values and Social Change in Britain*. London: Macmillan.

Gerharz, G.P. (1970). Secularization as a loss of social control: Toward a new theory. *Sociological Analysis, 31*, 1–11.

Gerrard, N.L. (1968). The serpent-handling religions of West Virginia. *Trans-Action, 5*, 22–28.

Gerrard, N.L. (1970). Churches of the stationary poor in southern Appalachia. In J. Photiadis and H. Schwarzweller (eds) *Change in Rural Appalachia*. Philadelphia, PA: University of Pennsylvania Press.

Gibbons, D., and de Jarnette, J. (1972). Hypnotic susceptibility and religious experience. *Journal for the Scientific Study of Religion, 11*, 152–156.

Gibson, H.M., Francis, L.J., and Pearson, P.R. (1990). The relationship between social class and attitude towards Christianity among fourteen and fifteen-year-old adolescents. *Personality and Individual Differences, 11*, 631–635.

Gilbert, D.T. (1991). How mental systems believe. *American Psychologist, 46*, 107–119.

Gillin, J.L. (1910). A contribution to the sociology of sects. *American Journal of Sociology, 16*, 236–252.

Giorgi, L., and Marsh, C. (1990). The Protestant Work Ethic as a cultural phenomenon. *European Journal of Social Psychology, 20*, 499–517.

Glass, J., Bengtson, V.L., and Dunham, C.C. (1986). Attitude similarity in three-generation families: Socialization, status inheritance, or reciprocal influence? *American Sociological Review, 51*, 685–698.

Glassner, B., and Berg, B. (1980). How Jews avoid alcohol problems. *American Sociological Review, 45*, 647–664.

Glenn, N.D. (1964). Negro religion and Negro status in the United States. In L. Schneider (ed.) *Religion, Culture and Society*. New York: Wiley.

Glenn, N.D., and Alston, J.P. (1967). Rural urban differences in reported attitude and behavior. *Southwestern Social Science Quarterly, 47*, 381–400.

Glenn, N.D., and Gotard, E. (1977). The religion of blacks in the United States: Some recent trends and current characteristics. *American Journal of Sociology, 83*, 443–451.

Glenn, N.D., and Weiner, D. (1969). Some trends in the social origins of American sociologists. *American Sociologist, 4*, 291–302.

Glik, D.C. (1986). Psychosocial wellness among spiritual healing participants. *Social Science and Medicine, 22*, 579–586.

Glock, C.Y. (1962). On the study of religious commitment. *Religious Education, 57*, S98–S109.

Glock, C.Y. (1964). The role of deprivation in the origin and evolution of religious groups. In R. Lee and M.E. Marty (eds) *Religion and Social Conflict*. New York: Oxford University Press.

Glock, C.Y., and Siegelman, E. (1969). *Prejudice U.S.A.* New York: Praeger.

Glock, C.Y., and Stark, R. (1965). *Religion and Society in Tension*. Chicago, IL: Rand McNally.

Glock, C.Y., and Stark, R. (1966). *Christian Beliefs and Anti-Semitism*. New York: Harper & Row.

Glock, C.Y., Ringer, B.B., and Babie, E.R. (1967). *To Comfort and to Challenge*. Berkeley: University of California Press.

Gluckman, M. (1965) *Politics, Law and Ritual in Tribal Society*, Oxford: Blackwell.

Godin, A., and Hallez, M. (1964). Parental images and divine paternity. In A. Godin (ed.) *From Religious Experiences to a Religious Attitude*. Brussels: Lumen Vitae.

Goffman, E. (1971). *Relations in Public*. London: Allen Lane.

Goldman, R.J. (1964). *Religious Thinking from Childhood to Adolescence*. London: Routledge & Kegan Paul.

Goldschmidt, W.R. (1944). Class denominations in rural California churches. *American Journal of Sociology*, *49*, 348–355.

Goldsen, R.K., Rosenberg, M., Williams, R.M., jr., and Suchmen, E.A. (1960). *What College Students Think*. Princeton, NJ: Van Nostrand.

Goode, E. (1966). Social class and church participation. *American Journal of Sociology*, *72*, 102–111.

Goode, E. (1968). Class styles of religious association. *British Journal of Sociology*, *19*, 1–16.

Goodman, F.D. (1972). *Speaking in Tongues: A Cross-Cultural Study in Glossolalia*. Chicago, IL: Chicago University Press.

Gordon, J.S. (1987). *The Golden Guru: The Strange Journey of Bhagwan Shree Rajneesh*. Lexington, MA: Stephen Green Press.

Gorer, G. (1955). *Exploring English Character*. London: Cresset.

Gorsuch, R.L. (1968). The conceptualization of God as seen in adjective ratings. *Journal for the Scientific Study of Religion*, *7*, 56–64.

Gorsuch, R.L. (1988). Psychology of religion. *Annual Review of Psychology*, *39*, 201–221.

Gorsuch, R.L. (1995). Religious aspects of substance abuse and recovery. *Journal of Social Issues*, *51*, 65–83.

Gorsuch, R.L., and Aleshire, D. (1974). Christian faith and ethnic prejudice: Review of research. *Journal for the Scientific Study of Religion*, *13*, 281–307.

Gorsuch, R.L., and Butler, M. (1976). Initial drug abuse: A review of predisposing social psychological factors. *Psychological Bulletin*, *81*, 120–137.

Goss, E. (1907). *Father and Son*. London: Heinemann.

Graff, R.W., and Ladd, C.E. (1971). POI (Personality Orientation Inventory) correlates of a religious commitment inventory. *Journal of Clinical Psychology*, *27*, 502–504.

Granberg, D., and Campbell, K.E. (1973). Certain aspects of religiosity and orientations toward the Vietnam war among Missouri undergraduates. *Sociological Analysis*, *34*, 40–49.

Grasmick, H.G., Bursik, R.J., jun., and Cochran, J.K. (1991). 'Render unto Caesar what is Caesar's': religiosity and taxpayers' inclinations to cheat. *Sociological Quarterly*, *32*, 251–266.

Grasmick, H.G., Kinsey, K., and Cochran, J.K. (1991). Denomination, religiosity and compliance with the law: A study of adults. *Journal for the Scientific Study of Religion*, *30*, 99–107.

Grasmick, H.G., Davenport, E., Chamlin, M.B., and Bursik, R.J., jun. (1992). Protestant fundamentalism and the retributive doctrine of punishment. *Criminology*, *30*, 21–45.

Gray, J.A. (1971). Sex differences in emotional behaviour in mammals including man: Endocrine basis. *Acta Psychologica*, *35*, 29–46.

Greeley, A.M. (1975). *The Sociology of the Paranormal*. London: Sage.

Greeley, A.M. (1981). *Religion: A Secular Theory*. Beverly Hills, CA: Sage.

Greeley, A.M. (1991). Religion and attitudes towards AIDS policy. *Sociology and Social Research*, *75*, 126–132.

Greeley, A.M. (1993). Religion and attitudes toward the environment. *Journal for the Scientific Study of Religion*, *32*, 19–28.

Greeley, A.M., and Rossi, P.H. (1966). *The Education of Catholic Americans*. Chicago, IL: Aldine.

Greeley, A.M., and Rossi, P.H. (1972). *The Denominational Society*. Glenview, IL: Scott, Foresman.

Greeley, A.M., McCready, W.C., and McCovat, K. (1976). *Catholic Schools in a Declining Church*. Kansas City: Sheed & Ward.

Greenberg, J. (1977). The Protestant work ethic and reactions to negative performance evaluation on a laboratory task. *Journal of Applied Psychology, 62,* 682–690.

Greenberg, J., Pyszczynski, T., and Solomon, S. (1986). The causes and consequences of self-esteem: A terror-management theory. In R.F. Baumeister (ed.) *Public Self and Private Self*. New York: Springer-Verlag.

Greenberg, J., Pyszczynski, T., Solomon, S., Rosenblatt, A., Veeder, M., Kirkland, S., and Lyon, D. (1990). Evidence for terror-management theory II: The effects of mortality salience on reactions to those who threaten or bolster the cultural worldview. *Journal of Personality and Social Psychology, 58,* 308–318.

Gregory, P.N., and Ebrey, P.B. (1993). *Religion and Society in T'ang and Sung China*. Oahu: University of Hawaii Press.

Griffin, G.A.E., Gorsuch, R.L., and Davis, A.-L. (1987). A cross-cultural investigation of religious orientation, social norms, and prejudice. *Journal for the Scientific Study of Religion, 26,* 358–365.

Group for the Advancement of Psychiatry (1968). The use of religion in mental illness. *Group for the Advancement of Psychiatry Reports and Symposia, 6,* pp. 664–688.

Grupp, F.W., jr., and Newman, W.M. (1973). Political ideology and religious preference: The John Birch Society and Americans for Democratic Action. *Journal for the Scientific Study of Religion, 12,* 401–413.

Gustafsson, B. (1972). The cemetery as a place for meditation. *Lumen Vitae, 27,* 85–138.

Guthrie, S.E. (1993). *Faces in the Clouds: A New Theory of Religion*. New York: Oxford University Press.

Hadaway, C.K. (1978). Life satisfaction and religion: A reanalysis. *Social Forces, 57,* 636–643.

Hadaway, C.K. and Roof, W.C. (1979). Those who stay religious 'nones' and those who don't: A research note. *Journal for the Scientific Study of Religion, 18,* 194–200.

Hadaway, C.K., and Roof, W.C. (1988). Apostasy in American churches: Evidence from national survey data. In D.G. Bromley (ed.) *Falling From the Faith*. Newbury Park, CA: Sage.

Hadaway, C.K., Marler, P.L., and Chaves, M. (1993). What the polls don't show: A closer look at U.S. church attendance. *American Sociological Review, 58,* 741–752.

Haerich, P. (1992). Premarital sexual permissiveness and religious orientation: A preliminary investigation. *Journal for the Scientific Study of Religion, 31,* 361–365.

Hall, G.S. (1904). *Adolescence: Its psychology and its relations to physiology, anthropology, sociology, sex, crime, religion and education* (2 vols). New York: Appleton.

Hamilton, R.F. (1968). A research note on the mass support for 'tough' military initiatives. *American Sociological Review, 33,* 439–445.

Hammond, P., and Williams, K. (1976). Protestant ethic thesis: Social psychological assessment. *Social Forces, 54,* 579–589.

Hampson, S.E. (1988). *The Construction of Personality*. London: Routledge.

Hanson, A., and Hanson, A. (1981). *Reasonable Belief*. Oxford: Oxford University Press.

Haraldsson, E. (1981). Some determinants of belief in psychical phenomena. *Journal of the American Society for Psychical Research, 75,* 297–309.

Hardy, A. (1979). *The Spiritual Nature of Man*. Oxford: Clarendon Press.

Hardyck, J.A., and Braden, M. (1962). Prophecy fails again: A report of a failure to replicate. *Journal of Abnormal and Social Psychology*, *65*, 136–141.

Harlan, L. (1992). *Religion and Rajput Women: The Ethics of Protection in Contemporary Narratives*. Berkeley: University of California Press.

Harms, E. (1944). The development of religious experience in children. *American Journal of Sociology*, *50*, 112–122.

Harrelson, W. (1989). Worship. *Encyclopedia Britannica*, *26*, 819–824.

Harris, M. (1981). *America Now*. New York: Random House.

Harrison, J.E. (1927). *Themis, A Study of the Social Origins of Greek Religion*. Cambridge: Cambridge University Press.

Harrison, J.F.C. (1979). *The Second Coming: Popular Millenarianism 1780–1850*. New Brunswick, NJ: Rutgers University Press.

Harrison, M.I. (1974). Sources of recruitment to Catholic Pentecostalism. *Journal for the Scientific Study of Religion*, *13*, 49–64.

Hartmann, H. (1958). *Ego Psychology and the Problem of Adaptation*. New York: International Universities Press.

Hartmann, R.T., and Peterson, R.E. (1968). Religious preference as a factor in attitudinal and background differences among college freshmen. *Sociology of Education*, *41*, 227–237.

Hartshorne, H., and May, M.A. (1928). *Studies in Deceit*. New York: Macmillan.

Hashimoto, H., and McPherson, W. (1976). Rise and decline of Sokagakkai Japan and the United States. *Review of Religious Research*, *17*, 82–92.

Hassenger, R. (ed.) (1967). *The Shape of Catholic Higher Education*. Chicago, IL: University of Chicago Press.

Hay, D. (1982). *Exploring Inner Space*. Harmondsworth: Penguin.

Hay, D. (1990). *Religious Experience Today*. London: Mowbray.

Hay, D., and Heald, G. (1987). Religion is good for you. *New Society*, 17 April.

Hay, D., and Morisy, A. (1978). Reports of ecstatic, paranormal, or religious experience in Great Britain and the United States – a comparison of trends. *Journal for the Scientific Study of Religion*, *17*, 255–268.

Hayden, B. (1987). Alliances and ritual ecstasy: Human responses to resource stress. *Journal for the Scientific Study of Religion*, *26*, 81–91.

Haywood, C.L. (1983). The authority and empowerment of women among Spiritualist groups. *Journal for the Scientific Study of Religion*, *22*, 157–166.

Hazani, M. (1986). When prophecy fails: Leaders die, followers persevere. *Genetic, Social, and General Psychology Monographs*, *112*, 245–271.

Heaton, T.B., and Cornwall, M. (1989). Religious group variation in the socioeconomic status and family behaviour of women. *Journal for the Scientific Study of Religion*, *28*, 283–299.

Heaton, T.B., and Goodman, K.L. (1985). Religion and family formation. *Review of Religious Research*, *26*, 343–359.

Heaton, T.B., Jacobson, C.K., and Fu, X.N. (1992). Religiosity of married couples and childlessness. *Review of Religious Research*, *33*, 244–255.

Hebb, D.O. (1955). The mammal and his environment. *American Journal of Psychiatry*, *91*, 826–831.

Heider, F. (1958). *The Psychology of Interpersonal Relations*. New York: Wiley.

Heiler, F. (1932). *Prayer: A Study in the History and Psychology of Religion*. New York: Oxford University Press.

Heller, D. (1986). *The Children's God*. Chicago, IL: University of Chicago Press.

Henninger, J. (1987). Sacrifice. *Encyclopedia of Religion*, *12*, 544–545.

Henry, E.R., Sims, J.H., and Spray, S.L. (1971). *The Fifth Profession*. San Francisco, CA: Jossey-Bass.

Herron, S. (1955). What's left of Harringay? *British Weekly*, 10 February.

Herskovits, M.J. (1948). *Man and His Works*. New York: Knopf.

Hertel, B.R. (1980). Inconsistency of beliefs in the existence of heaven and after-life. *Review of Religious Research, 21,* 171–183.

Hertel, B.R. (1988). Gender, religious identity and work force participation. *Journal for the Scientific Study of Religion, 27,* 574–592.

Hertel, B.R., and Donahue, M.J. (1995). Parental influence on God images among children: Testing Durkheim's metaphoric parallelism. *Journal for the Scientific Study of Religion, 34,* 186–199.

Hertel, B.R., and Hughes, M. (1987). Religious affiliation, attendance, and support for 'pro-family' issues in the United States. *Social Forces, 65,* 858–882.

Herzbrun, M.B. (1993). Father–adolescent religious consensus in the Jewish community: A preliminary report. *Journal for the Scientific Study of Religion, 32,* 163–166.

Hickman, M.J. (1993). Integration or segregation? The education of the Irish in Britain in Roman Catholic voluntary aided schools. *British Journal of Sociology of Education, 14,* 285–300.

Hill, C. (1971a). Immigrant sect development in Britain: A case of status deprivation? *Social Compass, 18,* 231–236.

Hill, C. (1971b). From church to sect: West Indian sect development in Britain. *Journal for the Scientific Study of Religion, 10,* 114–123.

Hine, V.H. (1970). Bridge burners: Commitment and participation in a religious movement. *Sociological Analysis, 31,* 61–66.

Hirschi, T., and Stark, R. (1969). Hellfire and delinquency. *Social Problems, 17,* 202–213.

Hoben, A. (1970). Traditional Amhara society. In A. Tuden and L. Plotnicov (eds) *Social Stratification in Africa*. New York: Free Press.

Hogan, M. (1979). Australian secularists: The disavowal of denominational allegiance. *Journal for the Scientific Study of Religion, 18,* 390–404.

Hoge, D. (1974). *Commitment on Campus: Changes in Religion and Values Over Five Decades*. Philadelphia, PA: Westminster Press.

Hoge, D.R., and de Zulueta, E. (1985). Salience as a condition for various social consequences of religious commitment. *Journal for the Scientific Study of Religion, 24,* 21–38.

Hoge, D.R., and Keeter, L.G. (1976). Determinants of college teachers' religious beliefs and participation. *Journal for the Scientific Study of Religion, 15,* 221–235.

Hoge, D.R., and Petrillo, G.H. (1982). Transmission of religious and social values from parents to teenage children. *Journal of Marriage and the Family, 44,* 569–580.

Hoge, D.R., Dyble, J.E., and Polk, D.T. (1981). Organizational and situational influences on vocational commitment of Protestant ministers. *Review of Religious Research, 23,* 133–149.

Hoge, D.R., Petrillo, G.H., and Smith, E.I. (1982). Transmission of religious and social values from parents to teenage children. *Journal of Marriage and the Family, 44,* 569–580.

Hollenweger, W.J. (1972). *The Pentecostals*. London: SCM Press.

Hollingworth, L.S. (1933). The adolescent child. In C.A. Murchison (ed.) *A Handbook of Child Psychology*. Worcester, MA: Clark University Press.

Holm, N.G. (1991). Pentecostalism: Conversion and charismata. *International Journal for the Psychology of Religion, 1,* 135–151.

Holt, J.B. (1940). Holiness religion: Cultural shock and social reorganization. *American Sociological Review, 5,* 740–747.

Homan, R. (1986). Nineteenth century missions: The organizational response to the French Revolution. *Archives de Sciences Sociales des Religions, 62,* 151–160.

Homola, M., Knudsen, D., and Marshall, H. (1987). Religion and socio-economic achievement. *Journal for the Scientific Study of Religion, 26*, 201–217.

Hong, G.Y. (1995). Buddhism and religious experience. In R.W. Hood, jun. (ed.) *Handbook of Religious Experience*. Birmingham, AL: Religious Education Press.

Hood, R.W., jr. (1970). Religious orientation and the report of religious experience. *Journal for the Scientific Study of Religion, 9*, 285–291.

Hood, R.W., jr. (1973). Hypnotic susceptibilty and reported religious experience. *Review of Religious Research, 33*, 549–550.

Hood, R.W., jr. (1974). Psychological strength and the report of intense religious experience. *Journal for the Scientific Study of Religion, 13*, 65–71.

Hood, R.W., jr. (1975). The construction and preliminary validation of a measure of reported mystical experience. *Journal for the Scientific Study of Religion, 14*, 29–41.

Hood, R.W., jr. (1976). Mystical experience as related to present and anticipated future church participation. *Psychological Reports, 39*, 1127–1136.

Hood, R.W., jr. (1977). Differential triggering of mystical experience as a function of self-actualization. *Review of Religious Research, 18*, 264–270.

Hood, R.W., jr. (1978). Anticipatory set and setting: stress incongruities as elicitors of mystical experience in solitary nature situations. *Journal for the Scientific Study of Religion, 17*, 279–287.

Hood, R.W., jr. (1995). The facilitation of religious experience. In R.W. Hood, jr. (ed.) *Handbook of Religious Experience*. Birmingham, AL: Religious Education Press.

Hood, R.W., jr., and Hall, J.R. (1980). Gender differences in the description of erotic and mystical experiences. *Review of Religious Research, 21*, 195–207.

Hood, R.W., jr., and Morris, R.J. (1981). Sensory isolation and the differential elicitation of religious imagery in intrinsic and extrinsic persons. *Journal for the Scientific Study of Religion, 20*, 261–273.

Hood, R.W., jr., and Morris, R.J. (1983). Toward a theory of death transcendence. *Journal for the Scientific Study of Religion, 22*, 353–365.

Hood, R.W., jr., Morris, R.J., and Watson, P.J. (1991). Male commitment to the cult of the Virgin Mary and the passion of Christ as a function of early maternal bonding. *International Journal for the Psychology of Religion, 1*, 221–231.

Horney, K. (1964). *The Neurotic Personality of Our Time*. New York: W.W. Norton.

Hoult, T.F. (1958). *The Sociology of Religion*. New York: Holt.

Houston, J., and Masters, R.E.L. (1972). The experimental induction of religious-type experiences. In J. White (ed.) *The Highest State of Consciousness*. Garden City, NY: Doubleday Anchor.

Houtart, F. (1977). Theravada Buddhism and political power: Construction and destruction of its ideological function. *Social Compass, 24*, 207–246.

Howells, T.H. (1928). A comparative study of those who accept as against those who do not accept religious authority. *University of Iowa Studies in Character, 2*, no.2.

Hughes, R.A. (1990). Psychological perspectives on infanticide in a faith healing sect. *Psychotherapy, 27*, 107–115.

Hunsberger, B. (1976). Background religious denomination, parental emphasis, and the religious orientation of university students. *Journal for the Scientific Study of Religion, 15*, 251–255.

Hunsberger, B. (1980). A reexamination of the antecedents of apostasy. *Review of Religious Research, 21*, 158–170.

Hunsberger, B. (1983). Apostasy. *Review of Religious Research, 25*, 21–38.

Hunsberger, B. (1995). Religion and prejudice: The role of religious funda-mentalism, quest, and right-wing authoritarianism. *Journal of Social Issues, 51*, 113–129.

Hunsberger, B. (1996). Religious fundamentalism, right-wing authoritarianism, and hostility toward homosexuals in non-Christian religious groups. *International Journal for the Psychology of Religion, 6*, 39–49.

Hunsberger, B., and Brown, L.B. (1984). Religious socialization, apostasy, and the impact of family background. *Journal for the Scientific Study of Religion, 23*, 239–251.

Hunsberger, B., and Platonow, E. (1986). Religion and helping charitable causes. *Journal of Psychology, 120*, 517–528.

Hunsberger, B., McKenzie, B., Pratt, M.W., and Pancer, S.M. (1993). Religious doubt: A social psychological analysis. *Research in the Social Scientific Study of Religion, 5*, 27–51.

Hunt, R.A. (1972). Mythological–symbolic religious commitment: The LAM scales. *Journal for the Scientific Study of Religion, 11*, 42–52.

Hunter, J.D. (1983). *American Evangelicalism: Conservative Religion and the Quandary of Modernity.* New Brunswick, NJ: Rutgers University Press.

Hunter, F.T., and Youniss, J. (1982). Changes in functions of three relations during adolescence. *Developmental Psychology, 18*, 806–811.

Huntington, S.P. (1993). If not civilizations, what? Paradigms of the post-cold war world. *Foreign Affairs, 72*, 185–207.

Hutch, R.A. (1990). *Religious Leadership: Personality, History and Sacred Authority.* New York: Peter Lang.

Hutsebaut, D. (1972). The representation of God: Two complementary hypotheses. *Social Compass, 19*, 389–406.

Huxley, F. (1966). The ritual of voodoo and the symbolism of the body. In J.S. Huxley (ed.) *A Discussion of Ritualization of Behaviour in Animals and Men.* London: Philosophical Transactions of the Royal Society.

Hyde, K. (1990). *Religion in Childhood and Adolescence.* Birmingham, AL: Religious Education Press.

Hynes, E. (1989). Nineteenth-century Irish Catholicism, farmers' ideology, and national religion: Explorations in cultural explanation. In R.O'Toole (ed.) *Sociological Studies in Roman Catholicism.* Lewiston, NY: Edwin Mellen.

Iannaccone, L. (1990). Religious practice: A human capital approach. *Journal for the Scientific Study of Religion, 29*, 297–314.

Iannaccone, L. (1994). Why strict churches are strong. *American Journal of Sociology, 99*, 1180–1211.

Idler, E.L. (1987). Religious involvement and the health of the elderly: Some hypotheses and an initial test. *Social Forces, 66*, 226–238.

Idler, E.L. (1994). *Cohesiveness and Coherence: Religion and the Health of the Elderly.* New York: Garland.

Inglehart, R. (1990). *Culture Shift in Advanced Industrial Society.* Princeton, NJ: Princeton University Press.

Inhelder, B., and Piaget, J. (1958). *The Growth of Logical Thinking from Childhood to Adolescence.* New York: Basic Books.

ITA (1970). *Religion in Britain and Northern Ireland.* London: Independent Television Authority.

Jackson, L.E., and Coursey, R.D. (1988). The relationship of God control and internal locus of control to intrinsic religious motivation, coping and purpose in life. *Journal for the Scientific Study of Religion, 27*, 399–410.

Jackson, M.C. (1991). A study of the relationship between psychotic and spiritual experience. Unpublished D.Phil. thesis, Oxford University.

Jacobs, J.L. (1989). *Divine Disenchantment: Deconverting from New Religions.* Bloomington: Indiana University Press.

Jahoda, G. (1969). *The Psychology of Superstition.* London: Allen Lane.

James, W. (1897/1956) *The Will to Believe.* New York: Dover.

James, W. (1902). *The Varieties of Religious Experience: A Study in Human Nature* (2nd edn). New York: Longmans, Green.

Janosik, R.J. (1974). Religion and political involvement: A study of Black African sects. *Journal for the Scientific Study of Religion, 13,* 161–175.

Janus, S.S., and Janus, C.L. (1993). *The Janus Report.* New York: Wiley.

Jarvis, G.K., and Northcott, H.C. (1987). Religion and differences in morbidity and mortality. *Social Science and Medicine, 25,* 813–824.

Jennings, M.K., and Niemi, N.G. (1968). The transmission of political values from parent to child. *American Political Science Review, 62,* 169–184.

Jensen, G.F., and Erickson, M.L. (1979). The religious factor and delinquency: Another look at the hellfire hypothesis. In R. Wuthnow (ed.) *The Religious Dimension.* New York: Academic Press.

Jensen, L., Newell, R.J., and Holman, T. (1990). Sexual behavior, church attendance, and permissive beliefs among unmarried young men and women. *Journal for the Scientific Study of Religion, 29,* 113–117.

Jessor, R. (1992). Risk behavior in adolescence: A psychosocial framework for understanding and action. In D.E. Rogers and E. Ginzburg (eds) *Adolescents at Risk: Medical and School Perspective.* Boulder, CO: Westview Press.

Johnson, B. (1961). Do holiness sects socialize in dominant values? *Social Forces, 39,* 309–317.

Johnson, C.L., and Weigert, A.J. (1978). An emerging faithstyle: A research note on the Catholic Charismatic Renewal. *Sociological Analysis, 39,* 165–172.

Johnson, N.R., Choate, D.A., and Bunis, W. (1984). Attendance at a Billy Graham Crusade: A resource mobilization approach. *Sociological Analysis, 45,* 383–392.

Johnson, W.T. (1971). The religious crusade: Revival or ritual? *American Journal of Sociology, 76,* 873–890.

Johnstone, R. (1966). *The Effectiveness of Lutheran Elementary and Secondary Schools as Agencies of Christian Education.* St Louis, MO: Concordia Seminary.

Jones, E. (1926). The psychology of religion. *British Journal of Medical Psychology, 6,* 264–269.

Jones, E. (1951). *Essays in Applied Psychoanalysis.* London: Hogarth Press.

Jones, V. (1970). Attitudes of college students and their changes: A 37-year study. *Genetic Psychology Monographs, 81,* 3–80.

Josephson, M. (1962). *The Robber Barons.* New York: Harcourt, Brace & World.

Juergensmeyer, M. (1993). *The New Cold War: Religious Nationalism Confronts the Secular State.* Berkeley: University of California Press.

Kahoe, R.D. (1974). Personality and achievement correlates of intrinsic and extrinsic religious orientations. *Journal of Personality and Social Psychology, 29,* 812–818.

Kahoe, R.D. (1977). Intrinsic religion and authoritarianism: A differentiated relationship. *Journal for the Scientific Study of Religion, 16,* 179–182.

Kaldor, P. (1994). *Winds of Change.* Homebush West, NSW: Anzea.

Kamen, H. (1967). *The Rise of Toleration.* London: World University Library.

Kanagy, C.L. (1990). The formation and development of a Protestant conversion movement among the highland Quichua of Ecuador. *Sociological Analysis, 51,* 205–217.

Kanagy, C.L., Willits, F.K. and Crider, D.M. (1990). Anomia and religiosity: Data from a panel study of middle-aged subjects. *Journal for the Scientific Study of Religion, 29,* 226–235.

Kanter, R.M. (1972). *Commitment and Community*. Cambridge, MA: Harvard University Press.

Kaplan, B.H. (1965). The structure of adaptive sentiments in lower class religious groups in Appalachia. *Journal of Social Issues, 21*, 126–141.

Kaplan, M. (1983). A woman's view of DSM-III. *American Psychologist, 38*, 786–792.

Kardiner, A. (with R. Linton) (1939). *The Individual and His Society*. New York: Columbia University Press.

Kardiner, A. (1945). *The Psychological Frontiers of Society*. New York: Columbia University Press.

Kass, J.D., Friedman, R., Leserman, J., Zuttermeister, P.C., and Benson, H. (1991). Health outcomes and a new index of spiritual experience. *Journal for the Scientific Study of Religion, 30*, 203–216.

Kay, W.K. (1981). Psychoticism and attitude to religion. *Personality and Individual Differences, 2*, 249–252.

Kedem, P. (1991). Dimensions of Jewish religiosity in Israel. In Z. Sobel and B. Beit-Hallahmi (eds) *Tradition, Innovation, Conflict: Jewishness and Judaism in Contemporary Israel*. Albany: State University of New York Press.

Kedem, P., and Cohen, D.W. (1987). The effects of religious education on moral judgment. *Journal of Psychology and Judaism, 11*, 4–14.

Kelley, M.W. (1958). The incidence of hospitalized mental illness among religious sisters in the United States. *American Journal of Psychiatry, 115*, 72–75.

Kennedy, E.C., Heckler, V.J., Kobler, F.J., and Walker, R.E. (1977). Clinical assessment of a profession: Roman Catholic clergymen. *Journal of Clinical Psychology, 33* (Supplement), 120–128.

Kersten, L. (1971). *The Lutheran Ethic: The Impact of Religion on Laymen and Clergy*. Detroit, MI: Wayne State University Press.

Kieren, D.K., and Munro, B.M. (1987). Following the leaders: parents' influence on adolescent religious activity. *Journal for the Scientific Study of Religion, 26*, 249–255.

Kildahl, J. (1972). *The Psychology of Speaking in Tongues*. New York: Harper & Row.

Kilpatrick, D.G., Sutker, L.W., and Sutker, P.B. (1970). Dogmatism, religion, and religiosity: a review and re-evaluation. *Psychological Reports, 26*, 15–22.

King, S.H., and Funkenstein, D.H. (1957). Religious practice and cardiovascular reactions during stress. *Journal of Abnormal and Social Psychology, 55*, 135–137.

Kingsbury, F.A. (1937). Why do people go to church? *Religious Education, 32*, 50–54.

Kinsey, A.C., Pomeroy, W.B., Martin, C.E., and Gebhard, P.H. (1953). *Sexual Behaviour in the Human Female*. London: Saunders.

Kinsey, A.C., Pomeroy, W.B., and Martin, C.E. (1948). *Sexual Behaviour in the Human Male*. London: Saunders.

Kirkpatrick, C. (1949). Religion and humanitarianism: A study of institutional implications. *Psychological Monographs, 63*, no. 309.

Kirkpatrick, L.A. (1992). An attachment-theory approach to the psychology of religion. *International Journal for the Psychology of Religion, 2*, 3–28.

Kirkpatrick, L.A. (1993). Fundamentalism, Christian orthodoxy, and intrinsic religious orientation as predictors of discriminatory attitudes. *Journal for the Scientific Study of Religion, 32*, 256–268.

Kirkpatrick, L.A., and Hood, R.W., jr. (1990). Intrinsic–extrinsic religious orientation: The boon or bane of contemporary psychology of religion. *Journal for the Scientific Study of Religion, 29*, 442–462.

Kirkpatrick, L.A., and Shaver, P.R. (1990). Attachment theory and religion:

Childhood attachments, religious beliefs, and conversion. *Journal for the Scientific Study of Religion, 29,* 315–334.

Kitzinger, S. (1969). Protest and mysticism: The Rastafari cult of Jamaica. *Journal for the Scientific Study of Religion, 8,* 240–268.

Kivett, V.R. (1979). Religious motivation in middle age: Correlates and implications. *Journal of Gerontology, 34,* 106–115.

Klaf, F.C., and Hamilton, J.G. (1961). Schizophrenia: A hundred years ago and today. *Journal of Mental Science, 107,* 819–827.

Klauber, J. (1974). Notes on the psychical roots of religion, with particular reference to the development of Western Christianity. *International Journal of Psychoanalysis, 55,* 249–255.

Kligerman, C. (1957). A psychoanalytic study of the confessions of St Augustine. *Journal of the American Psychoanalytic Association, 5,* 469–484.

Kluckhohn, C. (1959). Recurrent themes in myths and myth-making. *Daedalus, 88,* 268–279.

Koestler, A. (1940). *Darkness At Noon.* Harmondsworth: Penguin.

Kosa, J. (1969). The medical student: His career and religion. *Hospital Progress, 50,* 51–53.

Kosmin, B.A., and Lachman, S.P. (1993). *One Nation Under God.* New York: Harmony Books.

Kotre, J. (1971). *The View From the Border: A Social-Psychological Study of Current Catholicism.* London: Gill and Macmillan.

Kris, E. (1952). *Psychoanalytic Explorations in Art.* New York: Schocken.

Kruglanski, A. (1989). *Lay Epistemics and Human Knowledge: Cognitive and Motivational Bases.* New York: Plenum Press.

Kuhlen, R.G., and Arnold, M. (1944). Age differences in religious beliefs and problems during adolescence. *Journal of Genetic Psychology, 65,* 291–300.

Kune, G.A., Kune, S., and Watson, L.F. (1993). Perceived religiousness is protective for colorectal cancer: Data from the Melbourne colorectal cancer study. *Journal of the Royal Society of Medicine, 86,* 645–647.

Kurtz, S.N. (1992). *All the Mothers are One: Hindu India and the Cultural Reshaping of Psychoanalysis.* New York: Columbia University Press.

Labaki, B. (1988). Confessional communities, social stratification and wars in Lebanon. *Social Compass,* 35, 533–561.

La Barre, W. (1938). *The Peyote Cult.* New Haven, CT: Yale University Press.

La Barre, W. (1962). *They Shall Take Up Serpents.* Minneapolis: University of Minnesota Press.

La Barre, W. (1970). *The Ghost Dance: The Origins of Religion.* New York: Doubleday.

La Barre, W. (1991). *Shadow of Childhood: Neoteny and the Biology of Religion.* Norman: University of Oklahoma Press.

Lacan, J. (1982). God and the jouissance of woman. In J. Mitchell and J. Rose (eds) *Feminine Sexuality: Jacques Lacan and the Ecole Freudienne.* London: Macmillan.

Lamb, M.E., and Oppenheim, D. (1989). Fatherhood and father–child relationships. In S.H. Cath, A. Gurwitt, and L. Gunsberg (eds) *Fathers and Their Families.* Hillsdale, NJ: Analytic Press.

Lambert, W.W., Triandis, L.M., and Wolf, M. (1959). Some correlates of beliefs in the malevolence and benevolence of supernatural beings: A cross societal study. *Journal of Abnormal Social Psychology, 58,* 162–169.

Lang, K., and Lang, G.E. (1960). Decisions for Christ: Billy Graham in New York City. In M. Stein, A.J. Vidich, and O.M. White (eds) *Identity and Anxiety.* Chicago, IL: Free Press.

Larsen, L., and Knapp, R.H. (1964). Sex differences in symbolic conceptions of the deity. *Journal of Projective Techniques and Personality Assessment, 28,* 303–306.

Lasagna, L., Mosteller, F., von Felsinger, J.M., and Beecher, H.K. (1954). A study of the placebo response. *American Journal of Medicine, 16,* 770–779.

Lazerwitz, B. (1961). A comparison of major United States religious groups. *Journal of the American Statistical Association, 55,* 568–579.

Leak, G.K., and Fish, S. (1989). Religious orientation, impression management, and self-deception: Toward a clarification of the link between religiosity and social desirability. *Journal for the Scientific Study of Religion, 28,* 355–359.

Lehman, E.C., jr. (1972). The scholarly perspective and religious commitment. *Sociological Analysis, 33,* 199–216.

Lehman, E.C., jr. (1980). Patterns of lay resistance to women in ministry. *Sociological Analysis, 41,* 317–338.

Lehman, E.C., jr. (1993). *Gender and Work: The Case of the Clergy.* Albany: State University of New York Press.

Lehman, E.C., jr., and Shriver, D.W. (1968). Academic discipline as predictive of faculty religiosity. *Social Forces, 47,* 171–182.

Lehrer, E.L., and Chiswick, C.U. (1993). Religion as a determinant of marital stability. *Demography, 30,* 385–404.

Lemert, C.C. (1974). Cultural multiplexity and religious polytheism. *Social Compass, 21,* 241–253.

Lenski, G.E. (1953). Social correlates of religious interest. *American Sociological Review, 18,* 533–544.

Lenski, G.E. (1963). *The Religious Factor.* New York: Doubleday.

Leuba, J.H. (1912). *A Psychological Study of Religion.* New York: Macmillan.

Leuba, J.H. (1925). *The Psychology of Religious Mysticism.* New York: Harcourt Brace.

Leuba, J.H. (1934). Religious beliefs of American scientists. *Harper's, 169,* 297.

Levin, J.S. (1993). Age differences in mystical experience. *Gerontologist, 33,* 507–513.

Levin, J.S. (1994). Religion and health: Is there an association, is it valid, and is it causal? *Social Science and Medicine, 38,* 1475–1482.

Levin, J.S., and Schiller, P.L. (1986). Religion and multidimensional health locus of control scales. *Psychological Reports, 59,* 26.

Levin, J.S., and Vanderpool, H.Y. (1987). Is frequent religious attendance really conducive to better health? *Social Science and Medicine, 24,* 589–600.

Levine, B.C. (1986). Religious commitment and integration into a Jewish community in the United States. *Review of Religious Research, 27,* 328–343.

Levine, R.A., and Campbell, D.T. (1972). *Ethnocentrism: Theories of Conflict, Ethnic Attitudes and Group Behavior.* New York: Wiley.

Levine, S.V. (1981). Cults and mental health: Clinical conclusions. *Canadian Journal of Psychiatry, 16,* 534–539.

Levine, S.V. (1984). *Radical Departures.* New York: Harcourt Brace Jovanovich.

Levine, S.V., and Salter, N.E. (1976). Youth and contemporary religious movements: Psychosocial findings. *Canadian Psychiatric Association Journal, 21,* 411–420.

Levy, J.J., Dupras, A., and Samson, J.M. (1985). Religion, death and sexuality in Quebec: A research note. *Cahiers de Recherches en Science et de la Religion, 6,* 25–34.

Lewellen, T.C. (1979). Deviant religion and cultural evolution: The Aymara case. *Journal for the Scientific Study of Religion, 18,* 243–251.

Lewin, K. (1948). *Resolving Social Conflicts.* New York: Harper.

Lewis, I.M. (1966). Spirit possession and deprivation cults. *Man, N.S. 1,* 307–329.

Lewis, I.M. (1989). *Ecstatic Religion*. London: Routledge.

Lewis, R.E., Fraser, M.W., and Pecora, P.J. (1988). Religiosity among Indochinese refugees in Utah. *Journal for the Scientific Study of Religion*, 27, 272–283.

Ley, D., and Martin, R.B. (1993). Gentrification as secularization: The status of religious belief in the post-industrial city. *Social Compass*, 40, 217–232.

Liebman, C.S. (1983). Extremism as a religious norm. *Journal for the Scientific Study of Religion*, 22, 75–86.

Lienesch, M. (1993). *Redeeming America: Piety and Politics in the New Christian Right*. Chapel Hill: University of North Carolina Press.

Liff, Z.A. (1975). The charismatic leader. In Z.A. Liff (ed.) *The Leader in the Group*. New York: Jason Aronson.

Lindskoog, D., and Kirk, R.E. (1975). Some life-history and attitudinal correlates of self-actualization among evangelical seminary students. *Journal for the Scientific Study of Religion*, 14, 51–55.

Linn, L., and Schwartz, L.W. (1958). *Psychiatry and Religious Experience*. New York: Random House.

Lipset, S.M. (1964). Religion and politics in the American past and present. In R. Lee and M. Marty (eds) *Religion and Social Conflict*. New York: Oxford University Press.

Loehlin, J.C., and Nichols, R.C. (1977). *Heredity, Environment and Personality*. Austin: University of Texas Press.

Lofland, J. (1978). *Doomsday Cult*. New York: Irvington.

Lofland, J., and Stark, R. (1965). Becoming a world saver. *American Sociological Review*, 30, 862–874.

Loftus, J.A., and Camargo, R.J. (1993). Treating the clergy. *Annals of Sex Research*, 6, 287–303.

Long, D., Elkind, D., and Spilka, B. (1967). The child's concept of prayer. *Journal for the Scientific Study of Religion*, 6, 101–109.

Loomis, C.G. (1948). *White Magic: An Introduction to the Folklore of Christian Legend*. Cambridge, MA: The Medieval Academy Of America.

Lorenz, K. (1966). *On Aggression*. New York: Harcourt Brace Jovanovich.

Loukes, H. (1961). *Teenage Religion*. London: SCM Press.

Lovekin, A., and Malony, M.N. (1977). Religious glossolalia: A longitudinal study of personality changes. *Journal for the Scientific Study of Religion*, 16, 383–393.

Lowenthal, K.M. (1993). Religion, stress, and distress. *Religion Today*, 8, 14–16.

Lowy, M. (1984). Pour une sociologie de la mystique juive. *Archives de Sciences Sociales des Religions*, 57, 5–13.

Luckmann, T. (1967). *The Invisible Religion*. New York: Macmillan.

Lutzky, H. (1991). The sacred and the maternal object: An application of Fairbairn's theory to religion. In H.B. Siegel, L. Barbanel, I. Hirsch, J. Lasky, H. Silverman, and S. Warshaw (eds) *Psychoanalytic Reflections on Current Issues*. New York: New York University Press.

Lynch, F.R. (1977). Toward a theory of conversion and commitment to the occult. *American Behavioral Scientist*, 6, 887–907.

Lynd, R., and Lynd, H. (1929). *Middletown*. New York: Harcourt, Brace.

Lynn, P., and Smith, J.D. (1991). *Voluntary Action Research*. London: The Volunteer Centre.

Lynn, R., Hampson, S.L., and Magee, M. (1983). Determinants of educational achievement at 16+: Personality, home background and school. *Personality and Individual Differences*, 4, 473–481.

McAdams, D.P., Booth, L., and Selvik, R. (1981). Religious identity among students at a private college: Social motives, ego stage, and development. *Merrill-Palmer Quarterly*, 27, 219–239.

McClelland, D.C. (1961). *The Achieving Society*. Princeton, NJ: Van Nostrand.

McClelland, D.C. (1975). *Power: The Inner Experience*. New York: Irvington.

McClelland, D.C., and Kirshnit, C. (1982). Effect of motivational arousal on immune function. Cited by McClelland, D.C., *Human Motivation*, Cambridge: Cambridge University Press.

McClemon, J. (1988). A survey of Chinese anomalous experiences and comparison with Western representive samples. *Journal for the Scientific Study of Religion*, *27*, 421–426.

Maccoby, E.E. (1988). Gender as a social category. *Developmental Psychology*, *24*, 755–765.

Maccoby, E., and Jacklin, C. (1974). *The Psychology of Sex Differences*. Stanford, CA: Stanford University Press.

McCrae, R.R. (1984). Situational determinants of coping responses: Loss, threat, and challenge. *Journal of Personality and Social Psychology*, *46*, 919–928.

McCrae, R.R., and Costa, P.T. (1985). Updating Norman's 'adequate taxonomy': Intelligence and personality dimensions in natural language and in questionnaires. *Journal of Personality and Social Psychology*, *49*, 710–721.

McCreery, C. (1993). Schizotypy and out-of-the-body experiences. Unpublished D.Phil. thesis, Oxford University.

McDaniel, J. (1989). *The Madness of the Saints: Ecstatic Religion in Bengal*. Chicago, IL: University of Chicago Press.

MacDonald, A.P. (1969) Birth order and religious affiliation. *Developmental Psychology*, *1*, 628.

McFadden, S.H., and Levin, J.S. (1996). Religion, emotions and health. In C. Magai and S.H. McFadden (eds) *Handbook of Emotion, Adult Development and Aging*. San Diego, CA: Academic Press.

McGinn, B. (1987). Christian monasticism. *The Encyclopedia of Religion*, *10*, 44–52.

McGrath, E., Keita, G.P., Strickland, B., and Russo, N.F. (1990). *Women and Depression: Risk Factors and Treatment Issues*. Washington, DC: American Psychological Association.

McGuiness, D. (1993). Gender differences in cognitive style: Implications for mathematics performance and achievement. In L.A. Penner, G.M. Batche, H.M. Knoff, and D.L. Nelson (eds) *The Challenge of Mathematics and Science Education: Psychology's Response*. Washington, DC: American Psychological Association.

McGuire, M.B. (1977). Testimony as a commitment mechanism in Catholic pentecostal prayer groups. *Journal for the Scientific Study of Religion*, *16*, 165–168.

McGuire, M.B. (1983). Words of power: Personal empowerment and healing. *Culture, Medicine and Psychiatry*, *7*, 221–240.

McIntosh, D.N., Silver, R.C., and Wortman, C.B. (1993). Religion's role in adjusting to a negative life event: Coping with the loss of a child. *Journal of Personality and Social Psychology*, *65*, 812–821.

McLeod, H. (1981). *Religion and the People of Western Europe, 1789–1970*. Oxford: Oxford University Press.

McLoughlin, W.G., jr. (1959). *Modern Revivalism: Charles Grandison Finney to Billy Graham*. New York: The Ronald Press.

Mailloux, N. and Ancona, L. (1960). A clinical study of religious attitudes and a new approach to psychopathology. In H.P. David and J.C. Brengelmann (eds) *Perspectives in Personality Research*. London: International Union of Scientific Psychology.

Malinowski, B. (1925). Magic, science, and religion. In J. Needham (ed.) *Science, Religion, and Reality*. London: Macmillan.

Malinowski, B. (1935). *Coral Gardens and Their Magic*. New York: World Book Company.

Malony, H.N., and Lovekin, A.A. (1985). *Glossolalia: Behavioral Science Perspectives on Speaking in Tongues*. New York: Oxford University Press.

Makarec, K., and Persinger, M.A. (1985). Temporal lobe signs: Electroencephalographic validity and enhanced scores in special populations. *Perceptual and Motor Skills, 60*, 831–842.

Marcum, J.P. (1986). Explaining Protestant fertility: Belief, commitment, and homogamy. *Sociological Quarterly, 27*, 547–558.

Markides, K.S. (1983). Aging, religiosity, and adjustment: A longitudinal analysis. *Journal of Gerontology, 38*, 621–625.

Markle, G.E., Petersen, J.C., and Wagenfeld, M.O. (1978). Notes from the cancer underground: Participation in the Laetrile movement. *Social Science and Medicine, 12*, 31–57.

Markus, H., and Zajonc, R. (1985). The cognitive perspective in social psychology. In G. Lindzey and E. Aronson (eds) *Handbook of Social Psychology* (3rd edn, vol. 1). New York: Random House.

Martin, N.G., Eaves, L.J., Heath, A.C., Jardine, R., Feingold, L.M., and Eysenck, H.J. (1986). Transmission of social attitudes. *Proceedings of the National Academy of Sciences, USA, 83*, 4364–4368.

Martin-Baro, I. (1990). Religion as an instrument of psychological warfare. *Journal of Social Issues, 46*, 93–107.

Martinson, O.B., Wilkening, E.A., and Buttel, F.H. (1982). Religion and community-oriented attitudes. *Journal for the Scientific Study of Religion, 21*, 48–58.

Marty, M.E., Rosenberg, S.E., and Greeley, A.M. (1968). *What Do We Believe?* New York: Meredith Press.

Martz, L., and Carroll, G. (1988). *Ministry of Greed*. New York: Weidenfeld & Nicolson.

Marx, K. (1964). *Early Writings*. New York: McGraw-Hill.

Marx, K., and Engels, F. (1957). *K. Marx and F. Engels on Religion*. Moscow: Foreign Languages Publishing House.

Maslow, A.H. (1960). *Religions, Values and Peak Experiences*. Columbus: Ohio State University Press.

Maslow, A.H. (1970). *Motivation and Personality*. New York: Harper & Row.

Masters, R.E.L., and Houston, J. (1966). *The Varieties of Psychedelic Experience*. London: Turnstone Books.

Maton, K.I. (1989). The stress-buffering role of spiritual support: Cross-sectional and prospective investigations. *Journal for the Scientific Study of Religion, 28*, 310–323.

Matthews, R. (1936). *English Messiahs*. London: Methuen.

Mauss, A.L. (1968). Mormon Semitism and anti-Semitism. *Sociological Analysis, 29*, 11–27.

Meadow, A., and Bronson, L. (1969). Religious affiliation and psychopathology in a Mexican–American population. *Journal of Abnormal Psychology, 74*, 177–180.

Meissner, W.W. (1988). The cult phenomenon and the paranoid process. *The Psychoanalytic Study of Society, 12*, 69–95.

Meske, C., Sanders, G.F., and Meredith, W.H. (1994). Perceptions of rituals and traditions among elderly persons. *Activities, Adaptation and Aging, 18*, 13–26.

Miller, A.S. (1992). Predicting nonconventional religious affiliation in Tokyo: A control theory application. *Social Forces, 71*, 397–410.

Miller, A.S. (1995). A rational choice model of religious behavior in Japan. *Journal for the Scientific Study of Religion, 34*, 234–244.

Miller, A.S., and Hoffmann, J.P. (1995). Risk and religion: An exploration of gender differences in religiosity. *Journal for the Scientific Study of Religion, 34,* 63–75.

Miller, D.R. (1963). The study of social relationships: Situation, identity, and social interaction. In S. Koch (ed.) *Psychology: A Study of a Science* (vol. 5). New York: McGraw-Hill.

Miller, J.B. (1986). *Toward a New Psychology of Women.* Boston, MA: Beacon.

Mindel, C.H., and Vaughan, C.E. (1978). A multidimensional approach to religiosity and disengagement. *Journal of Gerontology, 33,* 103–108.

Moberg, D.O. (1962). *The Church as a Social Institution.* Englewood Cliffs, NJ: Prentice-Hall.

Moberg, D.O., and Taves, M.J. (1965). Church participation and adjustment in old age. In A.M. Rose and W.A. Peterson (eds) *Older People and Their Social World.* Philadelphia, PA: F.A. Davis.

Moehle, D. (1983). Cognitive dimensions of religious experiences. *Journal of Experimental Social Psychology, 19,* 122–145.

Moffatt, M. (1979). *An Untouchable Community in South India: Structure and Consensus.* Princeton, NJ: Princeton University Press.

Mol, H. (1970). Religion and sex in Australia. *Australian Journal of Sociology, 59,* 454–465.

Mol, H. (ed.) (1972). *Western Religion.* The Hague: Mouton.

Montague, H. (1977). The pessimistic sect's influence on the mental health of its members: The case of Jehovah's Witnesses. *Social Compass, 24,* 135–147.

Mooney, J. (1965). *The Ghost Dance Religion and the Sioux Outbreak of 1890.* Chicago, IL: University of Chicago Press.

Moore, R.L. (1986). *Religious Outsiders and the Making of Americans.* New York: Oxford University Press.

Mullin, J. (1995). Fear of 'demon forces' drove mother to kill children. *Guardian* (London), 12 May, p. 2.

Myers, D.G. (1992). *The Pursuit of Happiness.* New York: William Morrow.

Nassi, A. (1981). Survivors of the sixties: Comparative psychosocial and political development of former Berkeley student activists. *American Psychologist, 36,* 753–761.

Neal, A.G. (1970). Conflict and the functional equivalence of social movements. *Sociological Focus, 3,* 3–12.

Needham, R. (1972). *Belief, Language, and Experience.* Oxford: Blackwell.

Nelsen, H.M. (1973). Intellectualism and religious attendance of metropolitan residents. *Journal for the Scientific Study of Religion, 12,* 285–296.

Nelsen, H.M. (1981). Gender differences in the effects of parental discord on pre-adolescent religiousness. *Journal for the Scientific Study of Religion, 20,* 351–360.

Nelsen, H.M., and Everett, R.F. (1976). Impact of church size on clergy role and careers. *Review of Religious Research, 1,* 62–73.

Nelsen, H.M., and Kroliczak, A. (1984). Parental use of the threat 'God will punish': Replication and extension. *Journal for the Scientific Study of Religion, 23,* 267–277.

Nelsen, H.M., and Nelsen, A.K. (1975). *Black Church in the Sixties.* Lexington: University Press of Kentucky.

Nelsen, H.M., Cheek, N.H., and Au, P. (1985). Gender differences in images of God. *Journal for the Scientific Study of Religion, 24,* 396–402.

Nelsen, H.M., Yokley, R.L., and Madron, T.W. (1971). Rural–urban differences in religiosity. *Rural Sociology, 36,* 389–396.

Nelson, G.K. (1972). The membership of a cult: The Spiritualist National Union. *Review of Religious Research, 13,* 170–177.

Nelson, L.D. (1988a). Disaffiliation, desacralization, and political values. In D.G. Bromley (ed.) *Falling from the Faith. Causes and Consequences of Religious Apostasy*. Newbury Park, CA: Sage.

Nelson, L.D. (1988b). Religion and foreign aid provision: A comparative analysis of advanced market nations. *Sociological Analysis*, *49*, 49–63.

Nelson, L.D., and Cantrell, C.H. (1980) Religiosity and death anxiety: A multi-dimensional analysis. *Review of Religious Research*, *21*, 148–157.

Nelson, M.O. (1971). The concept of god and feelings toward parents. *Journal of Individual Psychology*, *27*, 46–49.

Nelson, M.O., and Jones, E.M. (1957). An application of the Q-technique to the study of religious concepts. *Psychological Reports*, *3*, 293–297.

Niebuhr, H.R. (1929). *The Social Sources of Denominationalism*. New York: Holt.

NORC (1994). *General Social Survey Data*. Chicago, IL: National Opinion Research Center.

Nordheimer, J. (1974). Experts feel Miss Hearst may have undergone brainwashing. *New York Times*, 28 May, p. 30.

Norman, W.T. (1963). Toward an adequate taxonomy of personality attributes: Replicated factor structure in peer nomination personality ratings. *Journal of Abnormal and Social Psychology*, *66*, 574–588.

Northover, W.E. (1974). Variations in beliefs among Roman Catholics. In C. Beattie and S. Crysdale (eds) *Sociology Canada: Readings*. Toronto: Butterworth.

Northover, W.E., and Gonzalez, L.M. (1993). A cross-cultural comparison of religious belief: Canadian and Spanish students' responses to the Hunt scale. *International Journal for the Psychology of Religion*, *3*, 187–199.

Nottingham, E.K. (1954). *Religion and Society*. New York: Doubleday.

Nunn, C.Z. (1964). Child control through a 'coalition with God'. *Child Development*, *35*, 417–432.

Obeyesekere, G. (1984). *The Cult of the Goddess Pattini*. Chicago, IL: University of Chicago Press.

Obeyesekere, G. (1991). *The Work of Culture: Symbolic Transformation in Psychoanalysis and Anthropology*. Chicago, IL: University of Chicago Press.

Ochsmann, R. (1984). Belief in afterlife as a moderator of fear of death? *European Journal of Social Psychology*, *14*, 53–67.

Odham (1947). Unpublished report on survey of religious activity. London: Odham's Press.

Oksanen, A. (1994). *Religious Conversion: A Meta-Analytical Study*. Lund: Lund University Press.

Oliner, S.P., and Oliner, P.M. (1988). *The Altruistic Personality: Rescuers of Jews in Nazi Europe*. New York: Free Press.

Olsson, P.A. (1983). Adolescent involvement with the supernatural and cults. In D.A. Halperin (ed.) *Psychodynamic Perspectives on Religion, Sect, and Cult*. Boston, MA: John Wright.

Opie, I. (1993). *The People in the Playground*. New York: Oxford University Press.

Orbach, I., and Florian, V. (1992). Attitudes toward life and death, religiosity, and gender in Israeli children. *Omega*, *24*, 139–149.

Osarchuk, M., and Tate, S.J. (1973). Effect of induced fear of death on belief in afterlife. *Journal of Personality and Social Psychology*, *27*, 256–260.

Ostow, M. (1958). The nature of religious controls. *American Psychologist*, *13*, 571–574.

Ostow, M. and Sharfstein, B. (1954). *The Need to Believe*. New York: International Universities Press.

Otto, R. (1917). *The Idea of the Holy* (trans. 1923). London: Oxford University Press.

Oxtoby, W.G. (1987). Priesthood. *Encyclopedia of Religion, 11,* 528–534.

Ozorak, E.W. (1989). Social and cognitive influences on the development of religious beliefs and commitment in adolescence. *Journal for the Scientific Study of Religion, 28,* 448–463.

Pahnke, W.H. (1966). Drugs and mysticism. *International Journal of Parapsychology, 8,* 295–314.

Pahnke, W.N. (1967). The mystical and/or religious element in the psychedelic experience. In D.H. Salman and R.H. Prince (eds) *Do Psychedelics have Religious Implications?* Montreal: R.M. Bucke Memorial Society.

Palmer, S.J., and Finn, N. (1992). Coping with apocalypse in Canada: Experiences of endtime in la Mission de l'Esprit Saint and the Institute of Applied Metaphysics. *Sociological Analysis, 53,* 397–415.

Paloutzian, R.F. (1981). Purpose in life and value changes following conversion. *Journal of Personality and Social Psychology, 41,* 1153–1160.

Paloutzian, R.F. (1996). *Invitation to the Psychology of Religion* (2nd edn). Boston, MA: Allyn & Bacon.

Paloutzian, R.F., and Ellison, C.W. (1982). Loneliness, spiritual well-being, and the quality of life. In L.A. Peplau and D. Perlman (eds) *Loneliness: A Sourcebook of Current Theory, Research, and Therapy.* New York: Wiley.

Pargament, K.I., and Maton, K.L. (in press). Religion in American life: A community psychology perspective. In J. and S. Rappaport (eds) *Handbook of Community Psychology.* New York: Plenum.

Pargament, K.I., and Park, C.L. (1995). Merely a defense? The variety of religious means and ends. *Journal of Social Issues, 51,* 13–32.

Pargament, K.I., Kennell, J., Hathaway, W., Grevengoed, N., Newman, J., and Jones, W. (1988). Religion and the problem-solving process: Three styles of coping. *Journal for the Scientific Study of Religion, 27,* 90–194.

Park, C., Cohen, L.M., and Herb, L. (1990). Intrinsic religiousness and religious coping as life stress moderators for Catholics versus Protestants. *Journal of Personality and Social Psychology, 59,* 562–574.

Parrott, G.L. (1970). Who marches? A psychological profile of the San Francisco Moratorium crowd. *Proceedings of the Annual Convention of the American Psychological Association, 5,* 447–448.

Parsons, T. (1960). *Structure and Process in Modern Society.* Chicago, IL: Free Press.

Parsons, T. (1964). Age and sex in the social structure of the United States. In T. Parsons, *Essays in Sociological Theory.* New York: Free Press.

Pasqualli, L. (1981). The representation of God and parental figures among North American students. In A. Vergote and A. Tamayo (eds) *The Parental Figures and the Representation of God.* The Hague: Mouton.

Patrick, J.W. (1979). Personal faith and the fear of death among divergent religious populations. *Journal for the Scientific Study of Religion, 18,* 298–305.

Pattison, E.M., and Pattison, M.L. (1980). 'Ex-gays': Religiously mediated change in homosexuals. *American Journal of Psychiatry, 137,* 1553–1562.

Pattison, E.M., Lapins, N.A., and Doerr, H.A. (1973). A study of personality and function. *Journal of Nervous and Mental Disease, 157,* 397–409.

Peek, C.W., and Brown, S. (1980). Sex prejudice among white Protestants: Like or unlike ethnic prejudice? *Social Forces, 59,* 169–185.

Pepper, S.C. (1942). *World Hypotheses.* Berkeley: University of California Press.

Peres, Y. (1995). Religious adherence and political attitudes. In S. Deshen, C.S. Liebman, and M. Shokeid (eds) *Israeli Judaism: The Sociology of Religion in Israel.* New Brunswick, NJ: Transaction.

Perkins, H.W. (1985). Religious traditions, parents and peers as determinants of alcohol and drug abuse among college students. *Review of Religious Research*, 27, 15–31.

Perris, A. (1985). *Music as Propaganda*. London: Greenwood.

Persinger, M.A. (1987). *Neuropsychological Bases of God Beliefs*. New York: Praeger.

Pescosolido, B.A., and Georgianna, S. (1989). Durkheim, suicide and religion: Toward a network theory of suicide. *American Sociological Review*, 54, 33–48.

Petrovich, O. (1988). An examination of Piaget's theory of childhood artificialism. Unpublished D.Phil. thesis, Oxford University.

Pfister, O. (1948). *Christianity and Fear*. New York: Macmillan.

Photiadis, J.D., and Schweiker, W. (1970). Attitudes toward joining authoritarian organizations and sectarian churches. *Journal for the Scientific Study of Religion*, 9, 227–235.

Piaget, J. (1962). *Play, Dreams, and Imitation in Childhood*. New York: Norton.

Piaget, J. (1967). *The Language and Thought of the Child*. London: Routledge & Kegan Paul.

Piazza, T., and Glock, C.Y. (1979). Images of God and their social meanings. In R. Wuthnow (ed.) *The Religious Dimension: New Directions in Quantitative Research*. New York: Academic Press.

Pickering, W.S.F. (1974). The persistence of rites of passage: Towards an explanation. *British Journal of Sociology*, 25, 63–78.

Piker, S. (1972). The problem of consistency in Thai religion. *Journal for the Scientific Study of Religion*, 11, 211–229.

Pilkington, G.W., Poppleton, P.K., and Gould, J.B. (1976). Changes in religious beliefs, practices and attitudes among university students over an eleven year period in relation to sex differences, denominational differences and differences between faculties and years of study. *British Journal of Social and Clinical Psychology*, 15, 1–9.

Pittard-Payne, B.B. (1980). Nonassociational religious participation. In D.H. Smith and J. Macaulay (eds) *Participation in Social and Political Activities*. San Francisco, CA: Jossey-Bass.

Ploch, D.R., and Hastings, D.W. (1994). Graphic representations of church attendance using General Social Survey data. *Journal for the Scientific Study of Religion*, 33, 16–33.

Plomin, R. (1989). Environment and genes: Determinants of behavior. *American Psychologist*, 44, 105–111.

Poblete, R., and O'Dea, T.F. (1960). Anomie and the 'quest for community': The formation of sects among the Puerto Ricans of New York. *Sociological Analysis*, 21, 18–36.

Poling, T.H., and Kenney, J.F. (1986). *The Hare Krishna Character Type: A Study of the Sensate Personality*. Lewiston, NY: Edwin Mellen.

Pollner, M. (1989). Divine relations, social relations, and well-being. *Journal of Health and Social Behavior*, 30, 92–104.

Poloma, M.M. (1995). The sociological context of religious experience. In R.W. Hood, jun. (ed.) *Handbook of Religious Experience*. Birmingham, AL: Religious Education Press.

Poloma, M.M., and Gallup, G.H. (1991). *The Varieties of Prayer: A Survey Report*. Philadelphia, PA: Trinity Press International.

Poloma, M.M., and Pendleton, B.F. (1989). Religious experiences, evangelism, and institutional growth within the Assemblies of God. *Journal for the Scientific Study of Religion*, 28, 415–431.

Poloma, M.M., and Pendleton, B.F. (1991). *Religiosity and Well-Being: Exploring*

Neglected Dimensions of Quality of Life Research. Lewiston, NY: Edwin Mellen.

Ponton, M.O., and Gorsuch, R.L. (1988). Prejudice and religion revisited: a cross-cultural investigation with a Venezuelan sample. *Journal for the Scientific Study of Religion, 27*, 260–271.

Pope, L. (1942). *Millhands and Preachers*. New Haven, CT: Yale University Press.

Pope, L. (1948). Religion and the class structure. *Annals of the American Academy of Political and Social Science, 256*, 84–91.

Porter, L.S., and Stone, A.A. (1996). An approach to assessing daily coping. In M. Zeidner and N.S. Endler (eds) *Handbook of Coping: Theory, Research, Applications*. New York: Wiley.

Potvin, R.H. (1977). Adolescent God images. *Review of Religious Research, 19*, 43–53.

Powell, B., Steelman, L.C., and Peek, C.W. (1982). Fundamentalism and sexism: A reanalysis of Peek and Brown. *Social Forces, 60*, 1154–1158.

Poythress, N.G. (1975). Literal, antiliteral, and mythological religious orientations. *Journal for the Scientific Study of Religion, 14*, 271–284.

Pozzi, E. (1982). Secularization and rebuffs of the sacred: The collective suicide of Jonestown. *Cahiers Internationaux de Sociologie, 29*, 131–143.

Pratt, J.B. (1920). *The Religious Consciousness*. New York: Macmillan.

Pratt, J.B. (1923). Religion and the younger generation. *Yale Review, 12*, 594–613.

Pratt, K.C. (1937). Differential selection of intelligence according to denominational preference of college freshmen. *Journal of Social Psychology, 8*, 301–310.

Pratt, M.W., Hunbsberger, B., Pancer, S.M., and Roth, D. (1992). Reflections on religion: Aging, belief orthodoxy, and interpersonal conflict in the complexity of adult thinking about religious issues. *Journal for the Scientific Study of Religion, 31*, 514–522.

Pratto, F., Sidanius, J., and Stallworth, L.M. (1993). Sexual selection and the sexual and ethnic basis of social hierarchy. In L. Ellis (ed.) *Social stratification and Socioeconomic Inequality. 1: A Comparative Biosocial Analysis*. New York: Praeger.

Proudfoot, W. (1985). *Religious Experience*. Berkeley: University of California Press.

Prudo, R., Harris, T., and Brown, G. (1984). Psychiatric disorder in an urban and in a rural population: 3. Social integration and the morphology of affective disorder. *Psychological Medicine, 14*, 327–345.

Pruyser, P.W. (1968). *A Dynamic Psychology of Religion*. New York: Harper & Row.

Puhakka, K. (1995). Hinduism and religious experience. In R.W. Hood, jun. (ed.) *Handbook of Religious Experience*. Birmingham, AL: Religious Education Press.

Putney, S., and Middleton, R. (1961). Rebellion, conformity, and parental religious ideologies. *Sociometry, 24*, 125–135.

Rambo, L.R. (1993). *Understanding Religious Conversion*. New Haven, CT: Yale University Press.

Ragan, C., Malony, H.N., and Beit-Hallahmi, B. (1980). Psychologists and religion: Professional factors and personal belief. *Review of Religious Research, 21*, 208–217.

Rank, O. (1914). *The Myth of the Birth of the Hero: A Psychological Interpretation of Mythology*. New York: Nervous and Mental Diseases Publishing Co.

Ranson, S., Bryman, A., and Hinings, B. (1977). *Clergy, Ministers and Priests*. London: Routledge & Kegan Paul.

Rao, S., and Murthy, V.N. (1984). Psychosocial correlates of locus of control among college students. *Psychological Studies, 29*, 51–56.

Raschke, H.J. (1987). Divorce. In M.B. Sussman and S.K. Steinmetz (eds) *Handbook of Marriage and the Family*. New York: Plenum Press.

Rasmussen, L., and Charman, T. (1995). Personality and religious beliefs: A test of Flugel's superego projection theory. *International Journal for the Psychology of Religion, 5,* 109–117.

Rattner, J. (1983). *Alfred Adler*. New York: F. Ungar.

Rayburn, C.A., Richmond, L.J., and Rogers, L. (1986). Men, women, and religion: Stress within leadership roles. *Journal of Clinical Psychology, 42,* 540–546.

Rees, D.G. (1967). Denominational concepts of God. Unpublished M.A. thesis, University of Liverpool.

Rees-Mogg, W. (1992). *Picnics on Vesuvius*. London: Sidgwick & Jackson.

Reeves, E.B., and Bylund, R.A. (1992). Anonymity and the rise of universal occasions for religious ritual: An extension of the Durkheim theory. *Journal for the Scientific Study of Religion, 31,* 113–130.

Rhodes, A.L., and Nam, C.B. (1970). The religious context of educational expectations. *American Sociological Review, 35,* 253–267.

Riccio, J.A. (1979). Religious affiliation and socioeconomic achievement. In R. Wuthnow (ed.) *The Religious Dimension*. New York: Academic Press.

Richardson, J.T. (1973). Psychological interpretations of glossolalia: A re-examination of research. *Journal for the Scientific Study of Religion, 12,* 199–207.

Richardson, J.T. (1985a). The active vs. passive convert: Paradigm conflict in conversion/recruitment research. *Journal for the Scientific Study of Religion, 24,* 163–179.

Richardson, J.T. (1985b). Psychological and psychiatric studies of new religions. In L.B. Brown (ed.) *Advances in the Psychology of Religion*. Oxford: Pergamon.

Richardson, J.T., Stewart, M., and Simmonds, R.B. (1979). *Organized Miracles: A Study of a Contemporary Youth, Communal, Fundamentalist Organization*. New Brunswick, NJ: Transaction.

Rigney, D., and Hoffman, T.J. (1993). Is American Catholicism anti-intellectual? *Journal for the Scientific Study of Religion, 32,* 211–222.

Rizzuto, A.-M. (1984). *The Birth of the Living God*. Chicago, IL: University of Chicago Press.

Robbins, T.L. (1969). Eastern mysticism and the resocialization of drug users. *Journal for the Scientific Study of Religion, 8,* 308–317.

Robbins, T.L., and Anthony, D. (1972). Getting straight with Meher Baba. A study of mysticism, drug rehabilitation, and post-adolescent role conflict. *Journal for the Scientific Study of Religion, 11,* 122–140.

Roberts, B.R. (1968). Protestant groups and coping with urban life in Guatemala City. *American Journal of Sociology, 73,* 753–767.

Robertson, D.M. (1989). *The Chicago Revival, 1876: Society and Revivalism in a Nineteenth-Century City*. Metuchen, NJ: Scarecrow Press.

Robin, R.W. (1981). Revival movement hysteria in the Southern Highlands of Papua New Guinea. *Journal for the Scientific Study of Religion, 20,* 150–163.

Rochford, E.B., jun. (1982). Recruitment strategies, ideology, and organization in the Hare Kirshna movement. *Social Problems, 29,* 399–410.

Rochford, E.B., jr., Purvis, S., and Eastman, N. (1989). New religions, mental health, and social control. *Research in the Social Scientific Study of Religion, 1,* 57–82.

Rogers, C.R. (1961). *On Becoming a Person*. Boston, MA: Houghton Mifflin.

Rohner, R.P. (1975). *They love me, they love me not*. New Haven, CT: Hraf.

Rohner, R.P. (1976). Sex differences in aggression: Phylogenetic and enculturation perspectives. *Ethos, 4,* 57–72.

Rohner, R.P. (1984). Toward a conception of culture for cross-cultural psychology. *Journal of Cross-Cultural Psychology, 15,* 111–138.

Rokeach, M. (1960). *The Open and Closed Mind.* New York: Basic Books.

Rokeach, M. (1968). *Beliefs, Attitudes and Values.* San Francisco, CA: Jossey-Bass.

Rokeach, M. (1969). Value systems in religion. *Review of Religious Research, 11,* 3–23.

Rokeach, M. (1981). *The Three Christs of Ypsilanti.* New York: Columbia University Press.

Roof, W.C. (1974). Religious orthodoxy and minority prejudice: Causal relationship or reflection of localistic world view? *American Journal of Sociology, 80,* 643–664.

Roof, W.C. (1989). Multiple religious switching: A research note. *Journal for the Scientific Study of Religion, 28,* 530–535.

Roof, W.C. (1993). *A Generation of Seekers: The Spiritual Journeys of the Baby Boom Generation.* San Francisco, CA: Harper.

Roof, C.W., and McKinney, W. (1987). *American Mainline Religion: Its Changing Shape and Future.* New Brunswick, NJ: Rutgers University Press.

Roof, C.W., and Roof, J.L. (1984). Review of the polls: Images of God among Americans. *Journal for the Scientific Study of Religion, 23,* 201–205.

Rooney, E.A., and Gibbons, D.C. (1966). Social reactions to crime without victims. *Social Problems, 13,* 400–410.

Rosegrant, J. (1976). The impact of set and setting on religious experience in nature. *Journal for the Scientific Study of Religion, 15,* 301–310.

Rosenberg, M. (1962). The dissonant religious context and emotional disturbance. *American Journal of Sociology, 68,* 1–10.

Rosenberg, M. (1979). *Conceiving the Self.* New York: Basic Books.

Rosenzweig, S. (1945). The picture-association method and its application in a study of reaction to frustration. *Journal of Personality, 14,* 3–23.

Ross, C.E. (1990). Religion and psychological distress. *Journal for the Scientific Study of Religion, 29,* 236–245.

Rotter, J.R. (1966). Generalized expectancies of internal versus external control of reinforcement. *Psychological Monographs, 80,* whole no. 609.

Russell, E.W. (1971). Christianity and militarism. *Peace Research Reviews, 4,* 1–77.

Ryan, R.M., Rigby, S., and King, K. (1993). Two types of religious internalization and their relations to religious orientations and mental health. *Journal of Personality and Social Psychology, 65,* 586–596.

Sales, S.M. (1972). Economic threat as a determinant of conversion rates in authoritarian and non-authoritarian churches. *Journal of Personality and Social Psychology, 23,* 420–428.

Salzman, L. (1953). The psychology of religious and ideological conversion. *Psychiatry, 16,* 177–187.

Samarin, W.J. (1972). *Tongues of Angels and of Men.* New York: Collier-Macmillan.

Samuelsson, K. (1993). *Religion and Economic Action: The Protestant Ethic, the Rise of Capitalism, and the Abuses of Scholarship.* Toronto: University of Toronto Press.

Sanada, T. (1979). After prophecy fails: A reappraisal of a Japanese case. *Japanese Journal of Religious Studies, 6,* 217–237.

Sanai, M. (1952). An empirical study of political, religious, and social attitudes. *British Journal of Psychology,* Statistical Section, *5,* 81–92.

Sander, W. (1992). Catholicism and the economics of fertility. *Population Studies, 46,* 477–489.

San Giovanni, L. (1978). *Ex-Nuns: A Study of Emergent Role Passage.* Norwood, NJ: Ablex.

Sapir, E. (1937). Fashion. *Encyclopedia of the Social Sciences*, 6. New York: Macmillan.

Sargant, W. (1957). *Battle for the Mind*. London: Heinemann.

Saski, H., and Nagasaki, H. (1989). The mental distance: Its difference in educational circumstances. *Journal of Human Development*, *25*, 1–10.

Scanlon, R. (1966). Adolf Hitler and the technique of mass brainwashing. In D.C. Bryant (ed.) *The Rhetorical Idiom*. New York: Russell & Russell.

Schachter, S. (1967). The interaction of cognitive and physiological determinants of emotional states. *Advances in Experimental Social Psychology*, *1*, 49–80.

Scheidt, R.J. (1973). Belief in supernatural phenomena and locus of control. *Psychological Reports*, *32*, 1159–1162.

Schimel, J.L. (1973). Esoteric identification processes in adolescence and beyond. *Journal of the American Academy of Psychoanalysis*, *1*, 403–415.

Schneider, L., and Dornbusch, M. (1950). *Popular Religion: Inspirational Books in America*. Chicago, IL: University of Chicago Press.

Schoenfeld, C.G. (1962). God the father and mother: Study and extension of Freud's conception of God as an exalted father. *American Imago*, *19*, 213–234.

Schoenherr, R.A., and Young, L.A. (1990). Quitting the clergy: Resignations in the Roman Catholic priesthood. *Journal for the Scientific Study of Religion*, *29*, 463–481.

Scholem, G. (1973). Sabbatai Sevi: The Mystical Messiah, 1626–1676. Princeton, NJ: Princeton University Press.

Scholes, P.A. (1955). *The Oxford Companion to Music* (9th edn). Oxford: Oxford University Press.

Schreckengost, G.E. (1987). The effect of latent racist, ethnic and sexual biases. *Review of Religious Research*, *28*, 351–366.

Schumaker, J.F. (1990). *Wings of Illusion: The Origin, Nature, and Future of Paranormal Beliefs*. Amherst, NY: Prometheus.

Schumaker, J.F. (1991). The adaptive value of suggestibility and dissociation. In J.F. Schumaker (ed.) *Human Suggestibility*. New York: Routledge.

Schumaker, J.F. (1995). *The Corruption of Reality: A Unified Theory of Religion, Hypnosis, and Psychopathology*. Amherst, NY: Prometheus.

Schutz, A. (1951). Making music together: A study in social relationship. In M. Natanson (ed.) *Collected Papers II: Studies in Social Theory*. The Hague: Nijhoff.

Schverisch, P.G., and Havens, J.J. (1995). Explaining the curve in the U-shaped curve. *Voluntas*, *6*, 203–225.

Schwab, R., and Petersen, K.U. (1990). Religiousness: Its relation to loneliness, neuroticism and subjective well-being. *Journal for the Scientific Study of Religion*, *29*, 335–345.

Schwartz, G. (1970). *Sect Ideologies and Social Status*. Chicago, IL: University of Chicago Press.

Seaman, J.M., Michel, J.B., and Dillehay, R.C. (1971). Membership in orthodox Christian groups, adjustment and dogmatism. *Sociological Quarterly*, *12*, 252–258.

Seggar, J.F., and Blake, R.H. (1970). Post-joining nonparticipation: An exploratory study of convert inactivity. *Review of Religious Research*, *11*, 204–209.

Sethi, S., and Seligman, M.E. (1993). Optimism and fundamentalism. *Psychological Science*, *4*, 256–259.

Shaffir, W. (1991). Conversion experiences: Newcomers to and defectors from Orthodox Judaism. In Z. Sobel and B. Beit-Hallahmi (eds) *Tradition, Innovation, Conflict: Jewishness and Judaism in Contemporary Israel*. Albany: State University of New York Press.

Shams, M., and Jackson, P.R. (1993). Religiosity as a predictor of well-being and moderator of the psychological impact of unemployment. *British Journal of Medical Psychology*, 66, 341–352.

Sharot, S. (1980). Jewish millenarianism: A comparison of medieval communities. *Comparative Studies in Society and History*, 22, 394–415.

Shaver, P., Lenauer, M., and Sadd, S. (1980). Religiousness, conversion, and subjective well-being: The 'healthy-minded' religion of modern American women. *American Journal of Psychiatry*, 137, 1563–1568.

Sheils, D. (1980). The great ancestors are watching. A cross-cultural study of superior ancestral religion. *Sociological Analysis*, 41, 247–257.

Sherif, M., and Cantril, H. (1947). *The Psychology of Ego-Involvement*. New York: Wiley.

Shostrom, E.L. (1966). *Personal Orientation Inventory: An Inventory for the Measurement of Self-Actualization*. San Diego, CA: Educational and Industrial Testing Service.

Simmonds, R.B. (1977). Conversion or addiction?: Consequences of joining a Jesus movement group. *American Behavioral Scientist*, 20, 909–924.

Simpson, J.H. (1984). High gods and the means of subsistence. *Sociological Analysis*, 45, 213–222.

Simpson, M.E., and Conklin, G.H. (1989). Socioeconomic development, suicide and religion: A test of Durkheim's theory of religion and suicide. *Social Forces*, 67, 945–964.

Sims, P. (1991). *Can Somebody Shout Amen*. New York: St Martin's Press.

Singelenberg, R. (1989). 'It separated the wheat from the chaff': The '1975' prophecy and its impact among Dutch Jehovah's Witnesses. *Sociological Analysis*, 50, 23–40.

Sipe, A.W.R. (1990). *A Secret World: Sexuality and the Search for Celibacy*. New York: Brunner/Mazel.

Skinner, B.F. (1971). *Beyond Freedom and Dignity*. New York: Knopf.

Skorupski, J. (1976). *Symbol and Theory: A Philosophical Study of Theories of Religion in Social Anthropology*. New York: Cambridge University Press.

Sloane, D.M., and Potvin, R.H. (1986). Religion and delinquency: Cutting through the maze. *Social Forces*, 1, 87–105.

Slugoski, B.R., Marcia, J.E., and Koopman, R.F. (1984). Cognitive and social interactional characteristics of ego identity statuses in college males. *Journal of Personality and Social Psychology*, 47, 646–661.

Smelser, N.J. (1962). *Theory of Collective Behaviour*. London: Routledge & Kegan Paul.

Smidt, C.E., and Penning, J.M. (1982). Religious commitment, political conservatism, and political and social tolerance in the United States: A longitudinal analysis. *Sociological Analysis*, 43, 231–246.

Smith, C.B., Weigert, A.J., and Thomas, D.L. (1979). Self-esteem and religiosity: An analysis of Catholic adolescents from five cultures. *Journal for the Scientific Study of Religion*, 18, 51–60.

Smith, J.M., and Ghose, S. (1989). Religious experience. *Encyclopedia Britannica*, 26, 624–637.

Smith, P. (1986). Anglo-American religion and hegemonic change in the world-system c.1870–1980. *British Journal of Sociology*, 37, 88–105.

Smith, R.E., Wheeler, G., and Diener, E. (1975). Faith without works: Jesus people, resistance to temptation, and altruism. *Journal of Applied Social Psychology*, 5, 320–330.

Snow, D.A., Zurcher, L.A., jr., and Ekland-Olson, S. (1980). Social networks and social movements: A microstructural approach to differential recruitment. *American Sociological Review*, 45, 787–801.

Social Trends. (1995). London: HMSO.

Sorenson, R.C. (1981). Evangelical seminarians' philosophies of human nature and theological beliefs. *Journal for the Scientific Study of Religion, 20*, 33–38.

Spanos, N.P., and Hewitt, E.C. (1979). Flossolalia: A test of the 'trance' and psychopathology hypotheses. *Journal of Abnormal Psychology, 88*, 427–434.

Spellman, C.M., Baskett, G.D., and Byrne, D. (1971). Manifest anxiety as a contributing factor in religious conversion. *Journal of Consulting and Clinical Psychology, 36*, 245–247.

Spero, M.H. (1982). Psychotherapeutic procedure with religious cult devotees. *Journal of Nervous and Mental Disease, 170*, 332–344.

Spickard, J.V. (1991). Experiencing religious rituals. *Sociological Analysis, 52*, 191–204.

Spilka, B., and McIntosh, D.N. (1995). Attribution theory and religious experience. In R.W. Hood, jr. (ed.) *Handbook of Religious Experience*. Birmingham, AL: Religious Education Press.

Spilka, B., Addison, J., and Rosensohn, M. (1975). Parents, self and God: A test of competing theories of individual-religion hypotheses. *Review of Religious Research, 16*, 154–165.

Spilka, B., Brown, G.A., and Cassidy, S.A. (1992). The structure of religious mystical experience. *International Journal for the Psychology of Religion, 2*, 241–257.

Spilka, B., Hood, R.W., and Gorsuch, R.L. (1985). *The Psychology of Religion*. Englewood Cliffs, NJ: Prentice-Hall.

Spilka, B., Kojetin, B.A., and McIntosh, D. (1985). Forms and measures of personal faith: Questions, correlates, and distinctions. *Journal for the Scientific Study of Religion, 24*, 437–42.

Spilka, B., Stout, L., Minton, B., and Sizemore, D. (1977). Death and personal faith: A psychometric investigation. *Journal for the Scientific Study of Religion, 16*, 169–178.

Spilka, B., Ladd, K.L., McIntosh, D.N., Milrose, S., and Bickel, C.O. (1996). The content of religious experience: The role of expectancy and desirability. *International Journal for the Psychology of Religion, 6*, 95–105.

Spiro, M.E. (1965). Religious systems as culturally constituted defense mechanisms. In M.E. Spiro (ed.) *Context and Meaning in Cultural Anthropology*. Glencoe, IL: The Free Press.

Spiro, M.E. (1966). Religion: Problems of definition and explanation. In M. Banton (ed.) *Anthropological Approaches to the Study of Religion*. New York: Praeger.

Spiro, M.E. (1968). Virgin birth, parthenogenesis, and physiological paternity: An essay in cultural interpretation. *Man, 3*, 242–261.

Spiro, M.E. (1978). Religious systems as culturally constituted defense mechanisms. In B. Kilborne and L.L. Langness (eds) *Culture and Human Nature*. Chicago, IL: University of Chicago Press.

Spiro, M.E., and D'Andrade, R.G. (1958). A cross-cultural study of some supernatural beliefs. *American Anthropologists, 60*, 456–466.

Spray, S.L., and Marx, J.H. (1960). The origins and correlates of religious adherence and apostasy among mental health professionals. *Sociological Analysis, 30*, 132–150.

Stace, W.T. (1960). *Mysticism and Philosophy*. Philadelphia, PA: J.B. Lippincott.

Stacey, W., and Shupe, A. (1982). Correlates of support for the electronic church. *Journal for the Scientific Study of Religion, 21*, 291–303.

Stack, S. (1983). The effect of religious commitment on suicide: A cross-national analysis. *Journal of Health and Social Behavior, 24*, 362–374.

Stack, S. (1991). The effect of religiosity on suicide in Sweden: A time series analysis. *Journal for the Scientific Study of Religion, 30*, 462–468.

Stack, S., and Wasserman, I. (1992). The effect of religion on suicide ideology: Analysis of the networks perspective. *Journal for the Scientific Study of Religion, 31,* 457–466.

Stack, S., Wasserman, I., and Kposowa, A. (1994). The effects of religion and feminism on suicide ideology: An analysis of national survey data. *Journal for the Scientific Study of Religion, 33,* 110–121.

Stanley, G., Bartlett, W.K., and Moyle, T. (1978). Some characteristics of charismatic experience: Glossolalia in Australia. *Journal for the Scientific Study of Religion,* 17, 269–277.

Starbuck, E.D. (1899). *Psychology of Religion.* New York: Scribner's.

Stark, R. (1963). On the incompatibility of religion and science: A survey of American graduate students. *Journal for the Scientific Study of Religion, 3,* 3–21.

Stark, R. (1973). Age and faith: A changing outlook or an old process? In C.Y. Glock (ed.) *Religion in Sociological Perspective.* Belmont, CA: Wadsworth.

Stark, R. (1984). Religion and conformity: Reaffirming a *sociology* of religion. *Sociological Analysis, 45,* 273–282.

Stark, R., and Bainbridge, W.S. (1980). Networks of faith: Interpersonal bonds and recruitment to cults and sects. *American Journal of Sociology, 85,* 1376–1395.

Stark, R., and Bainbridge, W.S. (1985). *The Future of Religion: Secularization, Revival and Cult Formation.* Berkeley: University of California Press.

Stark, R., and Bainbridge, W.S. (1987). *A Theory of Religion.* New York: Peter Lang.

Stark, R., and Glock, C.Y. (1968). *American Piety: The Nature of Religious Commitment.* Berkeley: University of California Press.

Stark, R., Kent, L., and Doyle, D.P. (1982). The ecology of a 'lost' relationship. *Journal of Research in Crime and Delinquency, 19,* 4–24.

Stark, R., Foster, B.D., Glock, C.Y., and Quinley, H.E. (1971). *Wayward Shepherds: Prejudice and the Protestant Clergy.* New York: Harper & Row.

Stark, W. (1967). *The Sociology of Religion,* vol. 2. London: Routledge & Kegan Paul.

Steggarda, M. (1993). Religion and the social positions of women and men. *Social Compass, 40,* 65–73.

Steinitz, L.Y. (1980). Religiosity, well-being and *Weltanschauung* among the elderly. *Journal for the Scientific Study of Religion, 19,* 60–67.

Stephan, K.H., and Stephan, G.E. (1973). Religion and the survival of Utopian communities. *Journal for the Scientific Study of Religion, 12,* 89–100.

Stifler, K., Greer, J., Sneck, W., and Dovenmuehle, R. (1993). An empirical investigation of the reported mystical experiences among religious contemplatives, psychotic inpatients, and normal adults. *Journal for the Scientific Study of Religion, 32,* 366–372.

Stone, L. (1991). *Road to Divorce: England 1530–1987.* New York: Oxford University Press.

Stone, M.H. (1992). Religious behavior in the Psychiatric Institute 500. In M. Finn and J. Gartner (eds) *Object Relations, Theory and Religion: Clinical Applications.* New York: Praeger.

Stone, S. (1934). The Miller delusion: A comparative study in mass psychology. *American Journal of Psychiatry, 91,* 593–623.

Stouffer, S.A. (1955). *Communism, Conformity and Civil Liberties.* New York: Doubleday.

Stouffer, S.A., Suchman, E.A., DeVinney, L.C., Star, S.A., and Williams, R.M. (1949). *The American Soldier. 2: Combat and its Aftermath.* Princeton, NJ: Princeton University Press.

Straus, R.A. (1976). Changing oneself: Seekers and the creative transformation of experience. In J. Lofland (ed.) *Doing Social Life.* New York: Wiley.

Straus, R.A. (1979). Religious conversion as a personal and collective accomplishment. *Sociological Analysis*, 40, 158–165.

Struening, E.I. (1963). Anti-democratic attitudes in a Midwest university. In H.H. Remmers (ed.) *Anti-Democratic Attitudes in American Schools*. Evanston, IL: Northwestern University Press.

Strunk, O., jr. (1959). Perceived relationships between parental and deity concepts. *Psychological News Letter*, *10*, 222–226.

Stryker, R. (1981). Religio-ethnic effects on attainments in the early career. *American Sociological Review*, *46*, 212–231.

Stukat, K.G. (1968). Suggestion. *International Encyclopedia of the Social Sciences*, *15*, 369–375.

Suziedalis, A., and Potvin, R.H. (1981). Sex differences in factors affecting religiousness among Catholic adolescents. *Journal for the Scientific Study of Religion*, *20*, 38–51.

Swanson, G.E. (1971). Life with God: Some variation of religious experience in a modern city. *Journal for the Scientific Study of Religion*, *10*, 169–199.

Swanson, G.S. (1960). *The Birth of the Gods*. Ann Arbor: University of Michigan Press.

Swanson, G.S. (1967). *Religion and Regime*. Ann Arbor: University of Michigan Press.

Swenson, W.M. (1961). Attitudes towards death in an aged population. *Journal of Gerontology*, *16*, 49–52.

Symington, T.A. (1935). *Religious Liberals and Conservatives*, Contributions in Education, no. 64. New York: Columbia University Teachers College.

Tajfel, H. (ed.) (1978), *Differentiation between Social Groups*. London: Academic Press.

Tajfel, H. (1981). *Human Groups and Social Categories: Studies in Social Psychology*. Cambridge: Cambridge University Press.

Tallmer, M. (1992). The aging analyst. *Psychoanalytic Review*, *79*, 381–404.

Tamayo, A., and Desjardins, L. (1976). Belief systems and conceptual images of parents and God. *Journal of Psychology*, *92*, 131–140.

Tamayo, A., and Dugas, A. (1977). Conceptual representation of mother, father and God according to sex and field of study. *Journal of Psychology*, *97*, 74–84.

Tamminen, K. (1994). Religious experiences in childhood and adolescence: A viewpoint of religious development between the ages of 7 and 20. *International Journal for the Psychology of Religion*, *4*, 61–85.

Tamney, J., Powell, S., and Johnson, S. (1989). Innovation theory and religious nones. *Journal for the Scientific Study of Religion*, *28*, 216–229.

Taylor, G.R. (1959). *Sex in History*. London: Thames & Hudson.

Taylor, R.J., and Chatters, L.M. (1988) Church members as a source of informal social support. *Review of Religious Research*, *30*, 193–203.

Tawney, R.H. (1966). *Religion and the Rise of Capitalism*. London: Murray.

Terry, R.L. (1971). Dependence, nurturance and monotheism: A cross-cultural study. *Journal of Psychology*, *79*, 163–164.

Tetlock, P.E., and Boettger, R. (1989). Accountability: A social magnifier of the dilution effect. *Journal of Personality and Social Psychology*, *57*, 388–398.

Thomas, G.M. (1989). *Revivalism and Cultural Change: Christianity, Nation Building, and the Market in the Nineteenth-Century United States*. Chicago, IL: University of Chicago Press.

Thomas, L.E., and Cooper, R.E. (1978). Measurement and incidence of mystical experience: An exploratory study. *Journal for the Scientific Study of Religion*, *17*, 433–437.

Thompson, A.D. (1974). Open-mindedness and indiscriminate antireligious orientation. *Journal for the Scientific Study of Religion*, *13*, 471–477.

Thompson, E.H. (1991). Beneath the status characteristic: Gender variations in religiousness. *Journal for the Scientific Study of Religion*, *30*, 381–394.

Thompson, L. (1948). Attitudes and acculturation. *American Anthropologist*, *50*, 200–215.

Thorne, B. (1993). *Gender Play: Girls and Boys in School*. New Brunswick, NJ: Rutgers University Press.

Thornes, B., and Collard, J. (1979). *Who Divorces?* London: Routledge & Kegan Paul.

Thornton, A. (1985). Changing attitudes towards separation and divorce: Causes and consequences. *American Journal of Sociology*, *90*, 856–872.

Thornton, R. (1986). *We Shall Live Again. The 1870 and 1890 Ghost Dance Movements as Demographic Revitalization*. Cambridge: Cambridge University Press.

Thouless, R.H. (1923). *An Introduction to the Psychology of Religion*. Cambridge: Cambridge University Press.

Thouless, R.H. (1935). The tendency to certainty in religious beliefs. *British Journal of Psychology*, *26*, 16–31.

Thouless, R.H. (1971). *An Introduction to the Psychology of Religion*. Cambridge: Cambridge University Press.

Thrupp, S. (ed.) (1962). *Millenial Dreams in Action*. The Hague: Mouton.

Thun, T. (1963). *Die religiose Entscheidung der Jugend*. Stuttgart: Ernst Klett.

Thun, T. (1969). *Das Religiose Schicksal des alten Menschen*. Stuttgart: Ernst Klett.

Thurston, H. (1951). *The Physical Phenomena of Mysticism*. London: Burns Oates.

Tiger, L. (1979). *Optimism: The Biology of Hope*. New York: Simon & Schuster.

Tiryakian, E.A. (1993) American religious exceptionalism: A reconsideration. *Annals of the American Academy of Political and Social Science*, *527*, 40–54.

Tobacyk, J.J., Nagot, E., and Miller, M. (1988). Paranormal beliefs and locus of control: A multidimensional examination. *Journal of Personality Assessment*, *52*, 241–246.

Towler, R. (1985). *The Need for Certainty: A Sociological Study of Conventional Religion*. London: Routledge & Kegan Paul.

Towler, R., and Coxon, A.P.M. (1979). *The Fate of Anglican Clergy*. London: Macmillan.

Trent, K., and Scott, J. (1989). Structural determinants of the divorce rate: A cross-societal analysis. *Journal of Marriage and the Family*, *51*, 391–404.

Trevor-Roper, H. (1963). *Historical Essays*. London: Macmillan.

Triandis, H.C. (1972). *The Analysis of Subjective Culture*. New York: Wiley.

Truett, K.R., Eaves, L.J., Meyer, J.M., and Heath, A.C. (1992). Religion and education as mediators of attitudes: A multivariate analysis. *Behavior Genetics*, *22*, 43–62.

Turner, H.A. (1994). Gender and social support: Taking the bad with the good? *Sex Roles*, *30*, 521–541.

Turner, R.H., and Killian L.M. (1957). *Collective Behavior*. Englewood Cliffs, NJ: Prentice Hall.

Turner, V. (1974). *Dramas, Fields, and Metaphors: Symbolic Action in Human Society*. Ithaca, NY: Cornell University Press.

Turner, V.W. (1967). *The Forest of Symbols*. Ithaca, NY: Cornell University Press.

Turner, V.W. (1969). *The Ritual Process*. London: Routledge & Kegan Paul.

Turner, V.W. (1977). Symbols in African ritual. In J.I. Dolgin, D.S. Kemnitzer, and D.M. Schneider (eds) *Symbolic Anthropology: A Reader in the Study of Symbols and Meanings*. New York: Columbia University Press.

Tversky, A. and Kahneman, D. (1973). On the psychology of prediction. *Psychological Review*, *80*, 237–251.

Tygart, C.E. (1971). Religiosity and university student anti-Vietnam war attitudes: A negative or curvilinear relationship? *Sociological Analysis*, *32*, 120–129.

Ullman, C. (1982). Cognitive and emotional antecedents of religious conversion. *Journal of Personality and Social Psychology*, *43*, 183–192.

Ullman, C. (1989). *The Transformed Self: The Psychology of Religious Conversion*. New York: Plenum Press.

Underhill, E. (1911/1930). *Mysticism: A Study in the Nature and Development of Man's Spiritual Consciousness*. London: Methuen.

Underhill, R. (1975). Economic and political antecedents of monotheism: A cross-cultural study. *American Journal of Sociology*, *80*, 841–861.

Ungerleider, J.T., and Wellisch, D.K. (1979). Coercive persuasion (brainwashing), religious cults and deprogramming. *American Journal of Psychiatry*, *136*, 723–738.

Unwin, J.D. (1934). *Sex and Culture*. London: Oxford University Press.

Valentine, C.W. (1962). *The Experimental Psychology of Beauty*. London: Methuen.

van Fossen, A.B. (1988). How do movements survive failures of prophecy? *Research in Social Movements, Conflicts and Change*, *10*, 193–212.

Van Gennep, A. (1908/1960). *The Rites of Passage*. Chicago, IL: Chicago University Press.

Veevers, J.E., and Cousineau, D.F. (1980). The heathen Canadians: Demographic correlates of non-belief. *Pacific Sociological Review*, *23*, 199–216.

Verdieck, M.J., Shields, J.J., and Hoge, D.R. (1988). Role commitment processes revisited: American Catholic priests 1970 and 1985. *Journal for the Scientific Study of Religion*, *27*, 524–535.

Vergote, A. (1969). *The Religious Man*. Dublin: Gill & Macmillan.

Vergote, A., and Aubert, C. (1972). Parental images and representations of God. *Social Compass*, *19*, 431–444.

Vergote, A., and Tamayo, A. (1980). *The Parental Figures and the Representation of God*. The Hague: Mouton.

Vergote, A., Tamayo, A., Pasqualli, L., Bonami, M., Pattyn, M., and Custers, S. (1969). Concept of God and parental images. *Journal for the Scientific Study of Religion*, *8*, 79–87.

Vidal, D. (1983). *Le Malheur et Son Prophète: Inspirés et sectaires en Languedoc calviniste (1685–1725)*. Paris: Payot.

Volinn, E.P. (1985). Eastern meditation groups: Why join? *Sociological Analysis*, *46*, 147–156.

Vollmerhausen, J.W. (1965). Religion, perfectionism and the fair deal. *American Journal of Psychoanalysis*, *25*, 203–215.

Vrcan, S. (1994). The war in ex-Yugoslavia and religion. *Social Compass*, *41*, 413–422.

Wadsworth, M.E.J., and Freeman, S.R. (1983). Generation differences in beliefs: A cohort study of stability and change in religious beliefs. *British Journal of Sociology*, *34*, 416–437.

Wagner, M.B. (1983). *Metaphysics in Midwestern America*. Columbus: Ohio State University Press.

Wald, K.D., Owen, D.E., and Hill, S.S., jun. (1988). Churches as political communities. *American Political Science Review*, *82*, 531–548.

Walker, A.G. (1985). From revival to restoration: The emergence of Britain's new classical pentecostalism. *Social Compass*, *32*, 261–271.

Wallace, A.F.C. (1956). Revitalization movements. *American Anthropologist*, *58*, 264–281.

Wallace, A.F.C. (1966). *Religion: An Anthropological View*. New York: Random House.

Wallace, A.F.C. (1970). *The Death and Rebirth of the Seneca*. New York: Knopf.

Wallace, R.A. (1975). A model of change of religious affiliation. *Journal for the Scientific Study of Religion*, *14*, 345–355.

Waller, N.G., Kojetin, B.A., Bouchard, T.J., jr., Lykken, D.T., and Tellegen, A. (1990). Genetic and environmental influences on religious interests, attitudes, and values: A study of twins reared apart and together. *Psychological Science*, *1*, 139–142.

Wallin, P. (1957). Religiosity, sexual gratification, and marital satisfaction. *American Sociological Review*, *22*, 300–305.

Wallin, P., and Clark, A.L. (1964). Religiosity, sexual gratification, and marital-satisfaction in the middle years of marriage. *Social Forces*, *42*, 303–309.

Wallis, R. (1982). The social construction of charisma. *Social Compass*, *29*, 25–39.

Ward, C., and Kemp, S. (1991). Religious experiences, altered states of consciousness, and suggestibility: Cross-cultural and historical perspectives. In J.F. Schumaker (ed.) *Human Suggestibility*. New York: Routledge.

Ward, C.A., and Beaubrun, M.H. (1980). The psychodynamics of demon possession. *Journal for the Scientific Study of Religion*, *19*, 201–207.

Warner, L.W. (1961). *The Family of God*. New Haven, CT: Yale University Press.

Watson, P.J., Morris, R.J., and Hood, R.W. (1987). Antireligious humanistic values, guilt, and self-esteem. *Journal for the Scientific Study of Religion*, *26*, 535–546.

Watson, P.J., Hood, R.W., Foster, S.G., and Morris, R.J. (1988). Sin, depression, and narcissism. *Review of Religious Research*, *29*, 295–305.

Watson, P.J., Hood, R.W., Morris, R.J. and Hall, J.R. (1984). Empathy, religious orientation, and social desirability. *Journal of Psychology*, *117*, 211–216.

Watson, P.J., Howard, R., Hood, R.W., and Morris, R.J. (1988). Age and religious orientation. *Review of Religious Research*, *29*, 271–280.

Wearing, A.J. and Brown, L.B. (1972). The dimensionality of religion. *British Journal of Social and Clinical Psychology*, *11*, 143–148.

Weber, M. (1904–5). *The Protestant Ethic and the Spirit of Capitalism*. London: Allen & Unwin.

Weber, M. (1922/1956). *The Sociology of Religion*. Boston, MA: Beacon Press.

Weber, M. (1968). *Economy and Society* (3 vols). New York: Bedminster.

Webster, A.C., and Stewart, R.A.C. (1973). Theological conservatism. In G.D. Wilson (ed.) *The Psychology of Conservatism*. London: Academic Press.

Weigert, A.J., and Thomas, D.L. (1972). Parental support, control and adolescent religiosity. *Journal for the Scientific Study of Religion*, *11*, 389–393.

Weigert-Vowinkel, E. (1938). The cult and mythology of the Magna Mater from the standpoint of psychoanalysis. *Psychiatry*, *1*, 347–378.

Weimann, G. (1987). 'New religions': From fear to faith. *Canadian Journal of Sociology*, *12*, 216–228.

Weintraub, W., and Aronson, H. (1974). Patients in psychoanalysis: Some findings related to sex and religion. *American Journal of Orthopsychiatry*, *44*, 102–108.

Weiser, N. (1974). The effects of prophetic disconfirmation on the committed. *Review of Religious Research*, *16*, 19–30.

Weiss, A.S., and Mendoza, R.H. (1990). Effects of acculturation into the Hare Krishna movement on mental health and personality. *Journal for the Scientific Study of Religion*, *29*, 173–184.

Welch, K.W. (1981). An interpersonal influence model of traditional religious commitment. *Sociological Quarterly*, *22*, 81–92.

Wellings, K., Field, J., Johnson, A.M., and Wadsworth, J. (1994). *Sexual Behaviour in Britain*. Harmondsworth: Penguin.

Welsh, M.A. (1978). Religious non-affiliates and worldly success. *Journal for the Scientific Study of Religion, 17*, 59–61.

Westley, F. (1983). *The Complex Forms of the Religious Life: A Durkheimian View of New Religious Movements.* Chico, CA: Scholars Press.

Westoff, C.F., and Jones, E.F. (1979). The end of 'Catholic' fertility. *Demography, 16*, 209–217.

Whitam, F.L. (1968a). Revivalism as institutionalized behavior: An analysis of the social base of a Billy Graham crusade. *Southwestern Social Science Quarterly, 49*, 115–127.

Whitam, F.L. (1968b). Peers, parents and Christ: Interpersonal influence in retention of teenage decisions made at a Billy Graham crusade. *Proceedings of the Southwestern Sociological Association.*

White, O.K., jun., and White, D. (1980). Abandoning an unpopular policy: An analysis of the decision granting the Mormon priesthood to blacks. *Sociological Analysis, 41*, 231–245.

White, S., McAllister, I., and Krishtanovskaya, O. (1994). Religion and politics in postcommunist Russia. *Religion, State, and Society, 22*, 73–88.

Whitelock, F.A., and Hynes, J.V. (1978). Religious stigmatization: A historical and psychophysiological enquiry. *Psychological Medicine, 8*, 185–202.

Whiting, J.W.M., Kluckhohn, C., and Anthony, A. (1958). The functions of male initiations ceremonies at puberty. In E.E. Maccoby, T.M. Newcomb, and E.L. Hartley (eds) *Readings in Social Psychology* (3rd edn). New York: Holt, Rinehart & Winston.

Wiggins, J.S. (1966). Substantive dimensions of self-report in the MMPI item pool. *Psychological Monographs, 80*, whole no. 630.

Wigoder, G. (1989). *The Encyclopedia of Judaism.* New York: Macmillan.

Wilcox, C., and Jelen, T.G. (1993). Catholicism and gender equality in western Europe: A contextual analysis. *International Journal of Public Opinion Research, 5*, 40–57.

Willems, E. (1967). *Followers of the New Faith: Culture Change and the Rise of Protestantism in Brazil and Chile.* Nashville, TN: Vanderbilt University Press.

Williams, D.R., Larson, D.B., and Buckler, R.E. (1991). Religion and psychological distress in a community sample. *Social Science and Medicine, 32*, 1257–1262.

Williams, R.L., and Cole, S. (1968). Religiosity, generalized anxiety, and apprehension concerning death. *Journal of Social Psychology, 75*, 111–117.

Willits, F.K., and Crider, D.M. (1988). Religion and well-being: Men and women in the middle years. *Review of Religious Research, 29*, 281–294.

Willits, F.K., and Crider, D.M. (1989). Church attendance and traditional religious beliefs in adolescence and young adulthood: A panel study. *Review of Religious Research, 31*, 68–81.

Wilson, B.R. (1961). *Sects and Society.* London: Heinemann.

Wilson, B.R. (1966). *Religion in Secular Society.* London: Watts.

Wilson, B.R. (1967). *Patterns of Sectarianism.* London: Heinemann.

Wilson, B.R. (1970). *Religious Sects: A Sociological Study.* New York: McGraw-Hill.

Wilson, B.R. (1973). *Magic and the Millenium. A Sociological Study of Religious Movements of Protest Among Tribal and Third-World Peoples.* New York: Harper & Row.

Wilson, B.R. (1975). *The Noble Savages: The Primitive Origins of Charisma and its Contemporary Survival.* Berkeley: University of California Press.

Wilson, B.R. (1976). *Contemporary Transformations of Religion.* New York: Oxford University Press.

Wilson, E.O. (1978). *On Human Nature.* Cambridge, MA: Harvard University Press.

Wilson, J., and Clow, H.K. (1981). Themes of power and control in a Pentecostal assembly. *Journal for the Scientific Study of Religion, 20*, 241–250.

Wilson, J., and Sherkat, D.E. (1994). Returning to the fold. *Journal for the Scientific Study of Religion, 33*, 148–161.

Winter, G. (1962). *The Suburban Captivity of the Churches*. New York: Macmillan.

Winter, J.A. (1973). The metaphoric parallelist approach to the sociology of theistic beliefs: Theme, variations and implications. *Sociological Analysis, 34*, 212–229.

Winter, J.A. (1992). The transformation of community integration among American Jewry: Religion or ethnoreligion? A national replication. *Review of Religious Research, 33*, 349–363.

Winter, M., and Short, C. (1993). Believing and belonging: Religion in rural England. *British Journal of Sociology, 44*, 635–651.

Wittenberg, R. (1968). *Postadolescence: Theoretical and Clinical Aspects of Psychoanalytic Theory*. New York: Grune & Stratton.

Witter, R.A., Stock., W.A., Okun, M.A., and Haring, M.J. (1985). Religion and sub-jective well-being in adulthood: A quantitative synthesis. *Review of Religious Research, 26*, 332–342.

Witztum, E., Greenberg, D., and Dasberg, H. (1990). Mental illness and religious change. *British Journal of Medical Psychology, 63*, 33–41.

Wolf, J.G. (ed.) (1989). *Gay Priests*. New York: HarperCollins.

Worsley, P. (1968). *The Trumpet Shall Sound*. New York: Schocken.

Wright, D. (1971). *The Psychology of Moral Behaviour*. Harmondsworth: Penguin.

Wright, D., and Cox, E. (1967). A study of the relationship between moral judge-ment and religious belief in a sample of English adolescents. *Journal of Social Psychology, 72*, 135–144.

Wright, S.A. (1986). Dyadic intimacy and social control in three cult movements. *Sociological Analysis, 47*, 137–150.

Wright, S.A. (1988). Leaving new religions: Issues, theories, and research. In D.G. Bromley (ed.) *Falling from the Faith. Causes and Consequences of Religious Apostasy*. Newbury Park, CA: Sage.

Wright, S.A., and Piper, E.S. (1986). Families and cults: Familial factors related to youth leaving or remaining in deviant religious groups. *Journal of Marriage and the Family, 48*, 15–25.

Wrightsman, L.S. (1974). *Assumptions About Human Nature: A Social Psychological Approach*. Belmont, CA: Wadsworth Publishing.

Wulff, D.M. (1991). *Psychology of Religion*. New York: Wiley.

Wuthnow, R. (1976). Astrology and marginality. *Journal for the Scientific Study of Religion, 15*, 157–168.

Wuthnow, R. (1978). *Experimentation in American Religion*. Berkeley: University of California Press.

Yates, J.W., Chalmer, B.J., St James, P., Follansbee, M., and McKegney, F.P. (1981). Religion in patients with advanced cancer. *Medical and Pediatric Oncology, 9*, 121–128.

Yeaman, P.A. (1987). Prophetic voices: Differences between men and women. *Review of Religious Research, 28*, 367–376.

Yinger, J.M. (1957). *Religion, Society and the Individual*. New York: Macmillan.

Yinger, J.M. (1970). *The Scientific Study of Religion*. London: Collier-Macmillan.

Young, F.W. (1965). *Initiation Ceremonies: A Cross-Cultural Study of Status Dramatization*. New York: Bobbs-Merrill.

Young, R.L. (1992). Religious orientation, race and support for the death penalty. *Journal for the Scientific Study of Religion, 31*, 76–87.

Zajonc, R.B. (1976). Family configuration and intelligence. *Science, 192*, 227–236.

Zavalloni, M. (1972). Social identity: Perspectives and prospects. *Social Science Information*, *12*, 65–91.

Zavalloni, M. (1975). Social identity and the recording of reality: Its relevance for cross-cultural psychology. *International Journal of Psychology*, *10*, 197–217.

Zeidner, M., and Beit-Hallahmi, B. (1988). Sex, ethnic, and social class differences in parareligious beliefs among Israeli adolescents. *Journal of Social Psychology*, *128*, 333–343.

Zusne, L., and Jones, W.H. (1982). *Anomalistic Psychology*. Hillsdale, NJ: Lawrence Erlbaum Associates.

Zygmunt, J. (1970). Prophetic failure and chiliastic identity: The case of Jehovah's Witnesses. *American Journal of Sociology*, *75*, 926–948.

Zygmunt, J.H. (1972). When prophecies fail: A theoretical perspective on the comparative evidence. *American Behavioral Scientist*, *16*, 245–268.

Author index

Aaronson, B.S. 85, 88
Acock, A.C. 102
Addison, J. 108, 165
Adityanjee, X. 200
Adlaf, E.M. 212
Adler, A. 29, 108
Adorno, T.W. 18, 23, 137, 165, 222
Aguirre, B.E. 226
Ajzen, I. 8, 109
Al-Thakeb, F. 165
Albrecht, J.C.N. 188
Aleshire, D. 218, 219
Alland, A. 140
Allison, J. 121
Allport, G.W. 31, 44, 45, 115, 150, 196
Almquist, E.M. 156
Alston, J.P. 160, 226
Altemeyer, B. 218
Altman, I. 84
Altstaedten, M. 207
Alwin, D.F. 102
Ancona, L. 192
Anderson, R.M. 55, 157, 223, 245
Anthony, A. 53
Anthony, D. 122
Antonovsky, A. 32
Apprey, M. 121
Argyle, M. 6, 36, 39, 50, 60, 68, 69, 122,
    152, 176, 185, 217, 221
Arjomand, S.A. 161, 182
Arnold, M. 150, 151
Aronson, E. 53
Aronson, H. 183
Ashby, J.A. 229
Astin, A.W. 224
Au, P. 140, 160
Aubert, C. 107

Babie, E.R. 162, 245

Back, C.W. 42, 73, 140, 157, 159, 160
Bacon, M.K. 145
Baer, H.A. 132, 159, 223
Bahr, H.M. 165, 200, 211
Bainbridge, W.S. 6, 16, 25, 125, 133,
    155, 199, 212
Bakan, P. 232
Balch, R.W. 126, 134
Balkwell, J. 176
Ball, D. 107
Ball, P. 57
Balswick, J.O. 176
Baltzell, E.D. 156
Barber, B. 131
Barfoot, C.H. 142
Barker, E. 124, 134
Barkun, M. 132, 157
Barron, F. 174
Barry, H. 145
Bartlett, W.K. 56
Baskett, G.D. 120
Bateman, M.M. 176
Batson, C.D. 45, 46, 47, 84, 91, 116,
    121, 167, 170, 171, 174, 189, 195, 200,
    201, 202, 218, 219
Baumeister, R. 244
Beard, A.W. 93
Beaubrun, M.H. 240
Beck, S.H. 204
Becker, E. 16
Beckford, J. 125
Beecher, H.K. 172
Beeghley, L. 205, 206, 212
Beit-Hallahmi, B. 1, 6, 14, 15, 23, 25,
    26, 28, 29, 34, 35, 36, 39, 96, 120, 122,
    130, 133, 135, 136, 142, 152, 160, 180,
    182, 189, 217, 221, 228, 234, 238, 240,
    243, 245, 251, 253, 254
Bell, H.M. 102

Bellah, R.N. 27, 32
Belle, D. 143
Bello, F. 180
Bem, D.J. 8
Bendix, R. 128
Bengtson, V.L. 95, 100, 102
Benson, H. 188
Benson, P. 165, 239
Bereiter, C. 182
Berg, B. 213
Berger, P.L. 13, 32
Bergin, A.E. 174
Berkman, L.F. 188
Bernard, J. 143
Bernt, F.M. 201
Berry, J. 67
Bibby, R.W. 103, 123, 233
Bickel, C.O. 96
Bilu, Y. 116, 240
Bird, F. 126, 134
Birky, I.T. 107
Blackbourn, D. 244
Blacking, J. 62
Blackwood, L. 214, 215
Blake, R.H. 123
Block, J.H. 143
Blocker, T.J. 225
Bloom, H. 16
Bock, E.W. 212
Boettger, R. 170
Boisen, A.T. 157, 158
Boling, T.E. 159
Bolt, M. 201
Bonami, N. 107, 108
Bonaparte, M. 137
Booth, L. 151
Bopegamage, A. 132
Bord, R.J. 222, 249, 252
Borhek, J.T. 97
Bouchard, T.J. jr. 163, 175
Bourque, L.B. 42, 73, 140, 157, 159, 160
Braden, M. 134
Bram, J. 158
Brandon, S.G.F.B. 53
Brannon, R.C.L. 219
Brinkerhoff, M.B. 123, 221
Bronfenbrenner, U. 98
Bronson, L. 190
Brown, D.E. 231, 237
Brown, D.R. 228
Brown, G. 191
Brown, G.A. 84, 90, 121
Brown, L.B. 8, 31, 41, 42, 89, 95, 97, 99,
  100, 102, 110, 121, 136, 149, 160, 165,
  176, 232, 247, 251
Brown, S. 225
Broyles, P.A. 187, 188
Bruce, S. 112, 123, 129
Bryman, A. 64, 68, 69
Bucke, R.M. 116
Buckler, R.E. 190
Buckley, P. 55
Bunis, W. 130
Burgess, E.W. 154
Burkett, S.R. 211
Burnham, K.E. 224
Burris, C.T. 45, 207
Bursik, R.J. jr. 213, 226
Burton, J. 26
Burton-Bradley, B.G. 192
Butler, M. 212
Buttel, F.H. 228
Bylund, R.A. 51
Byrne, D. 120

Caldwell, R. 238
Camargo, R.J. 67
Cameron, P. 159
Campbell, C. 33, 136
Campbell, D.T. 218
Campbell, J. 238
Campbell, K.E. 224
Campbell, T.C. 161, 245
Cantrell, C.H. 193, 195
Cantril, H. 34, 172
Caplovitz, D. 135, 136
Carlos, S. 246
Carlton-Ford, S.L. 55
Carroll, G. 128
Carroll, M.P. 235, 238
Carter, M. 99
Cassel, J. 118
Cassidy, S.A. 84, 90, 121
Castelli, J. 14
Cavalli-Sforza, L.L. 99–100, 101, 112
Cavan, R.S. 154, 221
Cavenar, J.C. jr. 120
Census (1936) 141
Chadwick, B.A. 213
Chalmer, B.J. 189
Chamberlain, K. 185
Chamlin, M.B. 226
Chapman, L.J. 165
Charlton, J. 64
Charman, T. 173, 239
Chatters, L.M. 227

Chaves, M. 42
Cheek, N.H. 140, 160
Chen, K.-H. 99, 100, 101, 112
Chesser, E. 101
Child, I.L. 145
Chiswick, C.U. 210, 211
Choate, D.A. 130
Christensen, C.W. 116, 120
Christiano, K.J. 223
Christie, R. 166
Christopher, S. 245
Claridge, G. 92
Clark, A.L. 241
Clark, C.A. 102
Clark, E.T. 157
Clark, L.L. 187
Clark, W.H. 201
Clelland, D.A. 130
Clow, H.K. 155, 237
Cochran, J.K. 205, 206, 212, 213
Cochrane, G. 132
Coe, G.A. 171
Cohen, D.W. 203
Cohen, H.A. 203
Cohen, L.M. 150
Cohen, S.M. 111
Cohn, N. 158, 244
Cohn, W. 132
Cole, B.S. 204
Cole, S. 193
Collard, J. 210
Colquhoun, F. 129, 139
Comstock, G.W. 187, 188, 199
Conger, J.A. 128
Conklin, G.H. 200
Connors, J.F. III 224
Cooper, R.E. 74, 77
Cornwall, M. 208, 210
Costa, P.T. 164, 165
Coursey, R.D. 173
Cousineau, D.F. 137, 160
Covello, V.T. 229
Cox, E. 140, 240
Coxon, A.P.M. 64
Crandall, V.C. 164
Cranston, R. 59
Crapanzano, V. 127, 133
Crider, D.M. 150, 184
Croog, S.H. 196
Cross, W. 142
Cruise, R.J. 212, 213
Csikszentmihalyi, M. 54
Curtis, R.F. 97

Custers, S. 107, 108, 238, 239
Cutler, N.E. 185

Daly, M. 142
D'Andrade, R.G. 22, 107, 142, 238, 239
Danser, D.B. 102
Darian, J.C. 10
Darley, J. 47
Dasberg, H. 121
Davenport, E. 226
Davidman, L. 83, 125
Davidson, J.M. 232
Davidson, R.J. 232
Davis, A.-L. 220
Davis, K. 29
Day, L.H. 199
de Jarnette, J. 171
De Neuter, H. 107
de Vaus, D.A. 144, 145
de Zulueta, E. 252
Dearman, M. 223
Deconchy, J.P. 8, 47, 108, 115, 133, 146, 238
Deikman, A.J. 83
Delin, P. 176
Demerath, N.J. 137
Depression Guideline Panel (1993) 143
Deren, M. 244
Desjardins, L. 107
Deutsch, A. 121
Dewe, P.J. 67
Dewhurst, K. 93
Dillehay, R.C. 167
Dirks, D.H. 203
Dodson, M. 158, 161
Doerr, H.A. 59
Dollard, J. 159
Dollimore, J. 97
Donahue, M.J. 45, 46, 108, 173
Dornbusch, S.M. 99, 100, 101, 112, 223
Douglas, M. 19–20, 131, 237
Dovenmuehle, R. 72
Downing, J.J. 90
Draper, E. 32
Drenovsky, C.K. 187, 188
Dudley, R.L. 136, 212, 213
Dugas, A. 107, 108
Dull, V.T. 186, 191
Dunham, C.C. 99, 100, 102
Dupras, A. 195
Durkheim, E. 19, 32, 51, 54, 197, 227, 235, 248

Dwyer, J.W. 187
Dyble, J.E. 69, 101, 102, 103, 106, 112
Dynes, R.R. 158

Eagly, A.H. 143
Earle, J.R. 223
Eastman, N. 121
Eaves, L.J. 163
Ebaugh, H.R.F. 64, 125, 136
Ebrey, P.B. 236
Eckberg, D.L. 225
Eckblad, M. 165
Eckhardt, K.W. 222, 224
Edwards, H. 159, 228
Eibl-Eibesfeldt, I. 142, 143
Eisinga, R. 218, 220, 221
Eister, A.W. 131, 134, 250
Ekland-Olson, S. 125
Elder, G.H. 166
Eliade, M. 63
Elkind, D. 115, 148, 169
Ellingson, T. 62
Ellis, L. 212
Ellison, C.G. 103, 125–6, 165, 166, 186,
    188, 200
Ellison, C.W. 207
Emmons, C.F. 142
Engels, F. 29, 245
England, R.W. 247
Engs, R.C. 213
Epstein, D.M. 156
Erickson, J.A. 101, 103, 104–5, 111
Erickson, M.L. 212, 213
Erikson, E.H. 17, 18
Everett, R.F. 69
Eysenck, H.J. 163, 171

Farnsworth, G. 134
Faulkner, J.E. 222, 249, 252
Faupel, C.E. 199
Fazel, M.K. 186
Fearon, J. 245
Feather, N.T. 170
Featherman, D.L. 217
Feifel, H. 193, 195, 196
Feigelman, W. 137
Feingold, L.M. 163
Feldman, M.W. 99, 100, 101, 112
Felling, A. 218, 220, 221
Felsinger, J.M. von 172
Feltey, K.M. 140
Fenichel, O. 23, 61
Fenn, R.K. 250

Fenwick, P. 94
Ferenczi, S. 18, 136
Fernandez, J.W. 132
Ferraro, J.F. 188, 246
Festinger, L. 48, 133, 134
Fichter, J.H. 63, 99, 139
Field, J. 204
Fiese, B.H. 51
Finn, N. 134
Firth, R. 15
Fish, S. 45
Fishbein, M. 8, 109
Fisher, R.L. 13
Fisher, S. 13
Fiske, A.M. 132
Fiske, S.T. 12, 27
Fletcher, B. 67, 68
Flora, C.B. 122
Florian, V. 196, 197
Flory, J.D. 202
Flugel, J.C. 23, 24, 240
Follansbee, M. 189
Forbes, G.B. 200, 201
Fortes, M. 19, 236
Foster, B.D. 212, 220
Foster, R.A. 237
Fowler, J.W. 152
Francis, L.J. 65, 66, 99, 100, 102, 109,
    110, 111, 150, 164, 212
Frank, J.D. and Frank, J.B. 59, 117,
    121, 127, 223
Frankel, B.G. 187, 188
Fraser, M.W. 123
Freedman, M.B. 132
Freeman, D. 239
Freeman, S.R. 150
Freemesser, G.F. 121
Frenkel-Brunswik, E. 18, 23, 137, 165,
    222
Freud, S. 15, 16, 21, 28, 32, 36, 107,
    108, 116, 146, 239, 243, 248, 254
Friedman, R. 188
Fromm, E. 18, 28, 107
Fu, X.N. 208
Fukayama, Y. 161, 245
Funk, R.A. 240
Funkenstein, D.H. 176
Furneaux, W.D. 171
Furnham, A. 214, 215, 217

Galanter, M. 55, 120, 121, 122, 124
Gallenmore, J.L. jr. 120
Gallup, G.H. 82, 85, 140, 141

Galton, F. 47
Garai, J.E. 143
Garfield, S.J. 197, 203
Garrison, C.E. 111
Gary, L.E. 228
Gay, D.A. 186, 219
Gee, E.M. 144
Geertz, C. 5, 15, 98, 103
George, L.K. 188
Georgianna, S. 199
Gerard, D. 141, 156
Gerharz, G.P. 253
Gerrard, N.L. 157
Ghose, S. 75
Gibbons, D. 171
Gibbons, D.C. 225
Gibson, H.M. 99
Gilbert, D.T. 12
Gillespie, J.M. 150, 196
Gillin, J.L. 157
Giorgi, L. 215
Glass, J. 99, 100, 102
Glass, T.A. 186
Glassner, B. 213
Glenn, N.D. 159, 160, 182
Glik, D.C. 59
Gliksman, L. 213
Glock, C.Y. 30–31, 40, 41, 130, 133, 157, 160, 162, 212, 220, 223, 225, 245, 246, 251
Gluckman, M. 51
Godin, A. 107
Goffman, E. 51
Goldman, R.J. 148, 149
Goldschmidt, W.R. 158
Goldsen, R.K. 203
Gonzalez, L.M. 230
Goode, E. 161, 246
Goodman, F.D. 56
Goodman, K.L. 210, 211
Gordon, J.S. 193
Gorer, G. 140
Gorman, B.S. 137
Gorsuch, R.L. 65, 88, 90, 93, 102, 107, 121, 151, 212, 218, 219, 220, 252
Goss, E. 117
Gotard, E. 159
Gould, J.B. 145
Gozali, J. 164
Graff R.W. 172
Graham, B. 62, 129–30, 139
Granberg, D. 224
Grasmick, H.G. 212, 213, 226

Gray, J.A. 142
Gray, R.A. 202
Greeley, A.M. 14, 73, 76, 77, 78, 81, 89, 99, 110, 111, 161, 181, 225, 226
Greenberg, D. 121
Greenberg, J. 16, 17, 214, 220
Greer, J.E. 72, 111
Gregory, P.N. 236
Greil, A.L. 83, 125
Grevengoed, N. 191
Griffin, G.A.E. 220
Gromoll, H.F. 200, 201
Group for the Advancement of Psychiatry 192
Grupp, F.W. jr. 224
Gustafsson, B. 195
Guthrie, S.E. 20

Hadaway, C.K. 42, 137, 184,
Haerich, P. 206
Hall, G.S. 115
Hall, J.R. 80, 140
Hallez, M. 107
Hamilton, J.G. 192
Hamilton, R.F. 224
Hammond, J.A. 204
Hammond, P. 214, 215
Hampson, S.E. 165
Hampson, S.L. 177
Hanson, A. 6
Hanson, A. 61
Hanson, D.J. 213
Haraldsson, E. 173
Hardy, A. 73, 75, 77, 85, 89–90
Hardyck, J.A. 134
Haring, M.J. 184
Harlan, L. 237
Harms, E. 147
Harrelson, W. 54
Harris, M. 244
Harris, T. 191
Harrison, J.D. 236
Harrison, J.F.C. 122
Harrison, M.I. 122, 125
Hartmann, H. 32
Hartmann, R.T. 224
Hartshorne, H. 203
Hashimoto, H. 122
Hassenger, R. 181
Hastings, D.W. 152, 153
Hathaway, W. 191
Hay, D. 73, 74, 76, 77, 79, 80, 81, 85, 89, 90, 140, 157

Hayden, B. 54
Haywood, C.L. 247
Hazani, M. 134
Heald, G. 77, 79, 90
Heath, A.C. 163
Heaton, T.B. 208, 210, 211
Hebb, D.O. 14
Heider, F. 12
Heiler, F. 82
Heller, D. 108
Henninger, J. 60
Henry, E.R. 183
Herb, L.L 190
Herron, S. 129
Herskovits, M.J. 24
Hertel, B.R. 40, 108, 145, 206
Herzbrun, M.B. 101, 106
Hewitt, E.C. 36, 96, 242
Hewitt, W.E. 187, 188
Hickman, M.J. 228
Hill, C. 28, 161
Hill, S.S. jr. 222
Hine, V.H. 126
Hinings, B. 64, 68, 69
Hirschi, T. 213
Hoben, A. 236
Hoffelt, D. 91
Hoffman, T.J. 178, 179
Hoffmann, J.P. 144
Hogan, M. 137
Hoge, D.R. 69, 99, 101, 102, 103, 106,
   111, 112, 177, 182, 252
Hollenweger, W.J. 157, 223
Hollingworth, L.S. 150
Holm, N.G. 57, 59
Holman, T. 206
Holt, J.B. 158, 250
Homan, R. 221
Homola, M. 216, 217
Hong, G.Y. 95
Hood, R.W. jr. 37, 45, 65, 73, 75, 76,
   80, 84, 88, 90, 91, 93, 94, 102, 121,
   140, 151, 152, 174, 176, 195, 196, 198,
   200, 235
Hood, T.C. 130
Horney, K. 15, 23
Hoult, T.F. 158
Houston, J. 85, 86
Houtart, F. 10
Howard, R. 152
Howells, T.H. 171
Hughes, M. 206
Hughes, R.A. 135

Hunsberger, B. 99, 112, 136, 165, 167,
   169, 201, 208
Hunt, R.A. 43
Hunter, F.T. 98
Hunter, J.D. 160, 162, 245
Huntington, S.P. 27
Hutch, R.A. 18, 21
Hutsebaut, D. 150
Huxley, F. 60
Hyde, K. 111
Hynes, E. 10
Hynes, J.V. 242

Iannaccone, L. 157, 158
Idler, E.L. 189, 190
Inglehart, R. 184
Inhelder, B. 12, 115
ITA 195

Jacklin, C. 143
Jackson, L.E. 173
Jackson, M.C. 92
Jackson, P.R. 186
Jacobs, J.L. 235
Jacobson, C.K. 208
Jahoda, G. 7
Jahoda, M. 166
James, W. 6, 34, 44, 73, 74, 76, 115, 118
Janosik, R.J. 223
Janus, C.L. 204
Janus, S.S. 204
Jardine, R. 163
Jarvis, G.K. 68, 187, 188
Jennings, M.K. 106
Jensen, G.F. 212, 213
Jensen, J.S. 176
Jensen, L. 206
Jessor, R. 212
Johnson, A.M. 204
Johnson, B. 250
Johnson, C.L. 133
Johnson, N.R. 130
Johnson, S. 137, 161
Johnstone, R. 110
Jones, E. 19, 21, 108, 237
Jones, E.F. 209
Jones, E.M. 107
Jones, R.B. 196
Jones, V. 182
Jones, W. 191
Jones, W.H. 7
Josephson, M. 221
Juergensmeyer, M. 229

Kahneman, D. 14
Kahoe, R.D. 165, 173, 174
Kaldor, P. 55, 56, 141, 185, 226
Kanagy, C.L. 132, 228
Kanter, R.M. 134
Kanungu, R.N. 128
Kaplan, B.H. 143, 158
Kaplan, H.B. 121
Kardiner, A. 22, 239, 246
Kass, J.D. 188
Kay, W.K. 164
Keating, J.P. 237
Kedem, P. 96, 203
Keeter, L.G. 99
Keita, G.P. 143
Kelley, M.W. 68
Kemp, S. 172
Kennell, J. 191
Kenney, J.F. 120
Kersten, L. 220
Kieren, D.K. 106
Kildahl, J. 57
Killian, L.M. 171
Kilpatrick, D.G. 167
King, K. 191
King, S.H. 176
Kingsbury, F.A. 154
Kinsey, A.C. 204, 206
Kinsey, K. 212
Kirk, R.E. 92
Kirkland, S. 16, 17, 220
Kirkpatrick, C. 42, 224
Kirkpatrick, L.A. 21, 45, 107, 108, 120,
    175, 186, 219, 235, 241, 248
Kirshnit, C. 185
Kitzinger, S. 236
Kivett, V.R. 173
Klaf, F.C. 192
Klauber, J. 18, 241
Kligerman, C. 116
Kline, C.A. 5
Kluckhohn, C. 53, 231, 237
Knapp, R.H. 238
Knudsen, D.D. 216, 217, 223
Koch, J.R. 246
Koestler, A. 13
Kojetin, B.A. 46, 163, 165
Koopman, R.F. 151
Kosa, J. 182
Kosmin, B.A. 156, 245
Kotre, J. 136
Kowalsky, G.S. 199
Kposowa, A. 200

Kris, E. 15
Krishtanovskaya, O. 231
Kroliczak, A. 176
Kruglanski, A. 12, 31
Kuhlen, R.G. 150, 151
Kune, G.A. 188
Kune, S. 188
Kurtz, S.N. 237

La Barre, W. 15, 17, 22, 87, 131, 158,
    240
Labaki, B. 229
Lacan, J. 22
Lachman, S.P. 156, 245
Ladd, C.E. 172
Ladd, K.L. 96
Lamb, M.E. 102
Lambert, W.W. 238
Lang, K. 129
Lang, G.E. 129
Lapins, N.A. 59
Larsen, L. 238
Larson, D.B. 190
Lasagna, L. 172
Lazerwitz, B. 156
Leak, G.K. 45
Lehman, E.C. jr. 64, 181
Lehrer, E.L. 210, 211
Lemert, C.C. 236
Lenauer, M. 184, 186
Lenski, G.E. 102, 180, 214, 215, 217,
    221, 246
Leonard, R.C. 224
Leserman, J. 188
Leuba, J.H. 24, 115, 189, 241
Levin, J.S. 78, 173, 187, 188, 189
Levine, B.C. 227
Levine, R.A. 218
Levine, S. 196
Levine, S.V. 121, 122, 123
Levinson, D.J. 18, 23, 137, 165, 222
Levy, J.J. 195
Lewellen, T.C. 132
Lewin, K. 26
Lewis, I.M. 60, 63, 237
Lewis, R.E. 123
Ley, D. 137, 160
Liebman, C.S. 226
Liff, Z.A. 116
Lindskoog, D. 92
Linn, L. 118, 120
Linton, R. 22, 239
Lipset, S.M. 222

Lipsey, C.M. 130
Loehlin, J.C. 163
Lofland, J. 118, 127
Loftus, J.A. 67
Long, D. 148
Loomis, C.G. 6
Lorenz, K. 13
Loukes, H. 150
Lovekin, A. 57, 175
Lowenthal, K.M. 187
Luckmann, T. 13, 32, 144
Lutzky, H. 18
Lykken, D.T. 163, 175
Lynch, F.R. 126
Lynd, R. 156
Lynd, H. 156
Lynn, P. 201
Lynn, R. 177
Lyon, D. 16, 17, 220

McAdams, D.P. 151
McAllister, I. 145, 231
McClelland, D.C. 189, 214, 217, 224
McClemon, J. 78
Maccoby, E.E. 142, 143
McCovat, K. 99
McCoy, J. 245
McCrae, R.R. 164, 165, 234
McCready, W.C. 99
McCreery, C. 78, 92, 93
McDaniel, J. 192
MacDonald, A.P. 101
McFadden, S.H. 189
McGinn, B. 71
McGrath, E. 143
McGuiness, D. 143
McGuire, M.B. 60, 126
McIntosh, D.N. 46, 91, 94, 191, 193
McKenzie, B. 169
MacKie, M.M. 221
McKinney, W. 225
McLeod, H. 221
McLoughlin, W.G. jr. 128
McPherson, W. 122
Magee, M. 177
Mailloux, N. 192
Malinowski, B. 13, 16
Malony, H.N. 57, 175, 182
Marcia, J.E. 151
Marcum, J.P. 209
Markides, K.S. 154
Markle, G.E. 142
Markus, H. 12

Marler, P.L. 42
Marsh, C. 215
Marshall, H. 216, 217
Martin, N.G. 163
Martin, R.B. 137, 160
Martin, T.K. 165, 200
Martin-Baro, I. 222
Martinson, O.B. 228
Marty, M.E. 161
Martz, L. 128
Marx, J.H. 137
Marx, K. 27, 29, 245
Maslow, A.H. 29, 91, 137
Masters, K.F. 174
Masters, R.E.L. 86, 87, 88
Maton, K.I. 191
Maton, K.L. 203
Matthews, R. 193
Mauss, A.L. 220
May, M.A. 203
Meadow, A. 190
Meissner, W.W. 118
Mendoza, R.H. 121
Meredith, W.H. 51
Meske, C. 51
Meyer, J.M. 163
Michel, J.B. 167
Middleton, R. 102, 165
Mikulincer, M. 196
Miller, A.S. 122, 143, 247
Miller, D.R. 97
Miller, J.B. 143
Miller, M. 173
Miller, M.K. 187
Mills, J. 53
Milrose, S. 96
Mindel, C.H. 154
Minton, B. 193
Moberg, D.O. 63, 64, 68, 184
Moehle, D. 77
Moffatt, M. 236, 249
Mol, H. 24, 161, 241
Montague, H. 192
Mooney, J. 131
Moore, R.L. 157
Morisey, A. 80, 81
Morris, R.J. 37, 88, 152, 174, 176, 195,
    196, 198, 200, 235
Mostella, F. 172
Moyle, T. 56
Mullen, K. 212
Mullin, J. 192
Munro, B.M. 106

Murthy, V.N. 173
Mutch, P.B. 212, 213
Myers, D.G. 201, 202

Nagasaki, H. 108
Nagot, E. 173
Nam, C.B. 178
Nassi, A. 224
Neal, A.G. 127
Needham, R. 40–41
Nelsen, A.K. 223
Nelsen, H.M. 69, 103, 140, 160, 176, 178, 223
Nelson, G.K. 125
Nelson, L.D. 137, 193, 195, 222
Nelson, M.O. 107
Nevo, B. 120
Newell, R.J. 206
Newman, J. 191
Newman, W.M. 224
Nichols, R.C. 163
Niebuhr, H.R. 156, 223
Niemi, N.G. 106
Nobbe, C. 245
Nordheimer, J. 124
Norman, W.T. 165
Norris, A.H. 164
Northcott, H.C. 68, 187, 188
Northover, W.E. 155, 230
Nottingham, E.K. 246
Nunn, C.Z. 103

Obeyesekere, G. 21, 238
Ochsmann, R. 195
O'Dea, T.F. 158
Odham 41
Oksanen, A. 120
Okun, M.A. 184
Oliner, P.M. 203
Oliner, S.P. 203
Olsson, P.A. 118
Opie, I. 142
Oppenheim, D. 102
Orbach, I. 197
Osarchuk, M. 47, 195
Osmond, H. 85
Ostow, M. 16, 23, 24, 32
Otto, R. 74
Owen, D.E. 222
Oxtoby, W.G. 69
Ozorak, E.W. 150, 151

Pahnke, W.H. 85–6, 89, 90

Palmer, S.J. 134
Paloutzian, R.F. 59, 121, 207, 251
Pancer, S.M. 167, 169
Pargament, K.I. 191, 203
Park, C. 190, 191
Parrott, G.L. 224
Parsons, T. 32, 102
Partridge, K.B. 187, 188, 199
Pasqualli, L. 107, 108, 238, 239
Patrick, J.W. 195
Pattison, E.M. 59, 122
Pattison, M.L. 122
Pattyn, M. 107, 108, 238, 239
Pearson, P.R. 99, 164
Pecora, P.J. 123
Peek, C.W. 219, 225
Pendleton, B.F. 55, 57, 58, 82, 89, 90
Penning, J.M. 225
Pepper, S.C. 20
Peres, Y. 222
Perkins, H.W. 213
Perris, A. 62
Persinger, M.A. 12, 94
Pescosolido, B.A. 199
Peters, J. 218, 220, 221
Petersen, J.C. 142
Petersen, K.U. 186
Peterson, R.E. 224
Petrillo, G.H. 69, 101, 102, 103, 106, 111, 112
Petrovich, O. 147
Pfister, O. 246
Photiadis, J.D. 158
Piaget, J. 12, 14, 115
Piazza, T. 225
Pickering, W.S.F. 54
Piker, S. 40, 41
Pilkington, G.W. 145
Piper, E.S. 117
Pittard-Payne, B.B. 126, 134
Platonow, E. 201
Ploch, D.R. 152, 153
Plomin, R. 163
Poblete, R. 158
Poling, T.H. 120
Polk, D.T. 69, 101, 102, 103, 106, 112
Pollner, M. 186
Poloma, M.M. 55, 57, 58, 77, 82, 89, 90, 140
Pope, L. 156, 223
Poppleton, P.K. 145
Porter, L.S. 191
Potvin, R.H. 108, 144, 150, 212

Powell, B. 219
Powell, S. 137, 161
Poythress, N.G. 177
Pozzi, E. 135
Pratt, J.B 115, 148
Pratt, K.C. 178
Pratt, M.W. 167, 169
Pratto, F. 142
Proudfoot, W. 77
Prudo, R. 191
Pruyser, P.W. 118, 176
Puhakka, K. 83, 95
Purvis, S. 121
Putney, S. 102, 165
Pyszczynski, T. 16, 17, 214, 220

Quinley, H.E. 212, 220

Rabkin, F. 121
Rabkin, R. 121
Ragan, C. 182
Rambo, L.R. 125
Rank, O. 238
Ranson, S. 64, 68, 69
Rao, S. 173
Raschke, H.J. 210
Rasmussen, L. 173, 239
Rattner, J. 29, 108
Rayburn, C.A. 68
Raynor-Prince, L. 167
Rees, D.G. 108, 146
Rees-Mogg, W. 24
Reeves, E.B. 51
Reimer, B. 126, 134
Rhoads, J.M. 120
Rhodes, A.L. 178
Riccio, J.A. 216
Richards, P.S. 174
Richardson, J.T. 57, 106, 121, 122, 126,
  135
Richmond, L.J. 68
Riecken, H.W. 48, 133, 134
Rigby, S. 191
Rigney, D. 178, 179
Ringer, B.B. 162, 245
Rizzuto, A.-M. 22
Robbins, T.L. 122
Roberts, B.R. 122
Robertson, D.M. 130
Robin, R.W. 192
Robinson, J.A.T. 232
Rochford, E.B. jr. 121, 125
Rogers, C.R. 29

Rogers, L. 68
Rohner, R.P. 24, 142, 238
Rokeach, M. 8, 12, 98, 167, 168–9, 224,
  228
Roof, C.W. 107, 123, 136, 137, 220,
  225
Roof, J.L. 107
Rooney, E.A. 225
Rosegrant, J. 84
Rosenberg, M. 27, 203, 227
Rosenberg, S.E. 161
Rosenblatt, A. 16, 17, 220
Rosensohn, M. 108, 165
Rosenzweig, S. 24, 240
Ross, C.E. 137, 191
Rossi, P.H. 110, 111, 181
Roth, D. 167
Roth, R.M. 203
Rotter, J.R. 173
Russell, E.W. 224
Russo, N.F. 143
Ryan, R.M. 191

Sadd, S. 184, 186
St James, P. 189
Sales, S.M. 158, 159
Salter, N.E. 121
Saltzman, L. 116, 117, 120
Samarin, W.J. 56
Samson, J.M. 195
Samuelsson, K. 214
San Giovanni, L. 136
Sanada, T. 134
Sanai, M. 232
Sander, W. 208
Sanders, G.F. 51
Sandford, R.N. 18, 23, 137, 168, 222
Sapir, E. 125
Sargant, W. 55
Saski, H. 108
Scanlon, R. 124
Schachter, S. 48, 87, 94–5, 133, 134
Scheidt, R.J. 173
Scheinfeld, A. 143
Schiller, P.L. 173
Schimel, J.L. 118
Schneider, L. 223
Schoenfeld, C.G. 21
Schoenherr, R.A. 69
Schoenrade, P. 45, 46, 47, 84, 91, 116,
  121, 171, 174, 185, 195, 200, 201, 218,
  219, 244
Scholem, G. 132

Scholes, P.A. 62
Schreckengost, G.E. 65
Schumaker, J.F. 171, 190, 232, 233
Schutz, A. 54
Schwab, R. 186
Schwartz, G. 28, 157, 250
Schwartz, L.W. 118, 120
Schweiker, W. 158
Scott, J. 210
Scott, J.E. 165
Seaman, J.M. 167
Seggar, J.F. 123
Seligman, M.E. 175, 233
Selvik, R. 151
Sethi, S. 175, 233
Shaffir, W. 114
Shams, M. 186
Sharfstein, B. 23, 24, 32
Sharot, S. 131, 132
Shaver, P.R. 108, 120, 184, 186, 235
Sheils, D. 236
Sheppard, G.T. 142
Sherif, M. 34
Sherkat, D.E. 103, 125, 126, 136, 166
Sherrow, F. 135, 136
Shields, J.J. 69
Short, C. 243
Shostrom, E.L. 91
Shriver, D.W. 181, 223
Shupe, A. 245
Sidanius, J. 142
Siegelman, E. 223
Silver, R.C. 191
Simmonds, R. B. 106, 121, 122, 135
Simpson, J.H. 236
Simpson, M.E. 200
Sims, J.H. 183
Sims, P. 128
Singelenberg, R. 134
Singer, M. 223
Sipe, A.W.R. 67
Sizemore, D. 193
Skinner, B.F. 23
Skokan, L.A. 186, 191
Skorupski, J. 13
Sloane, D.M. 150, 212
Slugoski, B.R. 151
Smart, L. 244
Smart, R.B. 212
Smelser, N.J. 29, 128, 131, 255
Smidt, C.E. 225
Smith, C.B. 165, 203
Smith, E.I. 69, 101, 102, 103, 106, 112

Smith, J.D. 201
Smith, J.M. 75
Smith, P. 245
Smythe, C. 213
Sneck, W. 72
Snow, D.A.125
Sobal, J. 142
Social Trends 208, 209
Solomon, S. 16, 17, 220
Sorenson, R.C. 200
Spanos, N.P. 36, 96, 242
Spaulding, J.G. 120
Spellman, C.M. 120
Spero, M.H. 118
Spickard, J.V. 82
Spilka, B. 46, 65, 84, 88, 90, 91, 93, 94,
    96, 102, 108, 121, 148, 151, 165, 193,
    239
Spiro, M.E. 13, 22, 32, 33, 68, 107, 238,
    239
Spray, S.L. 137, 183
Stace, W.T. 74, 75, 88, 96
Stacey, W. 245
Stack, S. 199, 200
Stallworth, L.M. 142
Stanley, G. 56
Starbuck, E.D. 40, 115, 176, 177
Stark, R. 6, 16, 29, 125, 127, 133, 152,
    154, 155, 160, 161, 181, 213, 220, 229,
    233, 252
Starr, P.D. 199
Steelman, L.C. 219
Steggarda, M. 145
Steinitz, L.Y. 186
Stephan, K.H. 227, 249
Stephan, G.E. 227, 249
Stephens, K. 207
Stewart, M. 106, 121, 122, 135
Stewart, R.A.C. 65
Stifler, K. 71
Stock, W.A. 184
Stone, A.A. 191
Stone, M.H. 121
Stone, S. 192
Stouffer, S.A. 196, 225
Stout, L. 193
Straus, R.A. 126
Struening, E.I. 219
Strickland, B. 143
Strunk, O. jr. 107
Stryker, R. 217
Stukat, K.G. 171
Suchmen, E.A. 203

Sutker, L.W. 167
Sutker, P.B. 167
Suziedalis, A. 144
Swanson, G.E. 236, 250
Swenson, W.M. 196
Syme, S.L. 188
Symington, T.A. 172, 177

Tajfel, H. 26
Tallmer, M. 183
Tamayo, A. 107, 108, 238–9
Tamminen, K. 140, 149
Tamney, J. 137, 161
Tate, S.J. 47, 195
Taves, M.J. 69, 184
Tawney, R.H. 214
Taylor, D. 126
Taylor, G.R. 24
Taylor, R.J. 227
Taylor, S.E. 12, 27
Tellegen, A. 163, 175
Terry, R.L. 238
Tetlock, P.E. 170
Tevault, R.K. 200, 201
Thomas, D.L. 101, 165, 203
Thomas, G.M. 236
Thomas, L.E. 74, 77
Thompson, A.D. 13, 137, 167
Thompson, E.H. 144, 248
Thorne, B. 143
Thornes, B. 210
Thornton, A. 210
Thornton, R. 131
Thouless, R.H. 6, 115, 149, 169, 170,
    232, 241
Thrupp, S. 132
Thun, T. 150, 154
Thurston, H. 172
Tiger, L. 13
Tiryakian, E.A. 223
Tobacyk, J.J. 173
Top, B.L. 213
Towler, R. 64, 232
Trent, K. 210
Trevor-Roper, H. 244
Triandis, H.C. 24
Triandis, L.M. 238
Truett, K.R. 163
Turner, H.A. 143
Turner, R.H. 171
Turner, V.W. 1, 50, 52, 59
Tversky, A. 14
Tygart, C.E. 224

Ullman, C. 119, 235
Underhill, E. 82
Underhill, R. 236
Ungerleider, J.T. 124
Unwin, J.D. 240

Valentine, C.W. 62
van Fossen, A.B. 134
Van Gennep, A. 51-2
Vanderpool, H.Y. 187
Varacalli, J.A. 137
Vaughan, C.E. 154
Vaughan, S.L. 125
Veeder, M. 16, 17, 220
Veevers, J.E. 137, 160
Ventis, W.L. 45, 46, 84, 91, 116, 121,
    171, 174, 189, 195, 200, 201, 218, 219
Verdieck, M.J. 69
Vergote, A. 107, 108, 147, 148, 238–9
Vidal, D. 132
Volinn, E.P. 122
Vollmerhausen, J.W. 15
Vrcan, S. 228

Wadsworth, J. 204
Wadsworth, M.E.J. 150
Wagenfeld, M.O. 142
Wagner, M.B. 246
Wald, K.D. 222
Walker, A.G. 158
Wallace, A.F.C. 6, 16, 131, 132
Wallace, R.A. 122, 123
Waller, N.G. 163, 175
Wallin, P. 241
Wallis, R. 128
Ward, C. 172
Ward, C.A. 240
Warner, C.M. 201
Warner, L.W. 237
Wasserman, I. 199, 200
Watson, L.F. 188
Watson, P.J. 37, 152, 174, 176, 200, 235
Wearing, A.J. 42
Weber, M. 12, 51, 127–8, 142, 213
Webster, A.C. 65
Weigert, A.J. 101, 133, 165, 203
Weigert-Vowinkel, E. 21
Weimann, G. 118
Weiner, D. 182
Weintraub, W. 183
Weiser, N. 134
Weiss, A.S. 121
Welch, K.W. 125, 226

Wellings, K. 204
Wellisch, D.K. 124
Welsh, M.A. 137
Wesley, J. 55
Westhoff, C.F. 209
Westly, F. 20
Whitam, F.L. 129
White, D. 10
White, M. 211
White, O.K. jr. 10
White, S. 231
Whitelock, F.A. 242
Whiting, J.W.M. 53
Wiggins, J.S. 175
Wigoder, G. 61
Wilcox, C. 11
Wilkening, E.A. 228
Wilkins, S. 134
Willems, E. 157
Williams, D.R. 190
Williams, K. 214, 215
Williams, R.L. 193
Williams, R.M. jr. 203
Willits, F.K. 150, 184
Wilson, B.R. 131, 134, 142, 157, 236, 246, 250
Wilson, E.O. 14
Wilson, J. 136, 155, 237
Wilson, M. 142
Wilson, W.P. 120
Wimberley, R.C. 130
Winter, G. 156
Winter, J.A. 19, 227
Winter, M. 243
Wittenberg, R. 136

Witter, R.A. 184
Witztum, E. 121
Wohlwill, J.F. 84
Wolf, J.G. 67
Wolf, M. 238
Worsley, P. 131
Worthington, E.L. 102
Wortman, C.B. 191
Wright, D. 140, 143, 177, 240
Wright, S.A. 117, 126, 134
Wrightsman, L.S. 200
Wulff, D.M. 42–3, 65, 83, 85, 92, 154, 166
Wuthnow, R. 77, 78, 84, 90, 91, 120, 132, 142, 245
Wygand, W. 90

Yates, J.W. 189
Yeaman, P.A. 140
Yinger, J.M. 32, 142, 157
Young, D.M. 186
Young, F.W. 53
Young, J. 150, 156
Young, L.A. 69
Young, R.L. 226
Youniss, J. 98

Zajonc, R. 12, 178
Zavalloni, M. 26
Zeidner, M. 142
Zika, S. 185
Zurcher, L.A. jr. 125
Zusne, L. 7
Zuttermeister, P.C. 188
Zygmunt, J.H. 134

Subject index

academics 178ff.
adolescent initiation 53
adolescents and youth 150ff.
adults, beliefs of 152
Afro-Americans 55, 159, 228
after-life 186
age 147ff.
Alister Hardy question 73
altruism 200ff., 227
ancestor worship 3
anger 176
anxiety 15–16, 234
art, and religion 1
attribution 95
Augustine, Saint 118
Australia 185ff.
authoritarianism 165–166, 222

Bach, J.S. 1, 62
Baptists 186, 219
basic trust 17–18
Beethoven, L. van 62
beliefs 39ff; of children 147; gender differences 140
big five 164ff.
brain hemispheres 93
Bunyan, J. 118

Catholics 63ff., 69, 177ff., 208ff.
charismatic worship 54ff.
children 147ff; and prayer 148; and religious experience 149
church schools 109ff.
clergy 63ff.
cognitive complexity 167ff.
cognitive need 12–13, 232–233
cognitive structure 91
collective effervescence 54ff.

communitas 52, 75
community action 203
community size 160ff.
conversion 34, 114–128, 151
core religious experience 141
crime 211ff.
cross-cultural generalization 230

death, fear of 15–16, 154, 193ff., 234–235
denominations 80, 156, 188; and gender differences 141
deprivation 27–31, 244–247; types of 30
distress 84ff., 94
divorce 201ff.
dogmatism 167
drugs, abuse of 212
drugs, psychedelic 81

early childhood effects 17, 235
empathy 200ff.
employment 144ff.
epilepsy 93ff.
evolutionary optimism 13–14, 233
experimentation 47ff.
extraversion 164
extrinsic religiosity 35, 44, 173ff.
Eysenck Personality Questionnaire 164

female clergy 65
fertility 208ff.
Francis, Saint 172, 242
fundamentalists 43, 175ff.
funerals 53

Gandhi, 2
gender differences 80, 139ff.
giving money 201ff.

glossolalia 55ff.
guilt 176ff., 239–240

Handel, G.F. 1
happiness 89, 184
healing 59
health 187ff.
helping 200ff.
heredity 163ff.
homosexual clergy 67
honesty 203
hypnosis 88ff.

identity 25–26, 243–244
ideological dimension 40–41
incomes 211
intellectual dimension 41
intelligence 177ff.
intrinsic religiosity 35, 44, 173ff.
Israel 2, 133, 222

Jesus Christ 3, 43, 79, 108
Jews 178, 188, 213
job status 216

'Keech, M.' 48, 133, 134

Leonardo (da Vinci) 1
liminal stage 52
locus of control 173
liberal attitudes 43
literalism 166

McPherson, 'Sister', Aimee S. 156
marriage 53
Marxism 161
meditation 83
mental health 60, 189ff.
Messiahs 193
Michelangelo 1
minority groups 158ff.
moral values 89
Mormons 187, 208ff.
mortality 188
mothers and fathers 102
Muhammad (prophet) 3
music 61ff., 78, 82

nature 84
neural factors 11–12, 232
neuroticism 164
non-verbal symbols 50
Northern Ireland 2

NRMs 130–135, 157, 176, 245

occultism 6, 7
old age 152ff.

Palestrina 62
parareligious beliefs 7
parents, influence of 99ff.
peak experiences 78ff.
Pentecostals 56ff.
People's Temple 160
personality, gender differences 142ff.
personality factors 31, 117–119,
    164–173, 247–248, 251
politics 221ff.
prayer 82, 140, 148
prejudice 218ff.
pre-literate societies 51, 227
private devotions 186
projection 18–24, 235–239; parental
    146; superego 22–24, 239–240; types
    of 19
Protestant Work Ethic 214
Protestants 177ff., 208ff., 215ff.
psychiatric disorders 191ff.
psychic experiences 77ff.
psychoanalysis 8, 14, 20–24, 28,
    116–120, 235–239, 254
psychological healing 59ff.

Quest dimension 45ff., 169

racial attitudes 218ff.
religion as art 14–15, 233–234
religion, definition of 5–7
religious coping 191
religious education 109ff.
religious experience 8, 42–43, 73ff.; in
    children 149ff.; core 74ff.; and
    gender 140; physiology 73ff.; social
    aspects 95; triggers for 81ff.; varieties
    of 74ff.
religious healing 57ff.
religious orders 69
Religious Orienation Scale 44
revivals 171, 192ff.
rites of passage 50ff.
ritual 3–4, 49–62
ritualistic dimension 41–42

sacraments 50
sacrifice 60ff.
schizotypy 92

scientists 180ff.
sectarianism 157
sects 64, 156ff., 228
self-actualization 29
self-actualizers 91ff., 137–138
self-esteem 26–27, 165, 243–244
sensory deprivation 88
Seventh Day Adventists 187, 192
sexual behaviour 204ff.
sexual motivation 24, 240–241
social class 155ff.
social cohesion 61, 192, 199ff., 226
social integration 228ff.
social learning 24–25
social support 185
socialization 99ff., 145ff., 166, 242–243

stress, in clergy 68
suggestibility 59, 171–172
suicide 197ff.
'switching' 123
symbolism 59

Tolstoy, L.N. 118
tongues, speaking in 55ff.
trance states 62

Virgin Mary 3, 8, 37, 79, 87, 108, 146,
  235

war experience 196
work and achievement 213ff.
worship 54ff., 83ff.